Louis Massignon: Professor of the Collège de France, a noted Islamic scholar . . .

Jean Charlot: Professor of Art at the University of Honolulu.

The future of the world may very well depend on men and women like these. In a time when the struggle between diverse ideologies grows ever more bitter, here are examples of the human links that can and must be forged.

Anne Fremantle has written this series of recognitions and rejoicings with the intellectual seriousness and composed clarity for which she is noted. And to her homage to the ten, Mrs. Fremantle adds a study of three "bridge" places, where national, class, and religious differences are successfully spanned: examples of unity achieved with diversity respected.

Pilgrimage to People is an unusual and thoughtful search for those who enlighten and those who care.

PILGRIMAGE
TO
PEOPLE

Pilgrimage
to
People

BY ANNE FREMANTLE

DAVID McKAY COMPANY, INC.

New York

PILGRIMAGE TO PEOPLE

COPYRIGHT © 1968 BY ANNE FREMANTLE

LIBRARY OF CONGRESS CATALOG CARD NUMBER: 68-10539

MANUFACTURED IN THE UNITED STATES OF AMERICA

VAN REES PRESS • NEW YORK

for Paul Horgan

sine quo non

"... and it was here that Margaret hoped to help him. It did not seem so difficult. She need trouble him with no gift of her own. She would only point out the salvation that was latent in his own soul, and in the soul of every man. Only connect! That was the whole of her sermon."

E. M. Forster, Howard's End

Author's Note

This proposes to be a travel book with a difference, a series of recognitions and rejoicings, a pilgrimage to people around the world, a search for hyphen people. The Lord told Abraham He would save Sodom and Gomorrah should Abraham find ten just men. Had I such a chance to choose, these would be my ten just, for whose existence all their contemporaries should be glad and grateful. It is a poor heart that never rejoices, and I purr with pride and pleasure that I have known these ten hyphen people. Here are their names and avocations:

Jean Charlot	Professor of Art at the University of Honolulu, Hawaii.
Daisetz Suzuki	Japanese monk.
Swami Gauribala	German Protestant born, now a swami in Jaffna, Ceylon.
Dom Bede Griffiths	Benedictine monk now living as a *sannyasi* in an ashram in India.
Louis Massignon	Sometime Professor at the *Collège de France,* one of the greatest Islamic scholars the West has ever produced.
Jacques Maritain	French Protestant who married a Russian Jewess; both became Catholics. Professor, writer, ambassador.
Rev. Michael Scott	Anglican clergyman first identified with South African colored, now with Naga people of India.
John Howard Griffin	Novelist, musicologist, white Texan farmer who "passed" in the United States as a Negro.

vii

| Alexander Kerensky | President of the Provisional Revolutionary Government of the U.S.S.R.; devout Orthodox layman. |
| Dorothy Day | Founder of the Catholic Worker Movement in the United States. |

I also rejoice that I have visited these three bridge places: The Chinese Trappist Monastery on Lantao Island; the Benedictine Monastery at Toumliline in Morocco; the Center of Intercultural Formation at Cuernavaca in Mexico.

ANNE FREMANTLE

Chapter I

DICHOTOMY is today a permanently fashionable disease. Everything is divided into we-they: the West is opposed to the East, the Cold War hangs Iron Curtains galore, and every page of print is "slanted." It appears to be impossible to praise Peter without being thought to denigrate Paul. I want to make it clear from the onset that I have never wanted to take sides at all. If I praise the Orient, I am not, repeat not, thereby repudiating my Occidental heritage. I did not go to Asia from any hostility to Europe. Nor do I agree with those writers who smugly return home thanking their stars for their Judeo-Christian heritage and grateful that they are not Indians or Japanese, Hindus or Buddhists—instead of just feeling, as Ulysses so rightly did, happy that they had made a fine journey and were safely home.... Born a European, I have lived for a quarter of a century in the United States. Only recently was I able to fulfill a lifelong ambition to circle the globe. I went frankly on a pilgrimage to people. I went to look for, and I found, hyphen people and bridge places. Hyphen people are those who are links uniting cultures, creeds, or currents of thought. Bridge places are those that bridge national, class, or religious differences. The French have a good word for hyphen: *trait d'union,* a uniting line. Hyphen people are not mishmashes. They are not, above all, goulash people. On the contrary, they are, every one of them, people with a strong awareness of their own genes, their own identity, their own spiritual, cultural, and national commitment and history. It is only when you start from somewhere that you can expect to arrive anywhere; if you start from nowhere, that is where you will arrive at journey's end. You have to be yourself, you have to be intensely a person, before you can be a hyphen person. Similarly, a bridge place is a place with its own strong presence; the great bridge places have been magnets that drew almost every type of men and women. Athens, Iona, Jerusalem—as Dr. Samuel Johnson wisely said, the man whose piety is not quickened by these is poor indeed.

But why travel at all? After all, as St. Augustine wrote, fifteen hundred years ago, "The Lord did not say 'Go to the East and find salvation; voyage to the West to receive grace.' Where you seek, there you shall find, for to Him Who is everywhere present, one comes by love and not by sail." But I was not seeking salvation by my displacements. I was on a pilgrimage to people, in the plural, and, like other animals, people are best viewed in their native habitats. In New York or London one can meet people living happily, completely assimilated, who come from every race, class, creed, and color, just as in any good zoo one can find every type of bird, beast, fish, or reptile. But meeting people casually, like viewing animals at a zoo, is very different from tracking them to their lairs and getting to know them where they are at home. Watching people gives me the same immense pleasure that bird-watching gives some of my friends: there is nothing in the world I enjoy so much. And, wherever possible, I like to watch people in their own eyries or burrows.

So I set off from the fourth-floor walk-up railroad flat in Manhattan that has been my own peculiar and beloved eyrie for twenty years, on the feast of the Annunciation, the feast that is, above all others, the feast of our freedom. In England it is a quarter day, one on which rents are paid; in Rome it is the day on which the Vatican year begins, insofar as dating documents is concerned. But above all, it is the feast of the word *Fiat:* that four-letter word that created us and all things visible and invisible, and that on this day gave us back the liberty that is the only reason for our creation. Mary and her Father-Lover-Son used the same word. *Fiat,* said He, *be; fiat mihi,* qualified she, so be it done to me.

Because I was leaving it, the view from my kitchen window, of crisscrossed colored laundry lines and fire escapes mondrianing against the hard, enamel-blue bright March sky, with the still bare branches of ailanthus—that dear Japanese tree-of-heaven that accommodates itself to, and grows splendidly in, not only, praise be, Brooklyn, but in all the five boroughs—was particularly appealing. As we came out onto the pavement, the brownstones, in their variations of russet, ocher, rose-madder, and beige, burnished our street that ends, as all New York streets end, in sky or river. The morning sun polished the houses into a Canaletto, shining and high-toned, but I knew that by evening, when I would not be there to see, the sunset would soften the buildings to Claudes. And yet—without me there to see, could it be so? The rainbow is not, without my eye; are the sunsets? Every morning I had seen East 78th Street, but how often had I been aware of it? Perhaps the day I left was the first time. Yet it is I who was changed, not the street. Perhaps on my life's last day I shall see the dear world best of all, galvanized by my imminent departure from the vapid ablative of place, the static locative, to the brisk accusative of movement. Now I was answering not wherein am I, but whereto go I? Not *ubi,* but *quo.* And so it may be again in the hour of my death. For grammatical cases—what a pity we lack them in English—fix color and line and mood, as a photograph eternalizes a chance gesture.

How little, too, we appreciate New York who see it daily on our way to the office and back, who rush away from it for our every moment of leisure, bad citizens babbling of green fields

3

instead of rejoicing in our "dear city of Athens, dear city of God." Yet, as Stephen Spender so rightly pointed out years ago:

> When we have tired of the brilliance of cities
> Death and Jerusalem glorify also the crossing sweeper.

My tickets were of "open date," and I paid for a round trip but had not specified my itinerary around the world. For a journey should not have a what-did-we-see-yesterday and where-are-we-today ("If it's Monday, it's Rome, dear"— "Cairo?—That's where you lost your galoshes") context. Unless each new mountain, person, building, or ocean is seen objectively, not relatively to the traveler's timetable, Tokyo and Teheran and Xanadu too will, like Wordsworth's yellow primrose, be nothing more, or, worse still, will "dicotyledon be to him."

At Idlewild the 707 comes to a pier, so no driving out to it, nor the endless walking and scrambling up and down ramps or steps that one has at Orly or London or Rome. As I waited in that no-man's-land before takeoff, I wondered—for the umpteenth time—whether a place's identity was not only the sum of its inhabitants. Are dogs not right, after all, and cats wrong? Is New York anything more than its successive waves of immigrants, from Dutch to English to Irish to Jewish to Puerto Rican? What was Athens, peopled by any other race, or Oaxaca, or Warsaw? But for the creaking of a wooden horse and the shadow of Creusa, Troy would be powerless to draw men still, and it is not twenty centuries that look down from the pyramids, but the pharaohs who designed and the slaves who built them. These and these only bring men out today to the Egyptian deserts, as St. Anthony and St. Pachomius brought hundreds in the fourth century A.D. "Whom came ye forth to see?" our Lord asked, "a reed shaken by the wind?" No one ever did that; they came, as He knew, to find a prophet—and preferably more than a prophet.

Lack of ghosts, not of landscape or "scenic" beauties, makes

New Zealand meaningless, Australia tasteless, and the Canadian landscape a huge bore. New York's cities are called Babylon and Ithaca, Syracuse and Rome, in spite of the early indubitably staunch Englishry of their founders, because of the quality of those other cities, those other makers. Their names honor not the begetters of the flesh of American citizens, but the ancestors of their ideas.

Yet, as the 707 rose into the spring sunlight, the view over Long Island Sound made nonsense of my human arrogance. Contrariwise, I found myself arguing and admitting, it is not any human projection of man, not even of humanity's self upon earth's screen, that hallows it; it is this anonymous spring day, this light that is the hero of every picture. I will not, because Darius the king has put up his statue in the marketplace, even though it is of solid gold, fall down before it. It is the landscape that matters, not the figures. Places create values, they do not receive them; it is the fountain that is holy, not the nymph Arethusa. Had not its rivers flowed around Manhattan, that island would not have been worth even $24, let alone worthy to house a Melville, a Poe, a Mark Twain or a Thomas Wolfe. And Maurice Barrès is right when he says that every living being is born "of a race, a soul an atmosphere, and genius manifests itself as such only in proportion as it is closely linked with its land and its dead." Thus my mind ding-donged, contradicting itself. Anyway, I decided, let my first act, now that I may loosen my seat belt, be to make a salute to America, which we are crossing at the rate of 500 miles an hour and at the height of 30,000 feet—just a hundred or so feet higher than Everest.

In 1613 Sir Thomas Dale declared in a letter:

> I have seen the best countries in Europe. I protest unto you before the living God! Put them all together, and this country of America will be equivalent to them, if it be but inhabited by good people.

5

Good the American people certainly are, even if such ghastly public events as the assassinations of Evers and Kennedy and the civil-rights workers still take place among them. It was Wotan, the chief of the Aesir, the Norse gods, who told his companions, once their battles were done, "North you may go, to the country of snow and giants; south to blue sea and swallows; east, to the rising sun, or westward, home." And all the Aesir together shouted, "Westward, home!" Home, that one unique place where one hangs one's heart and one's hat, America has been to all comers since first it was discovered: home to John Fitzgerald Kennedy and Lee Oswald, home to Robert Welch and Norman Thomas, home to Barry Goldwater and Robert Oppenheimer, home to Helen Keller and Eleanor Roosevelt.

Looking out now on checkerboard country, like an illustration for *Alice Through the Looking Glass,* all snowbound still, seen in gaps between woolly clouds, I recalled my own first arrival here in 1936. I had just been defeated as a Labour candidate in Great Britain. I had stood (my American friends were quick to tell me I might have got in had I *run*) against Alfred Duff Cooper, later Lord Norwich, then Minister of War, a cousin of my mother's whom I had never met. As the youngest Labour candidate, I had been offered three equally hopeless seats: Ealing, Acton, and St. George's Westminster. The first two were rich London suburbs of no possible interest; the third had many associations for a dyed-in-the-wool Jacobite as I am. "I'll take Charles James Fox's old constituency," I brashly told the big boss, Herbert Morrison. I loved Fox even before I had learned what a great radical he was, because his first names were those of the two Pretenders—the last two Stuart princes who tried to regain the throne that was theirs by right of inheritance. "Charles James Fox? 'o's 'e?" asked Morrison. I was soundly trounced—I got 5,000 votes to Duff Cooper's 20,000—but I did not lose my deposit. In English elections every candidate has to put down fifty pounds, which he loses if he does not get 5 percent of the opponent's vote. Naturally, the parties insure with Lloyd's against such a contingency, but it is terribly *infra dig* to lose one's deposit, and one is rarely asked to stand again if it happens to one. Also I had kept Duff Cooper at least part-time in his constituency, instead of leaving him free to rush around helping everyone else, as he would have done had his seat been uncontested. I was also able to make him lose his temper frequently. For at that time he was Chairman of the League of Nations Union, which had issued a peace pledge questionnaire, but he had also told everyone to throw this questionnaire into the wastepaper basket (trash can to you). All I had to do was to send a spy to every Conservative meeting at which Duff Cooper was present. My spy asked him, "As Chairman of the League of Nations Union, why did you advise everyone to throw the current questionnaire in the wpb?" I always got my rise. The very next year, when the Abbey Division of Westminster was vacant, owing to the (Conservative) sitting member's death, I was asked to raise money for the young Labour candidate, just down from Cambridge. The very first person I wrote to was Duff Cooper, pointing out to him that if we didn't raise some money the seat would go uncontested, which he, as a true democrat, could not approve. By return mail he sent me a cheque for ten guineas, asking me not to broadcast his gift because it might annoy the Conservative Central Office! Later, when he resigned over Munich, I wrote congratulating him, and got a charming letter in reply, hoping we would never have occasion to fight again. Nor did we.

After my defeat, in order to lick my wounds, I accepted a lecture tour in the United States for the English Speaking Union. I was to speak on the British Social Services—almost all of them Fabian-initiated, all of them either Liberal- or Labour-produced. I was to be paid all my expenses, but somehow I had to find my own fare across the Atlantic and back. Luckily, my mother had shortly before asked me whether I would like to buy a Cézanne. She had been offered one by her

7

friend Flora Priestly, who had bought it in the artist's studio and now needed twenty pounds sterling for some charity. "I don't like Cézanne," Mama said firmly. "And I don't have twenty pounds," I said. "Offer her seventeen pounds." For that sum I obtained a charming little still life. Everyone laughed at my purchase, but when after two years, Venturi's catalogue was published, there was *my* Cézanne illustrated and its whole provenance given. So I took it to a dealer, who gave me 250 pounds sterling over the counter, with which I purchased my first trip across the pond. In the six weeks I was in America, I traveled over 24,000 miles, from Quebec, where I first landed, to Mexico City, and from New York to Los Angeles and San Francisco. I spoke in thirty-two states and, thanks to fabulous American hospitality, never spent a single night in a hotel. I traveled alone, meeting every kind of person. Businessmen talked to me about That Man in the White House; commercial travelers sounded off on race relations; sophomores argued about isolation and pacifism; garage boys were pro or anti the T.V.A.; taxi drivers were enthusiastic about the W.P.A. And everywhere I found peace. Peace such as Europeans could not imagine, involved as we were, emotionally or actually, in the Abyssinian war, in the Spanish Civil War. The previous summer, my husband and I had driven up from Savoy to attend the opening of the Kröller Müller museum at Arnhem, full of Van Goghs. We stayed in the lovely forest, in a tiny inn. All night long we heard troops marching by: the still night was full of the sound of muffled feet. Holland was holding massive maneuvers. And in England there were notices of air-raid drills on every lamppost, photographs of Air Raid Precautions in every daily paper, accounts of mock bombardments, mimic blackouts, the daily noise of practicing wailing sirens. We were all feverishly taking Red Cross courses and exams, learning about the effects of poison gas. We had all been issued gas masks. All the big stores had bombproof shelters, and every civilian was supposed to gas-proof one room in his own house. On arrival in the United States, like Christian at the gate, my burden of war hysteria rolled off. Experts disagreed about the vulnerability of the Maine coast, but in those remote, pre-Pearl Harbor, pre-atomic days, Europe seemed to most Americans a distant lunatic asylum, from which their ancestors had fled, for which their parents had fought and died, once only, once and for all. So Americans thought then, and how wrong they were. But the prewar climate was artificially prolonged, for when I returned to the United States in 1941, after the bombing of London had begun, after the fall of Europe, the Autumn Ball at Tuxedo was still making headlines in the New York press, and in the Middle and Far West there was still a general naive assumption that "we can keep out of this one."

But perhaps even more than the emotional or political peace, what first struck me about the United States was the actual physical peace. I had expected America—and I think most Europeans still expect America—to be a series of cities, Pittsburgh upon Newark upon Providence upon Baltimore upon Chicago upon Detroit, all linked by superhighways. I myself thought of America as all Route 1 between New York and Philadelphia, a megalopolis like the south coast of England from Margate to Southampton, or the French Riviera from Marseilles to Monaco. Very few Europeans have any idea of the beauty or the extent of the American country. When I exclaimed over it again and again to Americans, asking them "Why do you come to Europe for your vacation? We haven't anything like as lovely a country to offer you as you have here," the somewhat scornful reply was, "We don't come to Europe for the *scenery*." And later, when I returned to Europe in the company of Americans, I found it was true. They seek out our towns, or our palaces; our castles, not our countryside; our houses, not our gardens. I had expected America to be a bustling, fevered, restless nation, and instead found a land unimaginably peaceful and incredibly romantic, with a tempo— except in the biggest cities—much more eighteenth than twen-

9

tieth century. I arrived in New England just as the trees were turning, and from Vermont to Virginia the fall color was beyond any palette or picture I had ever seen. The white towns, each with a church whose javelined spire speared the nursery-teapot-blue sky, were set against backgrounds of lollopping low-wooded hills, furred with strange flames of sumac, hickory, maple, dogwood, locust, and mountain ash. The foliage died from the ground up, the parched grass golden first, then the low shrubs scarlet and crimson and yellow, the oaks translated to umber last of all. I traveled through the heart of this incandescence for seventeen days, and felt it as God-filled as the furnace of the three children. Nowhere in Europe is there such glory, nor is there anywhere such gloriously empty country; nowhere in Europe such rainbow splendor upon earth, with never a scab or wart of villa or tea shoppe for flaming mile upon mile. In the great stretches of color upon color upon color, to the horizon and beyond, one felt one had come to Lucretius's *flamantia moenia mundi*—to the flaming ramparts of the world. And the weather! Europe cannot in any part of it even imagine such weather. Every day sun-drenched, with a sky chicory blue by day, Sèvres blue by night, from October through December, and year after blessed year the same. The steadiness of American weather is astonishing. It is so predictable. It is rarely warm enough to swim before Decoration Day, rarely warm enough after Labor Day; but from Labor Day to Christmas the blue-and-gold succession of days is only occasionally interrupted (on the eastern seaboard) by brief torrential rains. Each day is a little brisker, there is more of a nip in the shining air, the leaves are crisper, and more of them fall. That is all.

Nature, which in Europe is a museum piece, a treasured prisoner in national park or preserved forest, hedged and fenced, labeled private, forbidden to trespassers, hemmed and hugged, here in America is wide open, free, and, for all man's boasting, is mistress yet. In Europe, there is little wildlife that survives, except such as is parasitic upon our own: lice, domestic animals, or household pets. In the United States, within forty miles of New York, last year the village policeman shot a bear. And wolf, eagle, coyote, moose, elk, puma, buzzard, skunk, chipmunk, rattler, and raccoon survive if, alas, ever more precariously. Deer still destroy the petunias in suburban gardens, still starve to death in suburban snow. South of the Mexican border, there is the same dearth of wildlife as in Europe. I have driven the length and breadth of Mexico and seen but one cacomixle in a whole week; presumably all other native fauna have been either eaten or killed because they, too, eat.

As the plane came down toward the beige towers of San Francisco, I realized that, for all their magnificence, it is not the towns that are most expressive of America. The canyons of New York, sunless by day, celestial honeycombs by night, convey a lifting of mind and heart as do mountains; the megalithic skyscrapers of Chicago that stare into cold, tideless waters or frozen spume have a monstrous glory; mile-high Denver, with its shining domes flashing like opulent dental work; San Francisco, its bridges soaring over peacock-colored water, and Washington, self-consciously white (though the majority of its population now is Negro) are no mean cities. But it is to the country that every American goes, Anteus-like, to recover his strength—above all, to the woods and to the shore. For us in Europe, the city is the hearth: it is from the city that men went forth in the morning to work in the fields or to sail the sea; to the "dear city" they came safe home at night. Only when the city gates were shut against the surrounding country or wilderness did those within sleep safe: the walls —of Jerusalem, Byzantium, Assisi, London, Paris, Kiev—gave their citizens a womblike security. And that Jericho's walls fell at his trumpet's sound made Joshua at least momentarily the equal of Moses. Whereas in America, men live outside the city, go into the city to their work, and leave it thankfully at day's end to sleep. Safety is not within the city (especially today!), but within the individual stockade, and it is an individual or family safety, not an urban one. Americans feel safe in the wilds; their camping, their sailing, and their fishing are economical, unorganized, easy-going—not "le" camping, with a flurry of gadgets, as is that of the French; not an ideological statement, as is that of Germans or Russians. In midwinter, grown American men go camping in sub-zero weather; Boy Scouts enjoy sleeping in igloos of snow. It is this abiding closeness to nature that is, I think, the true deep source of the average American's native lack of class consciousness and of his natural good manners. In Europe, those on the way up and those on the way down—the upstarts and the downstarts—are almost invariably touchy, unsure of themselves, and rude. Which leaves only peasants and princes (so to speak)—those with "abiding stations"—courteous and comfortable. In America, there is such a constant movement up and down every imaginable ladder—social, emotional, psychological, spiritual, and sexual—that travelers generally extend to each other, in self-defense if for no higher motive, the courtesies of the road. Americans rarely snub each other, the way Europeans do; they don't enjoy "scoring off" each other; by and large, few sneer, are snide or sarcastic, and few are "mean." This basic gentility, based on a real equality of opportunity, is also based on the geographical luxury of enough room in which to stretch minds, hearts, lungs, and legs. This has given every truck driver the superb self-confidence of an aristocrat, and every little air hostess the manners one would wish our duchesses had. St. Augustine declared peace to be the supreme good, the order which everywhere, in all creation, composes part to part, the diapason of the universe and the object even of war. That peace was America's birthright and her reason for existing. It was to seek peace and ensure it that the Pilgrims came, and the Pollacks, the Wasps, Wops, Krauts, Yids, Micks, Chinks, and Japs.

From San Francisco, where we halted for less than an hour, it took under six to cover the 2,100 miles to Honolulu. The luxurious, giant, comfortable planes have substituted danger for the discomfort that used to accompany every journey. Dirt, fleas, undrinkable water, long nights sitting bolt upright in a filthy dark, these used to be generally prevalent, the jewels of endurance of which every traveler boasted. I remember on one vacation from Oxford going to see the Passion Play at Oberammergau. Four of us traveled third-class by train for three days and two nights from Ostend, sleeping in turns on the floor between the seats when we could sit on the wooden benches no longer. I managed to climb up on to a luggage rack, and stretched out in temporary bliss, to be demoted by a sulky guard. "Call yourself light luggage," he growled. Men spent their winters alone in ice huts, eating nauseating pemmican, or spent their summers blown in Gobi sandstorms, or they hung exposed, toes dropping off their feet ripe-fig-like, to seek a saint cave-hidden in the perpendicular face of Mount Kailas or a mythical colonel long since decomposed in the Brazilian jungle. Whereas today, here and now, we have excellent seats with "cuppas" of tea and cat naps provided for all the way. Only fear remains, bound to us like our shadow, with centered in it the memory of all those we have known who perished in the air, from the Queen of England's uncle to Dag Hammerskjöld. A Victorian epitaph for a mountaineer epitomizes, perhaps, the feeling one has each time one flies for those whose flights have ended in fall.

> One moment stood he, as the angels stand
> High on the topmost pinnacle of air
> The next he was not; to the fatherland
> Translated unaware.

Or so one hopes. Unaware? *Quién sabe?* as they say in Spanish. One will never know, unless. . . .

The descent over Molokai, Father Damian's leper island, was through lyrical rainbows. How green the islands looked—so different from blue Mediterranean islands, Greek or Italian or

13

Spanish. Curiously, tropics are basically green, whereas in Europe even the colder South Downs or Hebrides are blue. What is it that turns green English grass blue in the distance and leaves Puerto Rican rain-forested hills green? No doubt the answer is smog.

Again the antithesis of people and places presented itself. Molokai, without Father Damian, is just one, and by no means the most interesting, of the Hawaiian islands. Sanctified by him, it is, perhaps, the *only* interesting island in the group. For here something real happened. One man deliberately chose pain, disgust, horror, and death. He truly was one of those men of whom O'Shaughnessy wrote, "We dreamers, we derided, we mad, blind men who see." For in making his choice he also made himself into what every man is supposed to be: a saint.

As we arrived in Honolulu, the tiny airport was blessedly warm—75°—and pretty girls hung scented leis on every arriving passenger. My lei was of tuberoses only, my son Hugh's of tuberoses and orchids. It was the first time in this life, and probably will be the last, that I have had *enough* tuberoses. They grew in the hottest of the seven hothouses in my childhood home, Possingworth, in Sussex, together with freesias, stephanotis, and gardenias, but how few there were of each, and how precious. Reed, our Scottish head gardener, himself cut these flowers when ready and sent them down in a special trug to the "Mansion." There they were sent up to Mama's boudoir, where she alone arranged them. Their scent had mixed meaning for me. For her "boudoir" was where Mama scolded. When one of us had been bad, we were sent for, and would nervously ask our beloved butler, Pink (always on our side, a real friend), "Pinkchen, is it *boudoir?*" All too often Pink, his long, sad face even longer and sadder, would solemnly say, "I am afraid so, Miss."

Today the heady smell, though it brought back memories, betokened no such wrath to come, and was, on the contrary, all gay greeting.

We were met by Jean Charlot and his wife, who found a hotel for us, installed us, and returned to fetch us the next day, insisting that we move to their house, which we did with the more delight as the two boys who were home, Martin and Peter, had been fellow students with my youngest son Hugh at St. David's in New York.

On our first day we tried to learn as much as we could about Hawaii, which entered Western history when the islands were discovered by Captain Cook in 1778. (He returned in 1779 and was killed in Kealakekua Bay.) Happy the land that has no history, says the proverb. Until 1778, each island was separately ruled by a chief. But Kamehameha, Chief of Oahu, by dint of acquiring European-type vessels—he built up a navy of twenty vessels from twenty-five to fifty tons each—subdued the chiefs of the other islands and became undisputed ruler of the whole group. He died in 1819 and was succeeded by his son, who abolished *tabu* and encouraged missionaries. In 1824 this king and his wife visited England, where both died of measles. Lunalilo, their successor, died without heirs in 1874 and was succeeded by King Kalakaua, who was elected by ballot in 1874.

Japanese immigration to Hawaii was furthered by a convention signed in 1881; today the Japanese and Chinese are the most numerous, the most prosperous, and the most enterprising of Hawaii's citizens. There is no native word for female virtue; polyandry and polygamy are both indigenous, as is leprosy. Exports used to average $125 per head when it was said (in 1885) that "no country in the world has as large a commerce as the Hawaiian Kingdom, in proportion to the population." Now every mouthful of food has to come by sea, and the 1962 shipping strike on the U.S. mainland caused such a run on supplies after only a few days that there was a hysterical fear of starvation, and much hoarding. Hawaii used to export sugar, rice, and coffee—to the tune of 142,655,000 pounds of sugar, 9½ million pounds of rice, and 146,000 pounds of coffee in a year.

Earlier, too, half a million pounds of wool and 61,740 hides were exported in one year. Today every ounce of sugar, rice, wool, and coffee, and every hide, has to be imported, because the United States discourages any form of crop-raising and offers no incentive to local productivity.

We betook ourselves to Waikiki beach, to a cold, rough sea, where beautiful young men were surfboard riding, and a few ugly old ones used sand and sea unenthusiastically and unaesthetically.

After supper on our first evening we watched hula dancers demonstrate the total depravity so-called civilization can bring. Two old painted Hawaiian harridans dragooned a batch of eight- to ten-year-old Lolitas, all made up like tarts, all dancing and acting in the lewdest way. Dressed in their lovely native costume, these moppets, performing their (originally) lovely and dignified native dances, were more suggestive than the most salacious of call girls. In a ravishing setting of magenta bougainvillaea and palms, this noisy, filthy spectacle was doubtless supposed to titillate the appetites of the watching, tired, flaccid American businessmen. It was such a horrifying, odious, and tasteless performance that we crept away, ashamed to have been present, still more ashamed that our Caucasian presences occasioned such nauseating and pornographic exploitation of small girls.

Next morning Mrs. Charlot came to take us to Mass and then on to their home. We were enchanted with the Charlots' house, which they built themselves, and which is small and perfect. The kitchen is completely decorated with handmade tiles designed by Jean Charlot. The dining-room table stands half inside the house and half outside, so meals can be independent of the weather; since there is much rain in Hawaii, a raincoat covers the outside half of the beautifully grained wood table top when it is not in use. The Charlots love entertaining. We met many of their friends and ate marvelously, as Mrs. Charlot is a superb cook. The house has three bedrooms and three baths, and a stepladder leads up to the boys' "den," where they have television, etc. The library is infinitely civilized, with a glorious Chinese silk rug on the floor and a Steinway grand piano. There is also a studio for Jean, yet the whole area of the house is only 3,500 feet. The Charlots took us to the highest point of Honolulu, and also to the University of Hawaii, where Jean is senior Professor of Art, and where he has painted a huge wall of frescoes in the university itself. His figures are bold, his colors cool, a good combination in Hawaii, where, because of the prevailing damp, the sky is pale, often overcast, with frequent sudden rainbows to lift heart and eye. We also went with Jean to see many others of his frescoes: some in a new hotel, others in a bank. We were then taken to the University's East-West Center, headed by an Indian, Dr. Saksena, a Hindu philosopher with a strongly ecumenical outlook. The East-West Center was founded as an answer to Moscow's Freedom University and is run on almost the same principles as those of Nanking University in China, though it is on a smaller scale (Nanking has 9,000 students) and accepts more foreigners. The Center has a U.S. Federal grant of $10 million and exists to implant U.S. values in those who attend it. It is remarkably free from racism of any kind, and the caliber of its reputation can be gauged from the fact that D. T. Suzuki taught for a year here. The Charlots—Mrs. Charlot is as markedly from the heartland of the United States as her husband is from Europe—have four children: a married daughter, a theologian son, who in 1967 married a French aristocrat, and two younger boys, Martin and Peter. Martin, born in 1944, started making movies at twelve with an 8 mm. camera his mother bought him. A year later a local television station sponsored and showed his film, *The Baby Dinosaur*. Two years later he completed his *Memento Mei*, a film about his own dreams. A third completed production, *Apocalypse 3:16*, started with a capital of forty dollars, took nine months to make, and takes an hour and fifty minutes to play. The chief actor is a Hawaiian of royal heritage,

17

Tom Kealiinohomoku. Both Martin and his friend Tom are painters, like Martin's father. Tom has had his pictures exhibited at the Downtown Gallery in New York; Martin has had a one-man show in Honolulu, and has also shown in several mixed shows in New York. Even though now in the Army, doing his military service, Martin keeps up his painting, spending every minute of leave at work. His younger brother Peter is Martin's opposite, being tremendously athletic and extroverted. Peter enjoys the Army for what it is and does not live for his leaves, like Martin.

Jean Charlot was born in France on February 7, 1898, of mixed French and Mexican ancestry. His mother's maiden name was Goupil. Her great-great-grandfather had gone to Mexico around 1820. One of his children married an Indian woman; another, Charlot's great-grandfather, a Sephardic Jewess of Spanish descent, with whom he returned from Mexico City to Paris. Their daughter married Jean Charlot's father, a Frenchman who had lived in Russia and sympathized with the Bolshevists. At the age of three, young Jean began to draw, and he remembers as his first loves the Mexican illustrated codices in the family collection. Dolled up in Little Lord Fauntleroy suits, he was taken to church, in Paris in the winters, in the country in the summers. He remembers the absurdities of feminine dress in those days as he struggled to kiss an aunt through "the pillowed hurdles of bosom, boas and plumed hat." His father was a freethinker and an anarchist, his mother "sweetly pious." This the child found an enviable combination, for he could thus simultaneously obey and rebel, be docile and choose a path of his own.

On the occasion of his first Communion, a friend of his parents', Désiré Charnay, who hunted—and claimed to find—Atlantean and Egyptian remains in the Maya jungles, and had made casts of stelae with wet newspapers, gave Jean Charlot some North American grave pottery. It seemed appropriate, he told the child, because he had found it in the grave of a child. Jean also had an early passion for Greek vases and spent every spare moment copying them in art galleries. He also strained his eyes copying medieval miniatures. He worked for the designer Poiret while in his early teens and won prizes for sculpture and for a series of woodcuts of the Way of the Cross, later to be published as a book.

One summer Sunday morning, clinging to the hand of a drafted cousin newly in town, Jean was taken as usual to the village church at Poissy, "more Romanesque than Gothic, where St. Louis of France with his mother Blanche had worshipped." To reach the church they had to cross the town square with its chestnut trees. In the square's center was a statue of the painter Meissonier, "glorious native son, his bifurcated, frizzled beard sweeping awry over a square palette that, in turn, seemed to drip its load of pigment over the velvet pants of the artist." In church, the Charlots knelt sideways and close to the altar, following Mass through the open woodwork of the chancel. Before climbing into the pulpit, the priest took off his chasuble and appeared in his white alb. Jean Charlot described the resulting crisis in his faith as follows:

Monsieur le Curé was neither beautiful, nor thin. His skin, sweating off the summer heat, gleamed with the deep veinous red of a florid complexion. It was already through the eye that I thought, and this spectacle of the ecclesiastic in his nightshirt, as it seemed, bibulous with *vin ordinaire,* his pug nose tipped with a blue highlight, loomed unbearably grotesque. How could a Faith represented by such a symbol have any truth in it? I should get up and go, never to come back. Physically the opposite happened. My muscles reacted in place of a distracted mind. My elbows dug a little deeper into the arm-rest of the *prie-dieu* and my knees into its cushion. As swiftly as the vision and revulsion had come, they went, and the matter of faith was settled, for some forty years to date, and, let us hope, for as long as Time.[1]

[1] *Born Catholics,* F. J. Sheed, ed. Sheed & Ward, Inc., 1954, p. 100.

In his late teens, Jean Charlot became a member of the Guilde Notre Dame, made up of sculptors, designers, embroiderers, decorators, and stained-glass designers. During World War I he was an artillery lieutenant; at the war's end he found himself in Germany with the French army of occupation, where he discovered for himself and became absorbed in Matthias Grünewald's pictures. On his return to France he found the making of liturgical art provided a common ground between his devotion and his vocation. But his career as a French liturgical artist was cut short when a priest, having ordered some murals for a new church in a Paris suburb, changed his mind. How often priests—and other people too— were to change their minds, not after (for that an artist can understand—the one who commissioned the work simply doesn't like it), but before seeing it! Especially this habit was exasperating for a muralist, who has to make so many preparatory sketches.

Before he left France at twenty-three, Jean Charlot had inwardly digested several French Catholic writers. At his pimpliest stage J. K. Huysmans, that purplepassaging overwriting Dutchman, who "disguised with a sauce of obscure adjectives the clear taste of clichés," spoke to his condition. Later, Jean came to admire Paul Claudel, whom God, W. H. Auden assures us, will pardon: "pardon him for writing well!" Claudel reciprocated by coming to admire Jean Charlot. Claudel wrote the introduction to the catalogue of Charlot's first New York exhibition, at the John Becker gallery in 1932; he also wrote a monograph on Charlot's painting in a series called *Peintres Nouveaux* published by the *Nouvelle Revue Française* in 1935. Charlot illustrated Claudel's *Christophe Colomb,* his *Légende de Prakriti,* and in 1946 *Les Révélations de la Salette.* A fruitful mutual admiration society indeed. Charlot says he learned a decisive lesson in mural composition from Claudel's *Processional* "as generous and lasting as a visit to Assisi." Also read was poor Léon Bloy, whose child died of cold and hunger, and who haunted the Paris bordellos looking for a latter-day saint and never found one, while all the time Pope Pius X, a genuine, certified saint, sat where Bloy would never, never have imagined one could—and never thought to look!—on the throne of St. Peter.

Jean Charlot arrived in Mexico in 1921 to live with an uncle, a man with a magnificent collection of antiquities, not yet housed in a museum. Landing from his ship, at Mass in the cathedral of Vera Cruz, Jean saw his first Mexican priest, a genuine Indian of the kind locally called *indio verde*. "All through Mass I watched lovingly the nape of dark green skin between the fringes of white hair and the gold galloon of the Sunday vestments." In Mexico Jean frescoed his first wall: he painted with revolver in hand, in order to discourage the displeasure of the spectators, who were horrified at his covering the walls of their old palace with a layer of cement. He also made woodcuts, illustrated the leading poems of an Estridentista poet, wrote reports of Mexican arts for Paris reviews, discovered an Indian model who became a "classic" native female in modern Mexican painting, and started the painting of murals in schools. He admired—and still admires—the Mexican painters who in these years frescoed the walls of their public buildings with the history of Mexico. "These men," he wrote, "living as craftsmen in close union with the master masons and workmen with whom they collaborated, did work of social import and forgot the ivory tower and were recognized as useful by their fellow men. And ... their plastic language, though fit for descriptive purpose, was not a surrender to the past." They anticipated by some years the United States W.P.A. experiment that democratized U.S. culture, converting it from a few millionaires' expensive hobby to a national appetite. Charlot thinks a general comeback to storytelling in painting is unavoidable. "The craft of painting is in its healthiest state," he wrote, "when painting is used to an end, just as a healthy body is put to work. Painting for painting's sake is like the man who is afraid of failing health and totters through desperate medication and endless build-up exercises. Both for art and for man an anatomical interest in one's own carcass is born of a pathological fear of death. Modern art has become thus a language of interrogation and exclamation signs, fit to express emotional climaxes or introspective states but lacking the articulations needed for objective description. To be vital the comeback to subject-matter must be linked with the creation of a fit plastic language."

In Mexico, Jean Charlot's first mural, of the massacre in the Temple, was in the Preparatoria school, on a wall 14 feet by 26. He went to work with Diego Rivera on the walls of the Ministry of Education, where he painted backgrounds and details, and three panels, one of which—the Dance of the Ribbons— Rivera later destroyed and repainted. Charlot kept his monumental style even when no more walls were available to him because of disagreements with the authorities. He became art editor of an English language magazine called *Mexican Folkways,* and in 1926 he was hired by the Carnegie Institute's archaeological staff at Chichén Itzá, in Yucatán, to copy Mayan frescoes and bas-reliefs that could not be satisfactorily photographed. He also discovered, with Erick J. Thompson, the important Mayan site of Macanxoc. Of other Mexican discoveries Charlot has written:

When I came to Mexico, I had a stage country in my head; feathers, blue, green, and tropical pantomine. I was shown the most popular actress, the National Theatre, and also many too-white young girls with enormously high heels; themselves wound round with ruffles of organdie. And they showed me gentlemen with false collars. One of these, very much a millionaire, said to me: "Here, there are the savages, and ourselves. How can one speak of equality?"

Very soon I knew that indeed there was no equality. One day I

22

went out upon the streets at six o'clock in the morning. At six o'clock in the morning the fair ladies and their automobiles are still asleep.

That morning he watched the Indian women coming out of early Mass:

At first sight they are entirely the color of the dust; it seems as if flesh and worn clothing had fused in this gray which is extreme poverty and humility. When the eye becomes accustomed and the soul also, this rebel race discovers to loving observation the beauty of its weaves, and of its flesh.

Their *rebozos*—wrapped in a thousand ways, always with nobility, never keep a fold not essential to the body and its movement, the reverse of those fashionable cloths which crinkle like poodle dogs. Apparently alike, they are really composites of fine taste and artistic self-restraint; gray upon gray, black and light brown, rose and tenuous violet, blue from midnight to pastel, pigeon's throat, mauve, but fused so wisely that a scarcely attentive glance confuses them. The fringes affirm the texture as a musical motif over again with more accentuation; from the back, the braided hair with its red cord rounding the shoulder implies the flesh; face to face, the ovoid or spherical ocher-pigmented countenance transfers into the basic tone of the warp, while the white of teeth and eyes match the surface finish. By itself the rebozo is like a broken wing; it needs the tension and the living folds which model the face, though the face be hidden.

Blessed too the cold days when the man wraps himself in a sarape: he looks then . . . clothed in the waves of the sea. A piece of green wool here is worth a toga in marble. The sarapes: of multiple colors which come together in a white-gray-black and certainly the most beautiful of them are those without design, whose surface and texture is like the thin skin of a hard-beaten little burro, with white threads interwoven like the scars of the blows. This garment away from its wearer is no more than the shirt of a dead man, still retaining the form of his torso. The decoration is always simple, taken from familiar things of nature

23

and craft; beauty of hard earth and birds, better than Solomon in all his glory; and put together with an abstract geometry such as only this people after the Greeks of Crete have possessed.

In France, Catholicism had been all blue and pink and pretty: Corpus Christi processions with little boys in blue satin and little girls in pink organdy showering rose petals before the Host. "In Mexico," he writes, "the climate of the Church was reminiscent of late Fall, red leaves decaying underfoot or heaped for burning. It also looked like the art of Zurbarán, a black battleground strewn with the guts of martyrs and of heretics." For, in the 1920s, Charlot witnessed the persecution of the Church. It made, he tells us, gory reading. He admired the Mexican priests, and has described them well:

The Mexican Church is at an uneasy traditional stage, with a highly groomed group of priests trained in United States seminaries, ready to give Mexico the blessings of what they have learned North—one could say the latest models of spiritual plumbing. But it is still the body of low church men, the country priests, missionaries in their own tropics, fluent at Indian tongues and as poor as Indians, that ministers to the great bulk of souls. As did the sixteenth-century priests, and at a scarcely slackened pace, they butt full-force against a pagan world in which there is more than an overtone of Satanism. In each village, as a matter of fact, the priest's white magic clashes with the black magic of the witch. I can swear to these men's zeal and to their squalor. I cannot swear in all cases to their scholasticism, or their sobriety. . . . No Mexican preacher will ever bore, ever fail to exalt or to edify. The public admission of the average United States priest that he too is a sinner seems made with a thin-lipped mental reservation. The length to which the Mexican priest will go to publicly prove that he is a sinner, his display of heart and organs and his tearful gesticulations, leave no doubt as to both his repentance and his frailty. Carried over by the redundancy of the Spanish language, fortified by the clipped sounds of the *nahuatl* tongue, the country priest is an instinctive mystic, apt at creating images as fragrant

24

as those of a John of the Cross. He will work himself hoarse as he describes the beauties of the spiration within the Trinity; he will well nigh fall off his perch as the rope tightens around Judas' neck.

Many of Charlot's Mexican sketches emphasize his discovery of the horrid inequalities: one, compounded of "artistic disdain and ethical censure," is called *The Rich in Hell;* in another, a preposterous lady in purple wears a large gold medal on her plump breast. For Paul Claudel, Mexico is the place where Jean Charlot found his vocation. "Charlot is a constructor," Claudel wrote and "even color is with him an architectural element"; for example, yellow in a certain proportion holds up pink, as an arch supports an architrave. "He is born to fresco. . . . His painting smells of fresh plaster. He needs great spaces to fill— so why not all the whole distance between the Atlantic and the Pacific? What a joy to translate a whole world into the sphere of the vertical and to scramble up a ladder to paint on such a scale!"

In 1929 Jean Charlot came to New York, and he was less than edified there by being confronted with "what seemed to be an army of salesmen in cassocks." He had missed two arts in his far-flung search: merchandising and packaging, but found them in the Catholic Church in the United States. To this day, he laments, he understands less about the mystery of duplex envelopes than he does about that of the Trinity. At a New York mission, he watched "in awe how Dominican Fathers, inventing a kind of perpetual movement, sold us candles that were put upon the altar but not lighted, being returned to the pile from which they were sold again, and this *ad infinitum.*" When he closed his eyes in St. Patrick's to pray, he was "rudely shaken by a beadle as tough as any bouncer" and, kneeling close to a statue of St. Teresa of Lisieux, was expelled because he was suspiciously near the money box. Yet while in New York, where he taught for a year at the Art Students League, Charlot became reconciled to looking like a toothpaste salesman and to reading crime stories and tabloids. In 1943 he married Zohmah Day. The Charlots moved to Hawaii in 1949, and he feels for the nature of the Hawaiians, for their kind of being, as sympathetically as earlier he felt for Mexicans. He has Englished three ancient Hawaiian plays; he has great feeling for Hawaiian objects, possessing bone and hair ornaments and an amber necklace that belonged in 1911 to the last queen and a hand-colored lithograph of the last king.

He has described Hawaiian piety in *Born Catholics:* [2]

> Hawaiians revel in a physicality that clothes somehow fail to divert, hide or sublimate. In the islands, beauty and bulk have ever been synonymous and enormous fatness a privilege of royalty.... The Hawaiian female may be shapeless in terms of a sculptural form and quite unlike the stable beauty of a marble Venus, but so is the swimming octopus. Arms that seem as boneless and untiring in their motion as tentacles taper delicately towards the agitated feelers of ever swaying fingers. Hawaiian bodies are most alive at the hips. For Hawaiians, the seat of noble sentiments is not the heart but the intestines. To prove that he is, as we say, of good heart, a man will not put his hand to the cage of the ribs, but heartily slap his belly, thus proclaiming that he is *na'au ao*, a man with intestines made of light: he will refer to a schemer as a *na'au po*, one whose intestines are compounded of darkness. Thus it is fitting that history and religion be perpetuated by the motions of the hula, or belly dance. When the ladies of a sodality close in around the Holy Sacrament and march in procession, fearlessly clothed in Van Gogh yellow, how the gingerbread bodies sway, hard put not to reproduce the dancing prayer of King David before the Arch.... In Hawaii, there is no need and no desire for masks, as it is the body as such, and not as a symbol, that is a prayer in motion. Even though the full-blown hula is not performed in church it is an expected ingredient of church bazaars.

Recently Charlot was invited by Monsignor Franz Wasner, the Trapp family singers' famous chaplain, to decorate the

[2] P. 111.

Catholic Mission Church of Naiserelangi on Fiji about eighty miles from Suva, the capital. Here he painted three frescoes, all over ten feet high. He was delighted, on arrival, to be welcomed by the ceremonial presentation of a whale's tooth by Fijians whose parents were still cannibals. He painted Christ black surrounded with breadfruit trees. Christ wears a *masi*, the Fijian loincloth. Jean Charlot entered completely into Fijian life, enjoying helping with the plaster-making and "fratting" with the inhabitants of the grass huts, which, with their soft woven mats, he found deliciously comfortable. Charlot painted his friends into his frescoes: a little girl in her blue school uniform next to a banana tree in flower, a small black choirboy in scarlet, holding a candle. St. Francis Xavier is modeled from Monsignor Wasner. All the background is of giant ferns: the curly fronds resemble croziers and miters.

The Charlots enjoyed the exiguous life of the island for more than half a year—a life of unremitting work to provide food, clearing the ground, planting and caring for bananas and copra, raising cattle, planting taro and manioc, fishing and hunting. Children work in the fields, weed, harvest, and search for edible roots. When the Vatican Council was described in a sermon, the parishioners murmured to each other, "How can the poor Holy Father feed all those bishops?"

On one of Jean's frescoes the Indian boy Peter is seen with his pair of oxen. He was one of a septet who lived very differently from the Fijians. The latter have mats on their floors; the Indians have bare boards, and tables and chairs. When the frescoes were completed, Monsignor preached a sermon saying the two races, Fijian and Indian, must remain as united as they appear in the frescoes, both present as witnesses to the Redemption. Jean Charlot thanked the islanders for having taught him so much while he was living among them. He had watched them weaving mats, building houses, singing and dancing—all things he did not know how to do. But he could, and did, depict others doing these things: a fair exchange!

27

In four different countries, Jean Charlot has painted some forty frescoes. He has written and/or illustrated 65 books. He stems from four separate cultures: French, Mexican, Jewish, Russian. A good hyphen man.

On this first lap of my pilgrimage to people I found people, certainly, but also a country that had completely lost its identity, owing to the "presence" of a much larger, alien, all-encompassing culture. Nationalism is the besetting sin of the post-medieval world, a world that was at first the successor to Christendom, and that now, in many senses, is already post-Christian. Nationalism confuses the territorial imperative with the sense of identity, and, like all confusions, vitiates both. Hawaii was once a people in a place. Their place. Now it is a tourist trap filled with trippers pandered to by those they have corrupted. I was prepared to find there few of the just. I was not prepared to find Sodom, Gomorrah, Babylon and Nineveh established as the four cardinal points of this Eden, radiating from its heart.

Would I find the same phenomena in Japan, in Hong Kong, in Ceylon? Has the West come off, everywhere, on the East like a dye, indelibly discoloring it? Are VD, TB and bad taste all civilization has to offer? *Our* civilization? *Vamos a ver,* we shall see, I thought.

Chapter II

WE left Hawaii with no regrets. Nothing has been added by the United States except plumbing, and a school system that genuinely offers equality of opportunity. Are these enough to compensate for total economic dependency and the removal—as though it had been a grumbling appendix—of national entity?

Seven and a half hours' flight to Tokyo: the longest now when girdling the globe.

The Far East, at last. All my life I had longed for this moment. Mother had a stone Buddha outside on the roof garden of our London house; she also had an indoor bronze Buddha that was set in the red lacquer cabinet in the drawing room. To these we children offered flowers and incense. I read all of Lafcadio Hearn before I was ten, and all the stories about Arabia and Ceylon, Egypt and India, China and Japan, in the Andrew Lang fairy-tale books—the red, green, blue, and yellow, and the others. My uncle Arthur was a British diplomat, and while he was away (at that time in China) he left his excellent library in our Sussex house; it included a first edition of Lane's *Arabian Nights*. This, too, I devoured. I became a Moslem at nine, being received into the Woking Mosque to my father's distress. He was Church of England and patron of two livings; as Mama was high and he low, we alternated weekly: sang Eucharist one Sunday, choral matins the next.

I would have gone immediately to the Far East, the Near East, the Middle East, any east, as soon as I came down from Oxford at twenty, but I married at once. Now here I was, in the Far East at last, and what a deception! A small, poky, inefficient airport, dusty from newly-poured concrete, cold, and dark; slow, inefficient customs officers, incompetent and impolite; a long wait, and, finally, when we emerged, massive incomprehension. It was bitterly cold, and raining cats and dogs. None of the taxi drivers spoke a word of English. Suddenly I saw a priest—and never was so glad to see anyone. He was a Jesuit from Jochi (Sophia University) who had come to meet us. Father Dressman, S.J., addressed our taxi driver in fluent Japanese, and off we set toward the University, about an hour's drive away. Ugly, crowded streets, one-story tatty houses: was *this* Asia? Father Dressman and I stopped off at a subway station where a friend with a car was waiting, since taxis are not allowed, nor any but "authorized personnel" on the U.S. naval base where Father had parked me with George and Ann Dempsey. George was in the F.B.I.; his wife and he are both active in the Catholic Family Movement. Their tiny house, on a building estate taken over by the United States, was near the Jara Juku gate of the Meiji shrine. The Dempseys gave me a wonderful welcome, blissful hot chocolate, and their only guest room. From the window I could see a baseball diamond, a wall, and beyond them, sweeping live oaks and pines.

Everywhere there was evidence of United States power. Japan is an occupied country. Over 3,000 troops are on this base; 45,000 in Tokyo alone. The islands are so dotted with American bases that, from the "hairy Ainu" in the north, to the students at Jochi, no one can move without the occupying powers being aware of it. Yet my host is an admirable example of a centurion. An Annapolis graduate, his wife a graduate of St. Mary's, Notre Dame, they are filled with apostolic zeal, give their evenings to religious meetings, encourage "fratting" with the natives, and pay their Japanese maid $30 a month. For that she takes total charge of their two children from 8 A.M. to 8 P.M. (Mary teaches on the base) and two evenings a week stays until midnight (no overtime). The United States has its own radio, in English. The houses on the base are allocated in order of length of waiting. More babies rate more bedrooms; children over fourteen or more than seven years apart rate separate rooms for separate sexes. All the food eaten by all the U.S. forces is brought from the United States; all the clothes worn, also. (It is the same everywhere. For example, Aldous Huxley's son Matthew described to me how the United States Protestant missionaries in Brazil had erected a small Levittown in the jungle there. First, men are dropped by helicopter. They clear the jungle and build an airstrip. Then planes fly in building materials, and the U.S. men put up prefabs; later, wives and children are flown in, and all the food. Live chickens, too, so the invaders are in no wise dependent on the natives.)

Yet the United States personnel are very tactful. English friends staying in Japan told me they had no idea there were any occupying troops left, and there seems to be none of the resentment prevalent here that the British felt when, during the war, they were "underfed, underpaid, undersexed and under Eisenhower." And Father Dressman, whose brother is a Jesuit missionary working at Katmandu in Nepal, was "as the owl discreet." But how far was bustling, materialistic, apist Japan from Lafcadio Hearn or even Madame Butterfly! Yet in the splendid crop of young novelists there is evidence of intellectual life, and the "new religions" are evidence of spiritual stirrings.

The Dempseys, however, are despondent about the future of Catholicism in Japan, or indeed of any religion. After the war, many Japanese converted, or were ready to convert, on St. Christopher's principle, because America was the strongest, because America had won, because America was Christian, and because the largest single Christian body in the United States or out of it were the Catholics. But then the Communists pointed out that, actually, it was the U.S.S.R. that had won the European war, so why not become Communist? And after Communists and Christians fell out, the Japanese became generally inclined to cry a plague on both your houses. Now Japan is almost entirely secularized. Buddhism—even Zen—is peripheral; in the whole of Japan there are only 75,000 monks. Tokyo has a population of ten million; currently there are probably not more than 100 Zen novices in the whole city. This secularization is nothing new, for both China and Japan are nonreligious in the Judeo-Christian sense of religion being "fear of power invisible" or the acknowledgment of a "power outside ourselves that makes for righteousness." For the Chinese and for the Japanese, that power is neither fearful nor invisible, nor visible either, but totally immanent and inherent in all things; and it is never outside ourselves except insofar as it is as completely in others—people or things—as in ourselves. Professor Nakamura of Tokyo University gives three factors "responsible for the almost total secularization of religion in Japan." These are: first, the acceptance of absolute values within the phenomenal world; second, the spirit of tolerance, which was so general that from A.D. 794, for 350 years (the whole of the Heian period) capital punishment was abolished. (This spirit made the Japanese reject the Jesuit missionaries' teaching of eternal damnation.) And third, the ready absorption of foreign elements.

One factor that stands in the way of any large-scale conversion of the Japanese to Christianity is their dislike for any form of disputation. "Rikutsu," to argue, is a term of contempt. Another factor standing in the way of conversions is the Japanese genius for syncretization. Although the Japanese are not part of the continent of Asia, and so, like the English, always feel themselves somewhat marginally Asians and different from the "mainlanders," yet they have none of that essentially European feeling best expressed by St. Thomas Aquinas in the single

32

word *distinguo*. The Japanese happily provide brothels in the shadow of temples; a specially popular nightclub "turn" is a striptease of the Crucifixion, which shocks no Japanese; and Tokyo newspaper ads show the Buddha reading the evening paper. Nor does it seem incongruous to a young Japanese to be a Communist Party member while studying at a Catholic college, just as while most Japanese are nominally Buddhist, almost all are married and buried in Shinto ceremonies at Shinto shrines.

Today the great Buddhist monasteries, such as Daitokuji and Enkakuji, number their novices in tens rather than in hundreds, even though celibacy is not incumbent upon Buddhist priests or even monks—Asahina, the abbot of Enkakuji, and Kabori, the abbot of Daitokuji, are both married. It is the religious life itself that seems to have lost its appeal. Yet, daily, hundreds of schoolchildren and college students and adult groups of both sexes are escorted by guides through the many hundreds of shrines and temples on sightseeing trips. It may even be that this new emphasis on religion as part of Japan's *cultural* heritage itself expresses a whole new attitude in the East similar to that by which, for many people in the United States, culture is the purest *ersatz* for faith, and a Sunday spent in an art museum is seriously thought to be a more spiritual and interior experience than attendance at church or synagogue. It may even be, too, that the actual crowds thronging through the temples alter the whole experience of temple-going even for the believer: Chartres Cathedral during Mass, with the trippers excluded, is a different experience—almost a different actual *place*—from Chartres crowded with bus-loads of guided tourists all talking and walking at once. And the same is true of Kamakura.

As a result of the disruption caused by losing the war, and the consequent downgrading of the Emperor from godhood by General MacArthur's *fiat,* there is great nervousness and much psychosis among Japanese students. Even at Sophia there are

33

several suicides each year, and the overall figure for the country is high. Curiously, since national "face" was lost in defeat, there is today an even greater sensitivity about personal "face." The Jesuits told me that it is unwise ever to scold a student or reprimand him, however gently, in public. For any Japanese if accused of a crime will admit it, and more, for only someone claiming to be innocent is blameworthy: how *can* he be innocent? But if he admits his crime, then the criminal is let off lightly; shame is punishment enough. One young man, newly elected at the age of 26 to the Diet, in his acceptance (maiden) speech stumbled over one word. He killed himself that evening, and his family were *pleased* because thus he had wiped out the disgrace. This feeling for "face" accounts for the intense professionalism which the Japanese students put into everything. For example, on the baseball diamond outside my window, Japanese boys practiced every morning before school, and every afternoon until the light went—not from love of the game, but because they *must* become good at it. Whatever it may be—languages, sports, work, the Japanese apply themselves to it with more than German thoroughness and dedication. The idea of the "amateur" is simply nonexistent in Japan.

Japan is a country with 99 percent literacy, and its total of 505 colleges and universities is second only to that of the United States. There are 670,000 university students in Japan, 33,000 of them in Tokyo. Among the universities, Sophia, or Jochi (as it is called in Japanese), is rather a unique phenomenon. Perhaps the only Jesuit university in the world that admits to a Communist cell on campus, it was founded in 1913 by the German province of the Society of Jesus. Its rate of growth since the end of World War II has been phenomenal: in 1949, only 754 students applied; in 1957, 900. In 1962 the University was able to accept only 5,500 of the more than 10,000 Japanese students who applied. Currently it is over 8,000 strong.

The University's president, Father Oizumi, and the president emeritus, Father Paul Tsuchihashi—now over 95—are both Japanese, as are many, indeed most, of the Fathers. Pursuant to the expressed desire of the Holy See, that missionary priests should abandon their own nationality for that of their flock, all of the non-Japanese Fathers among the Sophia Jesuits have become, or are becoming, Japanese citizens. This, of course, means, for the United States' citizens, the giving up of their U.S. citizenship, and even the giving up of their names, to receive new Japanese ones. Father Tsuchihashi—who still says his Mass in the chapel every morning, and how impressive it is —was for many years the editor of the *Monumenta Nipponica,* which is the outstanding scholarly historical and etymological journal of Japan. It is now edited by Father Schiffer.

All classes at Sophia are in Japanese, except the evening classes in the new International Division, which has taught a further 1,100 students in the past twelve years.

Jochi's Jesuit faculty of seventy priests from sixteen different countries is assisted by 160 lay instructors, who include three women. Jochi is located in the Kojimachi district, just inside the outer moat of the old city. The five-story main building is a modern concrete structure that stands on high ground. From the roof on a clear day—a rarity in smoggy Tokyo—Mount Fuji can be seen. A few pine trees still prevail among the astonishing variety of buildings that make up Sophia University: these include old quonset huts, bought cheap after World War II, a 900-meter-square workshop for the department of mechanical engineering and a splendid new faculty of science and technology building that houses four science departments, i.e., mechanical engineering, electrical engineering, chemical engineering and physics, with eighty students—the maximum that can be handled at the moment—enrolled in each. The admirable library building, completed in 1952, houses more than a quarter of a million books, plus a fine reading room and a number of research study rooms for graduate students. Sophia confers doctorates in theology, philosophy, Western culture, and economics. The department of education, added in 1951, is one of the twenty-three new departments recently added to the university; others are foreign languages—English, German, French, Spanish, Portuguese, and Russian—and a law faculty. The cafeteria seats 500, and the dormitory building provides beds for 300 students.

The Summer School (run annually during July and August) is popular with United States students as well as with the Japanese. Held in English, it costs only $883 for the round trip from Seattle, Washington, and for all expenses for the six weeks.

All this activity is really phoenix-like, for only one year after its foundation Jochi was disrupted entirely by World War I. Then, hardly had it drawn breath when it was totally destroyed by the great Japanese earthquake of September 1, 1923. Rebuilt, it was then, once more, demolished by fire in World War II. Three times unlucky, Sophia University has nevertheless grown in barely a decade from under one to over eight thousand students, and from seven to twenty-five departments.

From its inception, the University was planned to become an integrated part of the Japanese educational system, and now its president is *persona gratissima* with the Japanese Department of Education and, indeed, has an importance that the size of the University—one of the numerically smallest in the country—does not warrant. This is partly because the Jochi president does not change, whereas in Japan, for political and other reasons, presidents of educational establishments very frequently do! And it is partly because Jochi's policy is for all its faculty to get their degrees at Japanese universities. Its young European and American scholastics now study Japanese language and culture for three years in Japan before going away for their theological studies, so that when they return to Japan as priests, they are already fluent in Japanese. More and more return from Europe and the United States with doctorates already under their belts. The Jesuit motto, after all, has for four centuries been *age quod agis,* do well (professionally, thoroughly) what you do; and the Japanese, who are tremendous perfectionists themselves, recognize and admire this quality in others.

Although Jochi is a founding member of NIKKEREN (The Japanese Christian Colleges Students Federation), of which at this time a Jochi student is president, less than 5 percent of Sophia's students are Christians, and none is required to be, for Sophia, named for the Divine Wisdom, does not discriminate in any way on the grounds of religious beliefs. However, some distinguished Japanese Christians are connected with it: Mr. Kobayshi, for example, one of the first Catholics to run for the Diet, who is head of the economics department, and Mr. Tanaka, formerly Chief Justice of Japan, and now on the International Court of Justice at The Hague, who is one of Jochi's trustees.

Sophia students, like all Japanese, are very social-minded, and Sophia has an enormous number of sport and cultural clubs—over 70. The Japanese hate to be alone, even for a moment. Such sports as eikido, judo, kendo, and archery have many devotees, as have baseball—Japan's favorite sport—tennis, soccer, and chess. Music—from jazz combos to guitar—is very popular, and boys and girls take their instruments for a whole weekend of practicing to some country place. The Japanese are such perfectionists that they will not stop doing anything they have undertaken until they have really mastered it. This trait, however admirable, leads to an absence of *esprit de corps:* it is almost impossible to get an audience for, say, a Jochi baseball or soccer match, as the students are all dispersed practicing hard at their own preferences. It is also very difficult to get Sophia students to go home, for most of their homes are small, poky, and overcrowded, so the Fathers have to drive the boys and girls away from study rather than encourage them to it. Similarly, every library or reading room in Japan is jam-packed. Such places as the U.N. library or the British Council

37

library have daily queues waiting for every seat, as they are rightly regarded as oases of peace in which work can be pursued.

In a poll made by one of the four student magazines published at Sophia, the chief interests of the students were listed. Eighty percent said their chief interest was their own career. After this, in second place, came politics or economics. Thirty percent of the students professed some religion, as against a national average of 15 percent; 61 percent of Japanese in a national poll of all the major cities professed no interest *whatever* in *any* religion. Yet many Japanese drop into shrines to pray casually, and almost all observe the week when the dead spirits come to visit and are made welcome in homes, where they are fed and entertained. On the last day of their visit, paper boats are made, lighted candles are put inside, and they are floated down the river. The Japanese generally are fond of any and all reminders of mortality—loving, for example, mildew and moss and mushrooms growing in a damp wood.

Jochi boasts several scholars of international fame. One, Father Heinrich Dumoulin, a German, is an outstanding student of Zen, and the author of *A History of Zen Buddhism*, published in the United States in an English translation by Pantheon Books (1963). We had the great privilege of being shown Kamakura by him. First there was a suburban train ride through lovely, jerky small hills. The almond blossom was in bud, and the orange-twigged, green-tipped willows had a busy look. It was horrifying to find Japanese popular piety as tasteless as our own: a huge image of Kwannon, the goddess of mercy, on a hillside was as saccharinely revolting as any Barclay Street statue of our Lady of Lourdes. We went first to the Shinto shrine at Kamakura where in the thirteenth century young Prince Yoshituna hid behind a tree, while his faithful favorite, Shizuka, tried to distract his elder brother Yoritomo. In vain: Yoritomo saw his brother, and killed him. Yoritomo pacified the country and gave Japan a constitution and a hier-

38

archy, establishing the hereditary shogunate, the "dual system," which lasted until 1868. But he continued to have remorse for having killed his brother. So he ordered Shizuka, now in his power, to sing and dance in public in his honor. But the loyal girl, decked in her loveliest robes, instead sang of Yoshituna's innocence and betrayal. Yoritomo, in expiation, built this temple to Hachiman, god of war, and set up also an image of himself. Here, too, but outside the temple, is the great bronze Daibutsu, the gigantic Amida-Buddha built some fifty years after Yoritomo's death. Amida is Buddha in the form venerated by the Jodo School of Buddhism, which teaches the Pure Land. According to this teaching, everyone is born into the Pure Land, and nothing is to be *done* by anyone: the whole spiritual life and development of each human being consists simply in realizing what and where he already is. By saying the name "Namu-amida-butsu," the devotee not only is in the Pure Land, but

> When I worship thee, O Buddha
> This is a Buddha worshipping another Buddha

as Saichi put it. Amida the Daibutsu is the Buddha of the Infinite Compassion, the Daihi, *Tai-pei* in Chinese, *Karuna* in Sanskrit. This is the aspect of ultimate reality stressed by Shinran (1173–1262). The other aspect, infinite wisdom, or Daichi, in Chinese *t'ai-chi*, *prajna* in Sanskrit, is that stressed by Zen. But as D. T. Suzuki, the interpreter of Zen to the West, has put it (in a lecture delivered before the Emperor of Japan in 1946), "The wisdom flows from the compassion and the compassion from the wisdom for the two are in fact one." This "one" is no person, but "the field" or ground of our, and all, being. "Whom do you address, and for what do you ask?" Father Dumoulin once asked a Buddhist priest. "I address no one and I ask for nothing," was the reply. Meister Eckhart, the medieval Dominican, put it thus in Catholic terms, "God must be very I, I very God, so consummately one that this he and this I are one 'is'." Or, as Meister Eckhart quotes St. Dionysius Denys, the Areopagite, as saying: "God is a fountain flowing into itself."

I made my obeisance to the great bronze Buddha. Once it was protected by a temple, but after it had three times been destroyed by tidal waves it was left exposed to whatever might fall upon it, snow or sea or rain. The draperies fall simply about the figure; the forehead is broad, the mouth full; the palms are turned upward, thumbs together; the eyes are half closed. Yet there is no sensation of sleepiness: the calm is of total awareness; the self is gathered, absolutely present. Here is eternalized in bronze a human being in what Meister Eckhart called the "now-moment," eternity's day in which all time is contained. The image is of one who has arrived where he always was, and found the place "satisfactory," as T. S. Eliot put it of the Magi at Bethlehem.

After seeing the Buddha, we drove three miles up through the back streets of Kamakura and into the country to a little monastery founded in the eleventh century by Mozo (his name means "dream-window"). The garden was idyllic, with peach and cherry blossoms in flower, the first we had seen. (Cherry blossom time officially begins in Japan on April 1, and artificial cherry blossoms are tied to every city lamppost, as are artificial willow fronds in summer, and fall foliage in autumn.) The green grass was starred with scillas and hepaticas and grape hyacinths. Little groups of Japanese ladies, each with one Caucasian lady in tow, were lunching in bright kimonoed clusters. We were parked in a most agreeable damp cave; above us was a damp seat from which, on clear days, Mozo could see Mount Fuji. We had a marvelous lunch: no eggs, fish, meat, or milk, but vegetables grown in the garden, lots of tea-stalks, mushrooms, bamboo shoots, several sweets, and two kinds of fragrant tea. We fed cake crumbs to some bantam hens while their cocks fussed around them. We went on to Kenkhoji, built in

1253, where up three flights of broad, worn stone steps is a wooden statue of Kwannon, the sexless god-goddess of mercy, who wears for a crown ten faces of him/herself. In China, Kwannon is male; in Japan, she is female, providing the female element in the Buddhist pantheon. The word for *Spirit* is female in Hebrew, Arabic, and Sanskrit so that in Genesis the spirit of God that brooded over the waters is feminine, as is, in Islam, the spirit of God, Ruh' Allah. And when a Christian says the Nicene Creed in the original Greek, he states that he believes in the Holy Spirit (feminine). Gold-lacquered, the Kenkhoji statue of Kwannon is supposed to have been found in the sea by a fisherman. Outside the temple is a statue of Binzuru, who may not enter the sacred precincts, because, though one of Buddha's original disciples, he once admired a woman's beauty.

Buddhism's attitude toward sex seems ambivalent. On the one hand, a Buddhist monk may not even touch a woman. (At a UNESCO luncheon I had to sit opposite a young monk, Rahula, not next to him, in order to avoid even adventitious contact. And of course no monk shakes hands.) Yet Zen evangelist monks such as Suzuki himself, Dr. Ruth Sasaki, the priest of the American temple in Kyoto, whose late husband was also a priest, and J. Kapleau, from New Haven, another U.S. ordained Buddhist priest, are married. Perhaps the answer lies in the taking of temporary vows—one swears off sex as Christians used to in Advent and Lent (hence the proscription still observed against celebrating marriages in Lent) and as Moslems do during the month of Ramadhan, and while performing the pilgrimage to Mecca. *Quién sabe?* as the Mexicans say; who knows? I certainly do not.

Asahina, the abbot of Enkakuji, is a national figure—something of the order of an Archbishop in the Church of England. He had just returned from making a television appearance in Tokyo when we saw him. He lives with his family in a small building within the monastery compound. His head was shaven, and he wore a white vest, a white silk handkerchief around his throat, and black trousers. He was very gay, and giggled a great deal. He and Father Dumoulin seemed to enjoy themselves together hugely, and laughed a lot; their whole conversation was in Japanese. Asahina pretended not to know any English (I had my doubts about this, and Father Dumoulin confirmed them, saying he speaks it perfectly). He told me, via Father Dumoulin, I could ask any question I liked. I asked whether, in meditation, images should be used or subdued. He replied they should be controlled, but not dismissed, for we can only proceed by imagination. If we wipe away all images, we are not mindful, but mindless. He told us that at Enkakuji there are only sixteen novices. We were shown the great belfry, with its eight-foot bell, the Semmon Dojo or "seat of perfect wisdom" where the Buddhist monks are trained, the hall enshrining the Buddha image, and the zendo.

Kamakura is indeed a holy place, with something of the atmosphere of the Greek Olympia. Here is also the Tokeiji nunnery, founded by the widow of the second shogun of the house of Hojo, Tokimune (1251–1284), on a hill opposite Enkakuji. Here at Kamakura the great Buddhist revival began around 1185, and Enkakuji was built for the outstanding Chinese Zen master Tsu-yuan. The various Japanese Buddhist sects are said to equate the various classes: Tendai for the royal family, Shingon for the nobility, Zen for the warriors, and Jodo for the masses. The Kamakura period was the greatest flowering of religious life in Japan. Then Zen, protected by the militaristic shoguns, struck deep roots and flourished greatly. "Zen," Suzuki has pointed out, "is a religion of will-power, and will-power is what is urgently needed by warriors . . . enlightened by intuition." [1] Rudyard Kipling describes the *kami*, the "feel" of Kamakura in the following lines:

[1] *Zen and Japanese Culture*, D. T. Suzuki, Eastern Buddhist Society, 1938.

Whoso will, from pride released
Contemning neither man nor beast,
May hear the soul of all the East
About him at Kamakura
Yea, voice of every soul that sprung
From life that strove from rung to rung
When Devadatta's rule was young
The warm winds bring to Kamakura

We flew to Kyoto along the side of Fuji, chipmunk-striped in the melting snow, as perfect a mountain as Mexico's Popocatepetl, and even more impressive because it is alone, rising straight out of a plain, with blue sea beyond. From Osaka airport, market gardens and new factories line the way to Kyoto. There were masses of white cranes in the fields, and one small field was entirely filled with pink hyacinths. In Kyoto we went to the temple of one thousand and one Buddhas. Our pious young guide told us that Buddha always assumes the aspect best comprehended by his votary. "Humble myself, he offers me a humble aspect." When one has lost a loved one, one comes here to seek a Buddha most like the departed. If found, one makes it an offering. The temple of Daitokuji was founded by the Emperor Go-Daigo in 1324. The huge complex of monastery, zendo halls, and religious buildings of various sorts is full of tremendous works of art. Here are Mokkei's tiger and dragon, and his Fuyo plant drenched by rain. We went also to see Dr. Ruth Sasaki's first American Zen hall, where United States novices are helped with linguistic and wriggling problems. For if U.S. citizens accept invitations to "sit" (zazen) in Japanese zendos (meditation halls) they distract others by their wriggling. A minimum of two hours' perfect "sitting" is required by Dr. Sasaki of her students before they may accept invitations to "sit" elsewhere. We met Bill Leavitt, born a New York Jew, who gave us tea and proudly told us he could now "sit" for five hours, and was invited all around. The zendo had both heating and air-conditioning, also cushions on which to sit.

43

In the evening, we went with the British Council representative through the lovely old prostitutes' quarters—a walled wooden city with willows and lanterns, past lots of pachinko saloons offering pinball machines of various types, to a nightclub where only coffee and lemonade are drunk, and the two bands consisted of very young men imitating Frank Sinatra, Elvis Presley, Bobby Darin, Joan Baez, etc. They were singing in English, pronouncing it like Japanese, without understanding a word; the effect was curious.

The Sawubun, where we stayed in Kyoto, is the pleasantest hotel I ever met. Tiny, it offers no meals—just lots of tea, blissful sleep on the ground (with electric hot pads in the bedclothes), and a perfect Japanese garden outside the picture windows. There are also marvelous Japanese baths. Kyoto contains perhaps the loveliest of all Japanese gardens; it is close to the Ryoanji temple. Designed about 1499 by Soami for the temple's founder, a retired general, it is enclosed by a low clay wall. It is about 100 by 50 feet large, and has a view toward a pine wood and distant hills. There is nothing in it but sand and fifteen stones arranged in five groups, surrounded by some rather mangy moss. The sand is supposed to be water, the stones islands, the moss a forest. There is no path, as no one walks on the coarse white sand. Void, the garden is a symbol of the mind purged of encumbrances. It represents the world where opposites are "reconciled beyond the stars." The guide called it "the garden of the wading tiger," since the stones look like cubs the mother is leading through a ford. But such visual analogies are definitely *kitsch*. One must absorb the garden's *ethos* without too much explanation.

There is another famous garden in the Daitokuji complex, made about 1509. Here tiny trees combine with stones stood endwise to suggest crags and waterfalls; there, stones suggest bridges and banks with the sand as the stream.

At Daitokuji itself is Rikyu's (1521–1591) garden of a hundred stones. Here are moss-covered rocks, and three tiny hills

44

outlined by evergreen hedges, and still another group of stones purporting to be a bridge leading to the farther shore. Nearby is Rikyu's teahouse. The tea ceremony was brought from China to Japan around 1300; Ikkyu, abbot of Daitokuji (1394–1481), taught it to his disciples; finally Rikyu perfected it. Every tea-master still today gets his or her certificate from Rikyu's descendants.

We were subjected several times to the commercial tea ceremony, as it is performed in most of the big temples. Tourists walk in line to receive a small cup of what looks (and tastes) like thick spinach soup, plus a small rice cookie. This is not, repeat *not*, the tea ceremony as it traditionally occurs in Zen. The Zen ritual began in China. There Zen monks drank tea before the image of Bodhidharma, who brought Buddhism to China. "The few friends meeting in the dim tearoom are imbued with an exalted and gravely happy mood. What they engage on is a continuation of their meditation... the stark loneliness of the Zen hall is softened by the sense of communion with like-minded friends," wrote Dumoulin in his *History of Zen* (Pantheon, 1963, p. 191). D. T. Suzuki notes that tea symbolizes Buddhism as wine does Christianity: tea keeps the mind fresh and vigilant, but does not intoxicate; wine first excites, and then inebriates: "This contrast is also that between Buddhism and Christianity." (D. T. Suzuki, *Zen Buddhism and Its Influence on Japanese Culture,* Eastern Buddhist Society, 1938, p.124.) For Rikyu, the art of the tea ceremony consisted in nothing else but boiling water, making tea, and sipping it. A friend made the following verse at one of Rikyu's tea parties:

When tea is made with water drawn from the depths of the mind
Whose bottom is beyond measure
We really have the tea ceremony

When he was over seventy, Rikyu was commanded by the friend who wrote this verse, a "crude and cruel despot," to commit suicide. Rikyu retired to his room, made his last tea, enjoyed it, wrote farewell poems in both Chinese and Japanese, then fell on his sword.

The tea ceremony provided a curious and interesting link between Zen and Christianity, between Japanese and Spaniards, at the time of their first confrontation, in the sixteenth century. The Daimyo of Bungo (1530–1587) met St. Francis Xavier at the time of the flowering of the Way of Tea, and many Christians appeared on the lists of tea gatherings. One of them, the Jesuit Father Rodriguez Tçuzzu, wrote of the art of tea:

> This art of tea is a kind of religion of solitude. It was established by the originators in order to promote good habits and moderation in all things among those who dedicate themselves to it. They give themselves to contemplation of natural things. Of themselves they arrive at the knowledge of the original cause in that they come to see things in themselves. The Daimyo Bungo and his son were both baptized, while among the "seven wise men of tea" who gathered around Rikyu, five also became Christian. One of these, Prince Toshinaga, "loved to pray in the teahouse, and held this ceremony to be useful in acquiring the virtues of purity, simplicity, and judgment.

Another Daimyo, Gamo Ujisato, in addition to the tea ceremony, was well versed in the composition of poetry and in designing gardens. Yoshitaka, baptized Simon, wrote to his son:

> In this life I desire nothing except tranquility. I need neither gold nor silver, neither beautiful furniture nor clothing, nor yet a delicious meal morning and night. If only I may pass my life without hunger or cold and may refresh my mind.

The Way of Tea helped the Christian mission to turn inward, while Christianity promoted the development of personal self-awareness among the Buddhists. It was a happy blending that ended tragically with the massacres of Christians in the early sixteenth century. These were occasioned by Spanish sailors boasting in their cups that Spain would soon take over Japan, as the country had been well softened up by Christian priests.

This boast was repeated by spies to the Japanese authorities, who, naturally, took immediate action. Christianity was proscribed, large numbers of Christians were killed, and Japan's voluntary withdrawal from the West began. It lasted over four hundred years.

In 1962 the Japanese Government gave land for the building of a martyr's memorial at Nagasaki, the martyrs not being the thousands destroyed by the second atomic bomb dropped by the Americans, but St. Phillip of Mexico and a handful of other Catholic missionaries killed in 1622. During that anniversary year and month, just after the Japanese Government had made its first official donation to a Christian Church, atomic activity was resumed, first by the United States, and then later by the U.S.S.R.

We went on to Nara, a medieval walled city now wholly a historic monument. It is most beautifully kept up, and here is the largest image of Buddha (though certainly not the finest) in the world. Father Dumoulin brought up the question of whether a Catholic can bow before a Buddha. The problem had arisen because Robert Kennedy, visiting Nara, had lighted a joss stick and bowed low before the huge Buddha, having been told this was only a politesse. Obviously he acted in good faith, and Father Dumoulin had himself allowed a Catholic convert (Jochi averages about 60 converts a year, mostly women), who had entered a Zen monastery as a novice, to remain there after her conversion. Some of his colleagues demurred. (My own feelings were more cynical; as the young lady in question had refused to enter a Zen *nunnery*, I doubted her vocation. . . .) But these current instances brought into the discussion the tremendous statements made by Vatican II about the overriding importance of religious liberty and the absolute right of every human being to the exercise of freewill in the area of religion. Until Vatican II, the Church's total commitment to the principle of free will had been doubted for many centuries by many—perhaps most—non-Catholics. Yet it is there from

47

the beginning: "Faith cannot be forced," Tertullian said, and even earlier, St. Justin had declared that "where there is no freedom, there can be no religion." But for long ages the Church's commitment to religious liberty had not only been covered with the dust of subsequently imposed and irrelevant doctrines—such as *extra Ecclesiam nulla salus* (no salvation outside the Church)—but also smothered in the blood of martyrs like Galileo, John Huss, Latimer, Ridley, and so many others. These, handed over to the secular arm by the Church, must one day be acknowledged as no less her martyrs than Thomas à Becket, Thomas More, or John Fisher, all of whom died for their right to "choose you this day whom you will serve," the Lord God or the gods "your father served," as Joshua advised the children of Israel.

The relevant declarations of Vatican II on religious liberty, and the setting up of permanent secretariats in Rome to build bridges and continue the dialogue (or initiate it) between Christians and non-Christians, between Catholics and non-Catholic Christians, are based on two closely related fundamental Catholic premises. The first, of course, is that of human free will. Without the freedom to choose, a man is less than human—he is, as St. Bernard says, "in that case either a child before the dawn of reason, an idiot, or a man asleep." At all times, and in all circumstances, a human being is free to choose between yes and no, right and left. And he must do so, even if he dislikes the necessity. At an extremely permissive school—Dartington Hall in England—the children greeted a new teacher with "Please, no more free choice," which, indeed, has been humanity's despairing cry down all the ages, sadly exemplified by its passion for emperors, dictators, priests, prophets, slogans, and the use of torture, not less than by its addiction to drink, drugs, astrologers, and panaceas. Yet the inescapable fact of our free will remains, in spite of genetics, environment, conditioning, brainwashing, propaganda of all kinds, and our own passionate conformism. And this, our free-

48

dom to choose, is the explanation given by God Himself for our creation, and is also the reason for our redemption.

The other premise is a corollary. It is the acceptance by the universe of itself, as being in time and in space, which is also the acceptance of the creation in history. (Whether we prefer the "big bang" or the "continuous creation" theory makes no difference here.) "I accept the universe," Margaret Fuller cried, and Carlyle is said to have grunted, "Gad! She'd better!" But the universe does also accept itself. Time, as St. Augustine pointed out, is higher in the order of being than space, for it is in time that we make spatial choices. As does the sun. For since no direction of space is privileged, the dissymmetry of time permits the sun to choose to send more light in one direction of its axis or rotation than in the other. Cobalt, also, as Madame Wu discovered, emits the quasi-totality of its electrons toward the left, so that, when it comes to radioactivity, cobalt deliberately chooses to emit practically no electrons toward the right; this because, like the sun, cobalt is capable of distinguishing its future from its past—as are we. And for Christians, this fact of being in history, of the "only now," is of absolutely paramount importance for us and for "all things visible and invisible" which all share with us not only in the creation, but in the redemption.

To return to the problem of Robert Kennedy and his joss-stick, what mattered then was his choice of what to do at that moment and in that place, before the Nara Buddha. Just as at a different time, and in another place, what mattered to King Henry V was whether he recognized an old, fat, drunk knight, or said, "I know not the man."

Nara was where the first Japanese zendo was built, by Dosho, in A.D. 653. The Hoyruji temple here was founded by Prince Shotoku (593–621), who wrote commentaries on three of the Mahayana Sutras, one of which, the Vimala-kirti, is one of the basic Zen texts. There are altogether over 5,000 volumes of the Tripitaka in Pali. All of these have also been translated

49

into Japanese by the diligence of generations of monks. Prince Shotoku, the "father of Japanese Buddhism," was a great statesman, educator, architect, builder, social worker, and patron of the arts. The problem of the "self-identity of contraries" raised in the Vimala-kirti is one of the perennial problems, like grace and free will, and the Zen solution "consists in not solving it at all, ... and that is really the solving." (D. T. Suzuki, *The Essence of Buddhism,* published by the Buddhist Society, London, 1947, p.24.)

Kyoto is one of the loveliest of cities, with literally hundreds of temples, but it suffers from being a tourist trap, not only for foreigners—the Japanese crowd it also. Literally battalions of schoolchildren and processions of men carrying banners, of women in kimonoed droves, file through the temples at a great rate. Nara is the more peaceful, is smaller, and has *désuet* charm. The museum, unvisited by tourists, is admirable, and the park, full of tame, moth-eaten deer, damply agreeable.

An alarming feature of current Japanese life is the emergence of the New Religions, the adherents of one of which, Tenryyo, are centered in a big town, Tenri, near Osaka, where no one lives but members of the sect. Altogether, fourteen million Japanese belong to these New Religions, which are entirely lay organizations: every member is a priest—there is no priesthood. They seem to offer much the same, and to appeal to the same type of person, as do the Pentecostal sects, the Seventh Day Adventists and Jehovah's Witnesses.

The Japanese trade unions have declared they see the New Religions as their greatest adversary. These are, indeed, ultra-right-wing in politics. Soka Gakkai, the biggest, has ten million adherents, and has thirteen members in the Senate. Its technique is called *shakubuku,* breaking and subduing. It has already made United States converts and has spread to Latin America and Thailand. Altogether, there are over thirty representatives of the New Religions in the Diet, and over thirty New Religions.

50

The Right in Japan is far more violent than the Left. The televised murder of the Socialist Prime Minister, for example, and, indeed, all the public assassinations of the past few years, have every one of them been the work of extreme rightists. These extremists calmly publish lists of those they have murdered and those they intend to assassinate. Among these latter is the charming secretary of the Japanese P.E.N. club, Yoko Matsuoka, who is serenely certain she will be done away with in due course.

One person who did not care for Soka Gakkai was D. T. Suzuki. "Soka Gakkai is *not* Buddhism at all," he said, and he should have known, as he, more than any other person, interpreted Buddhism to the West. He died at 97, in July 1966, the foremost authority on Zen in the world. I had met him in 1949 when he came to the United States to attend the World Philosophical Conference, and now I took Father Dumoulin with me to visit him at Kamakura. He lived on a hill, and the approach to his house in the grounds of Enkakuji monastery was through a monastic gateway, then a long uphill climb through a bamboo grove, then through a flowered garden, full of poets' narcissus, jonquils, and daffodils in bloom. When we rang, a maid came and told us Meiko, Suzuki's Abishag, had gone to Tokyo for the day. She had written to us that we might come, but had forgotten—or neglected—to tell the sage. He sent a note by the maid as we stood outside the door, saying he was far from well and could not see us, but I answered him with another note, and he relented and came himself to the door to welcome us, led us in, and gave us delicious tea and "Christian cake." He looked like a tiny, holy, and agreeable dragon, with jutting eyebrows and lower jaw, and recessed bright eyes. He had the latest *Listener,* and was reading *Franny and Zooey.* He and Father Dumoulin had met at some conference in Germany and were glad to see each other again. At first they talked of translations of Zen texts, and Suzuki said all Western translations missed the point, because Christians had no real appreciation of God's immanence, in spite of St. Paul's having said of God that "in Him we live and move and have our being." Father Domoulin tried to counter by saying Buddhists do not realize God's transcendance, that He is the utterly other. But Suzuki asked, "How could He be utterly other, since we only have existence from and in Him? How can He be utterly other, who is wholly within?" The discussion ended with a marvelous monologue by Suzuki on "the inexhaustibility of the Emptiness." And in spite of the high seriousness of his talk, he had a delicious gaiety and was full of humor. I was reminded that "there are no sad saints."

Born in 1870, Daisetz Teitaro Suzuki was the youngest of five children. His father was a doctor who came from five generations of Confucian scholars. (Confucius said, "I can do whatever my heart desires without contravening principles." This means much the same thing as St. Augustine's "Love and do what you will.") Suzuki's father died when he was six, and his first job was as a high school teacher in a fishing village. He transferred to Tokyo University and graduated from the literature department in 1892. He entered Enkakuji as a novice and was sent to La Salle, Illinois, by the abbot, Shaku Soyen, in 1897. There he remained until 1909, working as a translator and copy editor for the Open Court Publishing Company. In 1905 he acted as interpreter for his abbot in San Francisco and translated Swedenborg into Japanese. In 1911 he married Beatrice Lane and lived in the compound of Enkakuji until Abbot Shaku Soyen's death in 1919. In 1921 he moved to Kyoto to become professor of philosophy and religion at Otami College. He founded *The Eastern Buddhist*, a magazine. In 1936 he attended the World Congress of Faiths in England. In 1939 his wife died. In 1949 he taught at the East & West Center in Hawaii for a year. From 1951 to 1957 he was professor of religion at Columbia. His lectures there "ignited the fuse that exploded in the Zen boom," as Mr. Kapleau has commented. His many books (over 100 in Japanese and 30 in English) include *Outlines of Mahayan Buddhism* (1907); 3 volumes of *Essays on Zen* (London, 1927, 1933, 1934); *Studies in the Lankavatara Sutra* (1930); *The Lankavatara Sutra* (1932); *The Training of the Zen Buddhist Monk* (1934); *Manual of Zen Buddhism* (London, 1935); *Zen and Japanese Culture* (1938); *The Essence of Buddhism* (1947); *An Introduction to Zen Buddhism* (1940); *Mysticism: Christian and Buddhist* (1957); *Japanese Buddhism* (1958); *Zen Buddhism and Psychoanalysis* (1960). Suzuki himself described the beginning of his quest for Zen. Such a beginning is called *angya,* or going on foot, in Japanese. First, he had to get a certificate from a Zen priest, saying he was a *bona-fide* disciple. Then he had to be equipped—with a bamboo hat, deep and large, a pair of straw sandals and cotton leggings, a staff, and a copper pitcher. His only luggage was a *papier-mâché* box 13 by 10 by 3½ inches. In it was his priestly robe, his razor, his home address, enough money to bury him if he died unexpectedly, two books. A set of eating bowls was tied outside the box.

"The worst passion we cherish is the desire to possess. Even when we know that our final destination is a hole not more than three feet square, we have the strongest passion for accumulation," he wrote. Zen undertakes to cure this and all other passions. Today Suzuki is sorry that traveling is no longer, as when he was young, done on foot. "All the charm, all the experience and all the education one gets from traveling are entirely lost" when one goes by train or air, he says.

What is this Zen that young Suzuki had come to study? One answer is "a form of Buddhism developed in China in the eighth century—whose spirit is *prajna,* wisdom, and *karuna,* compassion." Fa-yen (d. 1104) had another—and yet the same —explanation:

> If people ask me what Zen is like, I will say that it is like learning the art of burglary. A burglar's son saw his father getting old and thought, "Who will be the bread-winner when he is unable

53

to carry out his profession? I must learn the trade." His father approved the son's idea. One night the father took the son to a big house, broke through the fence, entered the house, and, opening one of the large chests, told the son to go in and pick out the clothing in it. As soon as he got into it, the lid was dropped and the lock securely applied. The father now came out to the court-yard, and loudly knocking at the door woke up the whole family, whereas he himself quietly slipped away from the former hole in the fence. The residents got excited and lighted candles, but found that the burglar had already gone. The son who remained all the time in the chest securely confined thought of his cruel father. He was greatly mortified, when a fine idea flashed upon him. He made a noise which sounded like the gnawing of a rat. The family told the maid to take a candle and examine the chest. When the lid was unlocked, out came the prisoner, who blew out the light, pushed away the maid, and fled. The people ran after him. Noticing a well by the road, he picked up a large stone and threw it into the water. The pursuers all gathered around the well trying to find the burglar drowning himself in the dark hole. In the meantime he was safely back in his father's house. He blamed his father very much for his narrow escape. Said the father, "Be not offended, my son. Just tell me how you got off." When the son told him all about his adventures, the father remarked, "There you are, you have learned the art."

Suzuki still recalls the severity of his reception at the temple of his choice. A monk-official came out to see the new applicant. Suzuki bowed over his baggage respectfully and presented his letter of introduction with the certificate from his master. He was politely but firmly refused acceptance: the zendo was too full, the temple too poor. Suzuki knew better than to try an-other monastery, for the form of refusal is just that: a form, everywhere the same. So he bent again over his baggage, his head down. Now he was ejected by force. But he put down his bundle, sat down cross-legged, and until nightfall was appar-ently absorbed in meditation. When the moon rose, he was in-vited in, but not to sleep. He passed the night facing the wall in the same attitude of meditation. In the morning, he put on his sandals, and spent all day bent once again over his baggage. "This period of probation ... this spending all day with the head down on the bundle is, to say the least, a most tiresome and trying procedure," he recalls. After this trial came another: the second night's lodging he spent in solitary confinement in a room called the *Tangwa-dzume*. Here he passed altogether three days alone. Only after five days was he at last permitted into the zendo, after paying his respect to the Buddhisattva enshrined near the front entrance. Now his admission was announced in a loud voice by an usher-monk, and a tea ceremony followed. Later he received his *koan*. What is the *koan?* Peculiar to Zen Buddhism, and a fairly late development (around A.D. 1051), there are about 1700 *koans* in existence. The word literally means "public announcement." *Koans* consist of anecdotes about the masters or conundrums posed by them. "What is the sound of one hand clapping?" is perhaps the best-known example. Father Dumoulin writes that *"koans* are clearly, introductory, auxiliary means and make no pretense of expressing the inexpressible. They are one great mockery of all the rules of logic." C. G. Jung identified the "great deliverance" in Zen as the liberation of the unconscious. Enlightenment, evoked by the enormous psychological strain of concentration on the *koan,* is experienced as a realization of the primal unity of human nature, in which the boundaries between the conscious and the unconscious disappear. According to Suzuki, the *koan* brought Zen down from metaphysics and made it a suitable means by which all could strive for enlightenment. "Aristocratic Zen was now turned into a democratic systematized, and to a certain extent, mechanized, Zen. No doubt to that extent it meant a deterioration, but without this innovation Zen might have died out a long time before. To my mind it was the technique of the *koan* exercise that saved Zen as a unique heritage of Far Eastern culture." (*Essays in Zen Buddhism,* II, London, 1933, p. 63.)

The chief support of the Zendo life is begging, which has a double aim: to teach humility to the beggar and to enable the giver to accumulate the merit of self-denial. On begging days, the monks, each carrying a bowl, walk in single file slowly through the streets, crying *Hō*. They wear their deep, broad hats, which allow them to see only a few feet ahead; this is so they may not see who gives them money or rice, and so, too, that the giver may not see to whom he is giving. The bowl, staff, and robe are symbols of priesthood. Around the zendo there are generally many houses whose owners regularly contribute a fixed amount of rice toward the maintenance of the monastery. Once a month the monks go with a bag over their shoulders, to collect these regular offerings. Suzuki notes that the bag can be quite heavy, especially when the monk has to walk along a stony or muddy road home! Often the monk is bitten by a watchdog. "Does the dog have the Buddha-nature?" somewhat maliciously asked the Master on one such occasion. In the fall, the monks go into the country to ask the farmers for the pumpkins, potatoes, turnips, and other vegetables that are unfit for market. These are piled on a handcart that is pulled to the foot of the hill below the monastery; later the load is carried on the monks' backs to the kitchen. Some vegetables are immediately eaten, others are pickled for the winter.

The monks all work. "A day of no work is a day of no eating." Eating, Suzuki explains, is a solemn affair in the zendo life, though there is not much to eat. The main meal takes place about 10 A.M. and consists of rice mixed with barley, miso soup, and pickles. Earlier there is breakfast of gruel and pickles; supper is leftovers. Zen monks are only supposed to eat twice a day, so the evening meal is called "medicinal food" and is allowed in China and Japan, though not in India or Indochina because of different climatic conditions. Prayers are said before every meal, and five meditations are proposed while eating: (1) Is the offering merited? (2) Let us reflect how imperfect is our virtue. (3) What is essential is to hold our minds in control and detach ourselves from our faults, such as greed. (4) Food is medicinal and is taken to keep our body in good health. (5) We accept this food in order to accomplish our task of enlightenment. No talking is allowed at any meal. What, indeed, is the object of the Zen monk's life? Daily he repeats the vows:

> Sentient beings are numberless
> I vow to save them all
> Delusions are inexhaustible
> I vow to destroy them all
> The Buddha way is supreme
> I vow to complete it

Suzuki compares the way of Meister Eckhart, the fourteenth century Dominican, with that of Zen. "The most trivial thing perceived in God, a flower for example, would be a thing more perfect than the universe; the soul who is in God's day, in the real now, in her the father bears his one-begotten son and in that same birth the soul is born back into God; it is one birth." As the Buddhidharma put it:

> As long as the mind tarries on the plane of relativity
> It forever remains in the dark,
> But the moment it loses itself in the Emptiness
> It ascends the throne of Enlightenment.

Zen insists on:

> A special transmission outside the Scriptures
> No dependence on words or letters
> Direct pointing at the mind of man
> Seeing into one's nature.

"What are you doing?" a disciple asked Tokusan of T'ang China. "I am not doing anything." "Then you are sitting in idleness." "Sitting in idleness is doing something." "Then what is that anything which you are not doing?" "Even ancient sages

57

knew not." "Zen," Suzuki has written, "is the art of seeing into the nature of one's being: for example," he told me, "the why of the fall is only understood when one has arrived back home. And when one arrives there, one knows that 'the now moment in which God made the first man, and the now moment in which the last man will disappear and the now moment in which I am speaking are all one in God, in whom there is only one now.'" So wrote Meister Eckhart, for that moment, the "only now" in which the soul perceives what it is in reality, is what the Zen monk seeks, as does the Christian. Suzuki's glory is that he brought to the West evidence of this search as expressed in Mahayana Buddhism, and brought to the Far East —as, for example, in two lectures he gave on Buddhism before the Emperor of Japan in 1946—evidence of an identical search in Christianity.

The Zen way is unique, in its use of paradox and violence. The Zen masters were always—are always—striking their disciples, throwing them down, shouting at them, hitting them, as this account written in A.D. 867 shows:

> Wherever I went I met words and did not understand them
> A lump of doubt inside my mind was like a willow-basket.

then

> the master rose from the rug on which he sat deeply absorbed in meditation
> Baring his arm he gave me a blow with his fist on my chest
> My lump of doubt exploded suddenly and completely into pieces
> Raising my head I for the first time perceived that the sun was circular
> Since then I have been the happiest man in the world, with no fears, no worries
> Day in, day out I pass my time in a most lively way [2]

[2] Daisetz Teitaro Suzuki, *Mysticism: Christian and Buddhist*, Harper & Bros., New York, 1957, p. 35.

So Van Gogh "perceived" a chair, and pitied the banker who could not see it. So the thirteenth-century Japanese painter Mokkei painted the hibiscus now at Daitokuji. "The secret," Suzuki writes, "is to become the plant itself. . . . The discipline consists in studying the plant inwardly with the mind purified of its subjective, ego-centered contents. The mind must be kept in unison with the Emptiness or suchness, or being, of the plant, so the painter feels the pulsation of the one and same life animating him and his object. Finally the object makes its own picture." The seventeenth-century Englishman Thomas Traherne too saw the corn as "orient and immortal wheat" and said, "You never enjoy the world aright, till the sea itself floweth in your veins, till you are clothed with the heavens, and crowned with the stars." Henri Matisse, Suzuki notes, looked at an object for weeks, even for months, until its spirit began to move him, to urge him, even to threaten him to give it an expression. Then he would begin to paint. Thus one learns "to see one's face which one has even prior to birth," as the Sixth Zen Patriarch put it. And so one may become as Eckhart described it, "ignorant with knowing, loveless with loving, dark with light." Toward that divine darkness, which is light eternal, D. T. Suzuki guided many human beings of many faiths. May he rest in peace, and may light eternal shine upon him.

Japan has assimilated all the horrors of the industrial revolution, from sweated labor to pornography. The whole gamut of materialism is rampant there. Yet perhaps its centuries of virtue (as defined by St. Augustine, "the right ordering of love") may counter-balance today's crass greed, terrifying efficiency and rigid professionalism. Here Christianity and Zen Buddhism, Confucianism and Shintoism, are driven together toward a desperate ecumenism by the triumphant alternatives of atheistic capitalism and atheistic communism.

Chapter III

WE flew from Tokyo, cold and wet, into glorious weather at Hong Kong—John Bull's other island. For today Hong Kong is one of Great Britain's few remaining colonies. Ceded by the Cantonese in 1840, described then by Lord Palmerston as "a barren island with hardly a house upon it," its population, which was 800,000 in 1931 (it fell to 600,000 during the Japanese occupation in World War II), is around four million today. The difference is mainly due to refugees, the greater number coming directly from China, some also via Macao, and some via Taiwan. The natural increase of births over deaths accounts only for 100,000 per annum. Over 98 percent of Hong Kong's population are Chinese, and 95 percent are Chinese speaking; a bare 9 percent also speak English; for only 1 percent is English the main language.

Hong Kong is one of the most dramatically beautiful of all possible islands, with its superb, bustling harbor, always crowded, for more than 36,000 vessels (totaling 38 million tons of shipping cleared) enter and leave it every year. Hong Kong has a year-round average climate of 72°, and its soil is enormously fertile. The total land area is 398 square miles, of which Hong Kong island occupies only 29 square miles. The New Territories, leased from mainland China for 99 years by the Convention of Peking in 1898, together with 235 small hilly islands, make up the other 369 square miles. Yet, although there are twelve towns of more than 10,000 inhabitants, and 901 villages, and although only 13 percent of the colony's land area is arable (41 percent is grass and scrub lands, 28 percent is too steep for planting), Hong Kong yet grows a quarter of all its food, but produces none of its water. The other three quarters of its food, and every drop of its water come, year in, year out, from mainland China. That Hong Kong grows as much as it does is the more remarkable since during the Japanese occupation most of the timber, both natural and established, was stripped, and erosion was terribly increased. The current afforestation program is only slowly remedying this situation. Yet six to eight crops are harvested annually from the intensely cultivated land. White cabbage, flowering cabbage, turnip, lettuce, and tomatoes are the main crops, but such local delicacies as taro, ginger, bitter cucumber, litchi, mushrooms, and lotus root are also grown, and many of these are now exported to the Chinese overseas, particularly in the United States. In 1961, the value of these exports was over $3,500,000 Hong Kong, from a mere 1,000 acres planted.

The Hong Kong Government is investing millions in reclaiming land from the sea, and many of the spectacular resettlement estates are built on such land. The Government's resettlement program, to provide new homes for the squatters, who are all refugees, began in 1954, after a series of disastrous "squatter fires" in the biggest of which, at Shek Kip Mei, 53,000 people lost their homes, but none their lives. These "homes" were—and in the tolerated areas on the outskirts of the towns still are—colonies of huts roofed with corrugated iron, sticks, sacking, even grass. In these, 50,000 or more people still live closely packed together. Sanitation is nonexistent; neither walls nor roof keep out the wind, rain, or damp, and the fire hazards are continual; as late as January 1962 there were several serious squatter fires. The last outbreak of cholera was in 1961, when Hong Kong declared itself an infected area from August 17 until October 12; 130 cases were treated, but there were only 15 deaths. Because of the increasing number of young people—40 percent of the population are under 15, and 16 percent are under 5—there has been a disturbing rise in the incidence of diphtheria. The Maryknoll sisters, working in free clinics among the squatters, declare that the incidence of tuberculosis among them is 80 percent, yet the general health is remarkably good, and infant mortality has declined by 40 percent since 1952.

About one seventh of the population are now in Government housing, and so far half a million people have been provided with low-rent flats; in the next five years, another half-million will be similarly housed. Another half-million refugees have been housed by private enterprise. The Government blocks of flats, each housing 2,500 persons, are put up at the rate of one every ten days. In these new blocks there is one room of 120 square feet for every five adults (twenty-four square feet per adult is the minimum allowed by law). Each room of five adults has a veranda, on which all the cooking is done (which lessens the fire hazards), and each of the seven floors in every block has communal latrines and washing facilities. Wong Tai Sin Estate has a population of nearly 60,000, and many blocks have nearly that amount. If there are five adults in a family, they rate a room to themselves; if there are not, they must make up that number, or the Government will. Two children count as one adult. There is a roof school in every block, and many squatters sleep on the roofs—as on any and every available roof throughout the colony. There is a shared concrete playground between each two blocks. Lighting and water are provided free of charge. The ground-floor rooms are set aside as clinics and libraries, and sometimes as supplementary schools and as noodle factories. These latter originated as the brainchild of an American Monsignor who worried because the flour sent by American and European charity to the refugees was generally unacceptable. Neither bread nor (shades of Marie Antoinette) cake is a staple of Chinese diet, and any kind of baking is impossible on the tiny stoves generally used. So the Monsignor set up noodle factories, and the excellent resulting noodles are distributed free, while the labor of making them gives employment and is paid for by the donors.

The rent charged per five-person room in Government flats is $14 Hong Kong per month—about U.S. $2.50. Many people object to this as too high, for as squatters they paid no rent at all. The enormous areas already covered by the resettlement blocks have altered the whole landscape of Hong Kong. Visiting musician Hepzibah Menuhin infuriated the local officials by declaring on the B.B.C. radio news that the Government was "not doing any welfare work among the squatters because they are squatting illegally. They simply pretend the problem does not exist." In fact, the Government has been most realistic about the squatters, in that it has not only re-housed them itself but has also worked with any and every agency, domestic or foreign, offering assistance. And already the United Kingdom has accepted, in Hong Kong alone, *since World War II,* more refugees than the United States has admitted in all the sixty-six years of this century! Whereas Chiang Kai-shek's Government which has been quoted in the United States press as saying it would accept any and all refugees caring to come to Formosa, has, since its establishment in Formosa seventeen years ago, actually accepted only 18,000 refugees—a total of barely more than 1,000 a year. Talking to local well-to-do refugees (for, as the Government notes, *"most* of the refugees arrived destitute, but *many* brought capital and technical skills") about the reasons for the only minute trickle of refugees to Formosa over the years, they gave as the first, the long screening process required by the Taiwan Government, which understandably regards any mainland Chinese who have lived under the Communists with a suspicion growing greater, not less, with every year that Mao Tse-tung's Government remains in power. A second reason given was that the very motives that impelled the mainland Chinese refugees to leave China was the one that also made them reject Taiwan: a dislike for regimentation, a wish to live as, and how, they pleased. Indeed, the more perceptive and literate Hong Kong Chinese live an unreconcilable dichotomy: they don't like being "under the British," living as British subjects on what they regard as Chinese soil, but they prefer the British Government to either of their own Governments, Communist or Nationalist.

Certainly Hong Kong is a shining example of the success of capitalism. There are, of course, many reasons for Hong Kong's spectacular industrial development: low taxation, a plentiful supply of productive and extremely industrious labor (there is no unemployment of people between 15 and 25 years of age, and 90 percent of the males over 15 are gainfully employed), a free port, excellent communications, and limitless markets. All the industry is the result of the presence of the refugees. Industry was unimportant before their arrival between 1946 and 1950; now it has assumed a dominant role, and three quarters of the colony's total exports are products manufactured or processed locally. The annual value of exports is now over three billion Hong Kong dollars. There are well over 6,000 registered factories, and who knows how many family enterprises unregistered! Indeed, Government regulation of trade is purposely reduced to a minimum.

The general air of purposeful activity in Hong Kong is tremendous, largely because the sea is at least as busy as the land. Marine fish is Hong Kong's main primary product, and there is a permanent establishment of over 10,000 fishing junks of various kinds, manned by nearly 100,000 people, while over 150,000 depend directly or indirectly on fishing. The "boat people" (there were 138,320 of them listed in the last census), as they are called, live the year round on their sampans, and, both in Hong Kong harbor and in Aberdeen, the waters are nearly as crowded as the city streets, so the sampans have to be parked in rows, to leave enough room for egress. Many families have

64

one sampan for sleeping, and one for living and fishing: the boy babies are tied in, the girl babies are not. How the small children of both sexes avoid falling overboard is a mystery—they run ceaselessly around and around. From the air the bright sampans look like tidy beetles. It is a curious sight to see a man rowed ashore from his sampan, dressed smartly in a suit for work in an office, and ball playing in sampans is a miracle of dexterity.

Shipbuilding and repairing is the oldest of Hong Kong's industries, and shipbreaking, with the concomitant steel-rolling of scrap, produces an estimated 7,300 tons of steel a month—every bit of which is used for the buildings going up around the clock.

Textiles are Hong Kong's largest industry, and about 42 percent of the total labor force is employed in "the spinning of cotton, silk, rayon and woollen yarns, weaving, knitting, dyeing, printing and finishing of piece goods." The cotton-spinning mills, with over 600,000 spindles, are very up-to-date and also unionized; on the other hand, anyone looking out of his hotel window can see tailors working night and day on their sewing machines in the open air in the smelly, dark side streets. The annual influx of tourists—over half a million a year ("We are beating Tokyo," one Chinese announced delightedly)—has increased the demand for suits to an all-time high. With one, or at most two, fittings, custom-made suits are made and delivered to the tourist in a maximum of two days, and one tailor alone reported making and selling 3,600 suits in a year.

Most of the refugees live in Hong Kong or Kowloon, for lack of the albeit microscopic bus or ferry fares that they would need to go to work from the more remote New Territories or islands. The recent riots (1966) highlight the marginal existence lived by most of the population. Moreover, the land in the New Territories is, much of it, owned by clans, who have been living on it since time immemorial; some families there of Tang and Sung, for example, have been continuously in the same spot since the eleventh century. These people mostly speak Hakka, as the boat people speak Hoklo, dialects not understood by the more recent Cantonese arrivals. The clans practice an earlier communism, all the proceeds of their labor being handled by the clan as a whole, part being set aside for the upkeep of ancestral halls, temples, and religious schools. It was to the clan system that Mao Tse-tung was referring when he declared that Communism was native and natural to China.

One of the curious facts about Hong Kong is that whereas 17 percent of all imports are from China—the largest percentage from any single country—Hong Kong exports nothing at all to China, but re-exports 9 percent. The only countries to which re-exports are larger are Malaya and Japan. The facts behind these·statistics were explained by an "overseas Chinese" who had recently spent fifty days inside China. The only railroad in Hong Kong links it, via the border at Fanling, with Canton, only 90 miles away. Canton started food rationing in July 1960, and Peking followed on August 16 of the same year. Until then, commodities had been spasmodically available in the stores in mainland China, but the moment they appeared they would instantly be bought up, and disappear. Now every mainland Chinese has to have a ration card, but only for rice, cereals, and clothes. The ration varies with the harvest. Since 1962 the harvests have been good, but not bumper. Only children and old people get milk; students, manual factory workers, peasants, and "high class intellectuals" get more rice than the average person. Not only is rice rationed, but also cloth, and coupons are also needed for such items as transistor radios, watches, and bicycles. Such items are not only expensive in money, but also require many coupons.

Now in Hong Kong there are many food stores—sometimes three or four per block—marked in red neon lights with the words *Tai chi yo pau*. At these stores food can be bought for delivery inside China. The British post office, too, is very generous indeed and has special rates for parcels to China, and allows these to be greater in bulk and weight than the average. So the Hong Kong Chinese can (and do) send a constant stream of food and clothing parcels into China.

Another way of supplying friends and relatives in China from Hong Kong is to go to the China Trading Company, for example, a huge Chinese department store. Thence the customer's order is simply transmitted to China, and the clothes, or transistors, or flour, or rice do not leave the shelves. The salesmen know the different requirements within China: for example, in the north, rice is obtainable, but not flour; in the south, the reverse is true—flour is obtainable, but rice is short. The age of the recipient also affects his needs: for example, "dragon-eye meat" (kwewan lungyen dried fruits), which are heavily rationed in China, are especially recommended for the aging. This is said to increase sexual potency, as are snapturtle meat and eggs (valued as aphrodisiacs). Red snapper, too, like the English red mullet, is considered "upstairs fish." Indeed, the Chinese regard all food not simply as nourishment, but also medicinally, and categorize it accordingly—such and such food is suitable for such and such an age group. Food, indeed, in China, has become something of a status symbol, and at the Peking Hotel where other "overseas Chinese" are honored guests—among these, Indians, Malayans, Siamese, and Vietnamese, all quite lowly people—"Mountain-treasure-sea-flavor" is on the menu (Shan-cheng-hai-wei), which is bear-paw and shark's fin, considered as medicinally valuable as they are rare. The nasty wine supposedly made from dragon's blood, phoenix blood, and tiger's blood (actually fortified with snake, chicken, and badger blood) is also available, and this can also be purchased in Hong Kong. Now that the seven traditional courses have been restored in China, each of these can be stretched to include a variety of dishes—for example, a whole selection of cold cuts can be supplied as hors d'oeuvres. Small wonder that a visit to China is a "once in a lifetime" occasion for the overseas Chinese, and they return—always via Hong Kong—tremendously impressed. Less humble Western guests are invited by the Chinese Government: the keeper of Oriental Art at the British Museum, for example, and the Duke of Wellington as well as Camille Abouassouan, the Lebanese representative of UNESCO were the guests for two months of the Chinese Government and shown whatever they wished to see. M. Abouassouan was also given a car and driver and allowed to visit whatever places he wished.

Since China's greatest present need is for foreign currency, the Chinese Government gives generous extra coupons to anyone receiving remittances from abroad (*chaio hwei*). When these remittances are cashed, the relative who receives them—from Hong Kong, England, Ceylon, India, Indonesia, or from any of the 56 countries that have recognized China—gets not only the $10 or whatever sum it may be, but the equivalent of the value in coupons, besides. Furthermore, the buyer of the remittance can pay, in Hong Kong, the Chinese taxes and duty, so that the relative gets the full amount, in food or money, plus the extra coupons.

Large numbers of Hong Kong Chinese who have relatives on the mainland visit them at least once annually, on one of the four family feasts: the Lunar New Year; the spring Ching Ming festival, when visits are paid to the graves of the family ancestors; the Mid-Autumn festival, when gifts of mooncakes are exchanged; and the Chung Yeung, or ninth day of the ninth moon, when graves are refurbished. On such days the trains to Canton are jam-packed, everyone carrying food in immense quantities. Many people have yokes around their necks, from which laden baskets or pails swing.

Another occasion when the trains to the border and into China are crowded is the Canton Fair, held twice yearly in the spring and fall; a thousand persons traveled on each of the two morning trains—the 7 A.M. and the 9 A.M.—on the fair's first day. Surprisingly, in 1965, there were large delegations of

West Germans and Japanese, as well as Africans, Australians, Canadians, Egyptians, Latin Americans, Mexicans, New Zealanders, Pakistanis, and others. For local Chinese, only border passes are required, similar to those issued to persons crossing the Mexican-U.S. frontier.

The "overseas Chinese," as they are called by the mainland Chinese—that is to say, Chinese from Cambodia, Ceylon, Indonesia, Vietnam, etc.—are very much encouraged to visit China, and, when there, are given V.I.P. treatment. They are the guests of the Government, and special hotels are reserved for them, or special areas in hotels. For example, at Hanchow, in the new and excellent hotel on the lake, the third floor is reserved for overseas Chinese and foreign diplomats. One such overseas Chinese visitor arriving one evening telegraphed an uncle in Shanghai, who arrived by 3 o'clock the next morning, in spite of the fact that transportation within China is very limited. Overseas Chinese who return to stay are naturally also made much of, and seem privileged. A doctor, Johns Hopkins trained, with his Catholic (Chinese) wife, said that many with special skills—doctors like himself, or scientists trained at M.I.T., Cal Tech, Columbia, or Cambridge (England)—had returned. Though some regretted the "fleshpots of Egypt"—as he put it—some did not, and he was among the latter, though his wife and daughter (also a medical doctor), while loyally approving his decision, admitted life was very different now at home from what it had been on the "outside." One Chinese woman, who travels often from Shanghai to Hong Kong on business, said that though she came, as she put it, "from the wrong [i.e., aristocratic] kind of family," whenever she returned from Hong Kong into China she felt she was awakening from a pleasant dream into a harsh reality. "But one cannot and should not live in a dream," she said, "even if one might prefer it."

Among refugees in Hong Kong there are political, economic, social, and even educational refugees—Chinese who want to bring up their children in non-Communist schools. I was present at a very interesting discussion between an overseas Chinese, going home to visit, and a Chinese refugee, an employee of one of the airlines. The returning Chinese was taking equipment for his doctor-brother into China: stethoscopes, a wheelchair, hospital apparatus, operating table equipment, as well as two bicycles and an enormous amount of vitamins. The refugee said he thought it unethical to bring articles other than food or clothing into China, as persons who desired such things did so out of personal ambition, for individual aggrandizement. He said it was the lack of such articles that had caused him, personally, to leave China, and he thought those who wanted them should do likewise. The overseas Chinese replied that he thought it was perfectly ethical, and even laudable, to want to improve one's skills for the sake of China and in order to become a more useful citizen.

The financing of voyages to the interior of China is interesting. Anyone crossing into Red China can deposit money in a bank in Hong Kong and can withdraw it in eleven different Chinese cities as required, then, on returning to Hong Kong, withdraw the remainder.

There is only a trickle of refugees from China entering Hong Kong now, and these are allowed freely past the border guards. Most of those leaving China at present are men and women who left the land for factory work during the Great Leap Forward and were obliged to return to agriculture during the bad years 1958–1962. Anyone unable to produce proof of having lived in a city before 1958 had to return to the land. Many of these ex-peasants, having tasted the joys of city life, did—and do—not wish to go back to the hard commune life, and so chose to emigrate. The Chinese authorities are glad to see them go: people is one commodity of which China has enough and to spare.

But though allowed to leave by the Chinese, many would-be refugees were, and are, turned back by the British (in Hong

Kong) or the Portuguese (in Macao). The British have also tightened up the loopholes by which many Chinese had been entering Hong Kong from Macao. It is thought that the Chinese Government put no obstacles in their would-be refugees' way for two reasons: one, the food shortage, and two, to convince the would-be refugees that they had no place to go except to go back to work on the land where they were needed. Today in China all young people are obliged to spend a minimum of three weeks a year living on the land, sharing the peasant's life and work. One reason given is that today's youth is too soft. They cannot remember the horrors of the Japanese war, of pestilence, of the 1942 famine, when people left the villages to walk the roads, starving, their only food earth, or "Goddess of Mercy": tree bark. Nor have any of today's children been sold by their parents for food. So they must be toughened by sharing the still hard peasant life, and above all, their "proletarian realism" must be strengthened, as peasant-born Chairman Mao insists, by physical contact with the peasants. The children are all examined by doctors before they are sent off—as much to protect their hosts as to ensure their own well-being. These young people are, if anything, overzealous and anxious to prove they are *not* the softies their elders think them. They overwork, often returning home exhausted. The younger children "learn by working" for from a third to a half of their school time, but under careful supervision—both so they may be of some use to their hosts and so they may not strain themselves.

Eighty percent of the Chinese are still peasants, and according to Chinese Communist doctrine, all peasants must be considered holy, much in the same way that, in *The Brothers Karamazov,* the soil of Russia was so considered by Alyosha, who stopped and crossed himself, not with holy water, but with the blessed earth. Yet though young people are exempt from sharing the peasants' laboring experience, there is no sentimentality about the peasant condition, however great the sentiment may be about the peasant status. A lovely 22-year-old

71

film star, daughter of a "state capitalist" living in Shanghai, who owns a charming house, a car, and has two servants, is obliged, like everyone else, to spend her three weeks living in a peasant's hut. She finds it enormously exhausting, for she—and all her companions from the cities—are expected to improve their "proletarian realism" not only by day-long hours of back-breaking hoeing or reaping, but also by instructing her contemporaries after work. These are, she declares, astonishingly naive, though living less than one hour from Shanghai by train. "If I dig down, will I reach America?" one girl asked her, and another, "America? Is it as far as Shanghai?" When she gets home, her mother says all she wants to do is to sleep, drink milk, and eat cake. After doing her day's work on film location or at the theater, she and her comrades have to criticize each other and, above all, themselves: these self-searching communal sessions often last until 2 A.M. or so. "I don't know when I am most exhausted," she said, "when I'm doing my own work or working on the land."

Hong Kong is a base not only for the British, but also for the U.S. fleet, and thousands of U.S. sailors put in there. They can be seen landing, every day and almost all day, at a special dock, where they are met by every kind of welfare organization so they have little chance of being "taken in and done for." They are touchingly well behaved, and their admirable manners and *tenue* is a matter for delighted surprise: a local Chinese told me there was practically never any trouble, year in, year out. He also said that this was the more remarkable as most of the sailors were under twenty. He vouchsafed that he thought they were so thoroughly scared by the indoctrination courses given them on board that when they walk the Chinese streets, especially such as Cat St. (Upper Lascar Road) with its medley of booths, its stores making everything from abacuses to red lettering on ivory to antiques, they seemed terrified. Although Hong Kong has a tremendous reputation as a dangerous place, where one's pocket will surely be picked, where one may be knifed in a dark alley, where drugs are peddled day-long professionally, actually it has a very small incidence of crime, and the population is curiously law-abiding. Indeed, the number of prisoners on Chi Ma Wan on Lantao Island remains fairly constant at 7,000; the inmates are excellently well behaved, and one Portuguese prison officer told me they had never had any trouble in the history of the prison—the only complaint was that the prisoners seemed to enjoy being there and were apt to come back! Prisoners serving sentences of under two years are put in open prisons with open-air work for all. An enormous amount has already been done by them on forestry and other projects. There were only 25 murders in the Colony in 1961 (population *4 million!*) and only 13,258 crimes of any kind reported, including prostitution and petty thievery!

The various private agencies cooperate with the Government in all the social services. For example, in 1961, four bungalows were built by prison labor, in the Siu Lam Valley, sponsored by the Christian Welfare and Relief Council, which has a membership of twenty-four Protestant churches. These bungalows were geared to the rehabilitation of cured drug addicts, by settling them on small holdings. The Salvation Army and the Lutheran and Presbyterian social workers also all cooperate in the provision of voluntary services to roof dwellers, hillside squatters, and boat people. The British Government pays the salaries of all the priest, nun, and lay teachers in the 168 Catholic schools, which are attended by 96,695 children.

Ninety-eight new schools have been built since 1951. There are only 174,000 Catholics in the Colony, but these include 362 priests, 634 nuns, and 108 brothers. The several universities offer degrees in almost every imaginable subject, and the hospitals are excellent. I got an infected toe and went to Matilda Hospital for two nights, and will, if I am able to afford the fare, fly there anytime I am seriously ill. Doctors, nurses, and equipment were the best I ever encountered anywhere.

A lovely fifty-minute ride on a ferry boat (cost 40 cents),

took us across seven miles of sea from Hong Kong to Lantao, an island bigger than Hong Kong itself but almost uninhabited. A handsome United States citizen, lay brother Yvo, meets the ferry in his brown habit and drives visitors up a steep road (made by the monks) in the Jeep to the guesthouse, most agreeably situated in the middle of a rose garden. Everywhere there are signs, "no radios," for the Chinese have a passion for transistors—in Hong Kong and in mainland China (as in Japan) everyone walks around playing a transistor all the time, and the gardeners and other workmen employed by the monks are no exceptions. We arrived at lunchtime on Good Friday and were given a superb meal of excellent homemade Reblochon-type cheese, fish, eggs, milk, and apples—all produced on their land or from their waters by our hosts. The monks themselves were on bread and water, and were apologetic that they had so little to offer. All the monks are Chinese, and only Dom Paulinus Lee, then Prior, and the guestmaster were allowed to meet visitors; Dom Paulinus alone spoke English. Brother Yvo took us all over the farm. The then British Governor, Sir Arthur Grantham, gave the Trappists seventy-five acres of completely barren land, uncultivated and uninhabited, in 1951. Within ten years the Trappists had twenty cows in milk (and the only pasteurized tuberculin-tested milk in Hong Kong), two bulls (one gored and killed one of the monks, Father Malachy, in 1961), quantities of pigs and chickens, plenty of vegetables and flowers. Every acre is under intensive cultivation, with the exception of the Chinese burial ground. The Chinese are very fussy about their graves, and consult soothsayers to determine the location. Every grave must have a view, water, and wind; therefore it must be on a hill or, at least, a hillock. When a man or woman reaches sixty, the relatives buy a coffin and give a party: after sixty it is "correct" to die—earlier it is a misfortune. A grave can only revert to the land if it is deserted. At Lantao, on the monks' land, each year people come from mainland China to visit the graves, so the monks keep the graveyard unplowed, a tiny sterile island in all their good earth. The monks sell their tomatoes, their flowers, their fruit—their apples are justly famed—and are entirely self-supporting, though they have received many gifts of equipment and machinery. The Jeep, for example, the forage harvester, and the silo filler were gifts from Gehl Brothers in West Bend; the tractor was the gift of the Metal Parts Corporation of Racine, Wisconsin; the boat was the gift of the Asiatic Petroleum Company. Other gifts include water turbines and a hydroelectric plant. The first thing the monks did was to plant grass, then trees, mostly fruit trees. They build continually: they have a huge church, lovely in the original granite, unfortunately most of it now covered with a bilious-yellow eggy-looking plaster. Inside, the church is hideous, full of *bondieuserie*. The monks are all from the monastery of our Lady of Liesse at Yang Kia P'ing. This abbey was founded by French trappists from Tamie in the Savoy Alps in 1883. Although the abbey was a three-day trip by mule from the nearest city, Kalgan, the monks flourished exceedingly, living on the sale of their apricots and the apricot kernels (used for making liqueur), so that by 1927 they were ready to make a new foundation. They bought acreage sufficient for 300 monks ten miles north of Chekiakaong, two miles northwest of Chengtu, 270 miles from Peking. The new priory was built on level sandy soil. The monks grew cotton, wheat, peanuts, and grapes and made wine, liquor, and cheese. In 1941 the new foundation had 70 monks, and Dom Paulinus Lee was elected Prior.

Dom Paulinus entered the Trappist order at thirteen. His family had already been entering the Trappist order for three generations; his nephew is a scholar at St. John's University, Collegeville, Minnesota, the biggest Benedictine abbey in the world. But this boy, even if he felt he had a vocation, could not become a monk, for in China the rule is that the eldest son must marry. Dom Paulinus's brother, this boy's father, remains in Peking; he has seven children. What life, Dom Paulinus asks, would there be for him or for his children outside China? Dom Paulinus is a scholar and knows many characters, but not those for baseball or betting, nor those for economics or sociology. "I never needed to know them," he said. (Another brother was pointed out by Brother Yvo: "He is quite a scholar. He knows more characters than any of the other monks.") Dom Paulinus is a good Latinist, and we had a cozy antivernacular jag together. He told me the destruction of Yang Kia P'ing began in 1947, and that same year, on April 9, the Reds occupied the Trappist seminary at Chengtu. "They were most correct," Dom Paulinus said. "It was the people brought the monks to judgment, never the State. The Communist discipline was perfect. They did not enter any territory forbidden to them by the monks; they respected our enclosure. One father was shot crossing the garden, when challenged by a sentry (he had forgotten the password) but he was only slightly wounded. When the Reds retreated, General Lu offered to ask for an UNRAA plane to evacuate the monks, but then the Reds returned. After four months the monks found themselves with no money and with nothing to do; their land was taken from them, and they were not allowed to teach or preach. Then, with Red permission, the monks got on a plane to Peking, took a boat to Shanghai, and went on to Chengtu, where Dom Paulinus found only forty monks. The others had left. In 1949 Dom Paulinus was invited to Gethsemane in Kentucky, and went there with eight Chinese monks, one Belgian priest, and one lay brother. The lay brother went to a monastery in Winnipeg; the monks were absorbed by the United States, but Dom Paulinus went back in May 1950 to Chengtu. Now only four monks and seven lay brothers were left. He got to Hong Kong with 17 monks in all, but the Bishop of Hong Kong sent Dom Paulinus back into China to look for more of his monks. He went to Canton disguised as a workman, and met thirteen of his monks in the Cathedral. On July 29, 1950, fourteen more monks of Dom Paulinus's priory at Chengtu got to Peking, where Dom Paulinus met them. He did not dare stay with his family or friends lest he endanger their lives, so he stayed for three days in a hospital. Then he went to Canton, where he began to work as a gardener in the seminary. Here eight lay brothers joined him, carrying little apple and grape plants. When interrogated by the police, they said they were going to work in a garden. However, all Dom Paulinus got out with him were eleven of his original forty monks, and with these he established the new community at Lantao.

Although Chengtu monastery was closed on February 28, 1951, all but five of the monks were released. The sub-prior, Father Vincent Che, was charged four times before the people's court, because he would not say, "Labor created the world," but insisted that "God made the world." He was jailed, and died in prison on August 7, 1951; his three brothers and one uncle were all Trappist monks. Another who died was Father Albert Wei. He was eight months in prison, but was released when he became seriously ill. Father Yvon Yu was tortured, kept hanging from his wrists until he became seriously ill. He, too, was released only to die. On February 9, 1956, more than 4,000 people came to the solemn dedication of Our Lady of Liesse, Lantao island.

Dom Paulinus in conversation told me he thought Communism was inevitable and necessary in China, but when I asked whether it had done away with corruption, he just roared with laughter. Only four of his monks had remained faithful of all those he was able to see in China. After the expulsion of the foreign missionaries, the Church was reorganized under the leadership of Chinese Christians. Freedom of religion was established by the new Chinese constitution, and religious institutions were declared "free to perform their religious activities insofar as they did not try to interfere with the new government's policies." Churches in China are open for services, generally closed in between. This is equally true of Buddhist, Christian, and Confucian temples and Moslem mosques. The Vatican has been most careful not to condemn or even admonish the Chinese clergy: there is no schism, and Mass is said daily in the cathedrals of mainland China, three masses on Sundays. No catechisms or church schools are allowed; there is no preaching. And, of course, foreign priests are either obliged to leave, or sent to jail (like Bishop Walsh). The last foreign nuns to leave were the Madames of the Sacred Heart who were expelled from Peking in 1966.

Dom Paulinus went to France to attend the General Chapter of the Cistercian Order in 1949, for the first time since he had become Prior. He met, he has written, "great misunderstanding from my superiors, great opposition from some of my confreres; I was destitute of financial assistance. I remember well now my moment of extreme agony when I seriously wondered, 'What good will it be for me to remain a Cistercian?' However, God was merciful. When I was at the shrine of Lourdes, I received something like an inspiration from our Lady: 'God wants the community of Liesse to live.' Now I have found the answer to my question. God wanted me to build up this Lantao monastery as a seed bed of the Cistercian vocation, for future China."

He is very revealing about his Cistercian vocation, writing to announce his retirement with deep simplicity:

Now after all these experiences of so many years, I believe that I can say that I have my final and personal conviction about my Cistercian vocation. I am sure you are very interested to know it.

First let me say I am no longer as enthusiastic in encouraging young people to join the Cistercian Order as I was when I was younger, for I have seen too many failures. I know many disappointments concerning many persons who have been in the Cistercian Order. During recent years many changes have come in the Cistercian rules and life, and even its purpose and claims seem somehow different from the ones when I entered the Order.

However I must say that I believe that it is a great mercy of

God and a choicest grace to call me into this Order. And I wish to tell all my young posterity about this.

First I believe that only in my Cistercian life did I find such peace of mind which makes me a little proudly satisfied of all my life's days spent for God's service. The Rules were a particular protection for me from all the dangers and unhappiness of life in the world. The duties and exercises, the manual work in a Cistercian house helped me to enjoy every moment of my life. I have found that spiritual training of the Cistercian tradition is really deeply practical asceticism, compared with all other systems that I know. So I feel that unlike many of my contemporaries, I have no regrets of my past life.

The greatest joy for me in the monastery is that I feel a great freedom to extend my love very widely to my brethren, to my relatives, to my friends. Sometimes I hear one or the other object to me that the Cistercian life is SELFISH. They say that a Cistercian monk is one who gets away from trouble to enjoy himself like an isolated island. I can answer such an objection from my own experience that this is a completely wrong idea of the Cistercian vocation. While only remaining inside of a small community a Cistercian monk by obedience has ample occasions to perform the duties of fraternal charity, all of which require more self-denial than more active work in many parish duties. But if one performs his duties with love in the monastery he can superabundantly give himself to others.

So in a word, I have been happily loving my brethren, my friends and my relatives and I am still loving them, and I can love all of you until the everlasting age without any change or loss.

The Lantao island Trappist monastery is one of the most stimulating and invigorating places imaginable. Here the strict Trappist life is led: the monks go barefoot, live marginally. They are truly bridge builders: Chinese and Christian, monks and farmers, guests and hosts. Lantao, truly a bridge place, may in God's good time become a bridgehead.

Hong Kong, capitalism's show-piece, is in immediate danger from purely destructive, purely negative forces. "Satan the

Waster" was the title of Vernon Lee's fine play about World War I, showing Satan as the Waster of all the virtues, the ruin of all kinds of good. The mobs lunging around Hong Kong in the summer of 1967 have nothing to offer—themselves, each other or other people. They can only cavil and smash. Perhaps Lantao alone will remain, as the Benedictine monasteries remained in Europe during the barbarian invasions, during the Dark Ages. Perhaps nothing will remain. *Sub specie aeternitatis,* it does not matter—it is that the monks came, that they were there, that they *are* there, that matters. Maybe the monks of Lantao themselves are a part of that "High that proved too high, the heroic for earth too hard" of which Browning wrote. At all events, they are a proof that not all our Western gifts are tainted, and that Christianity can be as naturally and beautifully Chinese as it is Greek, Latin, or Anglo-Saxon.

Chapter IV

CEYLON—the best of islands, essence of island—
has always enchanted the English. With a glorious climate, lots of food, flowers, and above all, an abun-
dance of rare and beautiful birds. Blue jays, kingfishers, crow-
pheasants (very chic in black and beige), green pigeons, red
sandpipers, peacocks, partridges, every variety of gold and red
finch and yellow canary, as well as cormorants, pelicans, and
vast numbers of other sea birds abound. Coming down through
the fat white monsoon clouds onto the greenest country ever,
with enough palm trees, was like at last arriving inside the perfect fairy tale. Everything the hymn says about

> ... the spicy breezes
> Blow soft o'er Ceylon's isle;
> [And] every prospect pleases,

is true. Only the last—and best-known—line is not, for man is
less vile here, on the whole, than elsewhere, because less harried
and more comfortable. Only saints become better through discomfort, misery, or want. For only saints can escape (though
the Sixth Chinese Patriarch assured us they do not impede)
causality. So the Singhalese, plump, glossy, mahogany-bodied
with abundant shining black hair, are able, agreeable, amiable.
For there are enough bananas, breadfruit, jackfruit, and coconuts to eat, enough coconut milk also to drink, and coconut

fiber from which to make copra. Copra for mats. Ceylon has also enough water. But too many people, and more, alas, to come. It has the highest birthrate in the world.

We drove with our hosts, the Canadian High Commissioner and his wife and their three children, to the sea. Their 11-year-old girl was learning Hindu dancing; the two boys played local musical instruments brilliantly. We spent a day in the sea in masks, watching fish, blazing blue, striped magenta and yellow, yellow with black edges, huge blue-finned black ones, all swimming among fan-shaped, mushroom-shaped, fern-shaped corals. Are these colors really only in our eyes? It was hard to believe in their nonexistence. We sailed astride our hosts' sailfish, ate hugely of curry at a rest-house, then took a tiny rowboat across a river to a Buddhist hermitage on an island in a big sweet-water lake. Founded by a German Buddhist convert, who became the monk Nyantiloka in 1906, Dodanduwa now contains only four monks, one old man, Nyanaponika, being a pupil of the founder. The monastery was touchingly simple—four beds, a big desk, and a good library of ola-leaf books written in Pali on palm leaves, delicious smelling and with thongs and sticks to read by. (*Tao* means the bindings on a book, *Yoga,* the yoke, *Re-ligio,* the binding Thing.)

The grave of Nyantiloka was a heavy granite monument, with an inscription in Pali, Singhalese, German, and English: 1878–1957. The Buddha image had been brought from Tokyo, for apparently Buddhism had been almost extinct in Ceylon until these German converts had brought it back. Now it is flourishing, and even militant. Suzuki had made much of the crucifix defying the turning world by its verticality and the dying Buddha identifying with it in his horizontality. But are not both valid symbols? Christ said, "And I, if I be lifted up from the earth, will draw all men unto me," and the dying Buddha's last words were, "Work out your salvation diligently." Where is there conflict?

Ceylon has many beautiful sixteenth-century Catholic

churches, dating from the time of St. Francis Xavier and his successors, and an indigenous Christian community over four centuries old. The four faiths—Buddhism, Christianity, Hinduism, and Islam—here seem to live, if not in complete peace, yet in a more edifying attempt at it than in most places.

Yet for a variety of reasons, religious as well as racial, the successive waves of invaders have never been completely fused, and though the Singhalese and the Tamils both came from India, the Singhalese adopted Buddhism, while the Tamils remained Hindus. Today there are 4 million Singhalese and about 1 million Tamils. The Portuguese settlers and their converts—mostly Singhalese—number nearly half a million, as do the descendants of the Moors with their converts to Islam. There are other divisions: location divides the Ceylon Tamils from the Singhalese; occupation separates the plantation workers from the small cultivators.

Yet Ceylon has always been less unhappy than India, less torn by racial and religious strife. The British succeeded the Dutch in 1802, and by 1833 an enlightened governor, W. M. G. Colebrook, had already made a beginning of constitutional government in which the Ceylonese had a share.

Ceylon and China were the first countries in the world to have a female as president and vice president respectively. Madame Sun Yat-sen, widow of the great reformer president, sister of Madame Chiang Kai-shek, and Madame Bandanaraike, widow of the murdered Singhalese president, are both very distinguished ladies indeed. Madame Indira Gandhi, Nehru's only child, is now even more famous, as prime minister of the second most populous country in the world. Curious that countries where women have always been so discriminated against should be the very ones where they are elevated so high. Or is perhaps the best way up to be down? "He that is down needs fear no fall," as Bunyan put it, and these three ladies had no place to go but up.

I had no success in meeting Madame Bandanaraike. Was it

perhaps because I am a Catholic? She was said to be very anti-Catholic, and there had been several recent church burnings and such like. Also, she was having trouble with the large Indian minority—over two million, mostly tea workers who had come some hundred years before from India, imported by the British to work the tea plantations. These very industrious folk had been refused Singhalese citizenship, so could not vote or join unions. The Indian Government refuses to have them back, and most of them could not remember even from what part of India their grandparents came. In Ceylon they receive no welfare and no education, and now the Tamil they talk—their only language—has been made illegal, so they must learn Singhalese or starve.

Ceylon is full of Buddhas. There are caves full, ceilings full, temples full. Some are most beautiful—for example, the Mahintale tenth-century ones, carved in wood, the fifty-foot-long ones carved in the rock at Pidurutalagala, the recumbent ones at Sigiriya. Others, thickly covered with treacle-colored paint, are vulgar beyond imagining—a great deception for me, who had been raised to think only the West was vulgar and that the East, mysterious, spiritual, esoteric, was remote from our twentieth-century materialism. But all the ancient buildings and statues and temples are tremendously impressive: Anuradhapura, for example, a holy city like Mitla or Monte Albán in Mexico, and the great rock palace of Sigiriya, with enchanting rock paintings of apsaras (nymphs). Here another sibling tragedy had taken place, as at Kamakura in Japan. And again, terrible remorse for the fratricide, remorse that uselessly built and built "palaces and towers."

We stayed at Kandy, the old capital, which enshrines, in a splendid temple, one tooth of the Buddha, brought to Ceylon as an offering by the sister of Asoka, the Indian emperor. (Asoka was a great conqueror, who on becoming a Buddhist gave up war and devoted his life to pacification, erecting huge monuments—steles—recounting his exploits but also his aspirations,

84

his longing to help all sentient beings.) We stayed with an Englishman married to a Singhalese. She teaches at the university; he takes care of their young son. They fed us Hindu food, vegetables only, but marvelously prepared. Their diet does not even include eggs. (I remember on the only occasion I met Gandhi, at Sir Victor Gollancz's house in London, my mother told him she was a vegetarian, "but I eat eggs." "Ah, Madam," he replied, "some day you will see the fallacy behind the egg.") We visited the Temple of the Tooth, but it was touristy, garish, and mercenary—the sound of money passing almost drowned out the various religious noises.

I went on by plane to Jaffna, which could not be more off the beaten track. It is really remote, at the northernmost tip of the island, the first town in Ceylon when the invaders came from India, now the last, offering no temptations to tourists. The one hotel was rat-ridden—I was quite alarmed at the size of the rodents—and there was an unappetizing beach leading to a shallow, muggy, mud-colored sea. The town itself was tepid, without beauty or buildings of any significance, but it housed several genuinely holy men, and they truly gave it atmosphere: one actually felt it a holy place. There were a Moslem holy man, an English peer's son turned swami, a pocketful of delightful Catholic monks in the Rosary ashram, who sold wine, vegetables, balm, cough medicine, candles, and soap, and there were two Hindu swamis, to meet whom I came to Jaffna.

The older, called Yoga Swami, was born John Pillai in Ceylon in 1874. He had been educated in St. Patrick's, the local parochial school, only through the fifth grade, and then had obtained a tiny job as a clerk in the Public Works Department. One day, when still in his teens, he was defending a smaller boy in a street fight, and slashed a bigger boy. He was sent for six months to jail, being set to break stones on the road in the hot sun. He said to himself, "I cut the stones, and now the stones cut me." When he got out, he got back his job. But one day, in 1897, when just twenty-three, he went to a lecture by

Swami Vivekananda. The lecturer announced he would only speak for fifteen minutes, and added, "The time is short, the subject is vast." John Pillai did not even wait out the fifteen minutes. He left the lecture hall and at once began his own search. First he had a rigorous ascetic phase, rubbing chili powder all over himself before lying in the sun to attract ants, and refusing the food his aunt put out for him. But in 1907 he attached himself to one Chellapa Swami and received initiation from him in 1908. In 1910 he went on the annual pilgrimage to Kataragama, 365 miles from Jaffna. The first day the walk is only seven miles or so. But the last days require a daily stint of about twenty-six miles in the hot sun. The walk is always made barefoot and begins two days after the full moon of May. It starts from the Mullativa temple of Shakti and ends where Murgam, son of Shiva, killed Asura-Iswara. (These are all gods in the Hindu pantheon.)

Between his initiation in 1910 and 1916 Yoga Swami was not allowed to see his guru Chellapa Swami, even on his deathbed, for once initiation has been given, a swami dismisses his disciple. When Chellapa Swami died, his disciples took his body and burned it and then got drunk and smoked big cigars. Yoga Swami lost his temper and went to beat them, but they ran away and hid in a haystack and set fire to it, and it was the police who beat them. In 1923 Yoga Swami's disciples built him the house where he still lived when I met him and where he remained until his death. He gave permission to a devout follower, Mrs. Narataram, to collect his songs, but when she appeared after four years with the manuscripts, he dismissed her, saying that words that have left our mouths are polluted like food that has been touched by the mouth.

In 1933 Yoga Swami made another pilgrimage to Kataragama, and in 1941 he made a pilgrimage to Benares and in 1946 to Mysore. The second Jaffna Hindu swami, called locally the German Swami, met Yoga Swami in 1947, and in 1951 received his initiation or *upadesha*.

I was taken to see Yoga Swami by this disciple, Swami Gauribala, often called "the German Swami." He looked like the St.
Peter in the Oberammergau Passion Play, rather fat, with dirty
white hair and a long beard. He lived in a nice concrete hut with
a tiled roof, but complained it got too hot; palm leaves were far
preferable, he said, because cooler. He sat on a dais in the hut
and talked and talked. He was from Berlin, from a rich Protestant family. As a young man, while on a holiday in Italy, he
read a Buddhist translation by Nyantiloka and wrote to him.
He received an answer and started out for Ceylon, then three
weeks' journey away by boat. He stayed six years at the island
hermitage, living as a Buddhist monk. Then came the war, and,
as a German, he was picked up by the British authorities and
interned in a prison camp at Dehra Dun. With Heinrich Harrer
and five other men he escaped, and they made their way to the
Himalayas and into Tibet. There the Tibetan authorities sent
five of them back. Only one man, who knew Pali, and Harrer,
who knew Tibetan, were allowed to stay. German Swami was
not imprisoned again, but lived off the land in India for the
rest of the war, by which time he had learned Pali and Sanskrit
and had changed from Theravaya Buddhism to Mahayana.
Now he knows ten languages: English, French, German, Greek,
Latin, Sanskrit, Pali, Hindustani, Singhalese, and Tamil. He
lived three years alone in a cave, and decided it was all humbug.
Then he came to Jaffna to stay with a friend. "All swamis are
humbugs," he told his friend. "Come and meet the number one
humbug, he is right here," said the friend. "That's my man,"
said the German. He met Yoga Swami, who spoke one phrase
only to him: *summa iru,* to be. He then began the study of
Tamil in order to discover the fourteen shades of meaning in
those two words. One day German Swami was browsing in a
bookshop, and Yoga Swami came up behind him and said, "It's
not in books," and took the book out of his hand. "Bloody fool,"
he added. From that moment the German became Yoga Swami's
disciple. Yoga Swami gave him the name Gauribala, which

means "son of Gauri." (Gauri is one of the names of Shakti, an aspect of the Supreme Being.)

Swami Gauribala fed me curry and toddy, a delicious drink like a celestial ginger beer, and then we went to see Yoga Swami. His was a small house with no furniture except a hospital brass bed. On the bed was an old man whose leg had been broken by his own pet calf jumping on him. He sat up very straight. The German Swami prostrated himself. I curtsied deeply. Yoga Swami's first words, looking at me, were, "There is nothing." Then, looking at me still, he asked, "Why you come here? Swamis are humbugs. How many Gauribalas, how many Buddhas, how many Jesuses have come? They don't leave room for you." Then to Gauribala, "Why you come?" "I came to worship you," replied the German Swami. Yoga Swami said, "Humbug. Who is worshipping whom? I have two ears, you have two ears; I have two eyes, you have two eyes; I have two how-do-you-call-it [pointing to his own nostrils], you also have two." Then he said to us both, "In the beginning was the Word, and the Word was God. [He repeated it twice.] That is the thing. Find out that word." Then to me, "Don't believe anyone else, believe yourself. Make yourself. Stand on your own feet. Sanyasis are all humbug. Why do people come? They give nothing. What do you have?" (I opened my hands to show nothing.) "If you have something, give it." Then again to us both: "In the beginning was the Word and the Word was God. The Kingdom of God is within you within you within you." Gauribala said the Georges had sent me to Yoga Swami. He replied, "Why are they running about? Why don't they sit still and say 'Who am I, who am I who am I who am I.'" (He went on saying "who am I" faster and faster and higher and higher, until it became "miau-miau," an animal noise. Yoga Swami roared with laughter—shook all over.) Then he said to all of us in general, (several other people were present) "Undescribable, unspeakable. There is nothing. Find out for yourself. Don't rely on anyone." Then to the German Swami, "Bloody humbug.

Don't lie, don't tell lies, tell truth. The Kingdom of God is within you within you." Then he sang:

> Keecchi maachi thampalam
> Keeyo mayo thampalam

(This is a jingle children sing when each makes a sand castle and one hides something in the other's and challenges him to find it.) Then Yoga Swami said directly to me, "Don't run here, don't run there. *Sit in one place and look into yourself.* There is nothing. Do your work. Do your work well." Then he made a gesture of dismissal. Gauribala made a half prostration (kneeling, like women do). Yoga Swami asked, "Why you prostrate like woman?" Gauribala replied, "I am half man and half woman." Yoga Swami: "Nonsense. You are no man, no woman. Don't lie. *Soonyam, soonyam,*" he said in dismissal (the word for the metaphysical zero) and *"sootchma, sootchma"* (very subtle, very subtle).

It was difficult to guess, from the cracked voice and cackling laugh of the old man, whether his reiterations that "there is nothing" came from the depth of some dark night of his soul, or were the conclusions of someone who had spent a lifetime trying to discover whether we made Him or He made us, and knew we can never know here. But he had made himself into an indubitably, tangibly holy man, and I count it among my most valid experiences to have met John Pillai and his disciple, Swami Gauribala.

Ceylon is astonishingly complicated: a microcosm of the world. On the one hand, it is one of the oldest of countries, with a civilization reaching back three thousand and more years. Physically self-supporting, yet with perhaps the most terrifyingly high birthrate in the world; a developing country, yet politically precarious and newly menaced by communal strife, yet with a capacity not only to produce saints and sages —the Spirit bloweth where it listeth and every country has that—but also to provide a people who love them and listen to

89

them, which is rare today. And not because they are dying of hunger, or so miserable they do not care what they do or to whom they listen. There, well-fed, sane, healthy bodies make intelligent listeners. Man, in Ceylon, is less vile than in most places, and there is a sanity about the Ceylonese that makes not only saints settle there but sinners happy.

Chapter V

FOR a German Protestant to become a Ceylanese swami, and a parochial schoolboy his revered guru, are metamorphoses indeed. For an English public schoolboy to become an Indian *sannyasi* (monk) is yet another. Dom Bede Griffiths, who now lives in the Kursumela Ashram in Kottayam, Kerala, South India, has made that transformation.

Dom Bede looks like one of the Old Testament prophets from Chartres, except that he has a long, thin, aristocratic English face instead of a medieval French one. He has deep-set, dark eyes and a high, noble forehead, and he looks at each person as if, for the duration of his glance, only that person existed: every meeting with Dom Bede is an encounter. He is bushy-bearded and appears tough and peaceful, both. He is a striking example of what a Moslem writer has called the prophetic, rather than the mystic, type of consciousness. "Mohammed ascended the highest heaven and returned. I swear by God that if I had reached that point, I should never have returned," wrote a Moslem saint, Abdul Quddus. Dom Bede has movingly described moments of such ascension, but he has returned. And his return, like the Buddha's, like Mohammed's, is creative. He returns bringing his vision, to share it, to be a witness to it. In his autobiography, which relates his life from his school days up to the time that he became a Benedictine monk, Dom Bede has described the life of a young boy growing up in twentieth-century England, and told also what he found, and what he failed to find, there.

The Golden String is a luminously sensitive book, and it opens with an account of a mystical experience. One day during his last term at school, Bede Griffiths walked out alone in the evening and heard the birds sing.

> It seemed to me that I had never heard the birds singing before . . . as I walked on I came upon some hawthorn trees in full bloom and again I thought I had never seen such a sight nor experienced such sweetness before. I came then to where the sun was setting over the playing fields. A lark rose suddenly from the ground beside the tree by which I was standing and poured out its song above my head, and then sank, still singing, to rest. Everything then grew still as the sunset faded and the veil of dusk began to cover the earth. I remember now the feeling of awe which came over me. I felt inclined to kneel on the ground, as though I had been standing in the presence of an angel; and I hardly dared to look on the face of the sky, because it seemed as though it was but a veil before the face of God. . . . It was as though I had begun to see and smell and hear for the first time.[1]

Like the Zen Buddhists who only after illumination saw the sun was round, young Bede had been made aware of the "presence of nature," as he called it. This gradually led to his giving up his adherence to any form of Christianity. He passed, in the nineteen-twenties, from the rejection of the Catholic Church at the Reformation, to the rejection of Christ in the French Revolution, to the rejection of God in the Russian Revolution. But together with the rejection came the continuing vision of Dame Kind, as W. H. Auden has called the experience of nature mysticism. At Oxford, Bede Griffiths found two like-minded friends and also a most understanding and sympathetic tutor, the late C. S. Lewis. Griffiths describes the joy of that Oxford life: his rooms at Magdalen

[1] Bede Griffiths, *The Golden String,* New York, Doubleday (Image), p. 9.

...overlooked the medieval cloisters and the lovely fifteenth century tower.... There was a broad open space of lawn in front, with the deer park on one side and the river walks on the other. Outside my window there was an almond tree, which came into pink blossom early in the spring before any other color had appeared, and...I could watch the procession of spring flowers coming out day by day from the snowdrops and crocuses at the end of January, followed by the small blue scylla and periwinkle in February, until the primroses and violets and daffodils came with March. There were nuthatches and treecreepers and birds of all kinds nesting in the trees, and once I saw a kingfisher rise from the water just beneath me, showing first the blood-red of its breast and then the blue glint of its wings.

When Oxford was over—dear, blessed Oxford that has made young people happy for over seven hundred years—the three friends decided to share a common life, in order to escape from the blight of industrialism and materialism, and to live by the work of their own hands on a farm. Together they bought a solid cottage of Cotswold stone with a good roof but without water, drains, or light.

The three friends rose at six and took turns milking the two cows they had bought. They rode everywhere, at first on bicycles, but later on a horse they also bought. For breakfast they had porridge cooked overnight in a hay-box, for lunch a vegetable stew and cheese. For supper they had eggs from four ducks that laid four eggs daily and bread made from wholemeal stone-ground flour. They did not use tea, coffee, sugar, or tobacco; they drank instead milk and honey. The three of them together had an income of three hundred dollars per annum, all told. They read each evening by candlelight and allowed themselves no modern books or newspapers or radios, but sang old English rounds and played recorders. Even their crockery was locally made by a friend. They read the Bible daily, as literature at first, but gradually their reading brought them to their knees. A definite break was made in their lives when they began to pray on their knees. They used to kneel on the bare stone floor, not in the kitchen, but out in the cold at the back of the house, and the words seemed to pierce the soul.

This life lasted for less than a year, for then his two friends married, and Bede Griffiths returned home to read himself into becoming a devout Anglo-Catholic. One day he suddenly had a conviction that he must go on a retreat. He didn't know what a retreat was, but asked a local clergyman and went to the Cowley Fathers, who were having one. He describes what happened to him:

> I went to confession for the first time in my life, and tears poured from my eyes, tears of a kind I had never known before. My whole being seemed to be renewed ... the buses in the street seemed to have lost their solidity and to be glowing with light.... I read the words of St. John: "Not that we loved God, but that He loved us," and suddenly the meaning of what had happened dawned on my mind.... Now I suddenly saw that all the time it was not I who had been seeking God, but God who had been seeking me ... now I felt that love had taken possession of my soul. It was as though a wave of love flowed over me, a love as real and personal as any human love could be, yet infinitely transcending all human limitations. My body seemed to dissolve ... and felt light and buoyant. When I lay down I felt as though I might float on the bed, and I experienced such rapture that I could imagine no ecstasy of love beyond it.

When he returned home, he thought all his troubles were now over. But far from it. He had developed a passion for fasting and for staying up all night praying. He read the mystics, not only the Christian, but also the Buddhist. Gradually he reduced his mind to chaos, not being able to establish whether God was a person, or impersonal (Brahma), or a state (Nirvana). He resolved to become a hermit, in order to try and find out experimentally. He left home with a knapsack on his back. It is extraordinary to think that in twentieth-century England, one of the most industrialized of countries, Bede Griffiths was able, first with two friends, and now entirely alone, to live almost perfectly the life of the Egyptian desert Fathers. In the Cotswolds, not far from his earlier farm, he found a two-room cottage, next to another similar one where a farm laborer was living with his wife and children. These agreed to provide him with food and to do his washing. He got his old bed and straw mattress, bought a sleeping bag, a table, a stool, and a clock, and installed himself.

He arranged his life in two-hourly periods, giving two hours to prayer, then two to reading and thinking, and two to walking. He tried to live on bread and milk and dried fruit alone, determined not to cook or eat a cooked meal unless it became absolutely necessary. His chief problem was with prayer. He found he got more and more addicted to it, and once or twice stayed up all night praying. He began to be afraid that this passion for prayer and fasting was a sign that he was becoming unbalanced. "The urge to pray was overwhelming; sometimes it seemed that all the powers of heaven were drawing me, and the whole world appeared transfigured." Yet after he had lived like this for several months, he still was unsatisfied. He had just decided to give up his experiment, when the thought came to him that he must really wrestle with God until he could get an answer out of Him. So he determined to pray without ceasing and not to get up from his knees until he had gotten an answer.

"I shut myself in a little closet, where there was only a skylight . . . and began to pray with all my strength. Immediately I seemed to be carried away by a great wave of prayer, and I lost consciousness of everything else." The "message" he had been looking for was quite simply that he should start work on the farm. When he looked at the clock, he found he had been praying for eight hours. "To this day," he confesses, "I do not know what happened to me during those hours."

In those measureless hours he had made his surrender. Earlier, on the retreat he had made, he had been brought to re-

nounce his reason. Now he had been made to renounce his
will

> ... to surrender the inmost centre of my being. Each renuncia-
> tion had been dragged out of me painfully.... I had struggled
> against it and felt it as an invasion of my being by an alien power.
> There was indeed something terrifying in this power which had
> entered my life and which would not be refused. It had revealed
> itself to me as love, but I knew now that it was a love which
> demanded everything and which was a torment if resisted. Once
> the surrender had been made, that power took over the direction
> of my life.

Now he went to work on a big farm, finding in contact with
his fellow laborers and with the blessed earth the warm, human
life he needed. In fact, he nearly married a South African girl
who rode into his life and spent whole days walking the hills
with him, but she went back to South Africa, married an author,
and later died from a fall from her horse. "When we parted, I
told her that even if we should never meet again in this world,
I should never feel really separated from her." But Bede Griffiths took another way than that of the householder. Reading
Newman, he made the same journey, and on Christmas Eve,
1931, was received into the Catholic Church at Winchcombe.
Less than a month later, he entered the Benedictine order at
Prinknash Abbey. He made his solemn profession on December 21, 1936 and was ordained a priest on March 9, 1940. Later
he returned, as monk and priest, to the study of Oriental
thought. And that which earlier had so confused and unsettled
him, reducing his thought to chaos before he had found himself, he now knew as infinitely nourishing and sublimely great.
Virtue is the right order of love, St. Augustine has said, and
once Bede Griffiths had set his love in order, had made that
surrender which Moslems call Islam, *the* surrender, he found
that "from a Christian point of view the importance of Indian

philosophy can hardly be over-estimated. It marks the supreme achievement of the human mind in the natural order in its quest of a true conception of God."

Here, Dom Bede discovered to his joy, was a great religious tradition, going back as far as the beginnings of Greek philosophy in the six century B.C., and continuing without a break to the present day. But whereas for the Greek, man was the center of the universe, and everything referred to him, for the Hindu the supreme reality was Brahman. The idea of ultimate reality as found in Sankara writing in the eighth century is that of *at,* absolute being, *chit,* absolute knowledge, and *ananda,* absolute bliss. This *sacchitananda* is one without a second, whom we can only acknowledge by saying *neti, neti,* not this, not that. Through the discipline of Yoga, the yoke, we can gradually dispel the illusions that compositely make up Maya, this world: for there is "really" no world and no creature at all that experiences the world. There is only the one reality. This *sacchitananda* has to be experienced, here and now—it cannot be otherwise perceived than by experience. All through Indian history there is this yearning to experience God in the depths of the soul. This experience is arrived at by the various disciplines of Yoga, which all aim at control of the breath (pranayama), of the posture (asana), of the senses (which includes sex and the control of the ejaculation of semen) and, final victory, the control of thought, *vijnana.* In reaction to Sankara, Ramanuja, in the eleventh century, sought to arrive at reality by *bhakti-marga,* or the way of personal devotion. Ramanuja stressed that everything is God, rather than that only God exists, and the way to the experience his followers sought is by *puja,* worship, rather than by control or detachment. There is a splendid description in E. M. Forster's account of his stay in India, *The Hill of Devi,* of doing puja to a cricket bat and to an umbrella. These too are God. I myself remember, as a child, worshipping a Chinese vase, quite certain not that God was in it or that it was in God (which is the Christian position "in Whom we live and move and have our being," as St. Paul put it), but that it *was* God.

The Buddhist finds in the blowing or the passing away of the relative and temporal that release from attachment that is the *bliss* of ananda for the Hindu. The Chinese idea of the Tao (way) is of the "beginning and end, transcendent and immanent," sustaining all things, but so remote that "the Tao that can be named is not the Tao." In a recent translation into Chinese of the New Testament, Dr. Wu, a Chinese Catholic convert, has translated the *logos* of I John, 1, as *Tao.* Dom Bede comments, "In thus substituting the Chinese *Tao* for the Greek *Logos,* which we translate as the Word, he has placed Chinese philosophy in the same relation to the Gospel as Greek philosophy was placed originally by St. John's use of the word *Logos* . . . he brought the Hebrew revelation into relation with Greek philosophy."

"In the Hindu conception of the Atma and the Chinese conception of the Tao we have perhaps the most profound of all insights into this mystery," Dom Bede writes, and he adds, "I would like to see the spirit of ecumenism enlarged so that we can see the mystery of Christ, which we try very imperfectly to realize in our lives, is hidden in all ancient religions. It is the mystery of God which was present from the beginning. There has never been a time when God's grace, when his Spirit, was not present in mankind, leading men toward the truth." And the Christian is professionally obliged to agree with St. Justin Martyr, who said, "All truth wherever it is found belongs to us as Christians," and with St. Augustine, who said that "We must accept truth, wherever we find it, hungrily." (The Latin word *esurientes* really means "as though starving.")

The perception of a mystery beyond and within the world, of which this world is only a sign, is for Dom Bede the root of all religion. He writes

It underlies the religion of primitive man. It is embodied in the ancient myths and legends, it is found at the basis of Egyptian and Babylonian religion, and it finally takes shape in the mystery religions.

With his vows Dom Bede recaptured his first perception of the spring as he had experienced it as a schoolboy; yet now he knows spring itself is a symbol of passing beyond the barriers of the finite, the relative, the temporal, to that place where heart and mind may be—indeed already are—one with absolute reality.

As the Sufi dervishes chant at Konya before their dancing:

> Thou art the unseen and the seen
> Had no clue
> Thou art hiding in bodies and souls
> Had no clue
> I was looking for sign of thine in this world
> At last I have found that the world itself is
>   a sign of thine
> Now I have a clue

This concept of the visible as a symbol of the invisible, of the created as simply analogical, was currently Christian as well as Moslem until the Cartesian dialectic of the sixteenth century, or, at all events, until the Renaissance. What Dom Bede was seeking with his wholewheat, stone-ground bread, and his flight from the machine, was the Greek acceptance of nature as the given. In nature, man is the perfect form, and on nature he may build the perfect form—Olympia, Delphi, Paestum. Yet Greek vision was never wholly identified with Christianity, though some Christian painters, like Masaccio, tried to fit the Crucifixion into it. But the Eastern view, whether Buddhist, Hindu, Moslem, or Taoist, was always whole, total. This view postulates as the perfect form an everlasting yea to nature, and a complete acceptance of the initial given whereas the West, since the Renaissance, conquers or surpasses nature, accepts nothing, and questions everything. In the East, man is born to his appointed time and place; in the West, man makes himself and separates himself from his origins. In the East, man is social before he is individual; in the West, man is an individual before he is social. Salvation, for the Oriental, consists in becoming consciously part of the cosmic design. For the Occidental, salvation is separation from creation. For the Oriental the universe is subjective, I am it and it is I. For the Westerner, the universe is objective. "I am one for whom the visible world exists," as Flaubert put it. The universe is even hostile to the self. Oriental man is thoroughly at home in the universe; Occidental man is everywhere a stranger. This is partly Christian: "Here we have no abiding city." But it is Christianity aggravated by the divorce between thought and feeling, reason and emotion. Yet, as Dom Bede discovered experientially, at the mystical level these contradictions disappear. "Myself is my smallest being; the universe, my greatest being. The former is my physical, the latter my spiritual, being," wrote Mao Tse-tung, China's poet-leader, and his words express a truth accepted by both India and China. But there the resemblance between the countries ends. India has no sense of a concern for, or duty to, my neighbor. Since reality is one, unique and single, for Indians the only work worthy of man is reaching that reality. In China, on the contrary, the Boddhisatt-vas—as also in Japan—prove their Buddhahood by refusing the bliss of Nirvana until they have brought to it "all sentient beings." As Mao Tse-tung put it, "No crime is greater than the repression of man's nature, either by oneself, or by someone else," and the Chinese have always regarded man as the supremely important fact and being.

Dom Bede Griffiths sees that this is an Indian problem and faces it squarely: "The trouble is that for the Hindu mind this experience of God has been so overwhelming that it has made it difficult for it to affirm the reality of the world." With the result, alas, that the most religious people in the world are the least charitable.

"In India I almost forgot that one could walk on a pavement without fear of stepping on a huddled figure," wrote Arthur Koestler. I myself found, whether staying with poor Indians— a Balliol friend of my son's, with three small boys—or with rich friends who sent their second-best Cadillac to the airport to meet me, so blatant and revolting a disregard of humanity in their treatment of their servants that my pleasure in the company of my friends was wholly marred thereby.

Dom Bede Griffiths lives now in his own ashram in Kerala, South India. He wears the orange robe of a sannyasi (Hindu monk) and eats only what Hindus eat—completely vegetarian food. He has already gathered around him a small community, and he is working together with the Syrian Church of South India. He considers this church of importance as providing an example of a Catholic Church with a distinctive Oriental liturgy, springing from a Christian tradition which is quite different from that of the Greek and Latin. Mass is celebrated in Malayam, and the marriage service has borrowed Hindu customs. The Syrian Church is supposed to have been founded by St. Thomas the Apostle, and therefore to be as ancient as the Roman Church. It stems from Antioch, where "the disciples first came to be called Christians," and during the first four centuries it spread over Palestine, Syria, Mesopotamia, and Persia, and the number of its martyrs was no less than that of the Western Church. It was carried also to China, where the Chinese Emperor himself almost became a Christian. The Syrian liturgy is full of poetry, some of the earliest Christian poetry, such as *The Odes of Solomon,* originating in Antioch in the second century. St. Ephrem in the fourth century was one of the greatest of all hymn writers, and to this day the Syrian liturgy is composed of songs, mostly profound meditations on the Scriptures. The Syrian worshippers, also, have characteristically Eastern gestures, very different from those of people of the Latin rite. For example, they stand with hands outstretched in prayer, palms upward, and bow in adoration by prostrating on both knees and touching the ground with their foreheads.

After 500 years of Christian penetration, at first Catholic, later both Catholic and Protestant, India is less than 2 percent Christian. Indeed, during all these centuries Christians have appeared to Indians as loud-mouthed, red-faced, meat-eating, alcohol-drinking presences, with unintelligible liturgies, whether Latin or English. Dom Bede considers that the real task "which awaits the Church in India is to construct a theology, using the philosophy of the Vedanta as its basis in the same way as the Greek Fathers and St. Thomas Aquinas used the philosophy of Plato and Aristotle." There is no doubt in his mind that the "Vedanta is the greatest system of natural theology in the history of the world."

The problem of relating God to the world without creation remains. And it is very real, in a country where many, many people die daily of hunger in the streets, where there are no old age pensions, there is no medicare, no unemployment insurance, and no compulsory education, and where communal strife killed at partition more than the Nazis did at home, where even Christians observe caste distinction, and where minorities—Nagas, Todas, and the like—are discriminated against.

It is quite possible to dislike the manifestations of Indian religion, as Arthur Koestler disliked watching a great guru (Krishna Menon) gargling and spitting into a cup held by a little girl. (Koestler was not allowed the favor accorded more serious disciples, of listening to the bathroom noises of the Swami's morning toilet.) Dom Denys Rutledge, like Dom Bede a Benedictine, disliked the Hindu belief that "Man is God and once man has developed his powers, realized his full stature, there is nothing outside or above him, nothing beyond him, a depressing thought." It is better to seek "What is there in it for *me?*" as Dom J. M. Dechanet did, in his little book on Christian Yoga, which is widely used today in Catholic monasteries from the United States to the Congo. But either way, as Dom Bede points out, the experience which underlies all Hindu religion and philosophy and which is sought no less earnestly today than in the past is *Tat tvam asi*, thou are that—the soul in the ultimate ground of its being is one with Brahma, the ground of all being. "It is only when we have met the Hindu *here*, in this ultimate ground of his experience of God, that we can hope to come to any understanding with him." And Dom Bede goes on to say:

For the first time in history the great religions of the world have come into global contact with one another and have begun to confront one another with mutual understanding. There are today five great religions in the world, Hinduism, Buddhism, Judaism, Christianity and Islam, to which one may perhaps add a sixth, Confucianism. Each of these religions has a certain claim to universality. With Judaism, Christianity and Islam this has always been explicit; Hinduism and Buddhism and Confucianism have so far been confined to Asia and Hinduism and Buddhism have only recently begun to lay claim to universality, yet one may say that the claim is in a sense implicit in them. Hindus called their religion *sanatana dharma*, the eternal religion, and it is their belief that it reveals the eternal nature of man and therefore can embrace all mankind. The Buddha also believed that he had discovered the final truth, the way of salvation for man, and Buddhism has always shown a strong missionary spirit.

These religions can be divided into two groups, which are sharply distinguished from one another, and form, as has been said, two "spiritual hemispheres." There are the three Western religions, Judaism, Christianity and Islam, which belong to the "prophetic" type and these three recognize one, supreme, transcendent, personal God, who reveals himself through his prophets; and on the other hand there are the three Eastern religions which are of a "mystical" character, recognizing the one, infinite, eternal Being which is immanent in nature and the soul of man and which is known in the experience of the soul in its depths.

The difference, however, must not be exaggerated. There is a mystical tradition in Judaism, Christianity and Islam, while Hinduism, and to a less extent Buddhism and Confucianism, have also their worship of a personal God. The antithesis, in fact, only brings out the fact that these religions are essentially complementary, representing the two sides of all genuine religion. One may believe that it is the task of the future to bring these two traditions into vital relation with one another. . . .

In other words, the Western religions, which have always tended to regard themselves as forms of the one true religion and to seek to impose their belief on others, have to learn to recognize that they can no longer ignore the spiritual wisdom of the East and have to come to terms with Eastern religion. On the other hand, the Eastern religions have to learn to face the reality of the prophetic message of the West and not to assume, as they tend to do, that it can be simply absorbed in the synthesis of their own religion. The difficulty which a Christian experiences in India today is that Hindus consider that all religions are but different forms of the one *sanatana dharma;* all are essentially the same, and differ only in their accidental forms, their "rites and dogmas." This is certainly attractive as a way of reconciling the differences in religion which divide mankind, but for a Christian, as for a Jew or a Muslim, it involves the denial of what he believes to be essential in his religion. The problem, then, is how this synthesis can be achieved without renouncing any of the essential values of the different religions. This is one great ecumenical problem of the world of today.

One may believe that India is in a privileged position in this matter, because in no other country is there such a deeply rooted diversity of religions. Hinduism, Buddhism, Jainism, Parseeism, Judaism and Christianity have all been in India for nearly two thousand years, and in no country is there such a profoundly religious culture surviving today. When one looks back over the history of India it is difficult not to believe that it holds a privileged place in the history of religion. From its beginnings in the first millennium before Christ, Indian religion has undergone a continuous evolution, giving birth to at least four different religions, Hinduism, Buddhism, Jainism and Sikhism, and to innumerable sects within Hinduism, each with its own doctrine and cult, and developing a continuous philosophical tradition, in which the religious genius of the race has found expression.

It would, I think, be possible to argue that all mystical religion has its source in India. Certainly the spiritual movement which gave birth to the Upanishads, to Buddhism, and to Jainism in the sixth century B.C. is unique in the history of the world. Then, for the first time, it seems that the human mind broke through the barrier of the senses and attained to an intuition of the ultimate reality.... Beyond this, it seems certain that it was from this source that Pythagoras drew the inspiration which introduced a mystical current into Greek thought and descended through Plato and Plotinus into the Christian Church. It can further be shown that it was from this source that a new mystical current entered into Islam and transformed Sufi doctrine.

Dom Bede Griffiths is not the only Western priest trying to witness to India not by teaching, but by being. As early as 1950, Father Jules Monchanin was joined by Father Henri le Saux, and together they founded the sacchi ananda Ashram at Kulittalai, in South India. This ashram practiced total poverty and contemplation, and is described in a book written by the two fathers jointly and called *An Indian Benedictine Ashram*. After Father Monchanin's death in 1957, Father le Saux (who had taken the Hindu name Abshiktananda, which means "the joy of the monk through God") has lived alone in a hut. He is a Celt from Brittany and says he therefore finds Hindu mysticism less alien than a Hellenist would: Father Monchanin used indeed to bewail his own Hellenism. In 1962 Father le Saux organized, first at Almora, then in 1963 at Jaipur, and in 1964 at Nagpur, meetings between Protestants, Catholics, and Orthodox during which, for a week of meditation, the Gospel of St. John is studied in conjunction with the Upanishads. Every year Father le Saux goes on pilgrimage to the holy places of the Himalayas and is present there among the Hindu swamis.

Another priest working in India in the same ecumenical way is the Jesuit, Father Raymond Panikkar. What is needed, these men agree, is to voyage inward, and to discover within one's own soul the void from which creation began.

The Church's doctrine on Hinduism and Buddhism has been succinctly stated by Vatican II in its *schema* on the attitude of the Church to the non-Christian religions. Herewith one of the most pertinent paragraphs:

> In Hinduism men scrutinise the divine mystery and express it in the inexhaustible riches of myth and in the profundities of philosophy; they seek liberation from the miseries of our conditions by divers forms of the ascetic life, by deep contemplation and also by seeking refuge in God, with love and confidence. In Buddhism, the radical insufficiency of this changing world is recognized and the way is shewn by which men, with devotion and confidence, by self-renunciation and by purifying themselves from transitory attachments, can attain freedom and a lasting peace. The Catholic Church rejects nothing that is true and holy in these religions. She ceaselessly proclaims Christ who is "the Way, the Truth and the Life" and in Whom God reconciled all things to Himself. Knowing the different modalities of salvation, the Church brings a sincere attention to all these ways of acting and living, these rules and these doctrines which, although they differ on many points from what she proposes, still offer a ray of the truth that illumines all men.

India and China, the two most populous nations in the world, containing between them far more than half the whole world: twelve hundred million people, and nearly a hundred thousand more every day, are as different as nations can be. India mystical, politically disunited throughout its history, constantly conquered, with no one language ever; China pragmatic, united for hundreds—nay thousands of years under one Emperor, rarely conquered (if ever!) and with the same written language over the whole huge area during most of its five thousand years of history. What religion China has, came out from India. But China early built a wall around herself, less to keep the barbarians from getting in than to discourage the Chinese from going out. The West can bomb and bomb them both and be a villain, but what else can it do to either—or for them? Trade, like religion, follows the flag. And neither China nor India to-day are in a position to trade, the one from anger, the other from hunger. As for our religion, it has followed the flag too long, and its "new look" suffers from the French behavior in Algeria and Indonesia, and now from that of the Americans in Vietnam. "By their fruits ye shall know them" was said by the Founder of Christianity. Against the Goliath of distrust created by Christian imperialism, by Cesaro-Papism, such in-dividuals as Dom Bede Griffiths shoot their sling-shots of real charity—let us hope not in vain.

Chapter VI

I FIRST came to Africa in 1948. That year I sought to follow physically the journeys made by Charles de Foucauld, whose life I was writing. He was a French Army officer, born in 1854, who became a Trappist and later left the order to turn hermit. For fifteen years he lived alone in the Sahara, then was—almost accidentally—murdered by the Tuaregs among whom he had settled. He was peripatetic, a gyrovague, and I started my pilgrimage in his pursuit at Casablanca, where there is a street named for him, then went on to Fez, where he lived in the 1880s disguised as a Jew, making a "reconnaissance" of Morocco—with compasses, charts, maps, altitudes, and elevations—that Marshal Lyautey found most useful when he annexed Morocco in 1912. From Fez I went on to Tlemcen, where I found a passionately nationalist Moslem university within the still medieval city. Then I went, via Oran (Albert Camus's city) to Algiers, and down through the desert, via Laghouat, Béni-Abbès, and the Mzab oases, to de Foucauld's tomb at El Goléa. Ghardaia, one of the Mzab towns, remains in my mind as one of the most beautiful places I have ever seen—rising palm-girt and green, small and white and clean, directly out of the desert.

In those days Casablanca, my first stop, was famous—or infamous—for its Bouzbir. This was the oldest in Morocco. It was the first the French had set up, and was the bustling seaport's only claim to fame. When, however, a tourist asked at Cook's if they had a tour of Bouzbir, they looked shocked. "You must make your own arrangements," they said. However, the Cook's man, when pressed, gave the name of a guide, always a burly gentleman, who appeared at one's hotel after dark. (It was preferable to see Bouzbir by moonlight.) It was essential to take a carton of American cigarettes with one. And it was emphasized that one must never, never, let go of the guide's arm. Those were orders, and he would not answer for the safety, or even the life, of any tourist who let go of his arm. Bouzbir was a whitewashed town within a town. It was quite large.

The entrance was imposing, some thirty feet high, with great carved wooden gates. Guards, armed, were posted at the doors. Once inside, the small town was deliciously neat and white and clean. Flowering hibiscus trees filled the little square; the bright, moonlit streets were lined with souks, stores, and bazaars; there were crowded cafés, hairdressers, a movie house, a market, and everywhere the pervasive smell of mint—for the ritual three cups of mint tea are offered every visitor, the glass half filled with the fragrant leaves, half with boiling water, syrupy sweet. The guide distributed handfuls of cigarettes, and the visitors would push their way through a chattering, gay crowd—unique in that it consisted only of very young girls. For Bouzbir was the red-light district, or *quartier reservé* of Casa, and its only inhabitants were prostitutes.

Night life was Bouzbir's reason for existing. Young girls were "entered" there by their parents at birth, and if a girl didn't get into Bouzbir by the time she was twelve, she was considered not much good for anything—or anyone! By the time they were seventeen, most of the girls had acquired one, or even both, armsful of gold bangles—thin, pure gold bracelets with which they left Bouzbir and made excellent marriages. For these gold bangles were a substantial *dot*, thought none the worse of for being well and truly earned. And Bouzbir girls were tremendously sought after as wives, for, as my taxi driver pointed out, "Those girls taught to enjoy being wives—then husbands enjoy, too."

Bouzbir was what it was, yet it must be admitted that the sight of it was frankly delightful. In the moonlight hundreds of very pretty, very lightly clad, and unveiled girls, roaming, running in the streets, or sitting in the cafés, could not have been more charming. All ordinary nightclub activities took place there also—native dances, music-hall turns, much singing, and of course, that endless sipping of cups of mint tea. Over these, the girls talked. Sometimes a rich patron, a certain M. Dupré, an elderly French bachelor, would pay for all the girls he knew, first hiring ALL the victorias in Casa, and then would take the young ladies driving through the whole city, to the embarrassment of the puritanical among his friends and acquaintances. Sunday afternoons the girls kept "open house"; families could visit; no business was done; "never on Sunday" was true there as elsewhere, and there was lots of dancing and singing.

But how fierce the girls could be was demonstrated whenever a man appeared—especially if American and young. He would literally be mobbed by a posse of girls. They would tear his clothes off, fighting for him—and the lovely kittenish creatures turned into harpies at the sight of their prey and at the possibility of one more bangle. However, the guides had no pity for the nice young Americans. Americans were said to wear out a girl in two months; before that, girls had lasted two to three years.

It was the French who built Bouzbir, after they occupied Morocco in 1912. The name came from a M. Prosper Ferrier, whose grandfather, Pierre Ferrier, came to Morocco in 1830, under Louis Philippe. Prosper—whose name the Arabs mispronounced as Bouztri—managed to become British, French, and Greek consul all at once—in those days no great problem. He built a big house near where the Royal Palace now stands, but, as he was very fond of hunting, and the town gates were closed at sundown, he also built himself a hunting lodge without the city walls, where he could pass the night when hunting late. He would hunt wild boar where the Anfa Hotel now stands—where Roosevelt, Churchill, and Stalin met to plan the invasion of Europe in World War II. At that Anfa meeting in January 1943, after a good dinner, Roosevelt had told Sultan Sidi Mohammed ben Youssef that the U.S. would approve and encourage Moroccan independence. (Elliott Roosevelt has described the scene in *My Father Told Me.*) Thereafter, Moroccan independence was thirteen years a-borning, and only happened when and how it did because the French parliament was told that it would be necessary to mobilize half a million men to prevent it, and that Algeria was more important to France. Also that it would be impossible to stem the revolt in Algeria if Morocco was also in revolt. So on June 5, 1956 Morocco became independent, and the Sultan, whom the French had arrested and deported to Madagascar in 1953, was brought back to become King Mohammed V.

Prosper Ferrier's son, Pierre, had still shot partridges where the big city swimming pool is today. Pierre Ferrier remembers the French bombardment of Casablanca in 1907, when the Ferriers' hunting lodge was badly shelled. When the French took over Morocco in 1912, M. Ferrier *père* sold them his town house and was asked if he would sell some of the land he owned around his hunting lodge to resettle the Moroccans whom the French were moving and relocating as far as possible from their own new city. Prosper Ferrier sold some thirty square acres, upon which about thirty thousand people now live. The natives called this part of their town "Bouzbir" since it was Prosper's land, and it became the first *medina,* or Arab ghetto. Later the French—to the fury of poor M. Prosper Ferrier, a respectable citizen—built the white-walled girls' town within their new city, and this red-light district came, then, to be called Bouzbir. And from *this* Bouzbir the red-light districts all over Morocco came to be called Bouzbirs; there was one outside of Fez, a street or two also so-called in Rabat, and a Bouzbir outside of Marrakech. But none was as large, as well-built, as well-policed, as safe, or as sanitary as the original Bouzbir of Casablanca.

A French woman doctor who for ten years—from 1947 to 1957—had been in charge of the periodic checking of some fifty of the Bouzbir girls said that during that whole decade they were absolutely free from disease. In 1957, immediately after independence, all Bouzbirs were abolished as being associated with the hated French colonialism. Now I learned that Bouzbir is the prefecture of police for the fifth district of Casablanca. Veiled women and girls scurry about its quiet streets, but they are the most respectable wives and daughters of municipal employees. As everywhere else in Morocco, the streets are full of children—some fifty percent of the population is under twenty years old. No one needs red-light districts today—the Americans are gone, also most of the French. Moslems, allowed by the Koranic law to practice polygamy (up to four legal wives are allowed at a time) do not need brothels.

Other things besides Bouzbir had changed in the more than fifteen years since I was first in Africa. Then, while there was plenty of food in Morocco, Algeria was starving. The nomads of the southern desert were dying out from hunger; in Gerryville alone more than 10,000 Arabs had already died of hunger. In fact, one of the reasons for the Algerian war was France's total failure to provide food. The Vichy government, at German orders, had stripped Algeria. Later the occupying armies had added to the crisis, which was aggravated by the birthrate that was then rising at the rate of 130,000 a year for a population of ten million. By 1945 Algeria produced only 20 percent of its annual grain requirements. The Algerian war, admitted as such only in 1951, actually began with the bombing of Sétif and Guelma in 1945, when the R.A.F. completely obliterated whole villages. As the schoolmaster (French) at El Goléa told me, "The British had so much practice on the northwest frontier, it's second nature to them—they were most efficient, and we escaped the onus." The Algerian war helped the population problem considerably by killing over one million Arabs and by leading to the withdrawal of some French *colons*.

Who today remembers the words of the Brazzaville Conference of October 1940, when the French solemnly declared that "the objectives of the work of civilization accomplished by France in her colonies eliminate any idea of evolution outside the French Empire bloc. The eventual constitution, however remote, of self-government for the colonies is not envisaged"? Nets to catch the wind are all memories!

I was anxious above all to see how the Church had adapted to her new, subservient role. For when in Africa before, I had stayed all over the Sahara in either monasteries or convents. Then their two attitudes were very different. The Fathers were colonialists, talking, kindly but paternally, of the *indigènes* (natives). The nuns were utterly different in their viewpoint, without any feeling of "we whose souls are lighted, with wisdom from on high." Working long hours in grim surroundings (one Sister sighed to me that her white habit was an advantage, because you could see the lice on it after a day at the dispensary), they had only maternal feelings. Perhaps that is one of the few advantages of being a woman: that if you are one, it is almost impossible to feel superior to anybody anywhere, ever. That certainly seems to be true of women the world over.

The Church took a long, long time—from 1789 to 1890, in fact—to wake up to the reality of revolution. So long as the foundations of society were secure, religion was far more concerned about individual relationships and ethical duties than about social obligations. Capitalist society in the nineteenth century was savage and cruel beyond belief, but it met no challenge, as a system, from Church or Chapel, from Catholic or Protestant (and still less from Orthodox) Christianity. Christian morality upheld and approved capitalism. I grew up with every other happy English child of the upper classes, singing the Protestant hymn:

> All things bright and beautiful, . . .
> The rich man in his castle,
> The poor man at his gate,
> God made them, high or lowly,
> And order'd their estate.

But even Christianity cannot escape causality. Such mistakes as the burning of Huss and the torture of Galileo led to the secession of whole nations from the Catholic Church; later mistakes, such as condemning Marx while condoning the evils he so graphically described, led to the loss to the Church in the nineteenth century of the whole working class. And today, alas! when we deplore lampshades made of human skin by the Nazis, or French torture in Algeria, or American racism in Alabama or brutality in Vietnam, we do not do so as Christians. Only as liberals, or possibly simply as human beings. No Church has condemned by name in any single case any capitalist *person:* neither Hitler, nor the O.A.S. nor General Westmoreland, though many priests, clergymen, and Christian laymen have individually witnessed nobly against their behavior, and many have been killed for their witness.

The Chilean hierarchy, in 1964, defined the whole world as being now in a State of Mission, that is, a state in which the Church is represented by a minority, not only in numbers, but also in real influence on various social structures and on the national communities. "Today," their statement reads, "the Church is for the first time in history called upon to collaborate in the building of a world in which Christians are a minority." To do this the Christian must not have one set of rules for his own country and another for all other nations. (As Adlai Stevenson did when he ticked off the British for retaliating against Yemeni guerrillas. He told them: "Even under provocation a major power should not retaliate against a weaker country." And then proceeded wholeheartedly to approve American use of napalm bombs in Vietnam.) Today's Christians can have only one attitude: "We have met the enemy. We are they." (Which immortal remark was made by Pogo!)

And above all the Christian must remain the watchdog of freedom, individual or collective. For, as Boethius (480–524) said, "There can be no reasonable nature unless it be ended with free-will." And as St. Bernard (1079–1153) pointed out, "The will has nothing free except itself." Christ, when He said, "Render unto Caesar that which is Caesar's," both gave the state an authority that was from God and gave the individual a liberty that was no less from God. From the moment that the letters A.U.C. (*ab urbe condita*) changed to A.D. (*anno domini*), the defense of liberty, as Lord Acton (1834–1902) pointed out, ceased to be the concern of "a few ineffectual philosophers" and became "the perpetual charge of a universal Church."

It was Pope John XIII who warned the Church to avoid the errors of the past. Discussing the just relations between nations in different stages of economic development, it was he, too, who warned "the highly developed nations" that they must take care lest, "while giving help to less developed nations, they turn the political situation that prevails to their own profit or imperial aggrandizement. This conduct must explicitly be labeled as an effort to introduce a new form of colonialism which would only be a repetition of that old, outdated type from which many peoples have recently escaped. It would have a harmful impact on international relations and would constitute a threat to world peace." (*Pacem in Terris*)

As I drove up through the wonderfully beautiful brown Moroccan hills above a high bare plateau, I reflected that the Church has actually had to tack three times between 1891 and 1961—in the seventy years beween *Rerum Novarum* and *Mater et Magistra*—in order to steer a straight course. *Rerum Novarum* emphasized the role of government in the defense of gravely threatened human rights. *Quadragesimo Anno*—forty years later—reaffirmed the individual's inalienable rights in the face of the totalitarian state. *Mater et Magistra* does a volte-face to warn the individual that his rights do not consist simply in the restricting of governmental function, but that the fact of his individual value should be seen as a principle which obliges him to cooperate with both national and international authority for the common good.

The encyclicals and their implications are some of the questions discussed at Toumliline, the Benedictine monastery in the Middle Atlas to which I was bound. Morocco has always been considered the Far West of Africa. The Straits of Gibraltar were the Pillars of Hercules, the farthest and remotest limits of the world. The Phoenicians provided the blue-veiled Tuareg with their language *tifinagh*. In the Tangier museum the strange prehistoric egg-burial urns can be seen, that are also found in China. Morocco is a very old country, full of Roman ruins. There is an Arabic saying that an Algerian is a man, but a Moroccan is a lion. The girls are so lovely: there is a local folk song that says of the girls in Taliwin that a man might well wish to be wounded so these would bend over him in pity.

There are more cedars of Lebanon in Morocco than in Lebanon, and the High Atlas are strange and savage still, a country where there are more castles than houses, more earth than water, and more sky than either. The mood is indigo, and responds to St. John of the Cross's paradox of silent music and sonorous silence.

The Moroccans are pious Moslems, and their state, like every other Moslem state, is a theocracy: that is to say, there is no separation of religious and secular authority. In a Moslem state, there is no priesthood—any male adult can lead the Friday prayer and conduct a marriage or burial ceremony. And the ruler—be he imam, sultan, king, or khalif, is a deputy always, regent for Allah, Lord of all worlds. Five duties, to say the shahada (the creed: There is no god but God, and Mohammed is His prophet); prayer (five times daily, and, when possible, communally on Fridays); payment of tithe (for the community poor); fasting (from sunrise to sunset for one lunar month—Ramadan—each year, during which time no food, drink, smoking, or sexual intercourse are allowed); and pilgrimage (once in a lifetime for each individual to Mecca) are incumbent on all Moslems. So is *jihad,* the effort against oneself, which, when Islam is attacked, becomes externalized as its defense.

Christian monastic life was invented in Africa, and there are still 200 Coptic monasteries in Ethiopia, 8 in Egypt. But in all of Africa, with over 200 million inhabitants, there are only 9 Benedictine and 9 Trappist foundations. Toumliline's history begins in 1945 when a lay Catholic at Casablanca wrote to the Benedictine abbot of En Calcat in France to ask whether a foundation could be made in Morocco. Largely through the generosity of one widow, a site was bought about two miles from Azrou in the Middle Atlas in a live-oak forest at an elevation of 5,000 feet. Here a monastery was built, a dispensary opened, and on October 26, 1951, the Feast of Christ the King, Toumliline was consecrated to Him. From the first, the monastery ran into political difficulties. Dom Denys Martin, the Prior, refused to accept French military protection. "You will be massacred," the local officer in charge told him. "We are obliged professionally to accept that risk," Dom Denys replied. Gradually local orphans gravitated to the infant monastery, and the monks felt compelled to start an orphanage to house the children. The children brought changes to the Benedictine usage. For example, the signs used by the monks to communicate without words (requests to pass food at meals, and such like) were misread by the children, so they were abolished. The tonsure, too, in Islam is part of the rite of circumcision, and also was given up. No attempt was, is, or ever will be made to convert anyone. Dom Denys believes in deepening, broadening, and accentuating every man's or woman's own religion or faith, not in altering or changing it. Take, for example, a young Moroccan, called Rachid. As a child he was first drawn to the monastery in the summers, as he liked to help the monks garden, dig, and build. Then he introduced his father to the monks. As his appetite for the religious life grew, he left his family, went to live in the mosque, and gave everything away except three pounds of sugar; these he exchanged for bread, and lived marginally, working when the bread came to an end. He would eat no meat. "It makes my eyes follow women," he told Dom Denys.

In 1953 one of a group of thirty prisoners, all members of the Nationalist Istiqlal party, doing forced labor in the neighborhood, begged for water from the monastery. He was given the water, and he and his companions were also offered mint tea. This led to furious recrimination by the French authorities, who tried to have the monks disbanded. When the French arrested and deported the Sultan on August 20, 1953, Dom Denys knew independence was near. The Sultan returned to Morocco on November 16, 1955. In 1956, after the declaration of independence, the Sultan, now King, visited Toumliline. He said, "It is natural that, in evolving, Toumliline should become a center of civilization where Moslem and Christian thought collaborate." Toumliline indeed has filled a tremendous gap.

In 1956 the first summer conference took place at Toumliline. The participants came from 26 nations, and among the intellectuals driving up, past the lovely Roman ruins of Volubilis, through the lunar landscape of Ito, to stay in the modern, functional simplicity of the monastery, were such great Arabists as Olivier Lacombe and Monsignor Journet, James Kritzeck and, greatest of all, Louis Massignon. It was an informal gathering, a meeting of shorts and soutanes, dresses and djellabas. But after it was over, the chief Boy Scout of Morocco said to Dom Denys Martin, "I want to conform my life to the love I witnessed among you." By 1959 there were 700 who came to Toumliline, and the monastery had grown so that the Prior had made a new foundation at Bouaké on the Ivory Coast.

It was Jacques Maritain who had suggested I write a life of Charles de Foucauld.[1] Louis Massignon had known de Foucauld well, so my first meeting with him was when I went to his book-lined, comfortable apartment in the rue Monsieur. He had the white skin, the incandescent pallor of Maritain, but otherwise they could not have been, or looked, more unlike. Maritain looks like a Gothic saint or a Merovingian king, or both; Massignon looked like a scholar, even to his black jacket and his stoop. Massignon was unbelievably, almost extravagantly, courteous and gentle. To be with him was to be soothed, to feel cherished. It was as though he made an act of faith in the real presence of everyone he met.

In the bibliography, published in 1956, of Louis Massignon there were 600 entries. These included 200 published works, review articles, and 150 published lectures. He was the greatest Arab scholar of his time, and possibly the greatest Arabist of all time. In 1919 Massignon was appointed surrogate to the Chair of Islamic sociology at the Collège de France, and on May 30, 1926 he succeeded to that chair, which he held until 1954. He drew around him hundreds, even thousands, of students who today from Morocco to the Punjab to Indonesia to the U.S. attest his incomparable influence. When Massignon died on October 31, 1962, the French papers, from the Communist *Humanité* to the Catholic *La Croix* and the *Lettres Françaises* (which had a special Massignon memorial issue), joined in a paean of praise. "One of the men who signified France is dead," wrote the Communist poet Louis Aragon. He added, "May I be permitted to mark the hour when Massignon's heart has been stilled, by an affirmation of that community of disparate hopes, of that great longing for reconciliation, which may serve as an image of humanity's future, and by a homage which above all expresses my belief in the *incarnation* of human dreams, for which this man of God worked better

[1] *Desert Calling*, published in 1949, Henry Holt, N.Y. It was the first life of de Foucauld written in English.

than many other men, his unbelieving brothers, but still his brothers." The Soviet Academy of Sciences, of which Massignon was a member, sent a message expressing their deep sense of loss; from El Azhar University in Cairo, which he had first visited in 1906, and from Baghdad, from Japan and from the United States came condolences.

Louis Massignon was born on July 25, 1883, at Nogent-sur-Marne. His father was a sculptor who took the name of Pierre Roche from a maternal grandmother; some of his works, notably a bronze statue at the Luxemburg and a bust of J. K. Huysmans, remain. Massignon's great-grandparents were Vexin peasants; his mother's folk, Flanders weavers. His father, though he no longer believed, made a pilgrimage to Domremy in 1889. Louis Massignon, studying the beliefs of the peasants of the Vexin in order to give his eldest son a feeling for their past, found that St. Joan of Arc was but one of the sacred virgins who were "local priestesses, like Bernadette of Lourdes, Mélanie of La Salette, Lucia of Fatima." He was to find these again as far back in history as Persephone and the mysteries of Eleusis, as far away in geography as Amaterasu-Omikami in Japan, and Kwan-yin in China.

As a high school student Massignon's greatest friend was Henri Maspero. Both boys were mad about the East; they walked home together daily and in their spare time frequented the library of the École des Langues Orientales. On March 17, 1945 Henri Maspero, who had become a great Sinologist, died in Buchenwald. His son, whom Massignon had hidden during the early part of the war, was killed in 1944, also by the Germans.

In 1899 Massignon passed the first, and in 1900 the second, *baccalauréat,* and after the second (Sciences) his father sent him to stay in Béarn with Dr. Elie Pecaut, a Kantian Protestant. On his return, Massignon visited on October 27, 1900 a great friend of his father's, the convert writer J. K. Huysmans, who described him as "the most charming young man imaginable." In 1901 Massignon went to Algeria, where his mother's godfather was a military doctor. There he met Alfred le Chatelier, who founded Ouargla and also the chair to which Massignon succeeded at the Collège de France. Massignon met, too, Henri de Castries, a friend of de Foucauld. In 1902 Massignon obtained his licentiate in letters and began the study of Sanskrit. In 1904, aged twenty, he went to Morocco in order to verify certain data in his thesis on "The Geographic outline of Morocco during the first fifteen years of the sixteenth century, according to Leo the African" (published in Algiers, 1906). It was on this trip, while traveling from Tangier to Fez, that, betrayed by an Arab guide, Massignon, aged twenty-one, took command of the caravan, which was under attack. He broke the wine bottles he had with him in order not to give scandal to the Moslems in his party, and also not to lead them into a temptation to betray their faith. And he himself never touched wine again. At that moment, too, he made a vow to learn Arabic; fifty-five years later he remarked, "I am still learning it." When he was checking his itinerary, prepared in Paris, he was overwhelmed by the "staggering superiority" of de Foucauld's survey of Morocco (*La Reconnaissance au Maroc*). When Massignon's book was published in 1906, he wished to thank de Foucauld. "Is he still alive?" Massignon asked de Castries, who replied, "Yes, but he has wrecked his life. He has retired to become a priest near Béni-Abbès." Massignon said he still wished to thank him. "Lyautey's dining with me tonight," de Castries said. "He'll take your book to de Foucauld." Massignon has written: "To my very pro-Colonializing introduction, de Foucauld replied in kind. It was the style then." But "he added that he offered his prayers to God, asking Him to bless me, my work and all my life."

In February 1906 Massignon, having obtained his diplomas of literary and spoken Arabic, set off for Cairo, where, at the Institute of Oriental Archaeology, he varied his linguistic and archaeological studies with what he described as "violent escapades, disguised as a fellah, which were descents into criminal circles." While Massignon was on leave in Paris during the summer of 1907, General de Beylie appointed him head of an archaeological mission to Baghdad. He sailed from Marseilles on the *Luristan*, for thirteen days endured strong gales and high seas, landed at Basra, and became the guest of a noble Moslem family, the Alusi. In March-April 1908, vaguely disguised in Turkish costume, Massignon rode into the desert seeking— and finding—the fortress of Okheidir. He analyzed and photographed it (it had disappeared from view since Pietro della Valle in the sixteenth century) and then turned south to Kut, where his letter of credit was not honored, as he was suspected of being involved in the Young Turk revolution which broke out two months later. He was arrested as a spy, thrown into jail, and threatened with death. He tried to commit suicide, disgusted with himself. Suddenly, as for Paul, Pascal, and Claudel, "My eyes were closed before an interior fire, which judged me and burnt my heart, the pure Presence, ineffable, creative, suspending my sentence." He went back up the Tigris toward Baghdad on a Turkish boat, gave up in front of Ctesiphon's Taq, and, groggy with malaria, remained a convalescent for some weeks. One evening, as the light reflected from the dappled waves of the river in spate danced on his ceiling, he heard the doves cooing in a palm tree outside his window. "In a moment, suspended in silence, I understood them and the reality of my pardon clearly emerged ... The Stranger who visited me, that May evening, cauterizing my despair that He clove, my interior mirror had already shewn him to me but masked by my own features. Had shewn him mounting like the phosphorescence of a fish rising from abysmal waters, from my own depths. Betrayed in my host's eyes by my make-up of scientific larceny, disguised as a spy, my mirror darkened before His fire. Nothing more, except the admission of His sacred loneliness and a recognition of my original unworthiness, that was the diaphanous winding-sheet between us, made iridescent

by His coming." Left for dead, unconscious, Massignon kept re-
peating the word *hak,* which in Arabic means debt. Later, he
said that the Stranger who, on that day of His wrath seized him,
motionless in His hand like a sand gecko, upset, little by little,
all his acquired reflexes, all his precautions, all his human
respect. By an overturning of values, "He changed my relative
propertied tranquility into the most miserable poverty." Massignon's noble friends the Alusi went surety for him to the
governor of Baghdad, gave him four carriages and sixteen
horses, and got permission for him to return to France the way
he wished, by the desert, along the Euphrates, to Aleppo and
Beirut. His hosts gave him also a crystal seal engraved with
his name and the one word "Abduhu"—"His slave."

Then Massignon settled down to write his doctoral thesis
(published later in two volumes), on Al-Hallaj, the Arab mystic poet tortured and crucified on March 25, 922 as a heretic
for having in his ecstasy cried out, "I am He." The thesis took
five years to write. While Massignon was working on it, de
Foucauld arrived on a four-day visit to Paris, his first for eight
years, and came straight to see Massignon, took him to meet the
Abbé Huvelin, who had converted him, and then to spend a
whole February night, "slow, dark, bare without consolation,
in that proud and icy mausoleum, the *Sacré Coeur.*" Foucauld
was convinced he had at last found his disciple and successor.
But Massignon was just as sure he did not want to abandon the
world, or to study Berber, but rather Arabic, and his spiritual
director agreed that Massignon's place was in the new university founded by King Fuad, and not living with de Foucauld in
the Sahara. In 1912–13 Massignon gave forty lectures in Cairo.
In March 1913, de Foucauld returned for the last time to Paris,
bringing with him a young Tuareg, Ouksem. Massignon served
a Mass said by de Foucauld in honor of a martyred great-
granduncle, during which "a strange sign from God came between us like a sword." Actually, for all their communion in
the Catholic faith and in love of Islam, de Foucauld and Mas-

signon grew more and more apart. Age was a great factor in their differences. Massignon, thirty years his junior, started where de Foucauld ended, in devout and devoted nationalism. Then, too, de Foucauld preferred the lax Berbers, barely Moslem in faith, thinking he could come nearer to them than to Arabs. For Massignon, Islam was one of the three prayers of Abraham, and the Arabs were as "chosen" a people as the Jews. Islam was expressive of faith, as Judaism of hope, as Christianity of charity. Yet both men could share a friend. Cheikh Baye, the Moslem saint who conquered de Foucauld, who "Islamized" the Hoggar during de Foucauld's lifetime, in spite of the priest's presence there—won recognition from both men, from Massignon as a true saint, and from de Foucauld as "an enormous and salutary influence."

De Foucauld had written he would never keep weapons in his hermit's cell. At Tamanrasset, during the last months of 1916, he filled his borj with arms, turning it into an arsenal, at the French General Laperrine's request. De Foucauld was killed by mistake, by a sixteen-year-old Tuareg, set to guard him while his arms were being stolen by the other Tuaregs. Laperrine avenged the hermit in true Christian fashion, writing in his notebook the names of the assassins in red as he "liquidated" each of them.

Massignon, always nonviolent, gradually grew out of such reactions. Married on January 27, 1914 to his first cousin on his mother's side, he was mobilized on March 15, 1915 and sent to the Dardanelles. Twice mentioned in dispatches for his courage, he received also the Serbian gold medal. In 1917 he was sent, with the rank of captain, to work in Syria with the Sykes-Picot Mission. This experience, which he movingly relates, included a tussle with T. E. Lawrence. Georges Picot had two career diplomats as well as Massignon on his staff; Sir Mark Sykes had only a Palestine Arab, G. Albina, and Lord Lloyd (part-time). Sykes and Picot cabled in cipher directly to London and Paris, over the heads of Allenby and the French Minister in Cairo. Massignon and Sykes hit it off from the first. Sykes (whom an English Arab scholar, Marmaduke Pickthall thought viciously, outrageously double-dealing), to test Massignon made him give verbatim reports of five conferences that took place on board Admiral Lord Weymss' yacht, the *Northbrook*. Three were with the Emir Faisal, and two with King Hussein. Sykes also made Massignon work on the regional *Handbooks* which gave Massignon the idea for his own *Annuaire du monde Musulman*. Massignon's competence in fulfilling these assignments decided Sir Mark to associate Massignon with T. E. Lawrence. He intended to name both men adjutants to the Arab command of the Northern Army, which was to be confided to Faisal after the taking of Gaza. As it turned out, General Murray's defeat at Gaza necessitated the transfer to Egypt of four British divisions. Thereafter, France only sent to the Gaza front a small detachment, for the Eastern theater was divided between Macedonia and Egypt. Still, even after this setback, it was essential that Lawrence accept Massignon. And here was the rub. On August 8 the two met face to face in the Arab Bureau. Massignon was surprised at how young Lawrence looked, how unconventional, both timid and brutal. They talked French, English, finally Arabic, but in none of these languages was conversation satisfactory. Massignon's Arabic was that of the modern literary periodicals; Lawrence spoke a staccato, not very correct, local dialect. Loyally, Lawrence told Massignon that Hussein intended to proclaim himself not caliph, but imam; in exchange, he wished to know about Massignon's archaeological finds at Okheìdir. But it was nine years since the latter had been in the desert, and he had nothing to tell. "You love the Arabs more than I do," Lawrence concluded. Later, at the end of September, Massignon was sent to the east shore of Suez, opposite Ismailia, to write a sociological memorandum on the so-called "volunteers" who were, when the time came, to go up with Faisal from Aqaba to Ma'an. Some of these were Mosul Christians; a few were Yemen Jews—these latter deserted. One day Massignon was suddenly ordered to report to headquarters at Gaza. Massignon had no illusions: his destiny depended on Lawrence. His chiefs wished to give him a large amount of gold "to corrupt the Syrian Bedouins"; he would certainly be assassinated; more certainly still, he foresaw his remorse at buying his friends—he who nine years earlier had been beholden for his very life to the sacred hospitality of the Arab. Massignon had just sent 950,000 gold francs in convoy to Suez for King Hussein. Later, Nasser was to describe to Massignon with what a gesture of contempt Lawrence poured these guineas into the outstretched palms. Massignon had two long interviews with Lawrence on October 12 in a tent in the desert in which only Lawrence talked. Next day Massignon learned that Lawrence had come, by plane, from Aqaba, just to say that he would resign if Massignon was appointed to Faisal's staff as Lawrence's equal. That very same day, Massignon met St. John Philby in his tent. Philby had arrived from India to persuade Great Britain to play the Saudi, and not the Hashemite, card. Seven years later Philby entered the Hejaz with the victorious ibn-Saud; twenty-five years later, the U.S.A. took Saudi Arabia, with all its oil, out of Great Britain's hands. Yet Philby was right in backing the Saudis and Lawrence wrong in his Hashemite hunch.

Massignon met Lawrence again on December 9, 1917. Lawrence already then foresaw the French occupation of Lebanon, and was prepared to accept that. But no more. On December 11, (Jerusalem had surrendered on the 10th) the Sykes-Picot Mission solemnly entered the Holy City—in the first car, Allenby and Picot; in the second car, Bols and Piepape; in the third, Sir Wyndham Deedes, Lawrence, and Massignon. They arrived at the Jaffa gate at 10:30 A.M., and Allenby insisted all enter the city on foot. Massignon spent the whole morning with Lawrence. Allenby declared martial law, and threatened Picot with arrest if he did not agree. Lawrence had been told to make King Hussein believe he would be given Jerusalem, but he had just learned of Lord Balfour's arrangements with Lord Rothschild for the Jewish Home. Thus his country had ordered him to deceive his host, and Lawrence felt bitterly this breaking of his plighted word. Massignon was to feel no less miserable and guilty with regard to Faisal at the time of Meisseloun.

Massignon's victory over Lawrence came swiftly. In 1919 Lloyd George handed Faisal over to the French, to Lawrence's fury. In November 1919 Clemenceau authorized Massignon to take up the mission to which he had been appointed in 1917, but which Lawrence had stymied, solely because Lawrence did not wish a French Orientalist, aware of the future worldwide repercussions of Arab nationalism, to get close to the Emir Faisal, on whom Lawrence then still hoped to keep only British tabs. In Paris every day for some six weeks Massignon saw Faisal daily. Two years of war had aged the Emir, who spoke more slowly, but with greater authority. His great charm, Massignon said, was an engaging and original way of anticipating any confidence he felt was being made him, of meeting his interlocutor courteously halfway.

After the signing of the French-Arab interim treaty between Clemenceau and Faisal on January 6, 1920, Faisal invited Massignon to come to Damascus to assist in the negotiations leading to the definitive treaty, but Massignon's appointment at the Collège de France prevented his accepting. In November 1920, Massignon was at Damascus on an official mission to try and save the cultural institutions founded by Faisal, but Faisal was not there; nor did Massignon see him again until 1927, when he visited him in his new capital of Baghdad, after visiting Faisal's brother at Amman. Massignon always had a special affection for Baghdad, the city where his aristocratic friends the Alusi had offered him so noble an introduction to classical Arab culture and Islamic traditional sociology. And he always admired Faisal, and wrote his eulogy when he died in 1933.

Massignon was to make many journeys to the East—he

visited Jerusalem 28 times, for example. He was a tremendous believer in what Moslems call *baraka,* the grace bestowed on places by the holy men who hallowed them. All his life Massignon was an eager pilgrim—to Christian shrines, like La Salette; Moslem, like the shrine of the Seven Sleepers at Ephesus; or Hindu, as, for example, the site of Gandhi's funeral pyre. It was Ephesus, perhaps, that was for Massignon the holiest place on earth after Jerusalem. For here the Moslems venerate the Seven Sleepers, seven Christians who hid in a cave during Diocletian's persecution, with their dog, and slept for 372 years, to awake to testify their faith and die peacefully almost immediately. They are celebrated in Chapter XVIII of the Koran, and there are shrines to them in many places—among others, in Massignon's own Brittany, at Vieux-Marché; Massignon was wont to lead a pilgrimage to them there (he did so annually from 1953 to 1961). Ephesus, too, contains the little house—rebuilt exactly as it was on the original foundations—where Our Lady lived with St. John after the Ascension until her death, and here was found, according to visions seen in 1821 in Dülmen, the actual location of Our Lady's Assumption, *Panaghia Kapouli,* as a shepherd boy described it to the priest who came on the poor ruins. "This place is called the gate (Turkish) of the all-holy (Greek)." Massignon visited Dülmen three times, Ephesus as many. Massignon himself led the pilgrimage to Vieux-Marché from 1953 to 1961; in 1962, not well enough, he allowed a younger man to substitute for him. The idea of substitution, too, was one of his most strongly held beliefs. He found it in both Christianity and in Islam, and down through history: from Jesus Christ to Al-Hallaj, and on to the Algerian partiots murdered by the French in the the 1950s.

The best description of Louis Massignon is by himself:

I am [he wrote] primarily an historian who was first an archaeologist and did some digging; later, I did some digging in my own personal psychology. I can see stages in my life, not only in my private, but also in my public, life, for I am not among those who believe that the authenticity of a scholar is limited by his desk.

So the last years of his life were passionately political. In 1953-54 he gave a course on the "Central role of Arabic thought in the future of Islam." From 1954 on, he became an apostle of nonviolence. He was one of the founders of the Committee France-Maghreb. Horrified by French cruelties in the Algerian war, he instituted fasts as much to save France from the consequences of its dishonorable conduct—consequences of hatred, bitterness, contempt—as to save Algerian lives condemned by France. When already in his seventies, he went several times a week to the *bidonvilles*—the slums around Paris—to teach the Algerians shivering there to speak and to read French. Demonstrating against police brutality, he was several times arrested and taken off to jail; once when this happened, he was taken by the police officer to the tomb of one of their number killed by an Algerian. Massignon prayed so sincerely for the dead policeman that he melted the heart of his brutal captors. Another time, while he was speaking, he was attacked by a "commando" who set upon the old man and broke his watch. Still another time, he was thrown to the pavement by police with truncheons and spent the night with other "Nordafs" in an internment camp for Algerians.

He was, from his conversion on, a daily communicant. Toward the end of his life, he became a priest, ordained in the Oriental rite, which permits married priests. Father de Lubac, S.J., described to me his discovery of this fact. "Professor Massignon used to come to my Mass," he said. "One day he failed to come. After a few days I got worried. Perhaps the poor old man is seriously ill, I thought. So I went around to call. 'Ah, Father,' he told me, a twinkle in his eye, 'now I no longer need to come to your Mass. I say my own.'" He had been ordained in the Greek rite; Greek rites priests say Mass in Old Slavonic.

His married life was very happy, and he was devoted to his wife, one of the most admirable and intelligent of women. They had two sons, one of whom died, and one daughter. He had a very un-French, almost mystical, respect for women, and one of the things that really made him furious was that Allenby set up brothels in Jerusalem for his troops as soon as he got there, and also that the French had set up *bouzbirs*. He was outraged, too, to the end of his life, by the fact that the Virgin Mary had been struck off the Megilloth of Nazareth as impure, and that Bar Cochebas killed indiscriminately all Jews and all Christians who would not declare Mary, mother of Christ, to have been an adulteress.

To Abraham, "this man of all the beginnings," Massignon devoted his most erudite and most moving pages. Of Abraham's three prayers, the prayer for Sodom was the first, Sodom that can be saved whenever there are ten just men to be found. The second prayer was at Beersheba, the "well of the oath," where the first *hejira*, the first journey into the desert, that of Hagar with Ishmael, began. This was the first of all exiles, of all pilgrimages. The third prayer, on Mount Moriah, marked the end of human sacrifice, and the beginning, with Isaac, of what modern Protestants would call "salvation history." Massignon concludes:

> In the last analysis, Abraham prayed for the social pact upon which all cities must be founded; for the peace that should end all fratricidal strife; and for a holy priesthood. These three prayers, at Mamre, at Beersheba, and at Moriah, are in reality one, as Abraham's visitors were one (*tres vidit et Unum adoravit*).

Massignon, as early as 1921, published in June the whole text of Gandhi's first statement on *satyagraha* (the pursuit of truth), in the *Revue du Monde Musulman*. In 1931 he met Gandhi twice in Paris. In 1945 Massignon went to India for the first time, but could not meet Gandhi there, as the latter was in jail. Only after Gandhi's death did Massignon return to India, to a seminar of Gandhi studies under the auspices of UNESCO in 1953. Massignon attached a great importance to Gandhi's last pilgrimage, made with Moslem women to the tomb of a Moslem saint, Qutb Bakhtiyar (d. 1235) who was buried at Mahrauli, seven miles south of New Delhi. The women, afraid of Hindu hostility, had told Gandhi they dared not attempt the pilgrimage. Gandhi, then 79, accompanied them, together with some Hindu women from his own ashram. At the tomb he made a short speech about peace; he recited some verses of the Koran, and three days later was murdered by a Hindu, exasperated by Gandhi's public concern for Moslems.

According to Massignon, Gandhi had learned the very idea of *satyagraha* from Islam, from the dying Al-Hallaj, who had cried apocalyptically from his cross the words *Ana'l haqq*, "I am the truth." Massignon became the founder in France of the Society of the Friends of Gandhi. His Badaliya, founded in 1934, is a society whose object is an exchange (*badal*) of prayers and fasts, between Christians, Jews, Moslems, and any others who care to share. For Massignon, man is a wholly religious being, whether working or praying; a wholly social being, whose dignity is not merely spiritual, but total: the whole man is always worthy of respect. However removed some of Massignon's themes seem to be—a tenth-century Moslem mystic, a third-century Christian saint, Mohammed's daughter, the plan of pre-Islamic Basra—he is always committed to the human, social, and even material aspects of his subject, as well as to the intellectual. Nor for him was there any division between the living and the dead. In Islam, as in Christianity, he points out, the dead require our prayers, and we need their intercession. So some of his most erudite and profound studies are of the City of the Dead today in Cairo, of the city of Baghdad in the time of Al-Hallaj. Massignon's whole work, including his archaeology, is indeed a plunge into those depths where time and eternity meet "the Presence that is at the bottom of our deepest excavation of our remotest past" as he described it (*Mardis de Dar as-Salam,* 1952, p. 23). For the archaeologist as for the mystic, time, that succession of instants, is suspended.

And always, Massignon was the most perfect of hosts, giving of himself with both hands, never refusing his time or his help, never learning how to defend himself from *chronophages,* those wasters of his precious time.

Louis Massignon, *abdul Rahman, abdul Muntaqim,* servant of the Merciful, servant of the Avenger: pray for us.

Chapter VII

I WAS born in France, in an old Saracen house in Savoie, called la Maison du Diable, the Devil's House, since the Moslem Saracens were thought, by the local peasants, to be devils. There were legends aplenty about the house. Its walls were over three feet thick, and it had a nasty dungeon. I left when I was a few months old, and did not come back to live there until after World War I, when we came each year for the summer holidays. My sister and I cared so desperately for the place, and for France, that we would refuse to speak English when dragged back to England. And whenever we could, by hook or by crook, we would go abroad. Even after I married, at twenty, my husband and I would dash to Europe as soon as we had saved up ten pounds, which is what it then cost to go to Paris. Most English people do not care for Europe; I even know many who have never been out of England. Europe is foreign, alien in creed and language. One girl I know, trained as a Red Cross nurse in World War I, was not allowed by her mother to cross the Channel lest she meet Catholics! And my mother once sat next to Lord Grey at dinner when he was Foreign Minister; she asked where he was going for the summer (she was going to Bayreuth), and his reply was, "England is good enough for me." Never for me. The White Cliffs of Dover always meant for me the end of the holidays, the horrid reality of school, of cold, of rain, of bad food and ugly clothes.

So when I got back to Europe, on this my round-the-world *randonnée,* I remembered all it had meant to me. For example, the discovery of the Middle Ages, in the yellow-pine Victorian library at Cheltenham Ladies College, where as a teen-ager I found Henry Osborn Taylor's *The Medieval Mind,* which rescued me from sodden playing fields and companions with Cardiff accents and took me back to a merrier and a holier company. Then and there I fell in love with medieval Europe and devoured Belloc and Chesterton. And soaked up Malory and More, and Kantorowicz and Chaucer, till I forgot where I was and learned to be happy though a fat and spotty schoolgirl. Later, I outgrew the Chester-Belloc monster, and even outgrew Europe, learning to love Byzantium more, and Byblos and Babylon. But France remained beloved. Not Paris, France, that Gertrude Stein found exciting and peaceful, but provincial France, the Angevin sweetness of Touraine, the green Loire valley, the chestnut hills of Savoy, the rocky calanques and the olive groves of Provence. Coming back now to France was a return to my first language and my first love. *Amor de terra londhana,* love of a far country, *per vos totz le cor mi dol,* for you my whole heart aches, wrote and sang Jaufre Rendel, the twelfth-century Aquitainian. And though my heart was longing now for another, and remoter, land, to which, as Thomas Traherne writes, one must go "by backward steps," I came back to France, in love with her again.

And now I could come back without feeling miserable at how she was behaving. All through the war, I had hated British imperialism: Churchill's denial that the Atlantic Charter applied to colored peoples and his brutal imprisonment of Gandhi, Nehru, and Mrs. Pandit revolted me. While I worked in the British Embassy in Washington by day and was ordered to prove Gandhi was in the pay of the Japanese (I failed to do so), in the evenings I toasted the Republic of India. I became an American citizen as soon as the war was safely won, because the United States was then behaving with restraint and decency, because then it had no imperialist stance, and because it had invented the Marshall Plan. When France began in the late forties to torture and massacre Algerians, I was glad I no longer had any part in her. But now France had redeemed herself, or at least had righted her present though no one could raise the million Algerian dead or even the few thousand French dead. So I was happy to return. Yet for me the best of France, —indeed, the best of Europe—was not General de Gaulle, wise and good though he was and is, but a gentle philosopher who preached socialism in the name of St. Thomas Aquinas and showed how Thomism teaches that tyrants may be killed, that a man must follow truth even if the Church burn him for it, and that charity is no substitute for justice withheld.

There are some people—alas, all too few!—who are palpably holy. Their spirit seems to shine through and to permeate their flesh. The first time I met Jacques Maritain he was living in New York and asked me to dinner somewhere near Washington Square. Maritain looked absolutely Merovingian. With his long thin body, his Gothic face, and his aureole of white hair he might have stepped down from above one of the porches at Chartres. His almost translucent pallor seemed illuminated from within. Later he came to stay one weekend. It was during World War II, and I was working at the British Embassy in Washington, sharing a little house in Georgetown with a female colleague from the French Embassy. Our lodger (now Sir) Isaiah Berlin, was away. When Isaiah returned on Monday and was informed who had occupied his room in his absence, he touched the bed with his fingertips and said (complete agnostic though he claims to be), "How nice that someone so saintly slept here."

So saintly and also so witty. While Maritain was in the Philosophy Department at Princeton, his lectures were a delight, not less for their wry humor than for their serious content.

(Unfortunately, they were also inaudible, except to those in the first rows of listeners.) When Maritain was leaving Washington at the end of the war—he had been appointed French Ambassador to the Holy See—he was accompanied by his great friend Father (now Monsignor) Jean de Menasce. Father de Menasce was returning to Rome as Maritain's chaplain: he had spent the war years in the United States, as he was a Jew, and in Italy his life was daily in peril. It was a cloudy, mean day when Maritain and Father de Menasce were to set off. The tiny aircraft the French Government had provided looked as though it had been tied together with string. Both men looked at it with despondent distaste. Then Maritain asked his confessor: "Jean, are you in a state of grace?" Father de Menasce replied, "Jacques, put on your galoshes at once, or you will get your feet wet and catch cold." Maritain then turned to me with a deep sigh and said, "You see how I, an Ambassador, am treated by my chaplain!"

Later, when we lived in Princeton, Jacques and his wife Raïssa Maritain would often dine with us when we had distinguished clerical visitors. I remember once, when the "other" Father de Menasce, the Dominican, came (he was a member for a year of the Institute for Advanced Study, and is the greatest living Pahlevi, and one of the greatest Sanskrit scholars) to meet Dom Aelred Graham, the Prior of Portsmouth, a Benedictine; the Maritains came, too, and I fed everyone lentils (it was a Friday in Lent). Both the Dominican and the Benedictine denied ever having eaten lentils before, but the Maritains knew the dish well! On another occasion, Walter Terence Stace, the English head of the Princeton Philosophy Department, was there, a professed atheist, though a student of mysticism. He and Maritain became great friends. Since Raïssa Maritain's death, after a four-month illness, on November 4, 1960, Jacques Maritain has divided his time between the novitiate of the Little Brothers of Jesus (the followers of Charles de Foucauld) at

Toulouse, and the home of the Gruneliuses at Kolbsheim in Alsace, where Raïssa is buried.

In all literary history, there has surely never been such a perfect union as that of Jacques Maritain and Raïssa Oumancoff, for all of its fifty-six years. As Jacques has put it, in the preface to his *Carnet de Notes,* "The help and the inspiration of my beloved Raïssa have penetrated all my life and all my work. If there is any good in what I have done, it is to her, after God, that I owe it." (This was written in 1954 when, as Jacques put it, "the word happiness still had a meaning for me." Elsewhere he writes that "Now I only live a sort of ghost's life." Raïssa, the first time she met Jacques, wrote that "he at once became my great comfort." Her account of their engagement follows:

> Our engagement took place in the simplest way, without any proposal. We were alone in my parents' living room. Jacques was sitting on the rug, close to my chair; it suddenly seemed to me that we had always been near each other, and that we would always be so. Without thinking, I put out my hand and stroked his hair; he looked at me and all was clear to us. The feeling flowed through me that always—for my happiness and my salvation—that always my life would be bound up with Jacques'. It was one of those tender and peaceful feelings which are like a gift flowing from a region higher than ourselves, illuminating the future and deepening the present. From that moment our understanding was perfect and unchangeable.[1]

Jacques and Raïssa were married on November 26, 1904. They were baptized together on Monday, June 11, 1906. Raïssa's only (and younger) sister Vera was baptized with them and joined them when they moved to Heidelberg, thereafter living with them until her death on December 31, 1959, in Princeton, New Jersey. Léon Bloy was the godfather of all three. Léon

[1] Raïssa Maritain, *We Have Been Friends Together.* Doubleday Image Book, 1961, pp. 84–85.

Bloy (1864–1914) was a Catholic writer, a professional pauper and professional curmudgeon. (Imagine a Catholic D. H. Lawrence and H. L. Mencken in one!) He grunted and growled, rejoicing in the burning alive of society women at a fair in aid of the poor, being deliberately rude to any priest who came within range, yet always writing well: singlehandedly he tore the *bondieuseries*—the sticky pieties—from the French Church and adumbrated such commonplaces of today as a Christian contrition toward the Jews, the articulate layman, and the worker priest. He saw his child die of starvation, and gave himself the most honorific titles: Pilgrim of the Absolute, the Unbuyable, etc., while castigating his environment; calling, for example, the village where he lived "Hogs-on-Marne." Until meeting Léon Bloy, Jacques had considered himself to be wholly atheistic, or at best, agnostic.

After her baptism Vera regarded her Marthadom as a religious state: not strong enough to be a nurse, she thought of her life with Jacques and Raïssa as her vocation, and thanked God for having given her "a sheep and a lamb" to cherish. Jacques wrote that he did not think there had ever been "between three human beings a closer or deeper union than that which existed between us ... Each one was extraordinarily sensitive to the other two, and prepared to give all for them. It was as if a single respiration kept us alive."

From the first, Raïssa and Jacques were admirable hyphen people. Raïssa brought to Paris the knowledge she had, even before she was ten, acquired of Russian literature, and her feeling for Jewish traditions. Her parents had decided to emigrate from Russia because of the pogroms. Jacques came from a family imbued with the republican spirit and passionately concerned with the struggle for political and intellectual liberty. He and Raïssa met when she was seventeen, already a student at the Sorbonne. He had her name on a list of students he was going to ask to join a committee to protest the ill-treatment suffered by Russian socialist students in their own country. Jacques's mother was a daughter (by his first wife, a Catholic) of Jules Favre. Born in 1809, Jules Favre became a lawyer and in 1830 a republican. He was elected republican deputy for Lyons after the revolution of 1848. With Victor Hugo he tried to organize armed resistance to Louis Napoleon in the Paris streets. In 1858 he became deputy for Paris, in 1863 head of the republican party, and a member of the French Academy in 1867. He opposed the Mexican war and the war of 1870. As vice-president of France after the fall of Napoleon III, his declaration that he would not yield an inch of territory to Germany was followed by Bismarck's demand for Alsace and Lorraine, to which he was obliged to accede. Favre jeopardized Gambetta's Army of the East of 80,000 men by not including it in the armistice terms. He subsequently withdrew from the government, but remained a deputy until elected senator in 1876. He died in 1880. Jules Favre's daughter Geneviève, who though her mother had been a Catholic, followed her father into Protestantism after his second marriage, briefly married Paul Maritain, a lawyer in her father's law office. After their divorce, she took back her maiden name. Jacques (born in 1881) and his sister Jeanne grew up on the fourth floor of their mother's apartment, 149 rue de Rennes, where Geneviève Favre's Thursday luncheons were justly famous for the brilliant literary stars that assembled there. Geneviève Favre died during the German occupation, in 1943. Among the many writers Jacques Maritain knew well as a child was Charles Péguy, who in 1900 had founded the *Cahiers de la Quinzaine*. This fortnightly journal occupied a focal position in French literary life until 1914. Geneviève Favre started a children's page called Jean-Pierre, edited by her at the large, green baize-topped table at 8 rue de la Sorbonne which was the *Cahiers'* office, where Péguy worked several afternoons a week. (Péguy was often teased for thinking that "the world's axis passed through his office.") Since Péguy's death in 1919, Georges Sorel, who worked in the *Cahiers'* business office, has become far better known, because of Lenin's and Mussolini's interest in his views. Georges Sorel (1847–1922) began life as a highway engineer, but in 1892 quit his job to write. His *Réflexions sur la Violence* was published in 1908. Gradually he became royalist, nationalist, and fascist. In 1912 Péguy and Sorel quarreled, Péguy writing a brief note, "Please do not come any more on Thursdays." The *Cahiers'* business manager, A. Bourgeois, quit in 1904 with the swag, and the children's page came to an end, though the *Cahiers* acquired another thief as business manager. (Did Péguy, in imitation of his Master, deliberately choose thieves for the post? It is impossible not to wonder.)

Péguy was a little square man, with huge feet, a tight hat, a clear peasant face with bright eyes, and a military walk. His grandmother could not read; his mother, barely. When little, he was afraid to learn to walk, "because one falls." He was raised on the contradictory tenets of the village schoolmaster, who declared that until 1789 France was a miserable country, and the village curé, who declared that since 1789 France was a miserable country. Instead of developing schizophrenia, Péguy developed an immense pride: he was quite certain—and how right he was!—that "a Catholic renaissance is being made through me."

Young Jacques Maritain first devoted himself to science, and it was on leaving a plant physiology class that Raïssa first saw him, with his shock of blond hair and his slight stoop. Jacques's greatest friend was Ernest Psichari, the grandson of Ernest Renan. Renan's daughter, like Geneviève, adored her father and had an adored only son: these sons were from the first close comrades. Raïssa wrote that young Psichari from his schooldays on said, "Jacques and I are one. What he thinks I think, what he does I do, what he feels I feel." Henri Massis, a contemporary, remembers young Maritain and young Psichari, in velvet trousers tight at the ankles, wearing red belts "to make them look like workmen," reading Baudelaire and Verlaine at the Union Prolétaire of the IX arrondissement. "The problem was to save oneself from the interior gulf," they claimed. After three years at the Sorbonne, Raïssa and Jacques, one sunny day at the Paris zoo, made a pact. If the meaning of life did not reveal itself, "the solution would be suicide." From this solution, Jacques and Raïssa were saved by Bergson. Henri Bergson (1859–1941), a small, dry man, with a large forehead, thin chin, and huge, high-bridged nose, wearing a high collar and black tie, lectured on Fridays at 5 P.M. at the Collège de France. His lectures had such a vogue that servants came ahead of time to keep places for high society ladies; students endured a dull lecture on economics which took place before Bergson's, just to be sure of having seats; the crowd of carriages made a traffic jam. Bergson spoke with absolutely no gestures, without notes, his hands folded in front of him.

Like Heraclitus, Bergson believed change is the basis of all reality, that time is a continuous flow in which past and present are inseparable to the consciousness and the memory. His courses were crowded with poets, artists, rich old maids, and Russian exiles. It has been said of him that he opened a door to a concept of physics locked since Descartes. For the first time, to postulate the existence of two separate realms of being, only one of which is marked by awareness, as Descartes did, came under suspicion as possibly a treacherous, and worse, an unreal dualism. Indeed, there might, Bergson suggested, be a single realm of continuous and mainly unconscious mental processes. But Bergson proceeded too slowly for these impatient young people. Bergson had said to Henri Massis, "Truth is arriving. It has already appeared in physics. Later . . ." But for Jacques Maritain, Raïssa Oumancoff, and Ernest Psichari, "later" was too late, and philosophy not enough. It was indeed enough to think about, but not, as Massis put it, "to live and die for." Yet the solution was to come through Bergson, though he himself was not to be immediately aware of it. Once a week Jacques and Raïssa attended a course Bergson gave on Greek texts. The year they were studying with him, Bergson was commenting on Plotinus. One day, reading the Enneads alone in her room, Raïssa suddenly experienced the God of Whom they speak. The book fell from her knees, and she onto them. Later, after she and Jacques had been baptized, Bergson asked her one day, "If *it* began with Plotinus?"—"it" being the way to the Church. The answer for her, as it was later to be for Bergson himself, was in the affirmative. But Bergson never publicly proclaimed his conversion, out of a feeling of solidarity for his suffering people. When World War II and the Germans came to Paris he did not flee. With immense courage, he returned all his honors and medals to the French Government (of Pétain), but he asked to be buried, when he died, according to the rites of the Catholic Church.

The Maritains' baptism was the beginning of an ever-increasingly devout life. From August 1906 through June 1908, they were in Heidelberg. Jacques had obtained a fellowship to study experimental embryology under Hans Driesch. Jacques was very much interested in the embryogenetic theory of neovitalism, which had led Driesch to "re-introduce into biology concepts of entelechy." But though they personally liked Driesch, the Maritains did not care for what Raïssa called "the coarse and saber-scarred university," and their daily life hardly echoed its rhythm. They rose at 6. Mass and communion at 7:15. Breakfast. Work until 10:30. 10:45-11:30, prayer. 12:30, lunch. After a brief rest, darning for the two ladies, a few psalms, more work: Latin, German ... 5 P.M., visit to the Blessed Sacrament. 7 P.M., supper. Preparation for the next day. Compline. Rosary. Raïssa and Vera were in bed by 8 P.M. Jacques worked on until 11.

Jacques's sister Jeanne also returned to the Church, and her daughter Eveline was baptized. When the Maritains returned to Paris, in May 1908, they found the Bloys down to their last three francs. They themselves were poor, too: Jacques notes "the microscope I took to the pawnbrokers only brought in twenty francs. I had hoped for fifty." Bloy doted on both the Maritains and touchingly wrote in his diary, "It's not natural to have such friends when one has worked hard for thirty years to make enemies." Jacques and Raïssa somehow paid for a new edition of Bloy's *Salut par les Juifs*.

In 1909 the Maritains moved to the ground floor of an old and noble house, 16 rue de l'Orangerie, at Versailles. Here Massis brought Ernest Psichari, to a "vast room empty and polished with high white panelling on which a picture of Pope Pius X stood out. In this monastic simplicity Jacques advanced towards us with his two hands stretched out, slightly bent, behind him his wife and sister-in-law. From these beings inhabited by grace emanated a luminous tenderness. They did not argue; they simply wove a web of love around us," Massis wrote of this visit. For three years after their return to France, Jacques worked on a Dictionary of Practical Life. He detested the work. "The dictionary suffocates me. I am furious I have no time for theology," he wrote in 1910. And in 1911 again, "Profoundly discouraged by my work on the Dictionary ... Revolting food for the intellect, that one is continually obliged to regurgitate ..." In 1910 Jacques's first article, on "Modern Science and Reason," after being refused by the *Correspondant*, was accepted in June by the *Revue de Philosophie*. It was the first of literally countless articles, and more than fifty books! In 1912 Maritain began his lectures at the Collège Stanislas and in 1913 at the Institut Catholique, where he became professor in 1914. At this time Ernest Psichari was received into the Church. On August 22, 1914, Psichari was killed in battle; on September 5 of the same year, Péguy.

Thanks to a considerable bequest made by a young man, Pierre Villard, who was killed at the front in June 1918, Jacques and Raïssa were able to give 50,000 francs to the *Revue Universelle*, which had a double function: to promulgate the ideas of *Action Française* in the political, and Thomist ideas in the philosophical, sphere. Jacques was also able, with this legacy, to open, with Raïssa and Vera, a center for Thomistic studies, in October 1919. In 1921 the monthly meetings became regular, and annual retreats of three weeks were started, to which some 250 to 300 people came regularly. In 1923 the Maritains bought a house at Meudon and established themselves there. Young people and old, students and professors, lay men and women and religious, philosophers and doctors, poets, musicians, politicians, learned and ignorant folk, all came— and were the guests of Raïssa: for they came to a home, not to an institution. Jews, Protestants and Catholics all came. For Jacques and Raïssa the years at Meudon—from 1923 to 1938 —were the happiest in their lives. On October 1, 1938 the Maritains and Vera left for the United States. They did not return until after the war, when, as already related, Jacques went to Rome by air, while Raïssa and Vera followed him by boat. After the liberation, François Mauriac was asked in France, "Who is Jacques Maritain?" And, indeed, he is probably better known now, and more read, in the United States than in France. In 1926 he had written to Jean Cocteau:

> Every one of us, just as he has the hairs of his head counted, has also his poor task of unworthy servant well defined. I have been tied to the most dogmatic and trenchant thought, while contemplating our fleeting time, not in order to dispense, but to reform and reconcile.

It has been well said of Maritain that he is "precise and pure like cut crystal." But also he is so kind that he notes in his diary for 1910 that Père Clerissac bade him not to be too "nice" to people! Jacques Maritain is absolutely one-pointed: although he has written about art, politics, race, religion, and every aspect of ethics, as well as philosophy, his constant "concern" is God Himself. He has added a sixth "proof" of His existence to the five Thomist ones in his little book *Existence and the Existent;* and now, over eighty, he is concerned with proving, in three lectures published in 1962, the absolute innocence of God, picking up Dmitri Karamazov's turned-back ticket with an apology for the Creator that is somehow touching.

How much Jacques Maritain's writings influenced Popes Pius XII and John XXIII is not yet known, but Pope Paul VI has publicly admitted Maritain's influence on him and his devotion to him. Maritain was offered a Cardinal's hat—the first layman to be so honored since the Reformation, and he refused it. At thirteen, Maritain was already a dedicated Socialist and in a letter preserved by Geneviève Favre, written to their cook's husband, who influenced him when Jacques fled from his mother's friends to sit in the kitchen, Jacques wrote: "There is no merit whatever in working when one pleases. If there is anyone to thank for what progress I can make, it is the immense proletarian mass that sweats while I delight to read . . . it is all the labor of humanity, all the intellectual labor accumulated by preceding and present generations which I freely enjoy, that I freely appropriate. Capitalist property can never appropriate that communism, the sublime and universal communism, of human pain and thought. But believe me, I am ashamed when I think that at my age children of the people work sometimes 11 hours a day (and until lately 12, 13 and 14 hours a day) and that it is thanks to their work, not remunerated at its just value, that I, idle, without doing anything, without creating anything, without sweating, with tepid satisfaction, nourish myself with the bread of the body and the bread of science! . . . this enormous debt never will and never can be paid, this debt that I contract with the proletariat. There are moments when I even wonder if I have the right to be a socialist . . ." Christianity, when he met it, delayed his socialist expansion. Though he had financially helped Péguy with the *Cahiers,* after meeting with the philosophy of St. Thomas Maritain he came to realize that the center of Christian life is the Beatific Vision of the three Divine persons and not the perfection of morality, that, indeed, the end of man is not an action but a contemplation. Maritain became politically minded again only during the Action Française crisis in 1926: his social and political concern revived after he was forty-five. During World War II, which he spent entirely in the United States, Maritain wrote once again of the people and for them, and if some of his students objected to his "constant association of philosophical discourse with apostolic concern," others approved. What the "Death of God" theologians are now trumpeting as the latest gimmick, Jacques Maritain found clearly stated in St. Thomas: *In finem nostrae cognitionis Deum tanquam ignotum cognoscimus.* "At the end of our knowledge we learn God is the unknown (and unknowable)." He, like St. Thomas, is continually careful to distinguish (indeed that one word *distinguo,* I distinguish, is probably the most important single word in all philosophy) between God as efficient principal and God as object—as the final term to which man moves. Nor is it less important to distinguish between the person, subsisting, entire, in his soul "and the individual in the species and the dust in the wind." Yet as the same God is both principal and object, so also the same man is all three—person, individual, and a handful of dust.

Perhaps one of the clearest expressions of Jacques Maritain's position, hyphening as it does East and West, Protestant and Catholic, socialist and Christian, is a manifesto called *Sagesse* (Wisdom) drafted during the summer of 1951 at Kolbsheim, and signed by all present. Among the signatories, besides Jacques and Raïssa Maritain, were Louis Gardet, Olivier Lacombe, Père de Menasce, O.P. and Mgr. (now Cardinal) Journet. The manifesto states, among other things, that:

> The wisdoms of the east, to which many of our contemporaries look for the salvation of western man, in themselves presume a capacity for overcoming the pathetic, without ignoring the anguish of destiny with which they, when they meet it, confuse the Passion of Christ. Asceticism for them takes on above all the value of a technique, and too often the ultimate significance of sin, which is an offense against infinite transcendence opening itself as a person to the love of its creature, escapes them.
>
> In Christian wisdom, serenity is rooted in the wounds of Christ.

It does not invite the Christian to escape the drama, but to consummate it in spirit and in truth...

It is unavoidable that, *in statu via,* a certain abruptness of dialectic, aggravated by original sin, should be established in the secret of man's heart, between the immanence arising from nature, and its ravishment by the God of grace. The Cross is the meeting place of this double movement. But it is intended that this tension be resolved in harmony, whose component parts it already comprises.

The true idea of divine transcendence therefore excludes the possibility that we can find, or even truly seek, the God of grace by way of pure immanence. But at the same time the true idea of immanence equally forbids it, for the presence of the immensity of God in His creature never ceases to be personal.

A transcendence which would not take immanence into account, would lose itself in the insignificance of an identity. Sanctifying grace, which in our beings is the created similitude of the interior Deity, is precisely that through which the twofold transcendence of the divine gift springs from the deepest recess of our nature, and makes the inaccessible God truly immanent...

Christian thought owes it to itself not to content itself with the purely speculative recognition of a truth which is so dear to it. It is incumbent upon it to assume the anxiety of material causality in the economic, technological and social order. Economics and technology are an integral part of Christian sociology, in as much as they closely condition our corporal life. But the thought of the masses themselves should be yet more fundamental to a humanism of the Incarnation. On the temporal plane these masses are today's equivalent of the crowds of the Gospel.

The Christian therefore must contribute to the movement of history according to its component parts. He must cooperate with the positive forces of the temporal city towards greater justice, towards a more complete participation of each individual in the common good, in civic, moral and cultural values. The law of their being is constantly to progress and to ameliorate themselves, or else to fall into decay. It is to go against the nature of temporal realities to make of them purely means to eternal life: obviously they prepare it, as the road leads to its end, but they form a true order, oriented to a proper end, an end subordinated or rather secondary, but which, nonetheless, within its limits, retains its loyal dignity as an end...

But our duty binds us also to the inferior degrees of life and of being. Not that they have real rights owed them by us, for rights belong only to persons, but they have the dignity of being, which concentrates and dwells in the soul of those who have life, and even more in their sensibility and their consciousness, where the slow ascent of nature towards the inaccessible frontiers of the spirit spreads its greatest waves.

A sensitivity of behaviour towards animals, plants and things, a respect for life, a care never to inflict unnecessary suffering, are manifestations of a human nobility which also must be called fraternal, to the full extent in which it implies an exquisite sense of the divine paternity and is a prelude to the transfiguration which will redeem all creatures and cause them to enter the freedom of the sons of God...

From the fraternity of the Little Brothers of Jesus in Toulouse Jacques Maritain wrote his *Le Paysan de la Garonne* (The Garonne Peasant) a post-Council study in which "an old layman" muses on the time being. He explains "old layman": "old" does not only refer to the author's age, but to the fact that he is an inveterate layman. Maritain begins by bending his knees in thankfulness for the visible and invisible Church, and in thankfulness for all the Vatican Council that ended on December 8, 1965, has decreed and accomplished. Above all because from henceforward the true concept of liberty will be recognized and reverenced as one of the great guidelines of Christian wisdom, as also will the true concept of the value, the dignity, and the rights of the human person. That this world is good, that man's intelligence is a valid instrument, that faith expresses itself not in doing but in being, and that "stupidity must never be taken too seriously" are among Maritain's themes. Above all, he emphasizes that since Vatican II, it is not human values which take on the defense of spiritual values, but spiritual values which purport to defend human values.

For all Maritain's saintliness, there is plenty of fight in him still. As St. Augustine remarked: "Nowhere are the differences so great as among those who have entered into the unity (of the Catholic Church)" and the main thrust of Maritain's innocently-titled book is against Teilhard de Chardin's ideas. I remember once taking Evelyn Waugh to tea with Jacques Maritain in Princeton, and the feeling of raised hackles on both. No two men could have been more antipathetic to each other: they hated each other in Christ. Maritain met Teilhard several times, but Teilhard's main idea, that the mystical body includes the whole universe in its process of hominism (and finally of divinization) is, for Maritain, frankly pantheistic. As Monsignor Jean Cattaui de Menasce wrote in the *Osservatore Romano* recently, the attempt to equate the universe in evolution with the mystical body of Christ is "an equivocation which should arouse a sacred horror." Maritain himself quotes Teilhard as writing that "what dominates my interests . . . is the effort to establish in myself, and to diffuse around me a new religion . . . where the personal God ceases to be the big neolithic landowner of old to become the soul of the world." [2] Maritain calls this "a *theology-fiction*," and doubts "more and more, the more I think about it" that Teilhard was a mystic in the sense that a Catholic theologian would use the word. Maritain concludes that Teilhard was *"un grand imaginatif,"* who was either ignorant of St. Thomas Aquinas or had forgotten him. It is a splendid sign of the vitality, not just of Jacques Maritain, but of the whole Church, that there should be such hammer-and-tong arguments and spiritual joustings and intellectual ding-dongs. *Le Paysan de la Garonne* may not be Jacques Maritain's best book, and it is not his last—he has already (1968) written two more! But

[2] Teilhard de Chardin: "Lettres à Léontine Zanta," Paris, Desclée de Brouwer, 1965.

it is both "peaceful and exciting"—as Gertrude Stein called the Paris where Jacques was born.

The Church wonderfully produces saints where sociologically necessary. In the beginning, in Judea, they were local men and women, fishermen, publicans, weavers of tents. Gradually, as the Greek and Roman milieux were evangelized, members of the intellectual classes, the nobility, and finally, of the imperial circle, were converted: some of these became martyrs and some, saints. In medieval Europe, saints were generally kings or popes or at least bishops or abbots; with the rise of the middle classes, St. Francis of Assisi appears, the first bourgeois founder. Perhaps the apotheosis of all the bourgeois saints occurred in St. Teresa of Lisieux, who has been called the saint of the antimacassars. The proletariat was canonized in the Curé d'ars and in Mother Cabrini. Now the pure lay man, the "thinking reed" of Pascal, is incarnate in Jacques Maritain: let us hope that he and Raïssa may not only from heaven but on our altars be invoked to "pray for us, the bourgeoisie." How lucky I am to have known them! Married saints are rare, not because marriage is an unholy condition, but because sanctity is hard work, and time-consuming, and for most saints it is a full-time job. The French painter Soulages, in an interview with Pierre Dumayet, was asked if he used black so much because of an "economy of means." Was it not true he preferred a "limited palette"? He replied that these were expressions that made him furious. There was no question of economy: when one passionately loved something, everything else was excluded, perfectly naturally. That also seems the best argument for celibacy, and one that, in their hearts, no doubt many saints have felt. But for Jacques and Raïssa each other was never "anything else." They were so completely one that their dedication to God was single, the whole devotion of male and female as He created them. What an example of happiness! What an example of holiness!

Chapter VIII

MY geography on this pilgrimage to people is, I fear, purely arbitrary, and deliberately so. It is of the essence of hyphen people that, though they originate from a specific culture and country, they should not be identified with it. For all the essentially national and racial qualities of each of the examples chosen (no one, for example, ever could think of Suzuki as other than completely Japanese, or of Maritain as other than primordially French, and the same goes for every hyphen person ever encountered) it is yet difficult to say whether Louis Massignon belongs most to Arab Asia, to Moslem Africa or to Paris. So, too, each of these great human beings has more than one country, perhaps for the reason given in the Epistle to Diognetus, written before A.D. 200. Writing of the Christians, the author notes: "They dwell in all countries, but only as sojourners; they bear their share in all things as citizens, and they endure all hardships as strangers. Every foreign country is a fatherland to them, and every fatherland is foreign." These words were written of the early Christians by one of their fellowship but it is unlikely that John Pillai or D. T. Suzuki would object to their being applied also to them.

So, though Michael Scott is as English as anyone can be with such a name, he belongs at least equally to the South Africa that jailed and expelled him in 1950 and to the India for whom he was a hero in 1946 and a criminal in 1966. For this "knight of the Holy Ghost," as the poet Heine would have called him, is no respecter of persons: for him injustice is to be denounced whether the perpetrator be a Briton in imperialist India, a South African in Durban, or an Indian army of 40,000 troops today suppressing the primitive Indian Nagas. I knew him for all the ten years I worked at the U.N., but include him here as a European, for it is from Europe that he originates.

Michael Scott was born in 1907, the youngest of three brothers, in a rural parish in southern England. His father was an Anglican clergyman, as was his grandfather. Michael's great-grandfather was one of Nelson's captains. His mother's people were all clergy and navy people, too. Michael grew up in a slum of Southampton, where his father's parish comprised 10,000 souls crowded into half a square mile, living in back-to-back houses, all the streets leading down to the river Itchen which periodically flooded them, leaving the streets and lower floors of the houses covered with thick evil-smelling slime. Michael's father had found his vicarage large, damp and dirty, his Church dark and dreary. But he and his wife soon changed all that. Michael remembers bright lighting, gay hanging banners and brocade curtains in the church, and to their hospitable home came everyone who was in trouble: as a very small boy Michael's earliest memory is of "grown-ups" crying in his father's study. Yet his father never himself raised what Michael, even when very young, had called to himself *the* question: how could death, disease, dirt and darkness coexist with the lovely countryside, with sailing, cricket (Michael's father was a superb athlete) and "our" garden, into which the parish children were not allowed, as they would trample the flowers and "even use it as a lavatory"? Michael was admonished for taking his tin soldiers into the street and "playing in the gutter"; he was punished for reading a book about the French Revolution. When he was nearly twelve and was being prepared for Confirmation, Confession, and Communion, his father chose this moment to tell him the "facts of life." He describes his reaction:

I was very much taken aback. I had often heard blasphemies and obscenities. They were commonplace talk in the streets, but I had never associated them with sex or the origin of life. I had never thought of the origin of life before, much less the origin of my own life. The thought that my own life was the result of what my father described, with the implication that this had taken place between him and my mother, simply did not bear thinking about.[1]

This sensitive boy also reacted violently to the Crucifixion.

The story itself was horrible but quite intelligible. What I could not understand was how my sins could have affected it or how Christ's death could bring about my salvation . . . I could not help a feeling of revulsion at the idea of eating His body and drinking His blood especially if I was responsible for His death. When I went up to receive the Holy Communion I would feel very self-conscious, and when I turned around to walk back to my place I would feel strangely flat. I ought to be feeling as if I could fly, but here I was putting one foot in front of the other and feeling rather foolish. On the other hand sometimes I had a strange sense of belonging to God when I got back to my place, and I would be filled with a great sense of wonder and joy. I could not relate it to the doctrine of the Crucifixion and of salvation by the Body and Blood. That seemed revolting, but there must be something wrong with me because of the fervour with which other people sang hymns about being "washed in the blood of the lamb." If people really believed that by their sins they were actually driving nails into His hands and feet, surely they would not keep on doing it. How could they all come trooping out of church and start talking and laughing as though it made no difference, or as if it were only true when we were in church? [2]

At King's School Michael won his football colors, but when it came to being a prefect he could not bring himself to inflict corporal punishment; later, as junior master in a prep school,

---

[1] *A Time to Speak,* Michael Scott: New York, Doubleday & Co., 1958 (p. 26).

[2] *Ibid.* (p. 27).

he again found beating the boys beyond him. His slum childhood now began to catch up on him: he had TB glands and also
had to have his gallbladder removed. To recuperate he was sent
to Switzerland and now *the* question came back, urgently: what
was reality? The might and majesty of the dazzling Swiss mountains, or the grey lines of Southampton slum slate roofs covering silent suffering and hopeless misery? Was truth life, beauty,
and creation, or was it disease, corruption, and death? Michael
went off to South Africa to work in a leper colony, leaving behind both his father and the unanswered question. But in the
leper colony he found again *the* question unavoidably present.
Some of the lepers were terribly disfigured: half a face would
be beautiful and sensitive, the other half had the flesh eaten
away, or was fixed in a leering grin; stumps for fingers, or no
hands; blind, black: how could God be so cruel to men? An
old Cambridge don, in coaching Michael, helped him by teaching him how to "doubt the very foundations of my faith and
yet to keep faith."

In 1929 Michael returned home, and on December 27, 1930
he was ordained a clergyman of the Church of England by the
Bishop of Chichester. For three years he was a fashionable curate, riding to hounds and playing tennis and cricket. Then he
was moved to the East End of London, and gradually became
aware that there were "two kinds of Christianity: there was the
religion that was the divine sanction of the *status quo,* and there
was the religion which was the divine instrument of change."
These were the thirties: the years in England of Hunger March-
ers who converged on London from the Tyneside and Scotland;
of the Unemployment Act and the Means Test; of the triumph
of Hitler in Germany, and of Gandhi's fasts in India. Michael
Scott sailed to India, acting as chaplain on an army transport.
Here he was vividly reminded of the Rev. John Newton, who
wrote that he had never known sweeter hours of divine communion than when he was Chaplain on a slave ship from
Guinea. A high proportion of his human cargo died, while the

Rev. Newton wrote his famous hymn: "How sweet the name of Jesus sounds, In a believer's ear!"

Michael Scott became domestic chaplain to the Bishop of Bombay, and one of his duties was to interview deputations. At that time political prisoners were mercilessly beaten with long canes by the police but when Michael mentioned the matter to the Bishop, His Lordship told him it was better "that comparatively few agitators should suffer in the jails than that whole tracts of country and innocent villages should have to be laid waste," which the Bishop thought was the only alternative —British repression on a large scale or on an individual scale. After Michael Scott had had a bad motor accident, the Bishop sent Michael to Kasauli, at the foot of the Himalayas, "where women and children were beaten and raped by our soldiers on their punitive expeditions to suppress the peoples' revolts against their decadent rulers." Whole villages were being laid waste there, the little mud huts burned. "I was all the time saying *Namaste* with folded hands," said an Indian woman to Michael, describing her beating by a British soldier. Michael was glad of the outbreak of war, which took him back to England. Having learned to fly, he was about to join the RAF when he was found to have ileitis. To convalesce, he went to stay with his father who now had a country parish in Buckinghamshire. His mother felt Michael's anguish, and begged him to have a "heart-to-heart" talk with his father. One evening in the summer of 1940 he did. His father's last words to him were "You must follow your conscience, dear boy," and Michael knew he must again enlist. His father had a stroke that night and never, in the nine years he had left to live, was able again to carry on a conversation.

After being accepted as A.1. by the RAF, Michael had a recurrence of ileitis and another operation, after which he was discharged and returned to South Africa, where he was appointed to St. Albans' Colored Mission. Here he formed a non-political party with a practical program based on the Government Commissions' reports, and centered it around a scheme of regional planning. A National Conference was called, and the scheme was taken over by the Government, which, however, did nothing whatsoever, from that day to this.

On a bare plot outside Durban, in 1946, Indian South Africans stood in passive resistance. Michael Scott, tall, thin, in poor health, stood with them, horrified by the mobs of hysterical white men and girls who were beating them up. Most of the mob had changed into rugger shorts to avoid getting blood on their good clothes: they used knuckle dusters and their own heavy boots. Michael Scott, after absorbing the brutality for several nights, cabled to Mahatma Gandhi for help. The Mahatma cabled Smuts, who sent his police to the plot, where they arrested, not the attackers, but the attacked: the Indians, together with Michael Scott. He was condemned in the magistrates court at Durban on July 1, 1946, and sentenced to three months for joining the Passive Resisters who were opposing the new Asiatic Land Tenure Act. On that occasion he said: "With regard to the personal references to myself from the bench, and to the surprise that was expressed at my association with people of another class, namely my fellow-prisoners, I must first declaim any such superiority of class or intelligence as that suggested, and state further that my religion knows no color bar. It recognizes no artificial barriers of class or race, indeed it must challenge any conception of racial inferiority, for there cannot be Greek and Jew, circumcision and uncircumcision, barbarian, Scythian, bond-man and freeman, but Christ who is all in all." While in jail, Scott wrote a 40,000-word memorandum on conditions in the prison. On his return, he resigned from parish work, and his bishop gave him a general license to preach in the Diocese of Johannesburg.

Soon after leaving jail, he received an appeal from a group of African ex-servicemen who were living in conditions of misery on a site which they had named Tobruk. He built a canvas church, and settled down in a shack beside them. Shack and church were burned by his fellow-whites and he was again arrested, this time for living in a non-European area. He then went to the Transvaal, where his investigations into the near-slavery conditions among the laborers in the Bethal district aroused violent opposition. European farmers threatened to lynch him, and he only escaped with police protection.

Toward the end of 1946 a report appeared in *The New York Times* questioning the conduct of the Referendum which had been held in South West Africa to discover native opinion on the South African Government's proposal to incorporate this territory. A section of natives was anxious that their representatives be allowed to put their case before the U.N., or that a U.N. Commission of Inquiry be appointed to visit the country. The tribesmen were not allowed to travel overseas, or to send representatives, and therefore asked the Rev. Michael Scott to make representations on their behalf. This he did, traveling at his own expense to the General Assembly of the U.N. in the U.S.A., in 1948 and again in 1949. There, at Lake Success, on the occasion of his second visit, he made a statement in the Fourth Committee, pointing out that the South African proposal to incorporate South West Africa into the Union had been rejected by the General Assembly, as previously by the League of Nations. For three successive years, South Africa had been requested to submit a Trusteeship Agreement for South West Africa, and had rejected this recommendation. On July 23, 1947, the Union Government had admitted that against the "clearly expressed wish of the overwhelming majority of all the native races in South West Africa, and by unanimous vote of the European representatives the Territory be incorporated," thereby flouting the wishes of those who under the Mandate had been committed to their charge. The Union Parliament then immediately passed an act stating that "It is now recorded for the world to see that we no longer recognize the existence of the Mandate." Michael Scott declared this unilateral declaration to be contrary to the words and spirit of the Charter, and he asked that the Africans of the Herero, Nama, and Berg peoples be given a chance to state their case.

Michael Scott became a perennial at the U.N. Tall, remote, gentle, blue-eyed, he was not allowed by the State Department to move across New York or out of it (the same restrictions as are placed on all the delegates from Iron Curtain countries) and I remember one day wanting to take him to dinner with the Reinhold Niebuhrs at Union Theological, and having instead to ask them all to come to our East Side fourth floor walk-up as the Niebuhrs were "out of bounds" for Michael Scott. Dr. Fabregat, the ambassador of Uruguay, used to say suddenly, "And now I am going to talk to God." He then would be seen conferring with Michael Scott. If anybody ever brought a measure of union and peace and a sense of spirituality to the divided glass house on the East River, it certainly was the Rev. Michael Scott. U.N. people generally referred to the South West Africans as "the people of Michael Scott," so completely had he identified with them. He was the only white man to be invited by Ben-Bella, when newly elected president of Algeria, to the big Afro-Asian dinner he gave. "Here is one man who has shed his skin," Ben-Bella said of Scott. For thirteen years Scott petitioned for the liberation of South West Africa, and was finally able to get the question brought to the International Court of Justice at The Hague. He was also entrusted by Zambia and Southern Rhodesia to plead when their leaders were in jail or silenced. On a continent where Christians have mostly preached white supremacy, and have used the Scriptures to defend *apartheid*, it is little wonder that the Zulus chant:

> The Committee
> is at the school
> we are plagued
> by Christians

Michael Scott is indeed as unique a phenomenon in Africa as he was at the U.N. and in India. As soon as The Question of

South West Africa had been transferred to The Hague Court, he went to India directly from the United Nations and thus describes Christmas at Sevagram:

There the first thing I saw was a well with a blindfolded bullock harnessed to a shaft, interminably walking round and round in circles with a young boy walking behind it with a switch.

I was afflicted with a sense of futility which nothing could allay. It remained with me, this dreadful sense of futility, mounting towards panic, with the fuller realization of what I had come to find, of what millions in the world were anxiously looking for ...

As we stood in the darkness among the cowsheds somebody chanted from the *Swetaswatara Upanishad*:

Him I have known, the Great Spirit
Him who is Light, who is beyond all darkness.
To know Him, and Him alone, is to pass beyond death.
There is no other way.
He is the Whole, other than He is naught,
Greater or smaller there is nothing other.
Still as a tree, unshaken in the heavens,
His living being fills the Universe.

Which was the reality? My mind recalled the long rows of shanties in Karachi. In Calcutta my friend Sudhindranath Datta, a Bengal divided between India and Pakistan. He had been in charge of a relief squad. His mother had been saved by a kindly Englishman extricating her in his car. The trains had been coming into Calcutta from Pakistan with mangled bodies hanging from the doors and windows. In the streets of both dominions children had been crucified on doorways. Women had been flogged to death and disemboweled while still alive.

Near me was standing Dr. Tomiko Kora, a woman delegate from Japan. She had given an account of Hiroshima which was even more terrible than that published in an entire issue of the *New Yorker*. She told us also of Japan's population problem following the loss of her colonies. An energetic birth control campaign by the American occupation authorities had now even reached the stage of practising abortion on grounds of poverty, she told us . . .

My mind returned to Sevagram. The chanting went on, a never-ending river, telling of the perennial struggle of the human spirit striving towards perfection. It was from the *Dhammapada* now:

> Wakefulness is the way to immortality;
> Heedlessness is the way to death:
> Those who are wakeful die not,
> From craving is born grief;
> From craving fear is begotten
> There is no grief for him who is freed from craving:
> Whence then can there come fear?

. . . In a land torn and tortured by fear and hatred Gandhi had discovered in South Africa that love is an active revolt. The fruits of his discovery were his *satyagraha* movement, based upon love and respect for his enemies. Britain and India had learned much from one another through his *satyagraha* movement. But Gandhi was shot, just as Socrates was poisoned by his own people.

The message of all of them to us who had come from all over the world in search of peace seemed to be first, before all practical questions, a need for those who would be prepared to give themselves to the uttermost in the service of peace and the methods of peace. Only an army of the trained, disciplined, efficient, and of those wholly consumed by a love which is unearthly and universal, having no reservations, no racial or other barriers, but dedicating themselves through selfless action to the creative purpose in human history, could save the world.[3]

Michael Scott has built up the Africa Bureau in London. Forbidden since 1950 to return to South Africa, he has demonstrated against nuclear warfare both in England and in the Sahara.

On May 3, 1966, the Indian Government expelled Michael Scott because he "had persisted in taking a partisan attitude toward the Naga question." The Nagas have been in rebellion

[3] *Ibid.* (pp. 303 *et seq.*).

ever since Indian independence. They have fought sporadically for twelve years. Two years ago the Nagaland Baptist Church set up an unofficial peace mission, hoping to bring the punitive destruction of villages and crops to an end. Two Indians—Mr. Chalila, chief minister of Asaam, and Mr. J. Narayan, a disciple of Gandhi—together with the Rev. Michael Scott, were appointed to the mission. Scott came into India with at least the tacit approval of the Indian Government, which endorsed the efforts of the mission. The mission was successful in bringing about a cease-fire. It is entirely in keeping with Scott's whole life that the Indian people who hailed him as hero and martyr twenty years ago, now having tasted power, being top dog instead of bottom donkey, are against him, as passionately as they were for him when they were a subject people and he, a member of the governing race and class.

Only Indian reporters are allowed into Nagaland today, and the *London Observer* comments: "The reverend hero now transformed by the course of Indian history into a meddlesome and unwelcome intruder . . . may in the long run be missed."

As W. H. Auden has put it: "A pity we are not nice." Hardly ever. And never for long—not even the blackest and most persecuted of us. Let us do unto others as they did unto us, is the First Commandment of Causality that we all keep. Yet, as George Bernanos put it: "There is only one sorrow, that we are not saints." Because if we were, we would be freed from causality, set free from the horrid sequence of evil breeding evil.

But since we are not saints, since we are not even nice, those few of us that are have a pretty thin time—at our own hands. From those in high places—Gandhi, Hammarskjold, Kennedy —to the Bishop Walshes and the Michael Scotts. "No wonder You have so few friends," St. Teresa told God when she fell off her donkey, "the way You treat them."

Chapter IX

RETURNING to Mexico, whether from a round-the-world flight or simply from New York, is now for me coming home. Since 1955 my husband and I have been coming to Mexico at least once, and lately, twice a year, and have had a house there since 1957. It is very lucky to be born in one's favorite country, also very lucky to find it, and recognize it. Luckier still to be able to live there. For my mother, India was *mi tierra*, as the Mexicans say, where she was born, that she loved above all. But she lived there only a few years. For my sister, France is her *terre de prédilection*. For me, I consider myself most fortunate to have been born Savoyarde, in the high French Alps, and to have found Mexico, the only country I know with enough mountains and enough flowers.

I first went there in 1936, to stay with our then ambassador, Sir Owen O'Malley, the husband of that brilliant writer, Ann Bridge, whose novel, *Peking Picnic*, is a classic. It was not an auspicious time. President Calles was feuding with the Church, and dispossessing the British of their oil. Poor Sir Owen, who had been in love with my Aunt Iseult when both were young, and with whose daughter Jane I had been up at Oxford, was recalled six months after he had arrived, as Great Britain publicly sulked over the oil seizures, while Mexico put up tasteless —and graceless—huge monuments to *Los Petroleos*. However, the brief glimpse I had then, of that high country, was enough to whet an appetite that ten years have not slaked. Mexico is not to everyone's taste. It is a violent country—violent as is the United States in climate and in character and is both primitive and hypersophisticated—fiercely, almost gruesomely, gay, and at the same time perpetually tragic. The native Indians do not sit down—they fold up, like umbrellas. The religion is sad and savage. Christ is always bleeding, his Mother mourning. Always, for the time being, it is Good Friday or the Judgment Day. Even at a wedding, there may be, for no reason, a shooting, a death; there is a Chinese respect for family and a Chinese disregard for individual life. But such a love of life withal, and such gusto, and such a sense of beauty! Mexicans cannot make anything ugly (except for the foreign market or to ape the "yanqui" bourgeois). Ceramics, cloth, metalware, jewelry, furniture. In line and color and shape and texture, Mexicans seem unable to miss. And what complexity! "May God us keep, from single vision and Newton's sleep," wrote the poet William Blake, and I dote on the contradictions, complications, obfuscations, involutions, and convolutions of Mexican character and politics. The politics, indeed, are fabulously intricate. "I'm sure he's not in jail," a lawyer friend told me of a leading Mexican intellectual, "as he is high up in PAN. PRI bends over backwards to be nice to PAN, so everyone would know if he were in jail." PRI is the party in power, PAN the insignificant and, except at election times, inarticulate opposition.

Mexican politics are indeed a mystery even to Mexicans. For example, is PRI (the *Partido Revolucionario Institucional*) the only party? Luis Calvo, writing for the conservative Madrid daily, ABC, replied: "Yes and no. There are other parties (such as PAN, the *Partido de Acción Nacional*) Then is PRI the party to which most of the Mexicans belong? No. PRI is an official party composed of a small number of Mexicans. The people elect, in free elections, the candidate previously elected by PRI, the man PRI proposes to the voting public."

In fact, PRI has, for the past thirty-six years, nominated

163

the person who has been, in every election, elected by free and universal suffrage. PRI's members come from the "new" social class that in the revolution of 1910 replaced the landowners, businessmen, and bankers who had supported the dictatorship of Porfirio Díaz. This "new" social class, after directing the armed revolution, has held power ever since 1917. At first the syndicates—CTM—(*Confederación de Trabajadores Mexicanos*) were against PRI, but since the time of President Cardenas, CTM have been more and more taken over by PRI, especially in the provinces, where CTM provides the framework through which PRI functions.

PAN wants the "new" class, the progressive bourgeoisie that constitutes the main membership of PRI, to give up power. Yet PAN's presidential candidate José Gonzalez Torres, a lawyer from the agricultural state of Michoacán, had publicly to deny that PAN's campaign was sponsored by funds provided by PRI. And in the 1958 elections, it was widely rumored that PRI had provided the "straw" PAN candidate with the wherewithal to stand.

Does the extraordinary success of PRI's electoral machinery originate from a natural apathy of the voting public, or is this apathy the consequence of the infallible electoral machinery? Whichever is owl and which egg, no one in Mexico (except perhaps the extreme left) seriously objects to the present electoral system. As the Mexican magazine *Siempre* puts it: "Everyone accepts the show that PRI is running."

One of the strange facts of Mexican elections is that PRI, in spite of being certain of 80% of the votes in the ensuing election, sets about its electoral campaign with all the zest, publicity, candidate's nation-wide personal appearances, etc. of a party fighting for its life.

One reason for the confident optimism of today's Mexico is that it has at last digested its revolution. This took forty years— from 1910–1950—but now Mexico is sure it wants to keep what it has won, and wants more of the same. For example, during the six years that he was President, Adolfo Lopez Mateos distributed more land to landless communities than any president before him. Then too, all around Mexico City—the biggest city (over 6 million people) in the whole of Latin America both in area and population—there is not only a complex of super-highways that challenges any in Europe or the United States, but there are hundreds of acres of slum clearance projects, workers' dwellings, playing fields, parks and well-equipped playgrounds. Also there are numerous new hospitals, not only in Mexico City but even in towns as small as Chalco. Analphabetism has fallen in 25 years by 50%, in spite of the fact that many of Mexico's Indians do not even speak Spanish as their second language, and in spite of the multiplicity of these Indian languages quite apart from dialects. There is a huge State medical program, and many doctors, before qualifying, serve in country towns or even villages. This helps prevent too great a centralization in Mexico City of the medical social services. Of course, all is not rosy. For example, doctors and hospital care are free, and all patients coming under ISSTE (the *Instituto de Seguridad Social de los Trabajadores de l'Estado*) get 40% off the cost of all medicines prescribed. But many people still do not come under ISSTE, and for these, medicines are extremely costly when compared with the living wage. And these patients are generally those who require medicines most. In one small town in the State of Mexico, 46% of the population, when tested, had TB in one form or another.

The new schools, too, are numerous, and generally are good, simple buildings, well-staffed. In fact, one new school is built every two days. But it is almost impossible to compel the attendance of all, or even the majority of children in many districts. The truant officer—were there such a person—would have to proceed for many hours on horseback or by jeep, and might be even violently resented at the end of his journey.

Mexico is fortunate in that, re-election being forbidden by the Constitution, its ex-presidents seek behind-the-scenes or social outlets for their political activities. President Lopez Mateos appointed each one of Mexico's living ex-presidents to important jobs, a procedure which had the added advantage of keeping them also under his control. Ex-President Aleman, who was put in charge of tourism, is doing an admirable job of keeping Mexico in the public eye. Cardinal Tisserant's visit to Mexico and Madame Lopez Mateos's subsequent voyage to Greece, where she emphasized Mexico's free milk distribution program, are examples of Aleman's successful efforts in the field of public relations. The U.S. President's well-advertised 1966 visit is yet another. And now the Olympics!

Mexico is considered—and above all considers itself—the spokesman for the other Latin American states. Because it is *norteamericano*, and not central or South American, it stands in a very particular relationship to the Colossus to the North—the United States. Mexico is perfectly well aware that neither militarily nor economically can it resist Big Brother. But political gestures remain as a means of making it quite clear that Mexico does not like being pushed around. Such a gesture, demonstrating Mexico's *machismo*—its *he-man-ness*—is implicit in Mexico's repeated refusal to break off relations with Cuba in spite of the OAS decision. Mexico's declaration that it would await the International Court's verdict as to whether the OAS decision was binding on all members was based on Mexico's doctrine of non-intervention in the internal affairs of other countries called for its expounder, *doctrina Estrada*, formulated during the presidency of Cardenas. Mexico's stand was hailed with delight by the entire Mexican press, which jeered at Bolivia's change of heart, saying it was paid for by the U.S. promise to buy so much tin, just as Brazil's vote was paid for by the purchase of an unspecified amount of coffee. Mexico, the daily papers implied, was made of nobler stuff. The U.S. retaliation to Mexico's *machismo* by a sugar embargo was considered characteristic of Big Brother's behavior. It was viewed as tiresome, but not serious. The hasty declaration by the U.S.

166

that neither Mexico's action nor the U.S. unsweet reaction could possibly worsen relations between the two countries was dismissed as a hyena hope. It much increased Mexico's prestige as the one Latin American country able, even if only by a gesture, to assert its indifference to U.S. bullying.

As an ex-President of Colombia, Alberto Lleras Camargo, wrote on June 12, 1964 in *Vision:*

Mexico is a country which, in contrast to the rest of Latin America, shows no symptoms of exhaustion, paralysis, or regression. The stability of the political regime, strongly supported by a complex party machinery, has precluded any faltering in the will to do, to build, and to create. This does not mean that there is no misery, squalor, despair or ignorance in Mexico as in the rest of Latin America, but these forms of backwardness do not seem to be static, or growing and destroying the rest of the social set-up in Mexico.... On the contrary, there is an offensive battle to eliminate them.

One advantage of the one-party system, is that PRI has a very strong right, and a very strong left, wing. And the presidents who succeed each other, like Amurath to Amurath, generally alternate. Adolfo Lopez Mateos was inclined to the left; Gustavo Diaz Ordaz is distinctly right wing, the bankers' pet.

One of Gilbert and Sullivan's most famous generalizations was:

> That every boy and every gal,
> That's born into the world alive,
> Is either a little Liberal,
> Or else a little Conservative!

This is as true of Catholics as it is of Buddhists, Hindus, Jews or Muslims. And in a special way it is particularly true of Mexican Catholics. For the Church, which in the nineteenth century was Mexico's most powerful landlord and largest loan agency, had to fight for its life for forty years (1910–1950) in the twentieth. So that for many years to be a Catholic meant to be a conservative. The separation of Church and State was written into the constitution of 1857. Later, during the dictatorship (1876–1910) of Porfirio Díaz, the Church partially recovered her strength. But the Revolution of 1910 led to renewed conflicts between Church and State, and all the articles most objected to in the 1857 constitution (above all articles 3, 5, 72, 123, and 130) were reaffirmed in the new constitution of 1917. This led to the "Cristero" rebellion, which in three years cost Mexico over a million and a half dead.

The present era of peaceful co-existence began in 1938, when the Archbishop of Mexico, during the expropriation of the petroleum companies, urged his flock to support the Government. President Ávila Camacho was the first revolutionary president publicly to admit he was a believer; the present president, Gustavo Diaz Ordaz, has made the same admission. Yet it was not until 1951, when the Archbishop of Mexico organized a National Campaign for Morality, that the Catholic organizations appeared in public with a total membership of four and a half million: the largest assembly of Catholic leaders since the revolution. Since then "the Church has both recovered and increased her former influence. She is the only traditional organization which has survived the great social transformation taking place in contemporary Mexico." (Dr. P. Gonzalez Casanova: *La Democracia en Mexico,* p. 33).

Yet when President Kennedy and his wife came to Mexico, they terminated their State visit *before* going privately to the basilica of our Lady of Guadalupe, since article 130 of the Mexican Constitution does not recognize "religious groups referred to as Churches." Priests and nuns are still theoretically forbidden to wear clerical garb in public though more and more do so. Now Vatican II's approval of changes in clerical attire more than meets the Mexican state halfway. However, pilgrimages take place today "with the cross of Jesus going on before" in public streets without official protest.

Mexican Catholics, religious or secular, are fairly sharply divided between those who take a "traditionalist" stand and those who are "with it"—"it" being Vatican II. Mexico has 11 archbishoprics, 57 bishoprics, 1 cardinal, 6,347 priests, 18,000 nuns and 2,142 parishes, whose average size is over 300 square miles (Mexico is the seventh largest country, and Mexico City the tenth largest city, in the world). Some of the Mexican bishops were among the most liberal prelates at Vatican II; perhaps the most outstanding was the Bishop of Cuernavaca. At the other end of the ecclesiastical spectrum are such clerics as the Archbishop of Hermosillo and the Bishop of Zamora, who have publicly approved the Catholic traditionalist movement. This movement opposes such innovations as the taking of communion while standing, the wearing of lay clothes by religious, the substitution of the Rosary by the singing of Biblical psalms in the vernacular, and what it calls the "deformation" of the Gospel in the interest of Jews or people of Jewish background.

These religious disparities are partly geographical, for the politico-religious geography of Mexico is extremely varied. As Dr. Pablo Gonzalez Casanova puts it (op. cit., p. 35): "The unequal development of the different regions corresponds to different levels of religiosity. The most traditional and fanatic religious attitudes are found in central Mexico. In other areas, such as Nuevo Léon, there is a new political religiosity of a paternalistic nature ... closely linked to the factory system." One million Mexicans speak nothing but indigenous languages; two million are bilingual; about a million trilingual (speaking Mexicano—or Nahuatl—Spanish, and a local Indian language). All these, Dr. Casanova says, are polytheistic and totemistic. In the southern highlands, for example at San Cristobal de las Casas, there are Catholic churches which have completely reverted to pagan rites—Mass is no longer said in them. In the excellent Mexican film *Tarahumara*, winner of the Cannes Festival Award, the dispossessed Indians of the far north (Chihuahua) are shown as completely non-Christian as are the villainous Mexican *politicos* who murder them, and the young Mexico City journalist who espouses their cause (the bad are completely victorious!).

In certain areas, such as Puebla, the old nineteenth-century clerical-liberal strife is continued by today's young people. Here the local variant of the U.S. "panty-raid" was recently an invasion of the grounds of a convent school by young men from the State University, who tried to perform a so-called Black Mass in the garden. Puebla was the home, for over a hundred years, of a "hidden" convent, whose nuns, fed by the faithful, were never discovered by the authorities. Father Pardenas, S.J. of the Jesuit University, was recently stoned by Puebla Catholics for making too liberal a speech! Religious statistics in Mexico are subject to fluctuations. For example, the 1940 census recorded 433,671 individuals without religious affiliation, whereas the 1950 census indicated that all Mexicans were adherents of one religion or another! In the 1960 report, 192,965 citizens declared themselves to be without religious affiliation. Among the large Catholic secular organizations which play important roles in Mexican life are: Mexican Catholic Action, with 348,273 members; the National Union of Heads of Family —500,000 members; Knights of Columbus—3,500 members; The Christian Family Movement, which maintains 1,200 teaching centers and 35,000 lay teachers; and the National Association for a Good Press, which has put out an astonishing quantity of Catholic literature since 1952: 36,971,594 magazines, over two hundred million bulletins, and five million books. It publishes 13 magazines, 8 bulletins, and 2 books a month. There are also various "highbrow" Catholic magazines, such as *Dialogo*, edited by Ramon Xirau, whose father left Spain after the Civil War (he teaches philosophy), and the *Opus Dei* quarterly, *ISTMO*.

Education, as Dr. Betancur of UNESCO put it, "is the soundest cure for poverty, division and all forms of violent social revolution." Since 1930, illiteracy has dropped in Mexico from 66.5 to some 30%. Somewhere around 75% of the children receive primary school education, and some 20% go on to high school. The Mexican State spends one-fourth of its entire budget on education, and all schooling, including all school books, texts, and materials, are free. But there is no means of enforcing school attendance; the distances are too great, the children too poor, and often too ragged. Mexico has the lowest life expectancy (37 for men, 36 for women) of any Latin American country, and the second highest birth-rate in the world. So the question of Church education and Church schools is one of the gravest. Many Mexican bishops and priests have come to question the wisdom of Catholic schools. In a predominantly Catholic country they are divisive as well as expensive: only the middle classes can afford them, and many Catholics now suggest that a more practical plan for today would be State schools "infiltrated" by religious. This has already occurred, and is occurring, in some places. In Valle de Bravo, for example, the sisters teach daily in the state school; yet "religious bodies, ministers, companies and associations connected, with making propaganda for any religious creed are forbidden from intervening in establishments for elementary or secondary education or normal schools, or in the teaching of either workers or peasants." (Topic I of the *World Education Assembly,* paper presented by the Mexican Academy of Education.)

There are very few Communists in Mexico. The Mexican Communist Party founded in 1919 has never yet reached the total of 75,000 members which it needs to put up a presidential candidate, and party membership today is not a tenth of that. Some 80% of Mexican industry is financed by U.S. capital, and Mexico is an economic colony of the U.S. Yet there is a certain hard core of anti-U.S. feeling. Fifty-five percent of the population of Mexico live on the land, where wages are 6% lower than in the towns. The agrarian revolution, though slow, is still proceeding and consists "in nothing more than the incorporation of agriculture into the capitalist economy." In 1906, 97% of the land belong to 1,000 men; in 1965 there were over a million small proprietors (freeholders), and a million and a half *ejidatorios*-persons sharing in the communal ownership of land and water (the latter almost more important than the former, since 63% of the land needs artificial irrigation). The *Opus Dei* has a pilot *hacienda* at Santa Clara near Cuatla, where villagers are taught the most up-to-date agricultural methods, and the women are taught hygiene, sewing, and dietetics. But priests in most rural areas face terrible difficulties: parishes of over 18,000 souls are common, distributed in some 20 hamlets, to which the only access is on horseback.

Church architecture in Mexico is a delight. Whether it be the old, Spanish gloriously gilded *churrigueresque* architecture of such churches as the Carmen in Mexico City, Santo Domingo in Oaxaca, the Rosario chapel in Puebla, the great Jesuit Church of Tepozotlan, or the enchanting dozens of tiny chapels in the corn fields around Cholula, or the brilliant and audacious modern churches such as the Altillo Chapel of the Padres del Spirito Santo in Mexico or the new *fracciónamento* chapel in Cuernavaca, church architecture in Mexico really proves itself to be "the mistress art." The artist Siqueiros is currently building a rival to the Sistine Chapel (to be known simply as the Siqueiros chapel!) in Cuernavaca, and everywhere concrete and color, glass and sunlight are being combined to the greater glory of God.

Cuernavaca, about fifty miles by superhighway from Mexico City, has been described as a "sunny place for shady people." A city of almost 100,000 souls is built along wooded gullies called *barrancas*. Here are palaces and gardens year-long ablaze with bougainvillia, jacaranda, flamboyante, and tamarind, with wonderful views of the volcanoes Popocatepetl and Ixtacihuatl, eternally covered with snow. Here, too, are thousands of adobe huts, of tiny *tiendas* or stores. Here are the headquarters of the Centro de Investigaciones Culturales (CIF). The building, long, low, and white, with many balconies and arched verandas, covered with climbing plants in bright colors, has gardens where palm trees flourish and birds sing. The center is the altar, and at the daily Mass the Host is a large wheat tortilla, broken into small fragments and given to all.

CIF was established in the fall of 1960 as an independent educational institution, incorporated under the laws of New York State and sponsored jointly by Fordham University and the Bishops Committee for Latin America. The executive director is Monsignor Ivan Illich, a secular priest of the archdiocese of New York. I first met Monsignor (then Father) Illich at a cocktail party in New York. My husband met him first, came across to me and said, "You must meet this young priest. I think he will one day be a Cardinal." After meeting him, as I went home with my husband, I said, "You're so wrong about that young priest. He's not going to end up a Cardinal—he's going to be Pope." *Vamos a ver,* as they say in Mexico.

Trained at the Capranica, Pius XII's own college in Rome, Ivan Illich, born of a Slav Catholic father and Austrian Jewish mother, was destined for the Vatican foreign service. But he met Cardinal Spellman on one of his visits to Rome, and persuaded the Cardinal to take him back with him to New York, and appoint him curate in a Puerto Rican parish. Father Illich spoke neither English nor Spanish when he arrived in the United States; within three months he spoke both fluently. He also speaks French, German, Italian, Portuguese, and Russian, as well as his native Serbo-Croat. He holds three Ph.D degrees. Recently he went for a vacation to Patmos, to seek spiritual counsel from a holy Orthodox monk there, spent the first two days chatting in the cafés and reading the local newspaper, then when he could transpose ancient Greek into modern sufficiently, he proceeded to go to the Orthodox monastery to stay. Appointed Vice-Rector of the new Catholic University at Ponce, in Puerto Rico, he opposed his Bishop when the latter told his flock how to vote under pain of excommunication. Young Illich said to his superior: "I will write and object to the Holy Father. What you are doing is forbidden by theology." His

Bishop did not believe him until the Vatican sided with the Vice-Rector, who was promptly sacked.

The Centro de Investigaciones Culturales (CIF) at Cuernavaca was started in 1962 as an answer to John XXIII's appeal in 1961 to the Major Religious Superiors of the U.S.A., Canada, and Europe, requesting that they send at least ten percent of their members to Latin America during the next ten years. Its objective is to train priests, nuns, brothers, and lay people to work in Latin America. In its first five years it has trained 61% of all the church-related personnel going to Latin America, mainly Catholic, but also a substantial number of Protestants.

Latin America contains one third of all the Catholics in the world, served by one-seventh of the priests. It has the most rapidly growing population in the world, numbering two hundred million people at the present time. It is expected to number four hundred million by the year 2000. Today there is only one priest for every 45,000 Catholics (in the New York diocese there is one priest for every 700; in Europe, for every 925; and even in Africa, there is one for every 1,600 Catholics). In Guatemala the ratio is one priest to 11,000 lay Catholics; in Brazil, one to 5,500.

The training program at CIF consists of a four-months' course: two are held a year. The course has three major aspects: language, intercultural communication, and spiritual formation. The language training is grueling: six hours a day, five days a week, with one instructor to at most five students. Courses at Cuernavaca are currently being attended by priests, nuns, monks, and lay workers from Canada, France, Germany, Holland, and the United States as well as from Mexico and from all the Latin American countries. A representative of CELAM (the Latin American Bishops' Conference) is permanently in residence at CIF, and plans joint pastorals for the whole of Latin America; for a pool of articles, lecturers, and writers; plans for comprehensive theological and sociological training for all Latin America have already been worked out at

Cuernavaca. Luther College in Iowa sent a group to CIF last summer; the Episcopalians sent a clergyman now stationed in Costa Rica, and a German Lutheran with his family are the forerunners of a permanent Lutheran representation. What CIF can offer—and this is why it is, essentially, a bridge place even more, perhaps, than a study center—is an opportunity to become aware of the depth of cultural differences. Cultural, not theological: Latin America was Catholic before there was a single Catholic in the United States or Canada, and the Catholic Faith flourished there before the United States existed. Catholic traditions are far more deeply rooted in Latin America than in the U.S., and every community is fundamentally Catholic in a sense which no community is, ever has been, or ever will be in the United States or English-speaking Canada. But the Catholicism of Latin America ranges from the highly sophisticated Catholicism of some of the urban areas to that of illiterate Indians with no contact with what is known as contemporary civilization. It ranges "from an intensity of practice and devotion that is heroic, to an indifference that is difficult to conceive." Above all, the mores could not be more different. The double standard of sexual morality; the subjection of women; the often almost total disregard of efficiency, economy, and hygiene; the apparent apathy regarding living conditions, illnesses, and education; the constant lack of what may be regarded as the Anglo-Saxon virtues: truthfulness, honesty, prudence, or sobriety, irk the Yankee, the German, the Canadian, the Dutch, however noble their motives or intelligent their approach. Monsignor Illich sees the CIF courses as necessitating a "willingness to leave the womb of your own culture to be born again." When a Mother Superior complained, "I'm losing my faith," he merely replied, "I hope you're finding Christ instead." Of another sister he asked, "Do you realize you are a cursed people? You will never be as good as accepted by those you go among: at the best you will be adopted." He feels that there is no hope for the Church in Latin America—either for the native Church or the missionaries he is training—unless the Church ceases to be the most successful and, in some areas, the last remaining example of private enterprise.

First, he tells his students, you must learn what it means to be an adopted child. And here Christ is your example: He was Joseph's *adopted* son. An adopted child has to try harder, has to be more attractive, more obedient.

Since Cuernavaca began, a twin institute has been started at Petrópolis, in Brazil—in 1961. Those who come to Cuernavaca and Petrópolis are either religious (priests, nuns, or brothers), sent by their Superiors; members of the secular clergy sent by their bishops; or members of the laity working for a Church organization and financed by such an organization, which takes responsibility for them. Monsignor Illich does not suffer fools gladly, and has no use for do-gooders. Of the first 68 students, only 32 survived. He has himself described what generally happens either in Cuernavaca or Petrópolis to students coming from the United States.

JOE ARRIVES: He wants to give—he feels superior and secure—he is sure that he is needed—he feels accepted—he is sure that he is willing to give up anything.

HE STARTS TO LIVE HERE:
For 7 hours a day he must submit to accepting words and being corrected.
He finds out that he is inferior to *compesinos* in getting around Mexico, in surviving on their food and water, in making himself understood.
He is overwhelmed by the incredible degree of misery which he came to relieve; his contribution seems almost insignificant at best.
He comes to suspect that people will not welcome him but rather:

ridicule him,
reject him,
actually not need him.

He comes to see that there are more things one can give up than he had suspected (language, images, status).

WHAT IS REALLY HAPPENING TO HIM:

He has freely chosen to become "inferior"—to "ask for it."
He either is humble or feels humiliated.
He freely made himself a child or acts childish.
Probably he is both, with varying accent on one or the other.
He feels (subjective!) humiliated and acts childish (and knows it) . . .

So, Monsignor writes:

The formation of a missioner will be centered on the development of a capacity to leave his home at least spiritually and to talk to strangers. It is this he has to learn at a course aimed at missionary formation. Our purpose here will be to analyze the way in which all spiritual, intellectual and practical training of the missioner has to be organized around the development of the beatitude which makes the transition from a familiar to a foreign way of life easy and practical: and that is spiritual poverty in imitation of a special aspect of the Incarnation.

Very often the missioner has to learn a new language, always a new lingo. Modern linguistics have greatly shortened the time this takes. The missioner must also learn to understand hitherto unknown social, economic and geophysical forces. This is often easy on the surface but it is difficult for the missionary to accept the consequences these forces will have on his own life: the weather might frustrate him with tiredness, his social position put him into a goldfish bowl, the poverty force him to unaccustomed discomfort.

Most important of all, the missioner has to face a new culture. He has to learn to distinguish between that which is morally good everywhere and that which is socially acceptable to a particular ethnic group. He will have to know which of his habits among "his new people" are socially unacceptable, though they may be morally good and he may be used to them; and he might have to become willing to accept cultural taboos of his own home as everyday patterns of his new surroundings. This emotional and intellectual willingness to accept a new culture which does not come "natural" to anybody, can be greatly enhanced by a theoretical understanding of culture and a guided research of a local milieu.

However, the learning of a language, the acceptance *in toto* of a special "human climate," and specially the willingness to become part of a new culture present are much more than purely intellectual problems for the missioner. For him language, techniques and culture are not academic ends but first of all means to a practical purpose: communication. And to be more precise: communication of the Gospel. The missioner becomes part of his new surroundings in order to become able to speak, not just to survive. He is the man who is willing to witness with his life, to a foreign people, the relativity of human convictions in front of the unique and absolute meaning of the Revelation. He often is the man through whom the Incarnation of the Word becomes real in cultures other than that of the ancient Jews. (Is it for that reason that we have missioners to all nations but He has ever reserved for Himself the mission to the Jews?)

Sometimes the missioner lives among people who to him are foreigners but who have received the gospel before through priests from one culture and for a historical accident must now receive their priest coming from another. This is the case for instance in many parts of Latin America. In such situations the word "missioner" assumes a very special meaning. The priest from abroad remains "missioner" in the sense that he communicates the Gospel to those who are not of his own. The people among whom he lives might have received and absorbed the faith centuries before any of the missioner's ancestors entered the Church or the Church had any influence on the culture of the missioner's home. In such a situation the missioner's task is even more delicate than in a situation of first evangelization: many of the traits of the culture the missioner finds to be different from his own deserve respect not only because they are an intimate property of a people

178

but also because they were developed under the influence of the Catholic Church.

The full realization of such cultural relativity, especially in matters which are intimately connected with the unchangeable structure of the Church, requires great detachment. We all love to give absolute value to the things we have learned to love. We must. Because to love the immediate is human and therefore necessary. But we usually forget to ask ourselves if these values we treasure are absolute in relation to everybody else as well as to ourselves. The man, therefore, who is willing to be "sent" away from home as a "missioner" will have to subject his values to a careful scrutiny to determine their "catholicity." Just as he has to become indifferent to possessions and physical comfort; just as he has to become indifferent to being or not being with his family and his people, so he had to become indifferent to the cultural values of his home. This means that he has to become very poor in a deep sense.

Nor may he pretend to be what he is not: Monsignor has no use for "apostolic tourists who want to go native." Nor for those who come because they are misfits at home, or do not love their own country. Our Lord did not love His Father less for loving his human family; "If people can't love their own country and people, they can't love foreigners," Monsignor insists. Nor must they love people—any people, their own or those to whom they are sent—for God's sake. This is a denial of the natural order. If you love God in anyone or anyone for God, and not that person for him or herself, it is an insult.

Monsignor regards the first role of CIF to administer cultural shocks. It's no good going to Latin America and looking back at United States structures: little red schoolhouses and private hospitals à la Cabrini are useless in Latin America. It is no improvement, he says, to lead people from parish schools to higher wages, from promiscuity to contraception, from misery to the middle class. The Christian who leaves his own culture today seeks active participation, not rubbery accommodation.

For the Christian, all leaving of his own social group or community is a foreshadowing of death. And such death leads either analogically into the isolation of hell, or into the communion of saints.

Practically, too, the Anglo-Saxon coming into a Latin American culture must exchange the religion of the supermarket for the religion of the plaza. He must realize that the community is the unit, not the individual. Even if a Latin American never goes to Sunday Mass, he is aware from birth to death of his presence as a Catholic in a community that is Catholic. And this communitarian life and reality is something the Communists fully appreciate. For Communism gives hope for the others; it gives a sense of belonging to the alienated—the starving Indians who have crept down from the hills, to the slums of the big towns; to the proletarian poor who never see a priest from baptism to funeral. And, above all, it gives to the most miserable, the most insignificant, the most illiterate, a sense that HE can help, that he matters, that he has the right to work, the right to live and to eat. The proximity of food transforms hunger into anger. The Latin American poor—when they come down from the mountains because their children don't die fast enough—see food and luxury, and are aroused. So, for Monsignor, the first task in Latin America is to lead whole communities out of misery, not to help individuals to escape from it.

But the training of a new type of human cultural enzyme is only a part of the work that goes on at Cuernavaca. Monsignor is Vicar General to the Bishop of Cuernavaca, the Right Reverend Sergio Méndez Arced, and his students are assigned weekend work in parishes in the diocese. Work is being done on sociological surveys within the diocese; in many respects, Cuernavaca is a pilot diocese, where the CIF manpower can study, edit, and disseminate the material produced.

Some of the greatest problems for the clergy in Latin America stem from clerical celibacy. Clerical celibacy is itself one of the reasons for the paucity of vocations throughout Latin America—the lowest priest-people rato in the world prevails there. In many areas, too, clerical chastity is at an all-time low. Monsignor Illich has been seeking possible solutions to these dilemmas at Cuernavaca.

Much could be hoped for, he thinks, from the ordaining of mature married men—men with, say, fifteen to twenty years of successful married experience living within one community, a community which would recommend such men to the bishop. There is little to be said for a married clergy. Without wishing to offend our Orthodox or Protestant brethren, there do not seem to be enough advantages accruing from their experiments with a married clergy to indicate that the Church should follow their example in this instance. There is, however, much to be said in favor of ordaining men who have truly committed themselves, either to a woman or to God, and have proved their commitment in their lives. There is nothing to be said in favor of ordaining men merely because they are single: the Council of Calcedon's anathema on those who do not marry because they despise the married relationship might usefully be recalled in this context.

These distinctions—between ordaining married men and avoiding a married clergy; between ordaining the committed and avoiding the ordination of men who merely happen to be single—stem from an awareness that should be part of the theological equipment of clerics and laymen alike: an awareness of the importance of insisting on priestly chastity, as distinct from religious celibacy. Such an awareness would make it obvious that the ordination of already married men would neither render their marriage less chaste nor their priesthood less holy.

Another, and hardly less important problem is the civil service of the Church. That is, the vast body of men and women, religious and secular, called upon to assist in the administration of the Church. It is obvious that the Church cannot function without a dedicated, incorruptible, and international civil service. It should, however, be patent that not all those who are ordained must necessarily belong to it. A bishop, for example, can perfectly well have both a presbytery and a clergy; parish priests cannot and should not also be civil servants—nor can hospital almoners or prison chaplains. But the presbytery and the clergy, in each diocese, can and probably always will be overlapping, while remaining functionally separate.

Those who have dedicated themselves, full-time and forever, as clerics, should not, Monsignor Illich thinks, be married. But the Church has the right to impose its civil service rules even on those whom it employs on a full-time but impermanent basis: professors hired for a special course, men or women hired for specific clerical but non-sacerdotal functions of administration or instruction. Such functionaries can, of course, also be married. But the civil service rules imposed on such full-time, temporary ecclesiastical civil servants must closely and obviously parallel those imposed on, say, United Nations international civil servants. For example: not speaking in public, and not publishing anything without permission; not granting interviews or taking part in any activities that compromise the Church without permission from the ecclesiastical superiors.

The greatest needs of any bureaucracy are proper tools. Books, statistics, and other reference materials are the tools of every civil servant, lay or clerical, as of every intellectual. CIDOC—the Centro Intercultural de Documentation—is the head, as the students are the heart, of CIF. The documentation center is subdivided into the library, publications, and research. The library, in five short years, has become the most comprehensive and up-to-date in its specialized field, which is all aspects of the Church in all its relationships for the whole of Latin America. The library and the publications both enjoy, and exploit, what may be called ecclesiastical immunity from such trammels as publishing rights, translation rights, reproduction rights. As the circulation of documents is, so to speak, intro-mural, and as even the library has a very restricted readership, it is possible to possess and use highly explosive material. Everything produced at Cuernavaca is highly up-to-date. Monsignor says that the Christian was told to be poor, but not economical: cars are cheaper than buses, trains, and shabby planes that fall down; it is cheaper to buy a generator to run a deep freeze for 1,000 chickens; everything in the library is microfilmed; Monsignor records on tape while motoring and the lectures at Chula Vista have, since the first day, been simultaneously translated into the three working languages there—French, English, and Spanish.

The publications consist of a monthly report in two editions on all current material on the Church in Latin America, called CIF Reports, issued in English, French, Portuguese, and Spanish; in statistical data—and in books resulting from Cuernavaca Conversations. These conversations are excuses for the bringing together of people otherwise unable to meet. For example, the Bishops of Latin America number 850—one-third of all the bishops in the world—but it would be impossible for them to meet, as bishops, in Mexico, and quite difficult in several other Latin American countries. They can come to Cuernavaca to discuss education, for example, or to give talks on the planning of health services. Over two dozen Mothers Superior of major religious orders recently met in Cuernavaca, actually to discuss the implications of Vatican II on women religious. Nine Protestant Latin American leaders met for a weekend and discussed Christianity and culture; daily, in the chapel, at Monsignor Illich's invitation, one commented on the Gospel of the day. Preaching, of course, is forbidden to non-Catholics, but there is nothing to deter them from Gospel comment. During one "Conversation," the professor of Theology at Princeton spoke at length on the structure of the Protestant Churches in Latin America, which, he declared, were in profound crisis, owing to the fact that today, for the first time since medieval times, there is no culture or sub-culture in the whole of Latin America with which Christians can identify. The problem no longer is to Christianize a totally secular world, but to humanize a wholly materialistic one.

The research, the library, largely self-supporting with its volumes of maps, charts, and tables are all available to institutions the world over.

Between the regular four-month biannual training courses, there are held each year at Cuernavaca, besides the high-level conversations, workshops open to students. Last year's participants ranged from administrators, planners, and educational personnel (a workshop on educational planning in Latin America—lasting three weeks); a workshop in intensive Spanish, sponsored by Luther College, Decorah, Iowa; a workshop in the humanities addressed by (among some twenty others) Ramon Xirau, the philosopher; Erich Fromm, the psychologist; Carlos Fuentes, the novelist.

For Monsignor Illich, the call to Latin America could be a great grace to those churches sending "help"—a call which might shake their smugness, their conviction that basically their church is all it should be. "Are we, as we are when at home, those Christians Latin America basically needs?" This question, which should have some of the agony of Oliver Cromwell's appeal: "By the bowels of Christ, I beseech you to consider you may be mistaken" might prove, through a confrontation with the needs of Latin America, to be a means by which North Americans could be persuaded to take a second look at their own pastoral patterns. Missionaries are supposed to be the sowers of seeds, but as one of them perceptively put it: "We are all too often the carriers of germs." Or, as a Latin American wrote:

We need newcomers to become available, not to be just physically present. To enter our conversation, rather than force us into theirs. To come to meet our need for a Church of the future, rather than to create the image of their Church among us. To build the future of our nation, rather than sell us theirs. We need newcomers who learn to think with us as we are, rather than teach us their way of life and thought. To adopt the aspirations of our people, rather than sell us their own. We need newcomers who come as equals, to whom we can give, not those who come as rich uncles bringing us their leftovers. We want to learn from you, not be tools; we want to use your skill to build a world according to our plan.

All good things go in threes, and the focal tables at the Centro de Investigaciones Culturales are a spiritual table, the chapel; a physical table, the dining room, where people meet and talk; and a mental table, the library, where they learn to learn. This Centro is indeed a bridge place that is already a bridge-head, and a truly Christian answer to Communism. For it is only by proving to the world that Christians can be better and do better than Communists that the world will ever be convinced enough to "choose this day the Lord God."

I found Mexico perhaps the most exciting country I visited, and its religion the most alive. Here miscegenation—always a good thing—is a national quality. Very few Mexicans indeed are pure Indian, pure Spanish, or pure anything, and the Church has wisely ceased taking sides for the Spaniards against the Revolution. Now Mass has to be in the Indian dialects where the majority is Indian-language-speaking, and that is a further miscegenation, of Christian culture with pagan speech. "Fare forward, voyagers," T. S. Eliot urged in his *Four Quartets,* and Mexico, which spends under ten percent of its budget on armaments, and over thirty percent on education, is trying to do just that.

Chapter X

AND so, lest like poor Léon Bloy, who spent his life hunting for saints and never saw the one quietly occupying the throne of St. Peter, I decided to return "right back where I started from" to these United States, lest I miss the hyphen people living here, while seeking them at the far ends of the earth. I drove up from Mexico, as I have so often done before (best time for the 3,000 miles, 3 days). Across the border, in the heart of Texas, lives one of the most unique of hyphens, and the only living martyr I personally have the honor to number among my friends.

There is a well-known Negro anecdote, about a white man griping about his troubles to a Negro. Life was tough. He was broke. His only child was dying of leukemia, his wife was unfaithful. The Negro listened patiently, then commented succinctly, "You're still white." It is doubtful whether, since the world began, anyone has ever before had the courage and the imagination deliberately to stop being white—until John Howard Griffin, a white Texan, whose ancestors came to Mansfield, Texas, just after the Civil War. John went to a dermatologist in New Orleans, and had him deliberately darken his skin by giving him a medication which turned him so black that, after John had shaved off his hair, he could "pass" through the Deep South as a Negro. The account he wrote of his experiences, *Black Like Me,* is a bestseller in several languages. To its author the book has brought only terrible pain, suffering both physical and mental, and humiliation. Burned in effigy in his home town by his neighbors, his parents forced to leave their birthplace when old, John Howard Griffin has been repeatedly beaten up by his fellow-whites, the last time being dragged out of his car at a gas station in Mississippi and beaten on his kidneys with chains, so that it is doubtful whether he will ever completely recover from the effects of this assault. John Howard Griffin is indeed one of the twentieth century's authentic Christians. And patriots. During World War II he served in the U.S. Air Force in the Pacific for thirty-nine months, was twice wounded, and lost his sight for eleven years as the result of brain damage from enemy action. He has served his country faithfully both at home and abroad, and would, I think, agree with the nineteenth-century U.S. Congressman who said, "My country right or wrong: when right, to applaud and approve, when wrong, to set right." Bilingual from childhood, John Howard Griffin spent many years of his boyhood in France, became a medical student before the war, and intended, as soon as it was over, to become a doctor on the GI Bill of Rights. But increasing blindness compelled him to abandon his studies, and so he became a musicologist, and specialized in medieval music. A pupil of Nadia Boulanger, the harpsichordist, and of Robert Casadesus, he spent some time at the Abbey of Solesmes. In the spring of 1947, now completely blind, he returned to the U.S.A. to attend schools for the blind, and to study animal husbandry. While totally blind he wrote six books, plus many articles. He also married in 1953 and begot 4 children. He saw his wife for the first time four years after their marriage when he partially regained his sight in 1957.

John Howard Griffin is, surely, one of the most representative hyphen people alive. A hyphen between two languages and two cultures, he writes a great deal in French. Indeed, most of his first drafts are in French, then he translates, or recreates, in English. As a boy, he went to a French *lycée* and was also active in the French resistance. He is a hyphen also between the sighted and the blind, and one of the most moving things he has ever written is his account of a night-long visit he made to a beggar known only as *l'Aveugle,* in Tours. Griffin was himself going rapidly blind, and wanted to talk incognito to someone who was totally blind. Most of all, of course, himself intensely ethnically white American, he is a hyphen between black and white Americans. Being also intensely himself, he *is* himself, whether speaking French or English, whether sighted or blind, whether white or colored. And always he writes. And writes superbly well. And photographs, too, for he is also a superb photographer as is his young son, who at eight years old was the youngest honorary member of the Royal Photographic Society of Great Britain. John is too, by the dichotomy of charity, the other of whom he writes; thus he is both the "I and the thou" of whom Martin Buber wrote, and is not only a hyphen person, but the human being most committed to the dialogue whom I have ever met.

He recently wrote in his journals:

> In truth I practice and find my spiritual home in another time, one that is not held in very high esteem today, one against which there is even a revolution; and the strange thing is that I pray for the success of most elements of that revolution and support it—and yet all of my tissues draw away from it and back into the old houses of the soul—the *Precautions* of St. John of the Cross, the *Primitive Rule* of St. Benedict. This would appear to be a contradiction, and I suppose it is. The contradiction of yearning to withdraw from public life into a life of silence, solitude and obscurity—this yearning that has torn at me so many years; and yet my life and work, precisely because it was long ago given without reservation to God, is in the world, in activity. Somehow these contradictions are resolved within me, because there, at least, they are not contradictions.
>
> It is the same esthetically. How well I remember the winter afternoons with Pierre Reverdy, when he railed against me for

loving and drawing nourishment from the works of his generation: Braque, Blanchard, Reverdy, Maritain, Rouault. "You must go with your own age," he admonished. "These were for my time. You are too young. You must not latch on to the very end of the old. You must find your contemporaries, develop with them, take nourishment from them."

I never could.

John Howard Griffin looks like a romantic's idea of a Texan. He is large, burly, rugged, with a face that might have been roughcast in cement. He is simple, direct, straightforward, and at the same time nervous, a chain smoker, dynamic. At first sight he might be a truck driver, or the farmer he was for seven years—anything but a sensitive and accomplished pianist, a dedicated writer, deeply committed politically as well as a deeply religious man. But the eyes and the mouth are revealing: disciplined, devoted. These cannot lie. "Fate gave you your features," my mother used to say. "You make your own mouth." And she added, "Words can lie but eyes cannot."

John Howard Griffin was born in Dallas on June 16, 1920. His mother was a concert pianist, and he has inherited her deep love for music. He went through grade school in Fort Worth, to high school and college in France. He wished to become a doctor, and was keenly interested in the uses of musical therapy for the insane. When World War II broke out he was working in an asylum in Tours, and joined the French Resistance. As a member of the *Defense Passive* he helped many Jews to escape. Bedeaux, an acquaintance of John's in Tours, told the Nazis of John's work. He had gained John's confidence by promising to get Jewish refugees out through St. Nazaire. John's colleague, Jean Hussar, was forced to flee also, and was killed while fighting with the Free French. Bedeaux was later arrested in Africa but committed suicide before being brought to trial. John escaped through Ireland in 1940 when the Gestapo discovered his work, and he joined the U.S. Army in 1942. At the war's end, gravely wounded and with failing eyes he returned

189

to France. At Solesmes, the greatest center of Gregorian music in the world, he found not only the medieval musical manuscripts he sought, but also the setting for his first novel, *The Devil Rides Outside*. This takes its title from an old proverb "le diable rôde autour d'un monastère." It is a tremendous book, big in every sense of the word. It portrays a randy, virile, gifted young man, who comes to study medieval musical manuscripts at a Benedictine monastery, one pale golden October day. He is an unbeliever, but, as are most American Protestants by inheritance, a dyed-in-the-wool Manichaean: all that is pleasurable—women, wife, song, good food—is wrong. Life is real, earnest, and vastly disagreeable. At first all he feels is loneliness —he has left his girl in Paris—and cold. But the music is there, and asserts itself:

> ... the bright-toned baroque organ above ... building sound on sound with a clarity of fresh flute and oboe tones echoing from bare stone walls of the unlighted chapel. A final bright chord echoes forward through the chapel. But the sound is not allowed to die. Like a falling snowflake being billowed into the air as it touches earth, that tone, with a soft upswing of unisonal monks voices, is carried forward into the opening tones of the introit. Voices answering organ tone at first in quiet beginnings, gradually intensify the melody line, allowing the chant to ride on this fundamental rhythm as a feather might float on the waves of the sea ... This is my reason for being here. This, at least, I can understand. Many voices in perfect unison, breathing one melody, spreading in an ocean of sound without sharpness, to end again in silence. A fragility of black notes on white paper become a tender, awestricken chant of adoration. Stunning contrast of plainchant cantilena after the contrapuntal organ processional.

The student walks daily over to the local chateau, to give the son of the house, Jacques, a music lesson, and to practice as long as he will on Madame la Comtesse's piano. There comes a ghastly day when Jacques begs him to go to their farm, where the farmer's daughter, aged 10, is having what seems to be an epileptic fit. The parents are so stingy they grudge the towels asked to sponge her; they are furious when, dying, she wets the bed. Dead, their only concern is that the child wasn't baptized: if anyone knows, she will not get a Catholic burial. When the doctor comes he is furious; called too late, he can only sign the death certificate. The local people whisper against the young American, say it was he who caused the child's death—she had often had such seizures before and had come out of them. Later, he learns from a Latin-American doctor who comes to the monastery, that what the child really died of was congenital syphilis. It is a child's death to put beside the child's death in Camus's *The Plague,* and that other in Graham Greene's *The Heart of the Matter,* as one of the great pieces of contemporary virtuoso writing.

The young American finds chastity hard, but the cold and the boredom harder still. He is astounded that the monks know all his peccadilloes before the confesses them, that they never scold him or chase him out. Rather, the worse he behaves, the gentler and more understanding they become. Finally the cold wins: damp freezing mist penetrates his clothing. Enclosed in darkness and light rain, he goes into a coma for a week. The monks bring him to a fire, nurse him tenderly. When he recovers, everything is worse: the drunkenness, the lecherous excursions, the everlasting cold. But he begins to think, and thinking, as every dictator knows, and as Satan, the Waster of all virtue, the greatest dictator of them all, knows very well indeed, is dangerous. The young American contrasts what goes on "outside," where the devil rides, with the inside of the monastery.

On the outside there are things more valuable than truth: diplomacy, delicacy, and the outright denial of personal shortcomings. Man must be his own advocate, and totality of truth is a coward's device, a detestable and self-elevating repugnancy. Here there is nothing more destructive than the lie. It would be as faulty to tell a lie behind these walls as it would be to tell only the truth outside. For it is automatically presumed that truth is a naked and healthful cell; while in society it is automatically presumed that truth is merely the nucleus of the cell of politeness, a cell around which unlike personalities may revolve and mix.

In the world without, all of us must have certain acceptable desires. In the company of men we must first have a desire for women, indicating a fair amount either of real or of simulated success with them. In the company of women we must desire whatever it is that interests the woman—painting, architecture, some fascinatingly risqué joke—and possess a readiness to comply with hinted lechery.

We must have our ounce of piety and belong to some church, from the Catholic at the bottom, to the next high, the Baptist, and on up the ladder of Methodist and Presbyterian to the very stratosphere of the Episcopal. We must smile rather embarrassedly when we say, "Well, I've been made a deacon in my church—can you imagine that?" Or, "Junior's been appointed first acolyte. He has such a lovely manner, really, and he's so graceful at the altar. We're rather pleased."

We adapt ourselves, for there must be a constant modulation of character in accordance with the different planes of social strata. Our opinions must fluctuate in the company of Catholics, Jews, Negroes, and other inferior peoples. And in circles dominated by very advanced thinkers we must be able to express sincere and admirably balanced platitudes about segregation, birth control, premarital physical relations, and man's function in the cosmos. All very important topics. . . .

It's out there beyond the walls. And it's good and generous and beautiful—and a delusion of reality. For out there is the warmth of bellies and hearts, become glorious in the small frame of the unreal. And when we die, the moment we die, everyone says, "The community has suffered a great loss. He is irreplaceable." But who remembers our grandfather any more? We *have* to be replaceable and on the outside we always are, even with all the saliva we waste on the dead. Our success is measured by whether we were rich, civic-minded, generous, and by the number of children we so splendidly brought into the world by merely indulging our passion ...

And over and above, we are offered the freedom of choice. God, they say, gives us the freedom to choose. But this is a thing of the mind; these qualities of the outside are things of the mind. Can they legitimately be ugly, or even delusions? Can there be freedom of choice when the emotion, not the mind, has the thirsts? And aren't all these things tempered within us to a point where man lives his outside life with no need for consistency of ideal? Are not the smells of wet flesh, the comfort alternating with discomfort, the street sounds, the healthfulness of licentiousness to warm blood, the wonder of our miracle of livingness, enough? There's no freedom to choose until other knowledges insinuate themselves into the heart and the emotions, until other knowledges become other thirsts not to be denied. Then, and only then, can a choice be made.

Return to the inside, to our poor cloister and its world of the interior, its second portion of every man: the fog-filled interior known as man's health of soul. It too is a thing of the mind not yet ready to become a choice. Instead of riches we seek poverty, instead of the reeling insides we seek chastity, instead of sources of pride we seek sources of humility. But these aren't the end, as are wealth and success on the outside. They are the means to an end—the end being the destruction of all obstacles standing between us and the love of our life, which is God. ...

Two pictures, and a choice. The one which most of us know is brightly colored—brilliant, splashing—and satisfying to every cell of the human body. And over its hues death throws the shroud of an undetermined end. The other picture, the one within, is rather the color of the sun, white: the source of all colors before it is passed through the spectroscope and divided. It consumes the satisfaction of each cell of the body, so that the heat of many colors may become the Source of heat; burning the spirit into such a bliss as man may never know, but which, if we believe, is filtered through to us here on earth. It must not be contemplated lightly, for we shall never recover from it once it has seared us within. And the struggle is brief, for its fire becomes a process

193

inside: first a cleansing process, and then the curing of the intangible maladies of reserve and modesty, and with them the stinginess of our desire to remain individual unto ourselves . . .

The student goes to live outside, and gets involved, with one, two, three women, one good, one bad, one a peasant. It is too much, and he comes back with relief to the monastery. But he has realized it is not the women's flesh he is fleeing, but his own falseness. "Everything I do is counterfeit." The patient monks welcome him back.

This second part of the novel falls apart. There are too many, far too long, conversations between an elderly, lusting landlady, her son, and the "I" of the story. The villagers are almost all unrelievedly nasty, the "I" is the kind of innocent American hero who surely died (or should have!) somewhere between Henry James and *The Great Gatsby;* only the monastery remains real, a "very present help in trouble." Indeed, the whole novel is far too long, and the counterpoint between the landlady's son and "our hero" is never resolved: the son was pushed into a monastery at thirteen by his mother, and is now on his way out, and to marriage; the "hero" is on his way in. Somehow, it doesn't quite work, and the symbolism of the unnatural mother who wrongly drives one boy to the monastery by her love and the other by her lust, is unconvincing. Still and all, it is a powerful first novel.

In 1953, John Howard Griffin, now completely blind, living as a farmer in his native Texas, married. Three years later his second novel, *Nuni,* appeared. It is the story of a professor who survives a plane crash on a Pacific island, where he learns what innocence is, what experience is, and above all, what is civilization and what charity. It is an allegory, in the tradition of Samuel Butler's *Erewhon,* William Morris's *News from Nowhere,* Aldous Huxley's *Brave New World* and George Orwell's *1984.* Yet it is original in its resolution of the problem all these books pose: what to do about man. For, as Montaigne said,

"C'est toujours à l'homme qu'on a à faire." But in *Nuni* it is, surprisingly, the saintly savages who are, eventually, the least nice, and John Howard Griffin gives two cheers—not very loud ones and two, not three—for civilized, complicated man.

In 1957, after a series of operations, John Howard Griffin's sight was partially restored. He still has to wear very dark glasses at all times. On an assignment for the Negro magazine, *Sepia,* he went on November 1, 1959 to a dermatologist in New Orleans, who gave him medication to take orally, a medication used on victims of vitiligo, a disease that causes white spots to appear on the skin. For ten days he holed up at a friend's house without telling him what he was doing.

The doctor was sympathetic, but doubted the wisdom or the utility of John's project. Negroes, he said, had a destructive attitude to their own race. One minute they'd be friends, the next they'd be slashing each other with knives. As a young intern, many's the time he had been sent down to patch them up. Meanwhile, when not lying under a sun lamp, John was making friends with an elderly man who shined shoes for a living— a Negro, who had lost a leg in World War I. John intended to confide in him when he had crossed the great divide. By November 7th, John had a dark undercoating of pigment which he could touch up with stain. He shaved his head, as he had no curl, and looked at himself in the light. "A fierce, bald, very dark Negro glared at me from the glass. He in no way resembled me. The transformation was total and shocking." John had expected to see himself disguised, but this was no fancy dress. He was "imprisoned in the flesh of an utter stranger, an unsympathetic one," with whom he felt no kinship. His first contact with other Negroes, in the shower of a Negro hotel, initiated him into the civility of the despised toward each other, and into the bantering obscenity with which males habitually spoke to each other. He found the deliberate politeness everywhere, wary and resigned, as though the only way to reply to the unbelievable arrogance and bad manners of the whites was to be meticulously courteous to each other, both to affirm a superiority as civilized, rather than human, beings, and to try and deaden the hurt. He confided in his shoeshine friend, and never regretted it. He immediately started working with and for him. John's vignettes are unforgettable: the first meal, cooked in a gallon can on the sidewalk, of coon, turnips, and rice, brought in a milk carton. Across the street, a wino watching the feeding men: "Elevated in status by this man's misery ... we would feed our scraps to the poor." Many whites came to the shoeshine stand on that skid-row street in New Orleans. Many wanted John and his one-legged friend to find immoral pleasures for them—girls, gambling, "filthy pictures." These whites were much more friendly, so John learned to spot them. His one-legged black benefactor commented: "Oh yes, the whites are much more democratic in their sin than in their worship." John was terrified by the whites, insulted by the whites, and constantly consulted by whites, about Negro sex habits. He began to wonder if whites ever thought of Negroes except in terms of sexual performance.

But he was most shocked by racism among Catholics: a Negro Catholic church seemed a contradiction in terms, utterly monstrous and wrong. After a month of being a Negro, he went white again and developed a technique of "zigzagging back and forth. In my bag I kept a damp sponge, dyes, cleansing cream and Kleenex. It was hazardous, but it was the only way to traverse an area both as Negro and white. . . . I was the same man, whether white or black. Yet when I was white, I received the brotherly-love smiles from whites and the hate, stares or obsequiousness from the Negroes. And when I was a Negro, the whites judged me fit for the junk heap, and the Negroes treated me with great warmth."

More vignettes: the drunken one-man observer, trying to make up to the Negroes by drinking with them and buying their turkeys; cursing them when they would not grovel and be grateful. And the picayune racism of bus drivers; there is the bus driver who says, "Watch your step," to whites as they get out, but nothing to blacks. Until several white men and one old Negro lady get out together, and only she says "Thank you"—to the driver's fury. Once, when there was no room in the white section, a driver asked two Negroes to sit together so two white women could sit together. They did not budge. "She's welcome to sit here," said a Negro, pointing to the empty seat beside him and to one beside the woman across the aisle. The driver stopped the bus, walked to the rear, and told the Negroes: "They don't want to sit with you people, don't you know that? They don't want to, ain't that plain enough?" The Negroes did not react. If the women did not want to sit with them, then let one of the white men offer his seat and he could come and sit with the Negroes, thought John. A young white asked the driver: "Do you want me to slap these two jigaboos out of their seats?" But the driver demurred at "rough stuff." At Atlanta, the whites got off first. One held back, telling one of the Negroes, "Boy, I was on your side." By using the hated name of *boy,* he too, had revealed himself.

For John, it was the irony of it that hurt most. Here he was in the land of his forefathers—Georgia; the town of Griffin was named for one of them. The Governor, "no kin that I would care to discover," was also called Griffin and devoted himself energetically to keeping the Negroes in their place. Because of his success, because of this namesake, John Howard Griffin now badly needed a rest. He sought it in a monastery.

I arrived at the Trappist monastery with its two thousand acres of woods and farmlands and entered the courtyard as the monks were chanting Vespers. Their voices floated to me. A brown-robed Brother led me to a cell on the second floor and informed me supper would be at five.

The contrast was almost too great to be borne. It was a shock, like walking from the dismal swamps into sudden brilliant sunlight. Here all was peace, all silence except for the chanted prayers. Here men know nothing of hatred. They sought to make themselves conform ever more perfectly to God's will, whereas outside I had seen mostly men who sought to make God's will conform to their wretched prejudices. Here men sought their center in God, whereas outside they sought it in themselves. The difference was transforming.

We had supper at five—homemade bread, butter, milk, red beans, spinach and a peach. . . .

"Do Negroes often come here as guests, to spend a few days, Father?" I asked.

"Oh yes," he said. "Though I don't suppose many really know about this place."

"This is the Deep South," I said. "When you have Negro guests, do you have any trouble with your white guests?"

"No. No, the type of white man who would come to the Trappists —well, he comes here to be in an atmosphere of dedication to God. Such a man would hardly keep one eye on God and the other on the color of his neighbor's skin."

When John returned "home" he was hanged in effigy and the threats to life and limb were so troublesome he had to leave Texas. His aged parents were so harassed they moved to Mexico. But one thing had been permanently achieved. Both Negroes and whites had gained the certainty that because John had been a Negro for six weeks, he remained partly Negro or perhaps essentially Negro.

It is expedient, the Scriptures pointed out, that one man die for the people. John has not died for them yet, but he has been stripped and burned in effigy, and beaten with chains. And he goes right on.

John is not afraid of isolation. ". . . man is himself only when he is alone, completely alone. . . . Go it alone. It is the only hope. In the crowd there is nothing but comfort and mediocrity." Many Catholics take a dim view of John. He was asked to speak in Milwaukee, at a Sodality convention, then his speech was cancelled. The same thing happened to him at a Catholic University near Detroit.

198

John wrote *Black Like Me* in 1959. He warned of wrath to come:

> ... If some spark does set the keg afire, it will be a senseless tragedy of ignorant against ignorant, injustice answering injustice. We will all pay for not having cried for justice long ago.

Things are not exactly better in 1967.

Catholic racism is infinitely worse than any other, just as the mere suspicion—completely disproved—that Pope Pius XII was not sufficiently concerned at the German slaughter of Jews rouses everyone, however racist they themselves had been, however cowardly. For the least among Catholics is branded—yes, branded, for better, for worse, for richer, for poorer, with Christ's name. As John wrote:

> ... It is painful to see that your country does not practice what it preaches; it is infinitely more painful to see that your church does not.
>
> I learned the humiliating protocol. In areas where there was a Negro Catholic Church, it was made clear to me that I had better attend that one and no other. In areas where no such provision existed, I attended a "white" church. But I was instructed by other Negro Catholics. I was to sit to one side. If I wanted to receive Christ, I waited until the last white person had received him. Otherwise I would risk being passed at the altar rail.

On television recently (April 2, 1966) Negro wives of U.S. Army officers gently explained that while their husbands were overseas they had to find accommodation off the army reservations in the U.S. This they found very difficult. One airman's wife, being relocated, explained she and her husband—in his air force uniform—could not find a motel to take them in as they drove south: they had to spend the night in their station wagon and drive 100 miles before they could get breakfast anywhere. I remember when I worked in the British Embassy during the war, one of my colleagues was a lovely Indian girl, Sumita Devi, a great-niece of Rabindranath Tagore. She had been raised in Tagore's ashram, at Santeniketan, was gentle and very intelligent. When she wore her sari, everyone on the Washington buses was sweet to her and smiled; when she wore a coat and skirt, she was ordered to sit in the back. She complained each time this happened to the Ambassador, Lord Halifax, our boss. He told her to wear her sari. She refused. And was sacked.

John Howard Griffin has many sad tales to tell. Of the (Negro) Catholic priest whose sister Margaret had to leave the South for her studies because no Catholic hospital in the South would accept her for training. Of Negro Catholics who cannot attend retreats. This also happens in the North—for example, at Regina Laudis, the Benedictine nunnery in Bethlehem, Conn., the prioress' mother, who was in charge of the guest house, refused to accept a colored retreatant. A colored priest, Father August Thompson, explained to John Howard Griffin that he is not allowed to attend first communions, confirmations, or Cana conferences: he is, as he put it, "a second-class Christ."

John Howard Griffin lives on a farm, on a hillside, at the end of a road. He writes in a separate building, where he has a sink and a stove, a dark room for developing his photographs, a piano, and his work tools—desk, typewriter, etc. He needs, as he put it, "an infinite amount of uninterrupted time in front of him" to do his work, which has to come out of the framework of "the utter boredom of silence and solitude." He believes that not only the artist, but every individual, has a right to the maximum amount of freedom. As he told Dan Robertson in June, 1966: "We must see that all men truly have equal rights and then just leave everybody to hell alone." After the publication of *Black Like Me*, everyone was after John to explain his motives. And, as he puts it: "It was nobody's damned business what my motives were. I don't want my children becoming racists. And that's a good enough answer, even though it's not the real answer.... I do think it is a mistake to examine your motives too closely. If an act needs to be done and you do it from a neurotic motive, the effect of the act is still all right. The most damaging aphorism in history is 'Know Thyself.' The quicker you lose interest in yourself, the better you can function as a human being. You can examine yourself to a screeching halt."

John Howard Griffin is the most sensitive of friends. Jacques Maritain and Thomas Merton, to name but two, of different ages, are very close to him (Maritain is his second daughter's godfather), and John has done marvelous "photographic presentations" of them both. He is also an admirable journalist. His profiles of Francis Poulenc and of Arthur Lourie, the musicians, and of the Dominican Nobel Prize winner, Father Pire, are outstanding.

A good friend, a good companion, a good farmer, a good writer, a good musician, a good husband and father, a good photographer, a good Catholic, John Howard Griffin is a great American and one of this world's finest citizens.

Chapter XI

LECTURING at Yale on the Russian Revolution, Professor C. Driver described the Provisional Government, and explained that during its eight months of power, from March 12 to November 6, 1917, one man dominated the situation, the head of the Trudoviki (Labor) Party, first as Minister of Justice, later as Premier. Dr. Driver then stepped back and parted the curtains behind his desk. A man walked forward. "And here," Dr. Driver said, introducing the stranger to his students, "is that one man: Alexander Kerensky."

How many Americans realize that living here today is this one man who was the "absolute sole lord" of all the Russias, the real ruler of 170,000,000 human beings, of whom the *Saturday Evening Post* wrote in 1917 that "Never, in the history of the world before, has there been an elected representative of so many people"? This man, who for the Tsarist Secret Police was the most dangerous of all the Revolutionaries, who was jailed, and sentenced to exile in Siberia before being catapulted into power, now lives quietly in a brownstone house in the East Nineties in Manhattan.

I met him during my first month in New York, just after the end of World War II. Hélène Iswolsky, daughter of Imperial Russia's last Foreign Minister, was gathering Catholic, Orthodox, and Protestant friends together to form an ecumenical group called *The Third Hour*. This was named for that passage in the Acts when, hearing the first Christians talking in Pentecostal tongues, some members of the local synagogue claimed these men were drunk. Not so, others replied, for it is too early —only the third hour. It was early too, in 1946, to found an ecumenical society—almost twenty years earlier than any other such attempt here. It was a most intelligently organized religious group, meeting only when someone interesting was passing through town. Thus each year we heard the Reverend Michael Scott; thus we heard Father Voyaume, the founder of the Little Brothers of Jesus; thus we heard the young founders of Taizé, the French Protestant monastery that has now built an annex for the Orthodox. Alexander Kerensky was a founding member of *The Third Hour,* and I have known and venerated him now for over twenty years. He attended my son's wedding. He is a great hyphen, not only between Europe and the United States, where he has lived for so long, but also between Christianity and Communism, between generations, between cultures and between continents.

"I was never atheist," he told me. "To be a Menshevist or Bolshevist, one had to be atheist. For some time I was not communicant but never atheist." He is the author of many articles and books, the most important being *The Catastrophe, The Crucifixion of Liberty,* and his recent autobiography, *Russia and History's Turning Point.*

Today, over 85 years old, he is tall, handsome, upright, with a crew-cut stubble of white hair, very poor eyesight (he wears thick glasses), excellent hearing, and an old world courtesy. He kisses women's hands, European fashion, and still has his beautiful speaking voice, that was world famous. He has an astonishing memory, and plenty of humor. He does not look as if the description of him in the *Saturday Evening Post* for April 1917 can ever have been true. This told of his "pinched features, morbid and blotchy pallor," and said he walked with "short, nervous steps." Kerensky is scholarly, shy, a delicate and attentive host, a discreet and self-effacing guest.

Alexander Kerensky was born in 1881 on the Middle Volga, at Simbirsk, now called Ulyanovsk, after Vladimir Ilich Ulyanov (Lenin) born there eleven years before Kerensky, in 1870. Kerensky only saw Lenin once when Lenin was walking with Kerensky's mother. Kerensky's father was principal of the High School at Simbirsk to which both Lenin and his brother went. Kerensky's uncle, a priest, heard Lenin's first confession. In the Orthodox Church, babies receive communion as soon as baptized; first confession comes much later. Lenin had already lost his faith two years before his brother was executed for supposedly preparing an attempt on the life of the Czar. After the execution, Kerensky's father tried to help Lenin's mother.

Kerensky's father, while a seminarian, had decided to give up the Church as a career, leaving it to his brother. Instead, he entered the University of Kazan, where he got both a degree and a wife. She had been one of his pupils, the daughter of an officer. Her grandfather had been a serf who had bought his liberty and became a merchant. Kerensky and his brother sometimes visited his uncle, his father's brother, who had become a priest in his brother's stead. Kerensky told me he noticed, even as a very small child, the contrast between his rather comfortable home and his uncle's more straitened circumstances. But the uncle had an orchard, and the nephews much appreciated that.

Kerensky's mother read to her boys each evening, from pious storybooks or from the Gospels. Their Nanny, herself illiterate (she had been a serf), would scold Alexander when he beat up his brother: Jesus Christ would not like him to behave so, she told him. Once, on a walk, they met a dismal procession of convicts en route to Siberia, dirty, hairy, smelly, clanking their chains. The two little boys were scared. Nanny told them they must not be frightened, and gave the boys money from her own pocket to buy bread for the prisoners. "To give to them is to give to Jesus Christ himself," Nanny told them.

When Alexander was eight, his family moved to Tashkent,

where his father had been appointed head of the whole educational system of Russian Turkestan. He was subsequently ennobled for his services, being made *Dvorianstvo,* an honorific something like a British knight, but hereditary, for it appeared not only on Alexander's father's passport, but on his own. Kerensky remained for ten years in Tashkent. He remembers, at the age of eleven, experiencing his first moment of political consciousness. It was when, in an "open letter" to the newspaper, Tolstoy had protested the Franco-Russian alliance in 1892. Alexander Kerensky sneaked into the dining room to listen to his parents discussing Tolstoy's stand.

In 1897 Kerensky went up to the University of St. Petersburg. After one year there in the Faculty of Arts he changed to that of Law, and graduated in the spring of 1904. He remembers, as a moving experience, how once on his way home after a night of gaiety, in the gray of an early spring morning, he saw the (then) young Czar Nicholas, alone, looking out of a high window, brooding over his city in the cold dawn.

Soon after he became a lawyer, Alexander Kerensky's political activity began in earnest. His first briefs were in defense of people accused of political crimes following upon the 1905 uprising, and he was kept busy. In 1906 alone, 1,444 people were hanged for alleged participation. Kerensky was at that time also editing a surreptitious political newspaper. The police managed to get hold of the ninth issue to which he had contributed a particularly outspoken article. It was just before Christmas. Kerensky was at home decorating the Christmas tree with his wife, when the police came. They behaved "correctly," taking care not to wake the Kerenskys' eight-month-old son. While Mrs. Kerensky gave the police tea, Alexander packed a toothbrush, soap, and towel. Then he was taken off in a dingy cab to the Kresty jail. Here, in a cell six paces long and three wide, Kerensky was kept two weeks without being told the reason for his arrest. Legally, he could not be detained longer without explanation of the charge. So he wrote to the assistant prosecutor of the St. Petersburg District Court and warned him he would go on a hunger strike unless he was told within five days what the charges were against him. After five days had passed and he had heard nothing, he began his strike. At first the smell of food was agony, and, plagued by thirst, he sometimes sipped a little water. By the fourth day he had become semi-conscious. On the eighth, he was taken to the prosecutor and told the charge against him. But by then he could not hear it, for he had fainted. He was put under the care of the prison doctor, and so recovered. He has remembered those eight days ever after with the greatest pleasure. Fasting brought him to a state he had never reached before, nor has since regained, an "almost blissful" state. The four months' imprisonment that followed were very fruitful, as he writes: "They broadened my views and contributed to my understanding of what was going on." When he left jail he was no longer a romantic: "I knew that Russia would never achieve genuine democracy unless her people consciously strove for unity in pursuit of the common goal." Early in 1906, the electoral campaign for the first Duma was in full swing. The political prisoners, among them Kerensky, were "kept abreast of all developments" by prison officials favorable to their cause. When the newly-elected Duma members walked from the Tauride Palace to the reception given for them by the Czar in the Winter Palace, they had to walk past the tiny Kresty prison windows. The prisoners shouted and waved and cried out for an amnesty, which was not granted. Indeed, the Czar's intransigence made the first Duma "of popular wrath" unacceptable to him. He dissolved it July 8, 1906. Kerensky was eventually released but forbidden to live in St. Petersburg, Moscow, and other big cities. However, he was able to meet the director of the Police Department, who agreed to rescind the decree of exile, if Kerensky would agree to make himself scarce for a while. So with his wife and small son, he departed by train for a long stay with his father in Tashkent. In August 1906 Kerensky returned from Tashkent to St. Petersburg. He sat about waiting for briefs, like any other young lawyer. Then, one day, at the end of October 1906, he was offered the defense of some peasants in Estonia who had sacked an estate. Many had been flogged and shot, and a random selection from the village had been brought to trial. Kerensky accepted the brief, took a midnight train to Reval, and there met I. I. Poska, the defense attorney, future president of the Estonian republic. Kerensky got his peasants off, and no one would believe it was his first case. "This," he wrote, "was my debut as a lawyer and political speaker. Without false modesty I can say that my effectiveness as a public speaker was generally recognized. I may add that I never wrote my speeches down or rehearsed them."

After Kerensky's success in Reval, he had more cases than he could handle, and traveled all around Russia defending political prisoners. As a result of the 1905 revolts, district military courts had been set up where the defendants had no judicial guarantees of their right. Many of the military judges of these special courts were sadists, such as General Koshelev who studied pornographic photographs in court, and selected at random fifteen of the defendants to be hanged in retaliation for fifteen dragoons killed during the Tukum uprising.

In 1907 Leo Tolstoy and Leonid Andreyev were collecting thousands of signatures on a petition for the abolition of the death penalty. Kerensky not only signed it, but was deeply moved by it. Almost exactly ten years later, when he was Minister of Justice, he abolished the death penalty. In 1912 he defended the Armenian Dashnaksutyun Party, and was successful in proving that much of the evidence against the accused was false, and that the examining magistrate was guilty of perjury. Of the 146 defendants, 95 were acquitted. In April of the same year, the Lena Goldfields massacre of 200 workers occurred. These men, shot down unarmed, had merely wished to present a petition to the managers, complaining of bad meat in their rations. Kerensky was appointed to the commission to investigate the case. Here is his own description of his journey to the interior:

> We travelled by train, by troika, by steamboat and by a kind of gondola. The beauty that surrounded us on the Lena defies description. We saw houses on one bank and virgin woods on the other. At sunrise whole families of bears would come down to the river to drink.

The Governor of East Siberia, and the Governor of Irkutsk both helped young Kerensky. Kerensky told me that when he told this recently to a young student from the U.S.S.R., the youth would not believe that "in those days" it had been possible for such an impartial inquiry to have taken place. Kerensky wrote the commission's report. As a result of the inquiry, the Lena Goldfields Company monopoly was abolished and wages were increased. Now Kerensky was fast becoming a public figure, *malgré lui*. "My only desire . . . had been to serve my country," he writes. He was elected in 1912 to the Fourth Duma as a member of the Trudoviki (Labor) Party for Saratov Province, and quickly became head of that party. Soon after his election to the Fourth Duma he became a Free Mason. He was dogged night and day by the police, who placed him under "unflagging open observation." Always, he assured me, he was animated by two fundamental ideals: that of individual justice and that of transforming the State into a supra-national political power. He accepted neither the *laissez-faire* doctrine of the Manchester school, nor the Marxist view that the State is the weapon of the dominant class. He wanted, and he worked toward, something more like the Welfare state, "like Fabian concept of state," as he described it to me. He sublet one of the rooms of his apartment, but could never keep a tenant for long, as he could not afford to keep the apartment warm.

The years from 1912 to 1914 were years of strenuous revolutionary organization. From 1915 on, though dogged still by the *Obrana* (the secret police), Kerensky, as a member of the

Duma, enjoined immunity from political arrest, and was able to travel freely. However, since he was very poor, this condition gravely limited his capacity to travel.

He was, by all accounts, one of the greatest orators of all time, in the Demosthenes and Mirabeau class. He spoke not only superbly, but in beautiful Russian, a rare accomplishment even for an educated Russian, and much admired even by his political opponents. Kerensky spoke *extempore*, the sweat pouring down his pale face. He told me he never prepared a speech, never made notes.

His eloquence was much feared. The Empress wrote in her diary in February, 1917, that she hoped Kerensky "will be hanged for his dreadful speeches." Yet five months later the Czar wrote: "This man (Kerensky) is certainly in his right place at the present moment. The more power he gets the better it will be."

In 1915 he intervened in the Duma to obtain the release of 1,300 Poles. Still several thousand others were sent to hard labor in Siberia, including children aged twelve. About this time, Kerensky fell gravely ill and was for seven months in the hospital in Finland, where he had a serious operation. He returned to find conditions in Petrograd absolutely appalling. Aleksandr Protopopov had been made Minister of the Interior; Rasputin was at the height of his powers. The war was going badly. By the Czar's Ukase the Duma had been suspended. Its president, Rodzianko, telegraphed to the Czar that "the last bulwark of order has been eliminated." Then the sailors' mutiny occurred at the Kronstadt naval base on February 27, 1917. By the night of March 1, the revolutionaries in Petrograd had unanimously decided that, in the future, the state would be ruled by a constituent assembly. "Thus the monarchy was discarded forever," Kerensky wrote. On Monday, March 2, the Duma was dissolved at 6 A.M. after a stormy all-night sitting, but refused to disperse. Kerensky was awakened at 8 A.M. with the news that the Volynsky regiment had mutinied. He later told me that he reached the Duma in five minutes. During the next four days, no one ate or slept. "We were in a dream, a terrible and beautiful dream," Kerensky said. He told a friend to get to the Volynsky barracks and direct the men to the Duma. As they marched, other regiments joined them. The prisons were opened, the prisoners freed. At 11 A.M. Kerensky asked for all four Dumas to be summoned, but Milyukov, the Liberal professor who was head of the Progressive bloc, refused. Kerensky—since by now 80,000 people were on their way to the Duma—insisted that control must be maintained by the Duma: Was the Duma head of the revolutionary movement, or was it not? What should he tell the 80,000 people when they arrived? As he was given no answer, a "Provisional committee" was set up, and from that moment Kerensky was in charge. As he has written: "The door closed. I threw off my overcoat. There was no more day or night, morning or evening. Only by the ebb and flow of the crowds, by the coming and going of the human tides, could we feel that night had come or day returned. . . .We did not feel the need of food or sleep. We had suddenly become endowed with extraordinary mental clarity. We were able to grasp and understand everything in a flash . . . Afterwards, looking back . . . one could scarcely believe that all this chaos of happenings had been crowded into four days." (*The Catastrophe:* D. Appleton & Co., 1927, p. 3)

It was Kerensky who saved the loathed Minister of Justice from lynching, declaring that "the Imperial Duma does not shed blood." Twenty-four hours later, he saved (temporarily) the detested Protopopov from the crowd, by physically dragging him to safety, shouting, "Don't touch that man!" Kerensky was elected Vice-President of the Soviet, and Minister of Justice of the Provisional Government, the only man to be a member of the Executive of both bodies.

Maurice Paléologue, the French Ambassador to Russia, has given an interesting description of Kerensky as he appeared then. "One man alone among the members of the Provisional

Government appeared to be a man of action, with his bristling hair, wax complexion and half closed eyes through which he darted sharp and uneasy glances. He struck me all the more because he kept apart." However, Sukharov, a political opponent, gave another view. At a moment when there were accidental shots fired outside their window, Kerensky leapt up and shouted out to the crowd: "I, Kerensky, was speaking to you! Kerensky is speaking to you." Sukharov suggested that such words created a worse panic than the shots, but Kerensky "burst into a rage." "I demand," he shouted, "that everyone do his duty and not interfere when I give orders!" "Absolutely right," Sukharov heard someone remark approvingly. For indeed there was already a clear split between the Soviet and the Provisional Government. But Kerensky went into the Executive Committee, climbed on to a table, declared he was appearing before the Soviet as Minister of Justice in the Provisional Government and asked for a vote of confidence. He got it. But "in the midst of the ovations accorded me by the Soviet members, . . . I had already observed the faces of the angry leaders, foreboding vengeance. The fight had begun, the battle against me, against my influence, and my authority with the masses." As an example of his radical differences with Lenin, the latter declared that the first act of the Bolsheviks would be to arrest 50 to 100 capitalists and hang them. Kerensky's reply was: "You Bolsheviks recommend childish prescriptions. Arrest, kill, destroy. What are we—Socialists, or police of the old regime?"

Kerensky has said that it sometimes seems to him that the word "revolution" is not applicable to what happened to Russia at the beginning of March, 1917. "A whole world of national and political relationships simply sank to the bottom," he wrote. As Minister of Justice, Kerensky abolished the death penalty, and proclaimed unrestricted freedom of the press and of speech. "The Russian Revolution will astound the world by its magnanimity," he declared. Six months later he suppressed the Leninist papers, and suspended the right of public meeting;

before his fall he had reintroduced the death penalty. Certainly the six months of the Provisional Government can be divided into two periods: the first, bourgeois period when Prince Lvov was Prime Minister and the second, or socialist period, under Kerensky's premiership. Then double pressure, of the Germans at the Front and the Bolsheviks at the center, led to the triumph of what, for Kerensky, was the Bolshevik counter-revolution. Certainly it led to the War between the U.S.S.R. and the West, which began in 1917 and has never ceased. Hot first under Koltchak and Deniken, suspended between the German invasion of the U.S.S.R. and Yalta, then beginning again, cold at first, then warm, to hot in Vietnam. This war already stretches across forty years of the twentieth century.

As Kerensky notes, the French Revolution came before the Revolutionary and Napoleonic wars; the German Republic arose only after the German defeat. "Russian only revolution begun during World War," Kerensky told me. "At its most acute and critical moment, my first problem, continuation of war." All the time Kerensky was in the Government, the struggle against the Bolsheviks was for him part of the struggle against Germany. Indeed, Lenin came from Germany in a sealed train, and it was impossible, since the guards and customs officials had not yet been restored, to have prevented his entry into Russia on April 3, 1917. In return, Lenin considered Kerensky most dangerous: "Be wary of Kerensky above all," he wrote from Switzerland to friends in Stockholm, and pointed out that Kerensky was heading the "imperial war." "With Kerensky's help the government is duping the workers by pretending that the imperialist war is a defensive one," Lenin wrote in 1917. In fact, this was the central point of difference: should the new, revolutionary Russia continue the war with Germany, or not? For Kerensky, who became minister of war in May, 1917, and served as prime minister from July to November of the same year, the offensive against Germany and the continuation of the war were necessary for Russia's salvation. For him the war, too, was a great personal adventure, and he set off for the Front in a simple soldier's tunic in order to raise morale. His appeal to the millions of war-weary soldiers after three years of bitter suffering was: "I summon you, not to festivity, but to death; to sacrifice yourselves to save your country." Lenin's words were, "We appeal to you not to die, but to destroy—to destroy your class enemies." Kerensky went to the Southwestern Front, to Ternopol, Odessa, Sevastopol, then to the Northern Front. Near Dvina a puny peasant lad was pushed forward by his fellows, who urged him to speak. The General in command told Kerensky this boy was a Bolshevik agitator. The young soldier asked Kerensky: "You tell us we must fight the Germans so the peasants can have the land. But what's the use of land to peasants when they are dead? What good will this new freedom be to dead men?" "Comrade," Kerensky began, but the soldier interrupted: "What's the use of talking? Make peace quickly, that's all." "Silence when the Minister is talking!" shouted the Colonel. Kerensky ignored the soldier's question, and said to the Colonel: "Take this man and tomorrow issue orders saying he has been flung out of the ranks of the Russian Army. He is a coward. He is unworthy to defend the soil of Russia. Let him go home to his village and tell his fellow villagers we don't need cowards in the Russian Army." Kerensky repeated the word "coward," spitting it in the young soldier's face. The man fainted at his feet. Some days later, the Colonel asked Kerensky for permission to rescind his order, as the soldier had reformed, and was now a paragon of discipline. "Made very good soldier," Kerensky commented.

As a young man Kerensky had seen the harm done to the Russian Church by Dostoevsky's reactionary friend, Constantin Pobyedonostsev, who dominated the Church from 1881 to 1904. In 1905, a conclave of the Orthodox Church was organized, but was stopped by Rasputin. Kerensky's cousin, son of his priest uncle, had been very interested in the question of reunion between Old Catholic, Anglicans, and Orthodox. During his months in power, Kerensky called for a General Council of the Orthodox Church. "I play Emperor Constantine," Kerensky explained to me. This conclave elected as its head the Patriarch Tikhon—"certainly martyr, probably saint," as Kerensky called him. "The Church in Russia was never political," he said. "During Provisional Government never question of persecuting church. Even Genghis Khan never persecute church. Political dictatorship before Boshevists never touch souls of people."

Kerensky is convinced that Lenin received German funds to take Russia out of the war even before he came to power. He quotes the German Minister of Foreign Affairs, Baron von Kuhlmann, who in a telegram of December 3, 1917 to the Kaiser stated that: "It was not until the Bolsheviks had received from us a steady flow of funds through various channels and under varying labels that they were in a position to be able to build up their main organ, *Pravda* . . . the Bolsheviks have now come into power." Unfortunately, the archives of the German War Ministry and of the Intelligence Department of the German General Staff were destroyed by fire.

Kerensky has described at length the sad *dégringolade* of the Provisional Government. It was betrayed from the right by General Kornilov's revolt, in which Kerensky implicates the British Ambassador, saying that Kornilov was provided by the British with armored cars. From the left, the Bolsheviks attacked the Provisional Government and, though Kerensky was early aware of this danger, he was not able to persuade his colleagues to order the arrest of Lenin, Zinoviev, Parvus (a German working with the Soviets) Alexandra Kollontai, and others, until it was too late. By then Lenin and Zinoviev had already gone into hiding in a haystack and thence they fled to Finland.

Soon it was Kerensky's own turn to flee. On October 25— old style—the Bolsheviks attacked the Winter Palace. They took the cruiser *Aurora* up the Neva and bombarded the palace, simultaneously invading from the square. The palace was defended by young cadets and by a women's force. Kerensky had left for the front, to try to persuade Krasnow and the loyal troops to help him. He failed, and returned to find most of the military cadets shot and many civilians drowned. Kerensky escaped from Petrograd in a sailor's cloak, a sailor's hat and dark glasses. "The cloak is too short. The hat is too smll. But there is nothing to be done," he wrote. Kerensky escaped in a cab, while his loyal chauffeur drove his car as though in pursuit in the opposite direction. In a deep wood, near a peasant cottage, Kerensky hid in the thick undergrowth. There he lived for forty days and grew a beard and a moustache "to get a natural effect." He also wore the dark glasses. In early December he went by sled to the estate of Z. Belenky, a timber merchant near Novgorod. On January 5, 1918, the Constituent Assembly was to open, and Kerensky wished to appear and to "account for his activities to the people." But in the early morning hour of January 6, the Constituent Assembly was dispersed by force, the doors of the Tauride Palace locked, and the crowds assembled to acclaim the Assembly were scattered by gunfire. Kerensky escaped to Finland, to the estate of a Swedish Finn, who let him live on a corner of his estate. But soon he told Kerensky, "We have invited the Germans here, and when they come, this will be headquarters against the Russians." So Kerensky started on the move again.

First he returned to Petrograd, living at the apartment of a woman doctor. Then he went on to Moscow. But there he realized there was nothing more he could do. From R. Bruce Lockhart he obtained a British visa (Lockhart gave it to him on his own authority, in the absence of his ambassador, "because the visa application would have been rejected by the Foreign Office"). Disguised as a Serbian captain, Kerensky got to Murmansk, and there boarded first a French, then an English boat, in which he reached Thurso, in the Orkneys. It was the first time he had ever stepped on non-Russian soil. He took a train to London, and so began his long exile.

"And then?" I asked.

"I continue to do my duty of telling truth," he said.

Neither Philip Kerr (later Lord Lothian) who took him to see Lloyd George, then Prime Minister, nor Lord Milner, then Minister of War, nor any of the French whom he saw on a visit to Paris on July 10—Paul Painlevé, Georges Mandel, and Georges Clemenceau—were helpful. Clemenceau's line was that Russia was now a neutral country which had made a separate peace with France's enemies, and "the friends of our enemies are our enemies." Kerensky returned dejectedly to England.

Later he came to the United States where he has given of his time and intelligence in arranging the documents of the Russian Revolution at Stanford, and conducting a symposium there. He thinks Yalta in 1945 was a turning point as vital as 1917, and that the Bandung Conference in 1955 "may be said to mark the end of white hegemony." Above all, he thinks that, as Tolstoy put it, to overcome himself, "man must be transfigured."

Gentle, lively and witty, with a clear mind and a Christian heart, Kerensky at eighty-five provides living proof that even a politician can demonstrate in his own life the possibility of that transfiguration so necessary to every man. How admirably he has repaid America's hospitality—a grateful guest who has become a great asset.

And so, having traveled around the world to make my salaams to ten people, I came back to my beloved third floor New York railroad flat. I had resolved, for myself at least, the problem of places vs. people. People are infinitely more important, and places are, indeed, only important as a contributing factor to people's development. Sinai is holy because of Moses, Molokai because of Damien, not vice versa. People are much more important than anything they have made, including ideas, but *not* including other people! The old question, whether one would bomb Chartres to save a blind moron child is not a question at all.

And traveling has taught me, not the truth of any of the platitudes it has inspired, such as: "people are the same everywhere"; "a rolling stone gathers no moss, but sometimes gains polish"; "travel broadens the mind," etc., but the immense importance of the receiving, and if possible, the giving, of pleasure, delight, joy—in short, happiness. I found the company of hyphen people an enchantment, and I know of no pleasure so great as what it is now fashionable to call the "dialogue," but what in my outmoded way I prefer to call conversation. For the best conversation, here below, is already in heaven. Is heaven.

Chapter XII

IN Manhattan, citiest of all cities, Babylon hung with harps—Brooklyn Bridge, George Washington Bridge, Verrazano Narrows Bridge—is the only woman hyphen I know, who is as American as a malted.

The average American woman is an astonishing creature. She is far more sure of herself, far more reconciled to her female condition than the European woman because she knows her own value from childhood up. In Europe, "better luck next time" is peasant and peer's reaction when told his wife has presented him with a daughter. In Europe, a girl is educated only if and when her brother's education has been "taken care of," and no European parent spends as much upon a daughter as a son, whereas here a girl's education costs more. This makes the average American woman feel sure she is loved for herself alone, sure that no previous or subsequent brother will subtract from her value, or future husband enhance it. Two-thirds of American women are married and consider sex an enjoyable experience. Indeed, not to enjoy one's sex life is considered as queer as to prefer its deviations. And when marriage doesn't work, American women are, on the whole, less mean and bitter, and less broken by their failure, than the women of Europe, or of Asia (except China). Not that the American woman has greater inner resources of religion or philosophy—she has not. But she has greater objectivity, greater elasticity and more hope for a second chance. An American woman has to be simultaneously her husband's companion, housekeeper, often his business partner, his mistress and his hostess, as well as their children's nanny, chauffeur, and cook.

A European or an Asian or a Latin American man, whatever his means, can, and often does, keep several separate women for these various purposes. The average American expects his wife to be all women to him—while she lasts—which is one reason for the frequent turn-over in wives. An American often has three or four wives in succession. But much more rarely than men of other continents does he have a four-in-hand, all at once.

Dorothy Day is an All-American Woman, the most unicountried of my ten characters. She is a goddess of the hearth, if there still is an American hearth. And she is as perfectly average as she is absolutely singular.

In an admirable *New Yorker* profile on Dorothy Day, Dwight Macdonald had someone down at the *Catholic Worker* ask her "please to pass the butter." Submitting his article to Dorothy before publishing it, Dwight was firmly told there was one change he must make. "Pass the margarine" must be substituted. "The *Catholic Worker* never serves butter."

Dorothy Day, founder (with Peter Maurin, the French peasant philosopher) of the *Catholic Worker,* is a controversial figure, but a much beloved one. When I first became a Catholic, Monsignor de Menasce, the Alexandrian Jew who had received me into the Church, told me: "Go down to Dorothy Day at the *Catholic Worker* and tell her I sent you. See if she can give you anything to do." Obediently I took a subway downtown and arrived at Mott Street. A pleasant old-looking house with a sort of office-like entrance room. "Is Miss Day in?" I asked. "Dorothy's not here, is she?" the girl to whom I spoke yelled behind her. A boy came out and said, "She's off on a bus giving a lecture tour. Back sometime next week." I looked around. When I came back the next week I determined to ask to be allowed to scrub the very dirty floor. Good penance, I thought. A tough job, and one that really needed doing. But when I met Dorothy, she dismissed the idea instantly. "You'd be in everyone's way," she said, with truth, "and the bread line is about one thousand a day, tracking mud and dirt in from the street. Just a waste of time and soap." I was horrified. Raised in a (to me) sound Protestant belief that cleanliness was next to Godliness, and that to be dirty was to be wicked, I found Mott Street smelly and distasteful in the extreme. But I couldn't help loving Dorothy from the moment I saw her. She is like the great Greek statue of Demeter, the earth mother, in the British Museum, except that Demeter has no arms and Dorothy's are very strong and forceful. She looks like good homebaked bread and feels and smells and *is* like good homebaked bread. She is shapeless, heavy, wrinkled, yet has excellent bones to her face, lovely white hair, and a low, hesitant, gentle, very feminine voice and manner, clear blue eyes, and a glorious sense of humor. She attracts the most diverse people. Evelyn Waugh, about to be taken down to see her by Clare Luce with whom he was staying, telephoned to ask me whether Clare's large limousine should draw up at the door. "Better go by subway," I suggested. Later, when asked by Virgilia Petersen to appear on her television program, *Author Meets the Critic*, he said: "If I do, will you give me $100 for Dorothy Day?" "We don't pay authors," Virgilia replied. "They get the publicity for sole reward." "You get paid, don't you?" Evelyn asked Virgilia. "It's the way I earn my living," she replied. "Couldn't you do something more useful?" Evelyn asked her. "Great shortage of domestic staff in this country, isn't there?" "I do housework, and cooking," Virgilia replied, "but am paid for neither." "Well, if you won't give me any money for Dorothy Day," Evelyn said, "I won't appear on your program." And he did not. Summoned by her landlord to pay five hundred dollars for violations on her building, Dorothy was standing in court before the judge when Wystan Auden appeared and shoved an envelope into her hand. "Here's two-fifty," he murmured. She thanked him warmly, thinking he was offering her $2.50. It was, of course, $250.

Dorothy Day's life divides into two. For twenty-five years she felt that "sense of insecurity one hears so much about these days." Then, five years after she became a Catholic, she met Peter Maurin, and he was "my master and I was his disciple." He gave her a "way of life and instruction" which grew into the Catholic Worker Movement.

She came of sound stock. Her father was from Cleveland, Tennessee, and his father had been a surgeon who served in the Confederate army. Her mother was from Marlboro, New York, and her father, a chairmaker, had fought on the Northern side, coming home with TB of the larynx. Her mother's mother had married at fourteen, and bore eighteen children, of whom only six lived.

Dorothy was born on November 8, 1897. She had two older brothers and a younger sister. Her parents had a maid, Mary, who was Catholic, and once took Dorothy to Mass. But little Dorothy stood up on the pew, staring around her, and Mary was so embarrassed she never took her again. Dorothy and her family first lived in Brooklyn, where she started school.

She had a happy childhood, playing on the beach, fishing for eels in a creek, and playing house in an abandoned shack in a swamp. When she was six, her family moved to California, first to Berkeley, then to Oakland. Her father was a newspaperman: in New York he had worked nights on a morning paper; in San Francisco he lost his job after the earthquake, as the printing plant went up in flames. He was sports editor, and kept a horse at a stable near their bungalow. The night before the earthquake, the horses in the stable were restless. The earthquake the next morning lasted two minutes and twenty seconds. There was a deep rumbling, and the "earth became a sea which rocked our house." Dorothy's mother fainted, and her father, having got all the children safely out of the front door, carried his wife back to bed. Their house was damaged—chimneys fallen, the walls cracked from roof to ground. Luckily there was no fire in Oakland. But across the bay the great flames could be seen, and for days the refugees poured over and camped on the racetrack. Dorothy remembers best the "joy of doing good, of sharing whatever they had with others," for all the neighbors joined in serving the homeless. After the earthquake, Dorothy's family moved to Chicago. In Chicago they lived in a dingy, six-room apartment, and had no servant. They lived near a breakwater along the lake, where Dorothy remembers a brother and sister drowned in each other's arms.

Dorothy had begun, at eight, to be pious. She believed, but did not know in what she believed. She sang hymns and prayed, and went to Sunday School and church with a Methodist family next door, because none of her own family went to church. She was already afraid of God, of death, and of eternity. She longed to be a saint, and began to enjoy the housework she did to help her mother, who had been weakened by a series of miscarriages. One day, coming upon a neighbor on her knees, Dorothy "felt a feeling of gratitude and happiness" that warmed her heart. After that, she would plague her little sister by saying long prayers, and soon the two children practiced being saints, as a game.

Dorothy's father was a remote figure, as he worked at night and slept in the morning. She never really knew him until after she had graduated from high school at sixteen. She now went to the Episcopal Church, and when her family moved to the North Side, it was in this denomination that she was baptized and confirmed. Her family was poor no longer, as her father had found a good job as a sports editor, and they now had a cozy house with fireplaces and rooms for all. When Dorothy was fourteen there was a new baby, and also a first love: a musician to whom she never spoke. But how she hungered for his look! He led the park band, and Dorothy and her sister never missed a concert that summer. It seemed to her that her two loves, for her baby brother and for her musician, fused. Her heart, first awakening, loved equally a grown man and a baby boy. She describes enchantingly the baby in his crib discovering his toes, discovering the brass corner knob on his crib, and the singsong creaking of the spring and the peeping of the birds that he imitated, the jingle of the milkman's horse's harness and the metallic sound of bottles being deposited. Dorothy rose at four to feed the baby, then did her homework: Latin and Greek, which she loved; history, which bored her. At this stage she wrote long priggish letters to her school friend Henrietta, a butter-pat with blond curly hair and blue eyes, a frankly sensual girl. Dorothy, at fifteen, would write of "sensual love and the thrill that comes from the meeting of lips," but pronounced it wrong to think so much about mere human love. It was when she was fifteen, too, that she began to be aware of the labor movement. Her brother got a job on a Scripps-Howard paper that discussed working class conditions. Carl Sandburg wrote for this paper and Dorothy learned from it about Eugene Debs and the Industrial Workers of the World (the IWW, better known as the Wobblies). Dorothy at this time was reading Jack London, Upton Sinclair, and Frank Harris. Her first story, written in high school, was about a Russian revolutionary's martyrdom. After she went up to the University of Illinois on a scholarship, she joined the Socialist party. She was delighted to leave home. Her father's paper had folded, and now she was "on her own, no longer to be cared for by the family." The idea of earning her own living, by her own efforts, appealed far more to her than the idea of an education. How she worked! Dorothy was seventeen. For her board, she worked afternoons and evenings for a Methodist professor of languages, and took on extra jobs washing and ironing clothes and baby sitting. She read everything she could lay hands on by Dostoevski, Gorki, Tolstoi. Soon she moved, in order to gain more time to read and write, to the home of an instructor with five children. Her bare room had no carpet, only a bed, a table, a chair, and a little stove on which Dorothy cooked. She spent only forty cents a day on food: this she earned washing clothes at twenty cents an hour. Dorothy began writing as well as reading. She wrote at space rates for a local Urbana paper. When she criticized the existing order, her columns were not published; when she criticized the students' working conditions she was published, but her writings led to her being refused jobs by the Y, which controlled the employment bureau. Sometimes Dorothy was hungry, always she was cold, even in bed. And she was carrying her full University work load as well. Dorothy's mother sympathized. She had worked in a shirt factory as a girl, and had suffered from working ten hours a day for several years.

In 1916 Dorothy's family moved east to New York, where her father got a job on the *Morning Telegraph*. She decided to move with them, and got a job on *The Call*, a Socialist daily. The first thing she noticed about New York was the smell of poverty, a smell that has never ceased to affront her. A damp ooze coming from the very walls of tenements permeates everything, even clothes, and is a sepulchral stink. She found, however, that however poor she was in New York, she could live cheaply and well: a quick meal of roasted sweet chestnuts and a piece of fruit or a good bean soup and bread and butter with it, in those blissful days, cost but ten cents. And as a reporter she had no fares to pay. She covered protests: those against the conscription act of 1917, as well as streetcorner meetings and appeals. There were also plenty of strikes: transportation strikes, garment factory strikes, strikes in smelting factories. And there were food riots too. She met Trotsky, but did not become his follower, preferring to join the IWW, as being more indigenously American, more grass-rootsly concerned with poverty. She was at the great meeting at Madison Square Garden, on March 21, 1917, to celebrate the beginning of the Russian Revolution. I was at the similar celebration at the Albert Hall in London, and like Dorothy, can never forget the enormous sense of a new beginning: of one sixth of the world dismissing the bigoted rulers who jailed students simply because they were students, and condemned such men as Dostoevski to be shot, and by their pogroms showed Hitler what to do and how to do it. When her job on *The Call* folded, Dorothy joined the staff of *The Masses*. After *The Masses* was suppressed, she went again to Washington, to picket the White House as a suffragist. Her description of the thirty days she had to spend in jail for picketing is as graphic today as when she wrote it.

Our spokeswoman got up and began to announce that we were all going on hunger strike unless our demands were met, but before she could get the first words out of her mouth, Whittaker, the matron, had turned to the door and beckoned. Immediately the room was filled with men. There were two guards to every woman, and each of us was seized roughly by the arms and dragged out of the room. It seems impossible to believe, but we were not allowed to walk, were all but lifted from the floor, in the effort the men made to drag, rather than lead us to our place of confinement for the night.

The leaders were taken first. In my effort to get near Peggy I started to cross the room to join her, and was immediately seized by two guards. My instinctive impulse was to pull myself loose, to resist such handling, which only caused the men to tighten their hold on me, even to twist my arms painfully. I have no doubt but that I struggled every step of the way from the administration building to the cell block where we were being taken. It was a struggle to walk by myself, to wrest myself loose from the torture of those rough hands. We were then hurled onto some benches and when I tried to pick myself up and again join Peggy in my blind desire to be near a friend, I was thrown to the floor. . . .

I found myself flung into a cell with one of the leaders, Lucy Byrnes, a tall, red-haired schoolteacher from Brooklyn, with a calm, beautiful face. She was handcuffed to the bars of the cell, and left that way for hours. Every time she called out to the other women who had been placed up and down a corridor in a block of what we found out afterward were punishment cells, Whittaker came cursing outside the bars, threatening her with a strait jacket, a gag, everything but the whipping post and bloodhounds which we had heard were part of the setup at Occoquan ... It was not until the next day that we were offered food.[1]

Later, when living in Chicago, Dorothy had gone to an IWW rooming house to help a sick friend. The house was raided, and all found there arrested. Dorothy was thus a victim of the Palmer Red Raids, occasioned by the Red hysteria of the time. The Chicago jail was worse even than the Washington jail, and in a few words Dorothy etches the horror unforgettably:

We were driven first of all through the dark and silent streets of the city to the West Chicago Avenue police station. ... The next day we were photographed and fingerprinted and brought back to the cell. ... The room was foul. The beds had mattresses, but no sheets or pillow slips. It was summer so there was no need for blankets. Fortunately, open windows gave enough light and air. On one side was a niche in which there was a toilet, unscreened by any door. There was one wash basin ...

We were searched for drugs. We were stripped naked. We were given prison clothes and put in cells. The routine was to keep us locked in the cells, then leave us free to roam the corridors in alternate periods of several hours each ...

This particular experience lasted only a few days. Manny Gomez arranged our release by getting a lawyer, and the case was afterward dismissed.[2]

In 1918 her first novel was published and the movie rights were sold for $5,000. With the money Dorothy bought a little house on the beach on Staten Island and settled down, with a lover, to write. This was for her a time of natural happiness.

[1] *The Long Loneliness,* Doubleday, Image Books, 1959, pp. 73–74.
[2] *Ibid.* pp. 98–102.

There was love, and, later a child, and Dorothy wrote of her maternity so graphically for *The Masses* that when, four years later, in Mexico, she met Diego Rivera, he saluted her as the author of this article. There were friends too: Malcolm Cowley and his wife; Allen Tate and Caroline Gordon; Hart Crane, Kenneth Burke, and John Dos Passos. Staten Island in those days was idyllic, with lobster pots, clam bakes, spider crabs, and skunk cabbage, arbutus, and dandelion greens. Dorothy found she wanted more and more to pray. Gradually, the strain between herself and her atheist, anarchist lover became too great to bear. He left her repeatedly. Finally, one day when he returned "as he always had," she would not let him into the house. "My heart was breaking," she writes simply "with my own determination to make an end, once and for all, to the torture we were undergoing."

The very next day she was conditionally baptized, made her first confession, received communion. She was lonely and poor, but found work always, one time cooking for some Marist brothers, another time going to Hollywood, where a play of hers had been taken by Metro-Goldwyn-Mayer. But always:

> I was lonely, deadly lonely. And I was to find out then, as I found out so many times, over and over again, that women especially are social beings, who are not content with just husband and family, but must have a community, a group, and exchange with others.... Young and old, even in the busiest years of our lives, we women especially are victims of the long loneliness. Men may go away and become desert Fathers, but there were no desert mothers.[3]

She had been three years a Catholic, and felt she had nothing to show for it but a deep spiritual life and a few articles in *Commonweal*, when, in December 1932, when Dorothy was already 35, she returned from a hunger march to Washington and met the man whose "spirit and ideas" would dominate the

[3] *Ibid.* p. 153.

rest of her life. He very literally walked into her life. He was waiting for her in her tenement flat.

Peter Maurin was then a "short, stocky man in his mid-fifties," ragged and rugged. Although he had already been twenty years in America, he still spoke with a strong French accent, and always looked and behaved like the French peasant he was. I remember him only as a mindless old man, inert, fat, inarticulate, a helpless body treated with a mixture of hospital jollity and filial affection by all the Catholic Worker group. To Dorothy, he was Tolstoi and Gandhi, Thoreau and Trotsky, rolled into one. "He aroused in you a sense of your own capacities for work, for accomplishment," she wrote of him. He, meanwhile, went about comparing Dorothy to "a St. Catherine of Siena who would move mountains and influence governments." Together they began a paper. The first issue was twenty-five hundred copies of an eight-page tabloid that the Paulist Press printed for $57. This first issue appeared on May 1, 1933 and sold for one cent. There were "articles about labor, strikes, unemployment factual accounts, and half a dozen of Peter Maurin's Easy Essays"—short sentences, broken up to look like verse. Peter liked to think of himself as a "troubadour for Christ" and he wanted "nothing but his own essays to be printed, over and over, and broadcast throughout the country." He thought "everybody's paper is nobody's paper." Yet, within a few months, the *Catholic Worker*'s circulation rose to 150,-000, then 200,000 and during the first years the streets were "literally lined with papers" on May Day. Young people joined Dorothy and Peter, accepting only their carfare. They formed Campion Committees, and married each other. One seminarian sold the paper on a corner of Times Square, standing next to a comrade touting *The Daily Worker*. The seminarian shouted: "Read the *Catholic Worker* daily!" "Between sales, they conversed," Dorothy wrote happily. In 1933, Dorothy estimates the unemployed numbered thirteen million. Peter and Dorothy

228

started houses of hospitality, for the people they brought in off the streets. At first, Dorothy herself cooked and cleaned, edited the *Catholic Worker,* and sold it. Then a Lithuanian girl turned up, and made vast amounts of mashed potato with mushroom sauce "which filled everyone up nicely." Soon some twenty people of both sexes were sharing the house, and then other houses of hospitality began: within a few years there were thirty-three in the United States, one in England, and one in Australia. With World War II, most of the houses closed, but after the war's end others began. In 1950, there were still twenty houses and farms. When I first knew Dorothy, there were two farms near New York, both as nearly self-supporting as they could be made, one near Newburgh, N.Y. and one on Staten Island. There was another in Michigan. In every house of hospitality, all who come are made welcome, and may stay as long as they desire. But as long as they stay, they are invited to share in the alternation of work and of prayer, of Mass and dishwashing, of Benediction and ditchdigging. Nearly 100 couples, still working in various Catholic Action groups, met each other while working with Dorothy, and have founded *Catholic Worker* families.

Dorothy writes modestly:

> It has been said that it was the *Catholic Worker* and its stories of poverty and exploitation that aroused the priests to start labor schools, to go out on picket lines, to take sides in strikes with the workers.

Now the young Catholics in the United States are coming out as solidly for racial justice and for peace as their non-Catholic comrades. Indeed, Vatican II, following upon John XXIII's *Pacem in Terris* vindicated the *Catholic Worker*'s pacifist stand by declaring that:

> Any act of war aimed indiscriminately at the destruction of entire cities or of extensive areas along with their population is a

crime against God and man himself. It merits unequivocal and unhesitating condemnation.

Already, Pope Pius XII, in 1944, had approved not only Catholic conscientious objectors, but pacifist nations, by declaring that it was better to undergo injustice than to step down to the level of those who perpetrate injustice.

"It is good that we live in a country where we can be CO's," Dorothy says. And she tells how, in the Second World War, "We had lots of visits from the FBI at Mott St., and they were most interested in our discussions, and seemed most tolerant of our point of view." And the Vatican has sent the *Catholic Worker* a very full and special blessing, to all on the staff, and all connected with the paper.[4]

At thirty-eight, Dorothy wished she were married, living the ordinary happy life, and that she had not come under Peter Maurin's influence. But she overcame her discontent, reasoning with herself that she had had the love of a man, had had a child and must admit that: "I am a mother, and the mother of a very large family at that." Why she and Peter never married she has never explained; her daughter's father would not marry her because he did not believe in bourgeois ties. But when he was dying, he came back to Dorothy, and she nursed him tenderly to the end. She now has seven grandchildren, and still is as concerned as ever about the problem of evil: why does God permit the burning alive of babies in Vietnam?

She still writes every month in the *Catholic Worker,* and writes superbly, with humility, modesty, and clarity. Here is her appraisal—made in March 1966—of the *Catholic Worker's* situation: "To live in voluntary poverty among the involuntary poor, and to prepare the Christian revolution by learning to be Christians." This is the core of Dorothy's as it was of Peter's message.

[4] Anne Fremantle, "Dorothy Day's Workers for Revolution," *Catholic Digest,* April, 1950, Vol. 14, No. 6.

Fiercely decentralist, she wants factories to be part-owned by the workers, and set in green fields. Every worker also should have his own home, his garden, and ideally, his three acres and a cow.

"I don't want people just to want more things, but to want to make more things. I want people to grow more of their own food, and make more of their own clothes. When there's a war, we're all told to grow more and more food. As soon as it's over, we're told that we shouldn't grow any food, that it's uneconomical. That doesn't make sense," Dorothy says scornfully.

And she is indignant because it is only in prisons and in asylums that people are taught to make things. "Almost the only place flax is grown in America," she says, "is in prison yards and the grounds of institutions. In fact, when I meet anyone with a skill or a craft, I'm pretty sure he's done time." Everyone realizes the value of making things. Why, she asks, wait until people are naughty or nuts?

Begun in the depression, flourishing through hot war and cold war, Dorothy and her movement go on, declaring that the only cure for humanity is a Christian revolution.

Dorothy says:

> It's the only revolution that's never been tried. Its motto for the employer is, "Quit exploiting"; for the state, "Quit expanding"; and for us all, "Quit evil."

"It is essential that man be transfigured." Kerensky ended his autobiography with this quotation from Leo Tolstoi. "Only an army of those wholly consumed by a love which is unearthly and universal can help the human condition," wrote Michael Scott. "We have all known the long loneliness and we have learned that the only solution is love and that love comes with community," wrote Dorothy Day.

The Church defines sanctity as heroic virtue. Hyphen people, like saints, have to exceed the norm. And they do.

231

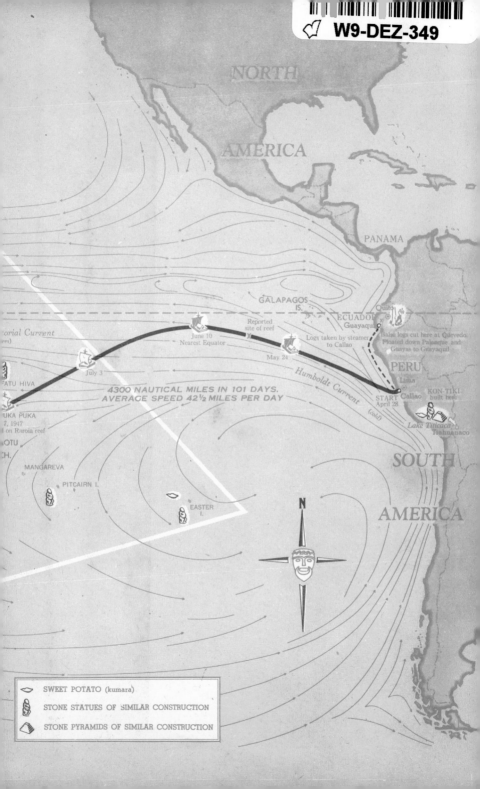

NORTH

AMERICA

PANAMA

GALAPAGOS
IS.

Quito
ECUADOR
Guayaquil

Reported
site of reef

Logs taken by steamer
to Callao

Balsa logs cut here at Quevedo.
Floated down Palenque and
Guayas to Guayaquil

orial Current
ern)

June 10
Nearest Equator

May 24

PERU
Lima

Humboldt Current

START Callao
April 28
(cold)

KON-TIKI
built here

FATU HIVA

July 3

4300 NAUTICAL MILES IN 101 DAYS.
AVERAGE SPEED 42½ MILES PER DAY

Lake Titicaca
Tiahuanaco

UKA PUKA
7, 1917
d on Raroia reef

OTU
CH.

MANGAREVA

SOUTH

PITCAIRN I.

EASTER
I.

AMERICA

N

SWEET POTATO (kumara)

STONE STATUES OF SIMILAR CONSTRUCTION

STONE PYRAMIDS OF SIMILAR CONSTRUCTION

KON-TIKI

ACROSS
THE PACIFIC
BY RAFT

KON-TIKI

ACROSS THE PACIFIC BY RAFT

By THOR HEYERDAHL
Translated by F. H. Lyon

Garden City Books, Garden City, New York

CONTENTS

LIST
OF PHOTOGRAPHS

I.

A Theory

ONCE IN A WHILE YOU FIND YOURSELF IN AN ODD SITUA-
tion. You get into it by degrees and in the most natural way but,
when you are right in the midst of it, you are suddenly astonished
and ask yourself how in the world it all came about.

If, for example, you put to sea on a wooden raft with a parrot
and five companions, it is inevitable that sooner or later you will
wake up one morning out at sea, perhaps a little better rested than
ordinarily, and begin to think about it.

On one such morning I sat writing in a dew-drenched logbook:
—*May 17. Norwegian Independence Day. Heavy sea. Fair wind.
I am cook today and found seven flying fish on deck, one squid on
the cabin roof, and one unknown fish in Torstein's sleeping bag. . . .*

Here the pencil stopped, and the same thought interjected itself:
This is really a queer seventeenth of May—indeed, taken all round,
a most peculiar existence. How did it all begin?

If I turned left, I had an unimpeded view of a vast blue sea with
hissing waves, rolling by close at hand in an endless pursuit of an
ever retreating horizon. If I turned right, I saw the inside of a shadowy cabin in which a bearded individual was lying on his back reading Goethe with his bare toes carefully dug into the latticework in
the low bamboo roof of the crazy little cabin that was our common
home.

"Bengt," I said, pushing away the green parrot that wanted to
perch on the logbook, "can you tell me how the hell we came to be
doing this?"

Goethe sank down under the red-gold beard.

"The devil I do; you know best yourself. It was your damned idea,
but I think it's grand."

3

He moved his toes three bars up and went on reading Goethe unperturbed. Outside the cabin three other fellows were working in the roasting sun on the bamboo deck. They were half-naked, brown-skinned, and bearded, with stripes of salt down their backs and looking as if they had never done anything else than float wooden rafts westward across the Pacific. Erik came crawling in through the opening with his sextant and a pile of papers.

"98° 46′ west by 8° 2′ south—a good day's run since yesterday, chaps!"

He took my pencil and drew a tiny circle on a chart which hung on the bamboo wall—a tiny circle at the end of a chain of nineteen circles that curved across from the port of Callao on the coast of Peru. Herman, Knut, and Torstein too came eagerly crowding in to see the new little circle that placed us a good 40 sea miles nearer the South Sea islands than the last in the chain.

"Do you see, boys?" said Herman proudly. "That means we're 850 sea miles from the coast of Peru."

"And we've got another 3,500 to go to get to the nearest islands," Knut added cautiously.

"And to be quite precise," said Torstein, "we're 15,000 feet above the bottom of the sea and a few fathoms below the moon."

So now we all knew exactly where we were, and I could go on speculating as to why. The parrot did not care; he only wanted to tug at the log. And the sea was just as round, just as sky-encircled, blue upon blue.

Perhaps the whole thing had begun the winter before, in the office of a New York museum. Or perhaps it had already begun ten years earlier, on a little island in the Marquesas group in the middle of the Pacific. Maybe we would land on the same island now, unless the northeast wind sent us farther south in the direction of Tahiti and the Tuamotu group. I could see the little island clearly in my mind's eye, with its jagged rust-red mountains, the green jungle which flowed down their slopes toward the sea, and the slender palms that waited and waved along the shore. The island was called Fatu Hiva; there was no land between it and us where we lay drifting, but nevertheless it was thousands of sea miles away. I saw the narrow Ouia Valley, where it opened out toward the sea, and remembered so well how we sat there on the lonely beach and looked out over this same endless sea, evening after evening. I was accompanied by my wife then, not by bearded pirates as now. We were collecting all kinds of live creatures, and images and other relics of a dead culture.

I remembered very well one particular evening. The civilized world seemed incomprehensibly remote and unreal. We had lived on the island for nearly a year, the only white people there; we had of our own will forsaken the good things of civilization along with its evils. We lived in a hut we had built for ourselves, on piles under the palms down by the shore, and ate what the tropical woods and the Pacific had to offer us.

On that particular evening we sat, as so often before, down on the beach in the moonlight, with the sea in front of us. Wide awake and filled with the romance that surrounded us, we let no impression escape us. We filled our nostrils with an aroma of rank jungle and salt sea and heard the wind's rustle in leaves and palm tops. At regular intervals all other noises were drowned by the great breakers that rolled straight in from the sea and rushed in foaming over the land till they were broken up into circles of froth among the shore boulders. There was a roaring and rustling and rumbling among millions of glistening stones, till all grew quiet again when the sea water had withdrawn to gather strength for a new attack on the invincible coast.

"It's queer," said my wife, "but there are never breakers like this on the other side of the island."

"No," said I, "but this is the windward side; there's always a sea running on this side."

We kept on sitting there and admiring the sea which, it seemed, was loath to give up demonstrating that here it came rolling in from eastward, eastward, eastward. It was the eternal east wind, the trade wind, which had disturbed the sea's surface, dug it up, and rolled it forward, up over the eastern horizon and over here to the islands. Here the unbroken advance of the sea was finally shattered against cliffs and reefs, while the east wind simply rose above coast and woods and mountains and continued westward unhindered, from island to island, toward the sunset.

So had the ocean swells and the lofty clouds above them rolled up over the same eastern horizon since the morning of time. The first natives who reached these islands knew well enough that this was so, and so did the present islanders. The long-range ocean birds kept to the eastward on their daily fishing trips to be able to return with the eastern wind at night when the belly was full and the wings

5

tired. Even trees and flowers were wholly dependent on the rain produced by the eastern winds, and all the vegetation grew accordingly. And we knew by ourselves, as we sat there, that far, far below that eastern horizon, where the clouds came up, lay the open coast of South America. There was nothing but 4,000 miles of open sea between.

We gazed at the driving clouds and the heaving moonlit sea, and we listened to an old man who squatted half-naked before us and stared down into the dying glow from a little smoldering fire.

"Tiki," the old man said quietly, "he was both god and chief. It was Tiki who brought my ancestors to these islands where we live now. Before that we lived in a big country beyond the sea."

He poked the coals with a stick to keep them from going out. The old man sat thinking. He lived for ancient times and was firmly fettered to them. He worshiped his forefathers and their deeds in an unbroken line back to the time of the gods. And he looked forward to being reunited with them. Old Tei Tetua was the sole survivor of all the extinct tribes on the east coast of Fatu Hiva. How old he was he did not know, but his wrinkled, bark-brown, leathery skin looked as if it had been dried in sun and wind for a hundred years. He was one of the few on these islands that still remembered and believed in his father's and his grandfather's legendary stories of the great Polynesian chief-god Tiki, son of the sun.

When we crept to bed that night in our little pile hut, old Tei Tetua's stories of Tiki and the islanders' old home beyond the sea continued to haunt my brain, accompanied by the muffled roar of the surf in the distance. It sounded like a voice from far-off times, which, it seemed, had something it wanted to tell, out there in the night. I could not sleep. It was as though time no longer existed, and Tiki and his seafarers were just landing in the surf on the beach below. A thought suddenly struck me and I said to my wife: "Have you noticed that the huge stone figures of Tiki in the jungle are remarkably like the monoliths left by extinct civilizations in South America?"

I felt sure that a roar of agreement came from the breakers. And then they slowly subsided while I slept.

✻   ✻   ✻

So, perhaps, the whole thing began. So began, in any case, a whole series of events which finally landed the six of us and a green parrot on board a raft off the coast of South America.

I remember how I shocked my father and amazed my mother and my friends when I came back to Norway and handed over my glass jars of beetles and fish from Fatu Hiva to the University Zoological Museum. I wanted to give up animal studies and tackle primitive peoples. The unsolved mysteries of the South Seas had fascinated me. There must be a rational solution of them, and I had made my objective the identification of the legendary hero Tiki.

In the years that followed, breakers and jungle ruins were a kind of remote, unreal dream which formed the background and accompaniment to my studies of the Pacific peoples. Although the thoughts and inclinations of primitive man can never be rightly judged by an armchair student, yet he can, in his library bookshelves, travel wider beyond time and horizons than can any modern outdoor explorer. Scientific works, journals from the time of the earliest explorations, and endless collections in museums in Europe and America offered a wealth of material for use in the puzzle I wanted to try to put together. Since our own race first reached the Pacific islands after the discovery of South America, investigators in all branches of science have collected an almost bottomless store of information about the inhabitants of the South Seas and all the peoples living round about them. But there has never been any agreement as to the origin of this isolated island people, or the reason why this type is only found scattered over all the solitary islands in the eastern part of the Pacific.

When the first Europeans at last ventured to cross this greatest of all oceans, they discovered to their amazement that right out in the midst of it lay a number of small mountainous islands and flat coral reefs, isolated from each other and from the world in general by vast areas of sea. And every single one of these islands was already inhabited by people who had come there before them—tall, handsome people who met them on the beach with dogs and pigs and fowl. Where had they come from? They talked a language which no other tribe knew. And the men of our race, who boldly called themselves the discoverers of the islands, found cultivated fields and villages with temples and huts on every single habitable island. On some islands, indeed, they found old pyramids, paved roads, and carven stone statues as high as a four-story house. But the explanation of the whole mystery was lacking. Who were these people, and where had they come from?

One can safely say that the answers to these riddles have been nearly as many in number as the works which have treated of them. Specialists in different fields have put forward quite different solutions, but their affirmations have always been disproved later by logical arguments from experts who have worked along other lines. Malaya, India, China, Japan, Arabia, Egypt, the Caucasus, Atlantis, even Germany and Norway, have been seriously championed as the Polynesians' homeland. But every time some obstacle of a decisive character has appeared and put the whole problem into the melting pot again.

And where science stopped, imagination began. The mysterious monoliths on Easter Island, and all the other relics of unknown origin on this tiny island, lying in complete solitude halfway between the easternmost Pacific islands and the coast of South America, gave rise to all sorts of speculations. Many observed that the finds on Easter Island recalled in many ways the relics of the prehistoric civilizations of South America. Perhaps there had once been a bridge of land over the sea, and this had sunk? Perhaps Easter Island, and all the other South Sea islands which had monuments of the same kind, were remains of a sunken continent left exposed above the sea?

This has been a popular theory and an acceptable explanation among laymen, but geologists and other scientists do not favor it. Zoologists, moreover, prove quite simply, from the study of insects and snails on the South Sea islands, that throughout the history of mankind these islands have been completely isolated from one another and from the continents round them, exactly as they are today.

We know, therefore, with absolute certainty that the original Polynesian race must at some time, willingly or unwillingly, have come drifting or sailing to these remote islands. And a closer look at the inhabitants of the South Seas shows that it cannot have been very many centuries since they came. For, even if the Polynesians live scattered over an area of sea four times as large as the whole of Europe, nevertheless they have not managed to develop different languages in the different islands. It is thousands of sea miles from Hawaii in the north to New Zealand in the south, from Samoa in the west to Easter Island in the east, yet all these isolated tribes speak dialects of a common language which we have called Polynesian.

Writing was unknown in all the islands, except for a few wooden tablets bearing incomprehensible hieroglyphs which the natives preserved on Easter Island, though neither they themselves nor anyone else could read them. But they had schools, and the poetical teaching of history was their most important function, for in Polynesia history was the same as religion. The people were ancestor-worshipers; they worshiped their dead chiefs all the way back to Tiki's time, and of Tiki himself it was said that he was son of the sun.

On almost every island learned men could enumerate the names of all the island's chiefs back to the time when it was first peopled. To assist their memories they often used a complicated system of knots on twisted strings, as the Inca Indians did in Peru. Modern scientists have collected all these local genealogies from the different islands and found that they agree with one another with astonishing exactness, both in names and number of generations. It has been discovered in this way, by taking an average Polynesian generation to represent twenty-five years, that the South Sea islands were not peopled before about 500 A.D. A new cultural wave with a new string of chiefs shows that another and still later migration reached the same islands as late as about 1100 A.D.

Where could such late migrations have come from? Very few investigators seem to have taken into consideration the decisive factor that the people which came to the islands at so late a date was a pure Stone Age people. Despite their intelligence and, in all other respects, astonishingly high culture, these seafarers brought with them a certain type of stone ax and a quantity of other characteristic Stone Age tools and spread these over all the islands to which they came. We must not forget that, apart from single isolated peoples, inhabiting primeval forests, and certain backward races, there were no cultures in the world of any reproductive capacity which were still at the Stone Age level in 500 or 1100 A.D., except in the New World. There even the highest Indian civilizations were totally ignorant at least of the uses of iron, and used stone axes and tools of the same type as those used in the South Sea islands right up to the time of the explorations.

These numerous Indian civilizations were the Polynesians' nearest neighbors to the east. To westward there lived only the black-skinned primitive peoples of Australia and Melanesia, distant relations of the Negroes, and beyond them again were Indonesia and the coast of Asia, where the Stone Age lay farther back in time, perhaps, than anywhere else in the world.

Thus both my suspicions and my attention were turned more and more away from the Old World, where so many had searched and none had found, and over to the known and unknown Indian civilizations of America, which no one hitherto had taken into consideration. And on the nearest coast due east, where today the South American republic of Peru stretches from the Pacific up into the mountains, there was no lack of traces if one only looked for them. Here an unknown people had once lived and established one of the world's strangest civilizations, till suddenly, long ago, they had vanished as though swept away from the earth's surface. They left behind them enormous stone statues carved in the image of human beings, which recalled those on Pitcairn, the Marquesas, and Easter Island, and huge pyramids built in steps like those on Tahiti and Samoa. They hewed out of the mountains, with stone axes, stone blocks as large as railway cars and heavier than elephants, transported them for miles about the countryside, and set them up on end or placed them on top of one another to form gateways, huge walls, and terraces, exactly as we find them on some of the islands in the Pacific.

The Inca Indians had their great empire in this mountain country when the first Spaniards came to Peru. They told the Spaniards that the colossal monuments that stood deserted about the landscape were erected by a race of white gods which had lived there before the Incas themselves became rulers. These vanished architects were described as wise, peaceful instructors, who had originally come from the north, long ago in the morning of time, and had taught the Incas' primitive forefathers architecture and agriculture as well as manners and customs. They were unlike other Indians in having white skins and long beards; they were also taller than the Incas. Finally they left Peru as suddenly as they had come; the Incas themselves took over power in the country, and the white teachers vanished forever from the coast of South America and fled westward across the Pacific.

Now it happened that, when the Europeans came to the Pacific islands, they were quite astonished to find that many of the natives had almost white skins and were bearded. On many of the islands there were whole families conspicuous for their remarkably pale skins, hair varying from reddish to blonde, blue-gray eyes, and almost Semitic, hook-nosed faces. In contrast to these the genuine Polynesians had golden-brown skins, raven hair, and rather flat, pulpy noses. The red-haired individuals called themselves *urukehu* and said that they were directly descended from the first chiefs on the islands, who were still white gods, such as Tangaroa, Kane, and Tiki. Legends of mysterious white men, from whom the islanders were originally descended, were current all over Polynesia. When Roggeveen discovered Easter Island in 1722, he noticed to his surprise what he termed "white men" among those on shore. And the people of Easter Island could themselves count up those of their ancestors who were white-skinned right back to the time of Tiki and Hotu Matua, when they first came sailing across the sea "from a mountainous land in the east which was scorched by the sun."

As I pursued my search, I found in Peru surprising traces in culture, mythology, and language which impelled me to go on digging ever deeper and with greater concentration in my attempt to identify the place of origin of the Polynesian tribal god Tiki.

And I found what I hoped for. I was sitting reading the Inca legends of the sun-king Virakocha, who was the supreme head of the mythical white people in Peru. I read:

. . . . Virakocha is an Inca (Ketchua) name and consequently of fairly recent date. The original name of the sun-god Virakocha, which seems to have been more used in Peru in old times, was Kon-Tiki or Illa-Tiki, which means Sun-Tiki or Fire-Tiki. Kon-Tiki was high priest and sun-king of the Incas' legendary 'white men' who had left the enormous ruins on the shores of Lake Titicaca. The legend runs that the mysterious white men with beards were attacked by a chief named Cari who came from the Coquimbo Valley. In a battle on an island in Lake Titicaca the fair race was massacred, but Kon-Tiki himself and his closest companions escaped and later came down to the Pacific coast, whence they finally disappeared oversea to the westward. . . .

I was no longer in doubt that the white chief-god Sun-Tiki, whom the Incas declared that their forefathers had driven out of Peru on to the Pacific, was identical with the white chief-god Tiki, son of the sun, whom the inhabitants of all the eastern Pacific islands hailed as the original founder of their race. And the details of Sun-Tiki's life in Peru, with the ancient names of places round Lake Titicaca, cropped up again in historic legends current among the natives of the Pacific islands.

But all over Polynesia I found indications that Kon-Tiki's peaceable race had not been able to hold the islands alone for long. Indications that seagoing war canoes, as large as Viking ships and lashed together two and two, had brought Northwest Indians from the New World across the sea to Hawaii and farther south to all the other islands. They had mingled their blood with that of Kon-Tiki's race and brought a new civilization to the island kingdom. This was the second Stone Age people that came to Polynesia, without metals, without the potter's art, without wheel or loom or cereal cultivation, about 1100 A.D.

So it came about that I was excavating rock carvings in the ancient Polynesian style among the Northwest Coast Indians in British Columbia when the Germans burst into Norway in 1940.

*　　*　　*

Right face, left face, about face. Washing barracks stairs, polishing boots, radio school, parachute—and at last a Murmansk convoy to Finnmark, where the war-god of technique reigned in the sun-god's absence all the dark winter through.

Peace came. And one day my theory was complete. I must go to America and put it forward.

2.

An Expedition Is Born

So it had begun, by a fire on a south sea island, where an old native sat telling legends and stories of his tribe. Many years later I sat with another old man, this time in a dark office on one of the upper floors of a big museum in New York.

Round us, in well-arranged glass cases, lay pottery fragments from the past, traces leading into the mists of antiquity. The walls were lined with books. Some of them one man had written and hardly ten men had read. The old man, who had read all these books and written some of them, sat behind his worktable, white-haired and good-humored. But now, for sure, I had trodden on his toes, for he gripped the arms of his chair uneasily and looked as if I had interrupted him in a game of solitaire.

"No!" he said. "Never!"

I imagine that Santa Claus would have looked as he did then if someone had dared to affirm that next year Christmas would be on Midsummer Day.

"You're wrong, absolutely wrong," he said and shook his head indignantly to drive out the idea.

"But you haven't read my arguments yet," I urged, nodding hopefully toward the manuscript which lay on the table.

"Arguments!" he repeated. "You can't treat ethnographic problems as a sort of detective mystery!"

"Why not?" I said. "I've based all the conclusions on my own observations and the facts that science has recorded."

"The task of science is investigation pure and simple," he said quietly. "Not to try to prove this or that."

He pushed the unopened manuscript carefully to one side and leaned over the table.

"It's quite true that South America was the home of some of the most curious civilizations of antiquity, and that we know neither who they were nor where they vanished when the Incas came into power. But one thing we do know for certain—that none of the peoples of South America got over to the islands in the Pacific."

He looked at me searchingly and continued:

"Do you know why? The answer's simple enough. They couldn't get there. They had no boats!"

"They had rafts," I objected hesitatingly. "You know, balsa-wood rafts."

The old man smiled and said calmly:

"Well, you can try a trip from Peru to the Pacific islands on a balsa-wood raft."

I could find nothing to say. It was getting late. We both rose. The old scientist patted me kindly on the shoulder, as he saw me out, and said that if I wanted help I had only to come to him. But I must in future specialize on Polynesia *or* America and not mix up two separate anthropological areas. He reached back over the table.

"You've forgotten this," he said and handed back my manuscript. I glanced at the title, "Polynesia and America; A Study of Prehistoric Relations." I stuck the manuscript under my arm and clattered down the stairs out into the crowds in the street.

That evening I went down and knocked on the door of an old flat in an out-of-the-way corner of Greenwich Village. I liked bringing my little problems down here when I felt they had made life a bit tangled.

A sparse little man with a long nose opened the door a crack before he threw it wide open with a broad smile and pulled me in. He took me straight into the little kitchen, where he set me to work carrying plates and forks while he himself doubled the quantity of the indefinable but savory-smelling concoction he was heating over the gas.

"Nice of you to come," he said. "How goes it?"

"Rottenly," I replied. "No one will read the manuscript."

He filled the plates and we attacked the contents.

"It's like this," he said. "All the people you've been to see think it's just a passing idea you've got. You know, here in America, people turn up with so many queer ideas."

"And there's another thing," I went on.

"Yes," said he. "Your way of approaching the problem. They're specialists, the whole lot of them, and they don't believe in a method of work which cuts into every field of science from botany to archaeology. They limit their own scope in order to be able to dig in the depths with more concentration for details. Modern research demands that every special branch shall dig in its own hole. It's not usual for anyone to sort out what comes up out of the holes and try to put it all together."

He rose and reached for a heavy manuscript.

"Look here," he said. "My last work on bird designs in Chinese peasant embroidery. Took me seven years, but it was accepted for publication at once. They want specialized research nowadays."

Carl was right. But to solve the problems of the Pacific without throwing light on them from all sides was, it seemed to me, like doing a puzzle and only using the pieces of one color.

We cleared the table, and I helped him wash and dry the dishes.

"Nothing new from the university in Chicago?"

"No."

"But what did your old friend at the museum say today?"

"He wasn't interested, either," I muttered. "He said that, as long as the Indians had only open rafts, it was futile to consider the possibility of their having discovered the Pacific islands."

The little man suddenly began to dry his plate furiously.

"Yes," he said at last. "To tell the truth, to me too that seems a practical objection to your theory."

I looked gloomily at the little ethnologist whom I had thought to be a sworn ally.

"But don't misunderstand me," he hastened to say. "In one way I think you're right, but in another way it's so incomprehensible. My work on designs supports your theory."

"Carl," I said. "I'm so sure the Indians crossed the Pacific on their rafts that I'm willing to build a raft of the same kind myself and cross the sea just to prove that it's possible."

"You're mad!"

My friend took it for a joke and laughed, half-scared at the thought.

"You're mad! A raft?"

He did not know what to say and only stared at me with a queer expression, as though waiting for a smile to show that I *was* joking.

He did not get one. I saw now that in practice no one would accept my theory because of the apparently endless stretch of sea between

17

Peru and Polynesia, which I was trying to bridge with no other aid than a prehistoric raft.

Carl looked at me uncertainly. "Now we'll go out and have a drink," he said. We went out and had four.

*　　　*　　　*

My rent became due that week. At the same time a letter from the Bank of Norway informed me that I could have no more dollars. Currency restrictions. I picked up my trunk and took the subway out to Brooklyn. Here I was taken in at the Norwegian Sailors' Home, where the food was good and sustaining and the prices suited my wallet. I got a little room a floor or two up but had my meals with all the seamen in a big dining room downstairs.

Seamen came and seamen went. They varied in type, dimensions, and degrees of sobriety but they all had one thing in common—when they talked about the sea, they knew what they were talking about. I learned that waves and rough sea did not increase with the depth of the sea or distance from land. On the contrary, squalls were often more treacherous along the coast than in the open sea. Shoal water, backwash along the coast, or ocean currents penned in close to the land could throw up a rougher sea than was usual far out. A vessel which could hold her own along an open coast could hold her own farther out. I also learned that, in a high sea, big ships were inclined to plunge bow or stern into the waves, so that tons of water would rush on board and twist steel tubes like wire, while a small boat, in the same sea, often made good weather because she could find room between the lines of waves and dance freely over them like a gull. I talked to sailors who had got safely away in boats after the seas had made their ship founder.

But the men knew little about rafts. A raft—that wasn't a ship; it had no keel or bulwarks. It was just something floating on which to save oneself in an emergency, until one was picked up by a boat of some kind. One of the men, nevertheless, had great respect for rafts in the open sea; he had drifted about on one for three weeks when a German torpedo sank his ship in mid-Atlantic.

"But you can't navigate a raft," he added. "It goes sideways and backward and round as the wind takes it."

In the library I dug out records left by the first Europeans who had reached the Pacific coast of South America. There was no lack of sketches or descriptions of the Indians' big balsa-wood rafts. They

had a square sail and centerboard and a long steering oar astern.
So they could be maneuvered.

Weeks passed at the Sailors' Home. No reply from Chicago or the
other cities to which I had sent copies of my theory. No one had
read it.

Then, one Saturday, I pulled myself together and marched into a
ship chandler's shop down in Water Street. There I was politely addressed as "Captain" when I bought a pilot chart of the Pacific. With
the chart rolled up under my arm I took the suburban train out to
Ossining, where I was a regular week-end guest of a young Norwegian married couple who had a charming place in the country.
My host had been a sea captain and was now office manager for the
Fred Olsen Line in New York.

After a refreshing plunge in the swimming pool city life was completely forgotten for the rest of the week end, and when Ambjörg
brought the cocktail tray, we sat down on the lawn in the hot sun.
I could contain myself no longer but spread the chart out on the
grass and asked Wilhelm if he thought a raft could carry men alive
from Peru to the South Sea islands.

He looked at me rather than at the chart, half taken aback, but
replied at once in the affirmative. I felt as much lightened as if I had
released a balloon inside my shirt, for I knew that to Wilhelm everything that had to do with navigation and sailing was both job and
hobby. He was initiated into my plans at once. To my astonishment
he then declared that the idea was sheer madness.

"But you said just now that you thought it was possible," I interrupted.

"Quite right," he admitted. "But the chances of its going wrong are
just as great. You yourself have never been on a balsa raft, and all of
a sudden you're imagining yourself across the Pacific on one. Perhaps it'll come off, perhaps it won't. The old Indians in Peru had
generations of experience to build upon. Perhaps ten rafts went to
the bottom for every one that got across—or perhaps hundreds in
the course of centuries. As you say, the Incas navigated in the open
sea with whole flotillas of these balsa rafts. Then, if anything went
wrong, they could be picked up by the nearest raft. But who's going
to pick you up, out in mid-ocean? Even if you take a radio for use in
an emergency, don't think it's going to be easy for a little raft to be
located down among the waves thousands of miles from land. In a
storm you can be washed off the raft and drowned many times over

before anyone gets to you. You'd better wait quietly here till some-one has had time to read your manuscript. Write again and stir them up; it's no good if you don't."

"I can't wait any longer now; I shan't have a cent left soon."

"Then you can come and stay with us. For that matter, how can you think of starting an expedition from South America without money?"

"It's easier to interest people in an expedition than in an unread manuscript."

"But what can you gain by it?"

"Destroy one of the weightiest arguments against the theory, quite apart from the fact that science will pay some attention to the affair."

"But if things go wrong?"

"Then I shan't have proved anything."

"Then you'd ruin your own theory in the eyes of everyone, wouldn't you?"

"Perhaps, but all the same one in ten might have got through be-fore us, as you said."

The children came out to play croquet, and we did not discuss the matter any more that day.

The next week end I was back at Ossining with the chart under my arm. And, when I left, there was a long pencil line from the coast of Peru to the Tuamotu islands in the Pacific. My friend, the captain, had given up hope of making me drop the idea, and we had sat together for hours working out the raft's probable speed.

"Ninety-seven days," said Wilhelm, "but remember that's only in theoretically ideal conditions, with a fair wind all the time and as-suming that the raft can really sail as you think it can. You must definitely allow at least four months for the trip and be prepared for a good deal more."

"All right," I said optimistically, "let us allow at least four months, but do it in ninety-seven days."

The little room at the Sailors' Home seemed twice as cozy as usual when I came home that evening and sat down on the edge of the bed with the chart. I paced out the floor as exactly as the bed and chest of drawers gave me room to do. Oh, yes, the raft would be much larger than this. I leaned out of the window to get a glimpse of the great city's remote starry sky, only visible right overhead be-tween the high yard walls. If there was little room on board the raft, anyhow there would be room for the sky and all its stars above us.

An Expedition Is Born

On West Seventy-Second Street, near Central Park, is one of the most exclusive clubs in New York. There is nothing more than a brightly polished little brass plate with "Explorers Club" on it to tell passers-by that there is anything out of the ordinary inside the doors. But, once inside, one might have made a parachute jump into a strange world, thousands of miles from New York's lines of motorcars flanked by skyscrapers. When the door to New York is shut behind one, one is swallowed up in an atmosphere of lion-hunting, mountaineering, and polar life. Trophies of hippopotamus and deer, big-game rifles, tusks, war drums and spears, Indian carpets, idols and model ships, flags, photographs and maps, surround the members of the club when they assemble for a dinner or to hear lecturers from distant countries.

After my journey to the Marquesas Islands I had been elected an active member of the club, and as junior member I had seldom missed a meeting when I was in town. So, when I now entered the club on a rainy November evening, I was not a little surprised to find the place in an unusual state. In the middle of the floor lay an inflated rubber raft with boat rations and accessories, while parachutes, rubber overalls, safety jackets, and polar equipment covered walls and tables, together with balloons for water distillation, and other curious inventions. A newly elected member of the club, Colonel Haskin, of the equipment laboratory of the Air Material Command, was to give a lecture and demonstrate a number of new military inventions which, he thought, would in the future be of use to scientific expeditions in both north and south.

After the lecture there was a vigorous discussion. The well-known Danish polar explorer Peter Freuchen, tall and bulky, rose with a skeptical shake of his huge beard. He had no faith in such new-fangled patents. He himself had once used a rubber boat and bag tent on one of his Greenland expeditions instead of an Eskimo kayak and igloo, and it had all but cost him his life. First he had nearly been frozen to death in a snowstorm because the zipper fastening of the tent had frozen up so that he could not even get in. And after that he had been out fishing when the hook caught in the inflated rubber boat, and the boat was punctured and sank under him like a bit of rag. He and an Eskimo friend had managed to get ashore that time in a kayak which came to their help. He was sure no clever modern inventor could sit in his laboratory and think out anything better than what the experience of thousands of years had taught the Eskimos to use in their own regions.

The discussion ended with a surprising offer from Colonel Haskin. Active members of the club could, on their next expeditions, select any they liked of the new inventions he had demonstrated, on the sole condition that they should let his laboratory know what they thought of the things when they came back.

That was that. I was the last to leave the clubrooms that evening. I had to go over every minute detail of all this brand-new equipment which had so suddenly tumbled into my hands and which was at my disposal for the asking. It was exactly what I wanted—equipment with which we could try to save our lives if, contrary to expectation, our wooden raft should show signs of breaking up and we had no other rafts near by.

All this equipment was still occupying my thoughts at the breakfast table in the Sailors' Home next morning when a well-dressed young man of athletic build came along with his breakfast tray and sat down at the same table as myself. We began to chat, and it appeared that he too was not a seaman but a university-trained engineer from Trondheim, who was in America to buy machinery parts and obtain experience in refrigerating technique. He was living not far away and often had meals at the Sailors' Home because of the good Norwegian cooking there.

He asked me what I was doing, and I then gave him a short account of my plans. I said that, if I did not get a definite answer about my manuscript before the end of the week, I should get under way with the starting of the raft expedition. My table companion did not say much but listened with great interest.

Four days later we ran across each other again in the same dining room.

"Have you decided whether you're going on your trip or not?" he asked.

"Yes," I said. "I'm going."

"When?"

"As soon as possible. If I hang about much longer now, the gales will be coming up from the Antarctic and it will be hurricane season in the islands, too. I must leave Peru in a very few months, but I must get money first and get the whole business organized."

"How many men will there be?"

"I've thought of having six men in all; that'll give some change of society on board the raft and is the right number for four hours' steering in every twenty-four hours."

He stood for a moment or two, as though chewing over a thought, then burst out emphatically:

"The devil, but how I'd like to be in it! I could undertake technical measurements and tests. Of course, you'll have to support your experiment with accurate measurements of winds and currents and waves. Remember that you're going to cross vast spaces of sea which are practically unknown because they lie outside all shipping routes. An expedition like yours can make interesting hydrographic and meteorological investigations; I could make good use of my thermodynamics."

I knew nothing about the man beyond what an open face can say. It may say a good deal.

"All right," I said. "We'll go together."

His name was Herman Watzinger; he was as much of a landlubber as myself.

A few days later I took Herman as my guest to the Explorers Club. Here we ran straight into the polar explorer Peter Freuchen. Freuchen has the blessed quality of never disappearing in a crowd. As big as a barn door and bristling with beard, he looks like a messenger from the open tundra. A special atmosphere surrounds him —it is as though he were going about with a grizzly bear on a lead.

We took him over to a big map on the wall and told him about our plan of crossing the Pacific on an Indian raft. His boyish blue eyes grew as large as saucers as he listened. Then he stamped his wooden leg on the floor and tightened his belt several holes.

"Damn it, boys! I should like to go with you!"

The old Greenland traveler filled our beer mugs and began to tell us of his confidence in primitive peoples' watercraft and these peoples' ability to make their way by accommodating themselves to nature both on land and at sea. He himself had traveled by raft down the great rivers of Siberia and towed natives on rafts astern of his ship along the coast of the Arctic. As he talked, he tugged at his beard and said we were certainly going to have a great time.

Through Freuchen's eager support of our plan the wheels began to turn at a dangerous speed, and they soon ran right into the printers' ink of the *Scandinavian Press*. The very next morning there came a violent knocking on my door in the Sailors' Home; I was wanted on the telephone in the passage downstairs. The result of the conversation was that Herman and I, the same evening, rang the doorbell of an apartment in a fashionable quarter of the city. We were received by a well-dressed young man in patent-leather slippers, wearing a silk dressing gown over a blue suit. He made an impression almost of softness and apologized for having a cold with a scented handkerchief held under his nose. Nonetheless we knew that this fellow had made a name in America by his exploits as an airman in the war. Besides our apparently delicate host two energetic young journalists, simply bursting with activity and ideas, were present. We knew one of them as an able correspondent.

Our host explained over a bottle of good whisky that he was interested in our expedition. He offered to raise the necessary capital if we would undertake to write newspaper articles and go on lecture tours after our return. We came to an agreement at last and drank to successful co-operation between the backers of the expedition and those taking part in it. From now on all our economic problems would be solved; they were taken over by our backers and would not trouble us. Herman and I were at once to set about raising a crew and equipment, build a raft, and get off before the hurricane season began.

Next day Herman resigned his post, and we set about our task seriously. I had already obtained a promise from the research laboratory of the Air Material Command to send everything I asked for and more through the Explorers Club; they said that an expedition such as ours was ideal for testing their equipment. This was a good start. Our most important tasks were now, first of all, to find four suitable men who were willing to go with us on the raft and to obtain supplies for the journey.

A party of men who were to put out to sea together on board a raft must be chosen with care. Otherwise there would be trouble and mutiny after a month's isolation at sea. I did not want to man the raft with sailors; they knew hardly any more about managing a raft than we did ourselves, and I did not want to have it argued afterward, when we had completed the voyage, that we made it because we were better seamen than the old raft-builders in Peru. Nevertheless, we wanted one man on board who at any rate could use a sextant and mark our course on a chart as a basis for all our scientific reports.

"I know a good fellow, a painter," I said to Herman. "He's a big hefty chap who can play the guitar and is full of fun. He went through navigation school and sailed round the world several times before he settled down at home with brush and palette. I've known him since we were boys and have often been on camping tours with him in the mountains at home. I'll write and ask him; I'm sure he'll come."

"He sounds all right," Herman nodded, "and then we want someone who can manage the radio."

"Radio!" I said, horrified. "What the hell do we want with that? It's out of place on a prehistoric raft."

"Not at all—it's a safety precaution which won't have any effect on your theory so long as we don't send out any SOS for help. And we shall need the radio to send out weather observations and other reports. But it'll be no use for us to receive gale warnings because there are no reports for that part of the ocean, and, even if there were, what good would they be to us on a raft?"

His arguments gradually swamped all my protests, the main ground for which was a lack of affection for push buttons and turning knobs.

"Curiously enough," I admitted, "I happen to have the best connections for getting into touch by radio over great distances with tiny sets. I was put into a radio section in the war. Every man in the right place, you know. But I shall certainly write a line to Knut Haugland and Torstein Raaby."

"Do you know them?"

"Yes. I met Knut for the first time in England in 1944. He'd been decorated by the British for having taken part in the parachute action that held up the German efforts to get the atomic bomb; he was the radio operator, you know, in the heavy water sabotage at Rjukan. When I met him, he had just come back from another job in Norway; the Gestapo had caught him with a secret radio set inside a chimney in the Maternity Clinic in Oslo. The Nazis had located him by D/F, and the whole building was surrounded by German soldiers with machine-gun posts in front of every single door. Fehmer, the head of the Gestapo, was standing in the courtyard himself waiting for Knut to be carried down. But it was his own men who were carried down. Knut fought his way with his pistol from the attic down to the cellar, and from there out into the back yard, where he disappeared over the hospital wall with a hail of bullets after him. I met him at a secret station in an old English castle; he had come back to organize underground liaison among more than a hundred transmitting stations in occupied Norway.

"I myself had just finished my training as a parachutist, and our plan was to jump together in the Nordmark near Oslo. But just then the Russians marched into the Kirkenes region, and a small Norwegian detachment was sent from Scotland to Finnmark to take over the operations, so to speak, from the whole Russian army. I was sent up there instead. And there I met Torstein.

"It was real Arctic winter up in those parts, and the northern lights flashed in the starry sky which was arched over us, pitch black, all day and all night. When we came to the ash heaps of the burned area in Finnmark, frozen blue and wearing furs, a cheery fellow with blue eyes and bristly fair hair crept out of a little hut up in the mountains. This was Torstein Raaby. He had first escaped to England, where he went through special training, and then he'd been smuggled into Norway somewhere near Tromsö. He'd been in hiding with a little transmitting set close to the battleship 'Tirpitz' and for ten months he had sent daily reports to England about all that happened on board. He sent his reports at night by connecting his secret transmitter to a receiving aerial put up by a German officer. It was his regular reports that guided the British bombers who at last finished off the 'Tirpitz.'

"Torstein escaped to Sweden and from there over to England again, and then he made a parachute jump with a new radio set behind the German lines up in the wilds of Finnmark. When the Germans retreated, he found himself sitting behind our own lines and came out of his hiding place to help us with his little radio, as our main station had been destroyed by a mine. I'm ready to bet that both Knut and Torstein are fed up with hanging about at home now and would be glad to go for a little trip on a wooden raft."

"Write and ask them," Herman proposed.

So I wrote a short letter, without any disingenuous persuasions, to Erik, Knut, and Torstein:

"Am going to cross Pacific on a wooden raft to support a theory that the South Sea islands were peopled from Peru. Will you come? I guarantee nothing but a free trip to Peru and the South Sea islands and back, but you will find good use for your technical abilities on the voyage. Reply at once."

Next day the following telegram arrived from Torstein:

"COMING. TORSTEIN."

Plans being discussed before the start in the Explorers Club in New York. From left to right: Chief of Clannfhearghuis, Herman Watzinger, the author, Greenland explorer Peter Freuchen.

Over the Andes for wood—our jeep on a mountain road 13,000 feet above sea level. Indians with pack donkeys, Indian women spinning wool as they walk, and flocks of llamas were the only living creatures we met.

In the Ecuadorian jungle we found our balsa logs. We felled the biggest trees we could find, peeled off the bark in Indian style, and built a makeshift raft on which we drifted down the Palenque and the Guayas to the Pacific.

Above: The six members of the *Kon-Tiki* expedition. From left to right: Knut Haugland, Bengt Danielsson, the author, Erik Hesselberg, Torstein Raaby, Herman Watzinger.

Below: Building the raft in Peru. We lashed the nine big balsa logs together with ordinary hemp ropes, using neither nails nor metal in any form.

Kon-Tiki ready to start in Callao Harbor. Like the Indians' prehistoric vessels on the west coast of South America, our raft had an open bamboo cabin and two masts lashed together with a square sail between. The woman secretary of the expedition, Gerd Vold (*inset*), named the raft by smashing a coconut against the bow. The raft received the name *Kon-Tiki* in memory of the Peruvian sun-god, who long ago vanished westward across the sea.

Above: Erik puts the finishing touch to the raft. A Peruvian sailor helps him to fix a tholepin of the hardest wood for the steering oar.
Below: Thank you and good-by! The tug *Guardian Rios* turns back and leaves us to our fate.

Under full sail out at sea. Nature was our only teacher, the last raftsmen having died several hundred years before, and we went through a hard school in our first weeks in the Humboldt Current off the coast of South America.

The kitchen department. Before our fresh fruit ran out, we had entered waters where fish abounded. We cooked our food on a couple of primus stoves, which stood on the bottom of a wooden box, and generally had our meals on the starboard side of the raft in front of the entrance to the cabin. Like our prehistoric forerunners, we also had with us sweet potatoes and gourds from Peru.

The other two also accepted.

As sixth member of the party we had in view now one man and now another, but each time some obstacle arose. In the meantime Herman and I had to attack the supply problem. We did not mean to eat llama flesh or dried *kumara* potatoes on our trip, for we were not making it to prove that we had once been Indians ourselves. Our intention was to test the performance and quality of the Inca raft, its seaworthiness and loading capacity, and to ascertain whether the elements would really propel it across the sea to Polynesia with its crew still on board. Our native forerunners could certainly have managed to live on dried meat and fish and *kumara* potatoes on board, as that was their staple diet ashore. We were also going to try to find out, on the actual trip, whether they could have obtained additional supplies of fresh fish and rain water while crossing the sea. As our own diet I had thought of simple field service rations, as we knew them from the war.

Just at that time a new assistant to the Norwegian military attaché in Washington had arrived. I had acted as second in command of his company in Finnmark and knew that he was a "ball of fire," who loved to attack and solve with savage energy any problem set before him. Björn Rörholt was a man of that vital type which feels quite lost if it has fought its way out into the open without immediately sighting a new problem to tackle.

I wrote to him explaining the situation and asked him to use his tracking sense to smell out a contact man in the supply department of the American army. The chances were that the laboratory was experimenting with new field rations we could test, in the same way as we were testing equipment for the Air Force laboratory.

Two days later Björn telephoned us from Washington. He had been in contact with the foreign liaison section of the American War Department, and they would like to know what it was all about.

Herman and I took the first train to Washington.

We found Björn in his room in the military attaché's office.

"I think it'll be all right," he said. "We'll be received at the foreign liaison section tomorrow provided we bring a proper letter from the colonel."

The "colonel" was Otto Munthe-Kaas, the Norwegian military attaché. He was well-disposed and more than willing to give us a proper letter of introduction when he heard what our business was.

When we came to fetch the document next morning, he suddenly rose and said he thought it would be best if he came with us himself. We drove out in the colonel's car to the Pentagon building to the offices of the War Department. The colonel and Björn sat in front in their smartest military turnout, while Herman and I sat behind and peered through the windshield at the huge Pentagon building, which towered up on the plain before us. This gigantic building with thirty thousand clerks and sixteen miles of corridors was to form the frame of our impending raft conference with military "high-ups." Never, before or after, did the little raft seem to Herman and me so helplessly small.

After endless wanderings in ramps and corridors we reached the door of the foreign liaison section, and soon, surrounded by brand-new uniforms, we were sitting round a large mahogany table at which the head of the foreign liaison section himself presided.

The stern, broad-built West Point officer, who bulked big at the end of the table, had a certain difficulty at first in understanding what the connection between the American War Department and our wooden raft was, but the colonel's well-considered words, and the favorable result of a hurricane-like examination by the officers round the table, slowly brought him over to our side, and he read with interest the letter from the equipment laboratory of the Air Material Command. Then he rose and gave his staff a concise order to help us through the proper channels and, wishing us good luck for the present, marched out of the conference room. When the door had shut on him, a young staff captain whispered in my ear:

"I'll bet you'll get what you want. It sounds like a minor military operation and brings a little change into our daily office peacetime routine; besides, it'll be a good opportunity of methodically testing equipment."

The liaison office at once arranged a meeting with Colonel Lewis at the quartermaster general's experimental laboratory, and Herman and I were taken over there by car.

Colonel Lewis was an affable giant of an officer with a sportsman's bearing. He at once called in the men in charge of experiments in the different sections. All were amicably disposed and immediately suggested quantities of equipment they would like us to test thoroughly. They exceeded our wildest hopes as they rattled off the names of nearly everything we could want, from field rations to sunburn ointment and splash-proof sleeping bags. Then they took us on an extensive tour to look at the things. We tasted special rations in smart packings; we tested matches which struck well even if they had been dipped in water, new primus stoves and water kegs, rubber bags and special boots, kitchen utensils and knives which would float, and all that an expedition could want.

I glanced at Herman. He looked like a good, expectant little boy walking through a chocolate shop with a rich aunt. The colonel walked in front demonstrating all these delights, and when the tour was completed staff clerks had made note of the kinds of goods and the quantities we required. I thought the battle was won and felt only an urge to rush home to the hotel in order to assume a horizontal position and think things over in peace and quiet. Then the tall, friendly colonel suddenly said:

"Well, now we must go in and have a talk with the boss; it's he who'll decide whether we can give you these things."

I felt my heart sink down into my boots. So we were to start our eloquence right from the beginning again, and heaven alone knew what kind of man the "boss" was!

We found that the boss was a little officer with an intensely earnest manner. He sat behind his writing table and examined us with keen blue eyes as we came into the office. He asked us to sit down.

"Well, what do these gentlemen want?" he asked Colonel Lewis sharply, without taking his eyes off mine.

"Oh, a few little things," Lewis hastened to reply. He explained the whole of our errand in outline, while the chief listened patiently without moving a finger.

"And what can they give us in return?" he asked, quite unimpressed.

"Well," said Lewis in a conciliatory tone, "we hoped that perhaps the expedition would be able to write reports on the new provisions and some of the equipment, based on the severe conditions in which they will be using it."

The intensely earnest officer behind the writing table leaned back in his chair with unaffected slowness, with his eyes still fixed on mine, and I felt myself sinking to the bottom of the deep leather chair as he said coolly:

"I don't see at all how they can give us anything in return."

There was dead silence in the room. Colonel Lewis fingered his collar, and neither of us said a word.

"But," the chief suddenly broke out, and now a gleam had come into the corner of his eye, "courage and enterprise count, too. Colonel Lewis, let them have the things!"

I was still sitting, half intoxicated with delight, in the cab which was taking us home to the hotel, when Herman began to laugh and giggle to himself at my side.

"Are you tight?" I asked anxiously.

"No," he laughed shamelessly, "but I've been calculating that the provisions we got include 684 boxes of pineapple, and that's my favorite dish."

There are a thousand things to be done, and mostly at the same time, when six men and a wooden raft and its cargo are to assemble at a place down on the coast of Peru. And we had three months and no Aladdin's lamp at our disposal.

We flew to New York with an introduction from the liaison office and met Professor Behre at Columbia University. He was head of the War Department's Geographical Research Committee, and it was he who pressed the buttons which at last brought Herman all his valuable instruments and apparatus for scientific measurements.

Then we flew to Washington to meet Admiral Glover at the Naval Hydrographic Institute. The good-natured old sea dog called in all his officers and pointed to the chart of the Pacific on the wall as he introduced Herman and me.

"These young gentlemen want to check up on our current maps. Help them!"

When the wheels had rolled a bit further, the English Colonel Lumsden called a conference at the British Military Mission in Washington to discuss our future problems and the chances of a favorable outcome. We received plenty of good advice and a selection of British equipment which was flown over from England to be tried out on the raft expedition. The British medical officer was an enthusiastic advocate of a mysterious shark powder. We were to sprinkle a few pinches of the powder on the water if a shark became too impudent, and the shark would vanish immediately.

"Sir," I said politely, "can we rely on this powder?"

"Well," said the Englishman, smiling, "that's just what we want to find out ourselves!"

When time is short and plane replaces train, while taxi replaces legs, one's wallet crumples up like a withered herbarium. When we had spent the cost of my return ticket to Norway, we went and called on our friends and backers in New York to get our finances straight.

There we encountered surprising and discouraging problems. The financial manager was ill in bed with fever, and his two colleagues were powerless till he was in action again. They stood firmly by our economic agreement, but they could do nothing for the time being. We were asked to postpone the business, a useless request, for we could not stop the numerous wheels which were now revolving vigorously. We could only hold on now; it was too late to stop or brake. Our friends the backers agreed to dissolve the whole syndicate in order to give us a free hand to act quickly and independently without them.

So there we were in the street with our hands in our trousers pockets.

"December, January, February," said Herman.

"And at a pinch March," said I, "but then we simply must start!"

If all else seemed obscure, one thing was clear to us. Ours was a journey with an objective, and we did not want to be classed with acrobats who roll down Niagara in empty barrels or sit on the knobs of flag staffs for seventeen days.

"No chewing-gum or pop backing," Herman said.

On this point we were in profound agreement.

We could get Norwegian currency. But that did not solve the problems on our side of the Atlantic. We could apply for a grant from some institution, but we could scarcely get one for a disputed theory; after all, that was just why we were going on the raft expedition. We soon found that neither press nor private promoters dared to put money into what they themselves and all the insurance companies regarded as a suicide voyage; but, if we came back safe and sound, it would be another matter.

Things looked pretty gloomy, and for many days we could see no ray of hope. It was then that Colonel Munthe-Kaas came into the picture again.

"You're in a fix, boys," he said. "Here's a check to begin with. You can return it when you come back from the South Sea islands."

Several other people followed his example, and my private loan was soon big enough to tide us over without help from agents or others. We could fly to South America and start building the raft.

The old Peruvian rafts were built of balsa wood, which in a dry state is lighter than cork. The balsa tree grows in Peru, but only beyond the mountains in the Andes range, so the seafarers in Inca times went up along the coast to Ecuador, where they felled their huge balsa trees right down on the edge of the Pacific. We meant to do the same.

Today's travel problems are different from those of Inca times. We have cars and planes and travel bureaus but, so as not to make things altogether too easy, we have also impediments called frontiers, with brass-buttoned attendants who doubt one's alibi, maltreat one's luggage, and weigh one down with stamped forms—if one is lucky enough to get in at all. It was the fear of these men with brass buttons that decided us we could not land in South America with packing cases and trunks full of strange devices, raise our hats, and ask politely in broken Spanish to be allowed to come in and sail away on a raft. We should be clapped into jail.

"No," said Herman. "We must have an official introduction."

One of our friends in the dissolved triumvirate was a correspondent at the United Nations, and he offered to take us out there by car for aid. We were greatly impressed when we came into the great hall of the assembly, where men of all nations sat on benches side by side listening silently to the flow of speech from a black-haired Russian in front of the gigantic map of the world that decorated the back wall.

Our friend the correspondent managed in a quiet moment to get hold of one of the delegates from Peru and, later, one of Ecuador's representatives. On a deep leather sofa in an antechamber they listened eagerly to our plan of crossing the sea to support a theory that men of an ancient civilization from their own country had been the first to reach the Pacific islands. Both promised to inform their governments and guaranteed us support when we came to their respective countries. Trygve Lie, passing through the anteroom, came over to us when he heard we were countrymen of his, and someone proposed that he should come with us on the raft. But there were billows enough for him on land. The assistant secretary of the United Nations, Dr. Benjamin Cohen from Chile, was himself a well-known amateur archaeologist, and he gave me a letter to the President of Peru, who was a personal friend of his. We also met in the hall the Norwegian ambassador, Wilhelm von Munthe of Morgenstierne, who from then on gave the expedition invaluable support.

So we bought two tickets and flew to South America. When the four heavy engines began to roar one after another, we sank into our seats exhausted. We had an unspeakable feeling of relief that the first stage of the program was over and that we were now going straight ahead to the adventure.

3.

To
South America

As our plane crossed the equator, it began a slant-ing descent through the milk-white clouds which till then had lain beneath us like a blinding waste of snow in the burning sun. The fleecy vapor clung to the windows till it dissolved and remained hanging over us like clouds, and the bright green roof of a rolling, billowy jungle appeared. We flew in over the South American re-public of Ecuador and landed at the tropical port of Guayaquil.

With yesterday's coats, vests, and overcoats over our arms we climbed out into the atmosphere of a hothouse to meet chattering southerners in tropical clothes and felt our shirts sticking to our backs like wet paper. We were embraced by customs and immigration of-ficials and almost carried to a cab, which took us to the best hotel in the town, the only good one. Here we quickly found our way to our respective baths and lay down flat under the cold-water faucet. We had reached the country where the balsa tree grows and were to buy timber to build our raft.

The first day we spent in learning the monetary system and enough Spanish to find our way back to the hotel. On the second day we ventured away from our baths in steadily widening circles, and, when Herman had satisfied the longing of his childhood to touch a real palm tree and I was a walking bowl of fruit salad, we decided to go and negotiate for balsa.

Unfortunately this was easier said than done. We could certainly buy balsa in quantities but not in the form of whole logs, as we wanted it. The days when balsa trees were accessible down on the coast were past. The last war had put an end to them; they had been felled in thousands and shipped to the aircraft factories because the wood was so gaseous and light. We were told that the only place where large balsa trees now grew was in the jungle in the interior of the country.

"Then we must go inland and fell them ourselves," we said.

"Impossible," said the authorities. "The rains have just begun, and all the roads into the jungle are impassable because of flood water and deep mud. If you want balsa wood, you must come back to Ecuador in six months; the rains will be over then and the roads up country will have dried."

In our extremity we called on Don Gustavo von Buchwald, the balsa king of Ecuador, and Herman unrolled his sketch of the raft with the lengths of timber we required. The slight little balsa king seized the telephone eagerly and set his agents to work searching. They found planks and light boards and separate short blocks in every sawmill but they could not find one single serviceable log. There were two big logs, as dry as tinder, at Don Gustavo's own dump, but they would not take us far. It was clear that the search was useless.

"But a brother of mine has a big balsa plantation," said Don Gustavo encouragingly. "His name is Don Federico and he lives at Quevedo, a little jungle town up country. He can get you all you want as soon as we can get hold of him after the rains. It's no use now because of the jungle rain up country."

If Don Gustavo said a thing was no use, all the balsa experts in Ecuador would say it was no use. So here we were in Guayaquil with no timber for the raft and with no possibility of going in and felling the trees ourselves until several months later, when it would be too late.

"Time's short," said Herman.

"And balsa we must have," said I. "The raft must be an exact copy, or we shall have no guarantee of coming through alive."

A little school map we found in the hotel, with green jungle, brown mountains, and inhabited places ringed round in red, told us that the jungle stretched unbroken from the Pacific right to the foot of the towering Andes. I had an idea. It was clearly impracticable now to get from the coastal area through the jungle to the balsa trees at Quevedo, but suppose we could get to the trees from the inland side, by coming straight down into the jungle from the bare snow mountains of the Andes range? Here was a possibility, the only one we saw.

Out on the airfield we found a little cargo plane which was willing to take us up to Quito, the capital of this strange country, high up on the Andes plateau, 9,300 feet above sea level. Between packing cases and furniture we caught occasional glimpses of green jungle and shining rivers before we disappeared into the clouds. When we came out again, the lowlands were hidden under an endless sea of rolling vapor, but ahead of us dry mountainsides and bare cliffs rose from the sea of mist right up to a brilliant blue sky.

The plane climbed straight up the mountainside as in an invisible funicular railway, and, although the Equator itself was in sight, at last we had shining snow fields alongside us. Then we glided between the mountains and over a rich alpine plateau clad in spring green, on which we landed close to the world's most unusual capital.

Most of Quito's 175,000 inhabitants are pure or half-breed mountain Indians, for it was their forefathers' own capital long before Columbus and our own race knew America. The city is filled with ancient monasteries, containing art treasures of immeasurable value, and other magnificent buildings dating from Spanish times, towering over the roofs of low Indian houses built of bricks of sun-dried clay. A labyrinth of narrow alleys winds between the clay walls, and these we found swarming with mountain Indians in red-speckled cloaks and big homemade hats. Some were going to market with pack donkeys, while others sat hunched up along the adobe walls dozing in the hot sun. A few automobiles containing aristocrats of Spanish origin, going at half-speed and hooting ceaselessly, succeeded in finding a path along the one-way alleys among children and donkeys and barelegged Indians. The air up here on the high plateau was of such brilliant crystalline clearness that the mountains round us seemed to come into the street picture and contribute to its other-world atmosphere.

Our friend from the cargo plane, Jorge, nicknamed "the crazy flier," belonged to one of the old Spanish families in Quito. He installed us in an antiquated, amusing hotel and then went round, sometimes with and sometimes without us, trying to get us transport over the mountains and down into the jungle to Quevedo. We met in the evening in an old Spanish café, and Jorge was full of bad news; we must absolutely put out of our heads the idea of going to Quevedo. Neither men nor vehicle were to be obtained to take us over the mountains, and certainly not down into the jungle where the rains had begun and where there was danger of attack if one stuck fast in the mud. Only last year a party of ten American oil engineers had been found killed by poisoned arrows in the eastern part of Ecuador, where many Indians still went about in the jungle stark naked and hunted with poisoned arrows.

"Some of them are head-hunters," Jorge said in a hollow voice, seeing that Herman, quite unperturbed, was helping himself to more beef and red wine.

"You think I exaggerate," he continued in a low voice. "But, although it is strictly forbidden, there are still people in this country who make a living by selling shrunken human heads. It's impossible to control it, and to this very day the jungle Indians cut off the heads of their enemies among other nomad tribes. They smash up and remove the skull itself and fill the empty skin of the head with hot sand, so that the whole head shrinks till it's hardly bigger than a cat's head, without losing its shape or its features. These shrunken heads of enemies were once valuable trophies; now they're rare black-market goods. Half-breed middlemen see that they get down to the buyers on the coast, who sell them to tourists for fabulous prices."

Jorge looked at us triumphantly. He little knew that Herman and I that same day had been dragged into a porter's lodge and offered two of these heads at 1,000 sucres apiece. These heads nowadays are often fakes, made up from monkeys' heads, but these two were genuine enough, pure Indians and so true to life that every tiny feature was preserved. They were the heads of a man and a woman, both the size of oranges; the woman was actually pretty, though only the eyelashes and long black hair had preserved their natural size. I shuddered at Jorge's warning but expressed my doubts whether there were head-hunters west of the mountains.

"One can never know," said Jorge gloomily. "And what would you say if your friend disappeared and his head came into the market in miniature? That happened to a friend of mine once," he added, staring at me stubbornly.

"Tell us about it," said Herman, chewing his beef slowly and with only moderate enjoyment.

I laid my fork carefully aside, and Jorge told his story. He was once living with his wife on an outpost in the jungle, washing gold and buying up the take of the other gold-washers. The family had at that time a native friend who brought his gold regularly and sold it for goods. One day this friend was killed in the jungle. Jorge tracked down the murderer and threatened to shoot him. Now the murderer was one of those who were suspected of selling shrunken human heads, and Jorge promised to spare his life if he handed over the head at once. The murderer at once produced the head of Jorge's friend, now as small as a man's fist. Jorge was quite upset when he saw his friend again, for he was quite unchanged except that he had become so very small. Much moved, he took the little head home to his wife. She fainted when she saw it, and Jorge had to hide his friend in a trunk. But it was so damp in the jungle that clusters of green mold formed on the head, so that Jorge had to take it out now and then and dry it in the sun. It hung very nicely by the hair on a clothesline, and Jorge's wife fainted every time she caught sight of it. But one day a mouse gnawed its way into the trunk and made a horrid mess of his friend. Jorge was much distressed and buried his friend with full ceremonies in a tiny little hole up on the airfield. For after all he was a human being, Jorge concluded.

"Nice dinner," I said to change the subject.

As we went home in the dark, I had a disagreeable feeling that Herman's hat had sunk far down over his ears. But he had only pulled it down to protect himself from the cold night wind from the mountains.

Next day we were sitting with our own Consul General Bryhn and his wife under the eucalyptus trees at their big country place outside the town. Bryhn hardly thought our planned jungle trip to Quevedo would lead to any drastic change in our hat sizes, but— there were robbers about in those very regions we had thought of visiting. He produced clippings from local papers announcing that soldiers were to be sent out, when the dry season came, to extirpate the *bandidos* who infested the regions around Quevedo. To go there now was the sheerest madness, and we would never get guides or transport. While we were talking to him, we saw a jeep from the American military attaché's office tear past along the road, and this gave us an idea. We went up to the American Embassy, accompanied by the consul general, and were able to see the military attaché himself. He was a trim, lighthearted young man in khaki and riding boots and asked laughingly why we had strayed to the top of the Andes when the local papers said we were to go to sea on a wooden raft.

We explained that the wood was still standing upright in the Quevedo jungle and we were up here on the roof of the continent and could not get to it. We asked the military attaché either (*a*) to lend us a plane and two parachutes or (*b*) to lend us a jeep with a driver who knew the country.

The military attaché at first sat speechless at our assurance; then he shook his head despairingly and said with a smile, all right—since we gave him no third choice, he preferred the second!

At a quarter past five the next morning a jeep rolled up to our hotel entrance, and an Ecuadorian captain of engineers jumped out and reported himself at our service. His orders were to drive us to Quevedo, mud or no mud. The jeep was packed full of gasoline cans, for there were no gasoline pumps or even wheel tracks along the route we were to take. Our new friend, Captain Agurto Alexis Alvarez, was armed to the teeth with knives and firearms on account of the reports of *bandidos*. We had come to the country peacefully in business suits to buy timber for ready money down on the coast, and the whole of our equipment on board the jeep consisted of a bag of tinned food, except that we had hurriedly acquired a second-hand camera and a pair of tear-proof khaki breeches for each of us. In addition, the consul general had pressed upon us his big revolver with an ample supply of ammunition to exterminate everything that crossed our path. The jeep whizzed away through empty alleys where the moon shone ghostly pale on whitewashed adobe walls, till we came out into the country and raced at a giddy speed along a good sand road southward through the mountain region.

It was good going all along the range as far as the mountain village of Latacunga, where windowless Indian houses clustered blindly round a whitewashed country church with palms in a square. Here we turned off along a mule track which undulated and twisted westward over hill and valley into the Andes. We came into a world we had never dreamed of. It was the mountain Indians' own world—east of the sun and west of the moon—outside time and beyond space. On the whole drive we saw not a carriage or a wheel. The traffic consisted of barelegged goatherds in gaily colored ponchos, driving forward disorderly herds of stiff-legged, dignified llamas, and now and then whole families of Indians coming along the road. The husband usually rode ahead on a mule, while his little wife trotted behind with her entire collection of hats on her head and the youngest child in a bag on her back. All the time she ambled along, she spun wool with her fingers. Donkeys and mules jogged behind at leisure, loaded with boughs and rushes and pottery.

The farther we went, the fewer the Indians who spoke Spanish, and soon Agurto's linguistic capacities were as useless as our own. A cluster of huts lay here and there up in the mountains; fewer and fewer were built of clay, while more and more were made of twigs and dry grass. Both the huts and the sun-browned, wrinkle-faced people seemed to have grown up out of the earth itself, from the baking effect of the mountain sun on the rock walls of the Andes. They belonged to cliff and scree and upland pasture as naturally as the mountain grass itself. Poor in possessions and small in stature, the mountain Indians had the wiry hardiness of wild animals and the childlike alertness of a primitive people, and the less they could talk, the more they could laugh. Radiant faces with snow-white teeth shone upon us from all we saw. There was nothing to indicate that the white man had lost or earned a dime in these regions. There were no billboards or road signs, and if a tin box or a scrap of paper was flung down by the roadside, it was picked up at once as a useful household article.

We went on up over sun-smitten slopes without a bush or tree and down into valleys of desert sand and cactus, till finally we climbed up and reached the topmost crest with snow fields round the peak and a wind so bitingly cold that we had to slacken speed in order not to freeze to bits as we sat in our shirts longing for jungle heat. For long stretches we had to drive across country between the mountains, over scree and grassy ridges, searching for the next bit of road. But when we reached the west wall, where the Andes range falls precipitously to the lowlands, the mule track was cut along shelves in the loose rock, and sheer cliffs and gorges were all about us. We put all our trust in friend Agurto as he sat crouched over the steering wheel, always swinging out when we came to a precipice. Suddenly a violent gust of wind met us; we had reached the outermost crest of the Andes chain, where the mountain fell away sharply in a series of precipices to the jungle far down in a bottomless abyss 12,000 feet beneath us. But we were cheated of the dizzy view over the sea of jungle, for, as soon as we reached the edge, thick cloud banks rolled about us like steam from a witches' cauldron. But now our road ran down unhindered into the depths. Always down, in steep loops along gorges and bluffs and ridges, while the air grew damper and warmer and ever fuller of the heavy, deadening hothouse air which rose from the jungle world below.

And then the rain began. First gently, then it began to pour and beat upon the jeep like drumsticks, and soon the chocolate-colored water was flowing down the rocks on every side of us. We almost flowed down, too, away from the dry mountain plateaus behind us and into another world, where stick and stone and clay slope were soft and lush with moss and turf. Leaves shot up; soon they became giant leaves hanging like green umbrellas and dripping over the hillside. Then came the first feeble advanced posts of the jungle trees, with heavy fringes and beards of moss and climbing plants hanging from them. There was a gurgling and splashing everywhere. As the slopes grew gentler, the jungle rolled up swiftly like an army of green giant growths that swallowed up the little jeep as it splashed along the waterlogged clay road. We were in the jungle. The air was moist and warm and heavy with the smell of vegetation.

Darkness had fallen when we reached a cluster of palm-roofed huts on a ridge. Dripping with warm water, we left the jeep for a night under a dry roof. The horde of fleas that attacked us in the hut were drowned in the next day's rain. With the jeep full of bananas and other tropical fruit we went on downhill through the jungle, down and down, though we thought we had reached bottom long ago. The mud grew worse but it did not stop us, and the robbers kept at an unknown distance.

Not till the road was barred by a broad river of muddy water rolling down through the jungle did the jeep give up. We stood stuck fast, unable to move either up or down along the riverbank. In an open clearing stood a hut where a few half-breed Indians were stretching out a jaguar skin on a sunny wall, while dogs and fowl were splashing about enjoying themselves on top of some cocoa beans spread out to dry in the sun. When the jeep came bumping along, the place came to life and some natives who spoke Spanish informed us that this was the Rio Palenque and that Quevedo was just on the other side. There was no bridge there, and the river was swift and deep, but they were willing to float us and the jeep over by raft. The queer contraption lay down by the bank. Twisted logs as thick as our arms were fastened together with vegetable fibers and bamboos to form a flimsy raft, twice the length and breadth of the jeep. With a plank under each wheel and our hearts in our mouths we drove the jeep out onto the logs, and though most of them were submerged under the muddy water, they did bear the jeep and us and four half-naked chocolate-colored men who pushed us off with long poles.

"Balsa?" Herman and I asked in the same breath.

"Balsa," one of the fellows nodded, with a disrespectful kick at the logs.

The current seized us and we whirled down the river, while the men pushed in their poles at the right places and kept the raft on an even diagonal course across the current and into quieter water on the other side. This was our first meeting with the balsa tree and our first trip on a balsa raft. We brought the raft safely to land at the farther bank and motored triumphantly into Quevedo. Two rows of tarred wooden houses with motionless vultures on the palm roofs formed a kind of street, and this was the whole place. The inhabitants dropped whatever they might be carrying, and black and brown, young and old, appeared swarming out of both doors and windows. They rushed to meet the jeep—a menacing, chattering tide of humanity. They scrambled on to it and under it and round it. We kept a tight hold on our worldly possessions while Agurto attempted desperate maneuvers at the steering wheel. Then the jeep had a puncture and went down on one knee. We had arrived at Quevedo and had to endure the embrace of welcome.

Don Federico's plantation lay a bit farther down the river. When the jeep came bumping into the yard along a path between the mango trees with Agurto, Herman, and me, the lean old jungle-dweller came to meet us at a trot with his nephew Angelo, a small boy who lived with him out in the wilds. We gave messages from Don Gustavo, and soon the jeep was standing alone in the yard while a fresh tropical shower streamed down over the jungle. There was a festive meal in Don Federico's bungalow; suckling pigs and chickens crackled over an open fire, while we sat round a dish loaded with tropical fruit and explained what we had come for. The jungle rain pouring down on the ground outside sent a warm sweet gust of scented blossoms and clay in through the window netting.

Don Federico had become as brisk as a boy. Why, yes, he had known balsa rafts since he was a child. Fifty years ago, when he lived down by the sea, the Indians from Peru still used to come sailing up along the coast on big balsa rafts to sell fish in Guayaquil. They could bring a couple of tons of dried fish in a bamboo cabin in the middle of the raft, or they might have wives and children and dogs and fowl on board. Such big balsa trees as they had used for their rafts would be hard to find now in the rains, for floodwater and mud had already made it impossible to get to the balsa plantation up in the forest, even on horseback. But Don Federico would do his best; there might still be some single trees growing wild in the forest nearer the bungalow, and we did not need many.

Late in the evening the rain stopped for a time, and we went for a turn under the mango trees round the bungalow. Here Don Federico had every kind of wild orchid in the world hanging down from the branches, with half-coconuts as flowerpots. Unlike cultivated orchids, these rare plants gave out a wonderful scent, and Herman was bending down to stick his nose into one of them when something like a long, thin, glittering eel emerged from the leaves above him. A lightning blow from Angelo's whip, and a wriggling snake fell to the ground. A second later it was held fast to the earth with a forked stick over its neck, and then its head was crushed.

"*Mortal*," said Angelo and exposed two curved poison fangs to show what he meant.

After that we thought we saw poisonous snakes lurking in the foliage everywhere and slipped into the house with Angelo's trophy hanging lifeless across a stick. Herman sat down to skin the monster, and Don Federico was telling fantastic stories about poisonous snakes and boa constrictors as thick as dinner plates when we suddenly noticed the shadows of two enormous scorpions on the wall, the size of lobsters. They rushed at each other and engaged in a life-and-death battle with their pincers, with their hinder parts turned up and their curved poisonous sting at the tail ready for the deathblow. It was a horrible sight, and not till we moved the oil lamp did we see that it had cast a supernaturally gigantic shadow of two quite ordinary scorpions of the size of one's finger, which were fighting on the edge of the bureau.

"Let them be," Don Federico laughed. "One'll kill the other, and we want the survivor in the house to keep the cockroaches away. Just keep your mosquito net tight round the bed and shake your clothes before you put them on, and you'll be all right. I've often been bitten by scorpions and I'm not dead yet," added the old man, laughing.

I slept well, except that I woke up thinking of poisonous creatures every time a lizard or bat squeaked and scrabbled too noisily near my pillow.

Next morning we got up early to go and search for balsa trees.

"Better shake our clothes," said Agurto, and as he spoke a scorpion fell out of his shirt sleeve and shot down into a crack in the floor.

Soon after sunrise Don Federico sent his men out on horseback in all directions to look for accessible balsa trees along the paths. Our own party consisted of Don Federico, Herman, and myself, and we soon found our way to an open place where there was a gigantic old tree of which Don Federico knew. It towered high above the trees round about, and the trunk was three feet thick. In Polynesian style we christened the tree before we touched it; we gave it the name Ku, after a Polynesian deity of American origin. Then we swung the ax and drove it into the balsa trunk till the forest echoed our blows. But cutting a sappy balsa was like cutting cork with a blunt ax; the ax simply rebounded, and I had not delivered many strokes before Herman had to relieve me. The ax changed hands time after time, while the splinters flew and the sweat trickled in the heat of the jungle.

Late in the day Ku was standing like a cock on one leg, quivering under our blows; soon he tottered and crashed down heavily over the surrounding forest, big branches and small trees being pulled down by the giant's fall. We had torn the branches from the trunk and were beginning to rip off the bark in zigzags in Indian style when Herman suddenly dropped the ax and leaped into the air as if doing a Polynesian war dance, with his hand pressed to his leg. Out of his trouser leg fell a shining ant as big as a scorpion and with a long sting at its tail. It must have had a skull like a lobster's claw, for it was almost impossible to stamp it under one's heel on the ground.

"A kongo," Don Federico explained with regret. "The little brute's worse than a scorpion, but it isn't dangerous to a healthy man."

Herman was tender and sore for several days, but this did not prevent his galloping with us on horseback along the jungle paths, looking for more giant balsas in the forest. From time to time we heard creaking and crashing and a heavy thud somewhere in the virgin forest. Don Federico nodded with a satisfied air. It meant that his half-breed Indians had felled a new giant balsa for the raft. In a week Ku had been followed by Kane, Kama, Ilo, Mauri, Ra, Rangi, Papa, Taranga, Kura, Kukara, and Hiti—twelve mighty balsas, all christened in honor of Polynesian legendary figures whose names had once been borne with Tiki over the sea from Peru. The logs, glistening with sap, were dragged down through the jungle first by horses and at the last by Don Federico's tractor, which brought them to the riverbank in front of the bungalow.

The sap-filled logs were far from being as light as corks. They must have weighed a ton apiece, and we waited with great anxiety to see how they would float in the water. We rolled them out to the edge of the bank one by one; there we made fast a rope of tough, climbing plants to the ends of the logs that they might not vanish downstream when we let them enter the water. Then we rolled them in turn down the bank and into the river. There was a mighty splash. They swung round and floated, about as much above as below the surface of the water, and when we went out along them they remained steady. We bound the timbers together with tough lianas that hung down from the tops of the jungle trees, so as to make two temporary rafts, one towing the other. Then we loaded the rafts with all the bamboos and lianas we should need later, and Herman and I went on board with two men of a mysterious mixed race, with whom we had no common language.

When we cut our moorings, we were caught by the whirling masses of water and went off downstream at a good pace. The last glimpse we had in the drizzle, as we rounded the first headland, was of our excellent friends standing on the end of the point in front of the bungalow, waving. Then we crept under a little shelter of green banana leaves and left steering problems to the two brown experts who had stationed themselves one in the bow and one astern, each holding a huge oar. They kept the raft in the swiftest current with nonchalant ease, and we danced downstream on a winding course between sunken trees and sandbanks.

The jungle stood like a solid wall along the banks on both sides, and parrots and other bright-colored birds fluttered out of the dense foliage as we passed. Once or twice an alligator hurled itself into the river and became invisible in the muddy water. But we soon caught sight of a much more remarkable monster. This was an iguana, or giant lizard, as big as a crocodile but with a large throat and fringed back. It lay dozing on the clay bank as if it had overslept from prehistoric times and did not move as we glided past. The oarsmen made signs to us not to shoot. Soon afterward we saw a smaller specimen about three feet long. It was running away along a thick branch which hung out over the raft. It ran only till it was in safety, and then it sat, all shining blue and green, and stared at us with cold snake's eyes as we passed. Later we passed a fern-clad hillock, and on the top of it lay the biggest iguana of all. It was like the silhouette of a fringed Chinese dragon carved in stone as it stood out motionless against the sky with chest and head raised. It did not as much as turn its head as we curved round it under the hillocks and vanished into the jungle.

Farther down we smelled smoke and passed several huts with straw roofs which lay in clearings along the bank. We on the raft were the objects of close attention from sinister-looking individuals on land, an unfavorable mixture of Indian, Negro, and Spaniard. Their boats, great dugout canoes, lay drawn up on to the bank.

When mealtimes came, we relieved our friends at the steering oars while they fried fish and breadfruit over a little fire regulated with wet clay. Roast chicken, eggs, and tropical fruits were also part of the menu on board, while the logs transported themselves and us at a fine speed down through the jungle toward the sea. What did it matter now if the water swept and splashed round us? The more it rained, the swifter the current ran.

When darkness fell over the river, an ear-splitting orchestra struck up on the bank. Toads and frogs, crickets and mosquitoes, croaked or chirped or hummed in a prolonged chorus of many voices. Now and again the shrill scream of a wild cat rang through the darkness, and soon another, and yet another, from birds scared into flight by the night prowlers of the jungle. Once or twice we saw the gleam of a fire in a native hut and heard bawling voices and the barking of dogs as we slid past in the night. But for the most part we sat alone with the jungle orchestra under the stars, till drowsiness and rain drove us into the cabin of leaves, where we went to sleep with our pistols loose in their holsters.

The farther downstream we drifted, the thicker became the huts and native plantations, and soon there were regular villages on the banks. The traffic here consisted of dugout canoes punted along with long poles, and now and then we saw a little balsa raft loaded with heaps of green bananas bound for market.

Where the Palenque joined the Rio Guayas, the water had risen so high that the paddle steamer was plying busily between Vinces and Guayaquil down on the coast. To save valuable time Herman and I each got a hammock on board the paddle steamer and steamed off across the thickly populated flat country to the coast. Our brown friends were to follow, drifting down alone with the timber.

At Guayaquil Herman and I parted. He was to remain at the mouth of the Guayas to stop the balsa logs as they came drifting down. Thence he was to take them, as cargo on a coasting steamer, to Peru, where he was to direct the building of the raft and make a faithful copy of the Indians' old-time vessels. I myself took the regular plane southward to Lima, the capital of Peru, to find a suitable place for building the raft.

The plane ascended to a great height along the shore of the Pacific, with the desert mountains in Peru on one side and a glittering ocean far below us on the other. It was here we were to put to sea on board the raft. The sea seemed endless when seen from a plane high up. Sky and sea melted into each other along an indefinable horizon far, far away to the westward, and I could not rid myself of the thought that even beyond that horizon many hundred similar sea plains curved onward round a fifth of the earth before there was any more land—in Polynesia. I tried to project my thoughts a few weeks ahead, when we should be drifting on a speck of a raft on that blue expanse below, but quickly dismissed the thought again, for it gave me the same unpleasant feeling inside as sitting in readiness to jump with a parachute.

On my arrival in Lima I took the street car down to the port of Callao to find a place where we could build the raft. I saw at once that the whole harbor was chock-full of ships and cranes and warehouses, with customs sheds and harbor offices and all the rest. And, if there was any open beach farther out, it swarmed with bathers to such a degree that inquisitive people would pull the raft and fittings to pieces as soon as our backs were turned. Callao was now the most important port in a country of seven million people, white and brown. Times had changed for raft-builders in Peru even more than in Ecuador, and I saw only one possibility—to get inside the high concrete walls round the naval harbor, where armed men stood on guard behind the iron gate and cast menacing and suspicious looks on me and other unauthorized persons who loafed past the walls. If one could only get in there, one would be safe.

I had met the Peruvian naval attaché in Washington and had a letter from him to support me. I went to the Ministry of Marine next day with the letter and sought an audience of the minister of marine, Manuel Nieto. He received in the morning in the elegant Empire drawing room of the Ministry, gleaming with mirrors and gilding. After a time he himself came in in full uniform, a short broadly built officer, as stern as Napoleon, straightforward and concise in his manner of speech. He asked why and I said why. I asked to be allowed to build a wooden raft in the naval dockyard.

"Young man," said the minister, drumming uneasily with his fingers. "You've come in by the window instead of the door. I'll be glad to help you, but the order must come from the foreign minister to me; I can't let foreigners into the naval area and give them the use of the dockyard as a matter of course. Apply to the Foreign Ministry in writing, and good luck."

I thought apprehensively of papers circulating and disappearing into the blue. Happy were the rude days of Kon-Tiki, when applications were an unknown hindrance!

To see the foreign minister in person was considerably harder. Norway had no local legation in Peru, and our helpful Consul General Bahr could, therefore, take me no farther than the counselors of the Foreign Ministry. I was afraid things would get no further. Dr. Cohen's letter to the President of the republic might come in useful now. So I sought through his adjutant an audience of His Excellency Don José Bustamante y Rivero, president of Peru. A day or two later I was told to be at the palace at twelve o'clock.

Lima is a modern city, with half a million inhabitants, and lies spread over a green plain at the foot of the desert mountains. Architecturally, and thanks not least to its gardens and plantations, it is surely one of the most beautiful capitals in the world—a bit of modern California or Riviera variegated with old Spanish architecture. The president's palace lies in the middle of the city and is strongly guarded by armed sentries in gaily colored costumes. An audience in Peru is a serious business, and few people have seen the president except on the screen. Soldiers in shining bandoleers escorted me upstairs and to the end of a long corridor; here my name was taken and registered by three civilians, and I was shown through a colossal oak door into a room with a long table and rows of chairs. A man dressed in white received me, asked me to sit down, and disappeared. A moment later a large door opened, and I was shown into a much handsomer room, where an imposing person in a spotless uniform advanced toward me.

"The President," I thought, drawing myself up. But no. The man in the gold-edged uniform offered me an antique straight-backed chair and disappeared. I had sat on the edge of my chair for barely a minute when yet another door opened and a servant bowed me into a large gilded room with gilded furniture and splendidly decorated. The fellow vanished as quickly as he had appeared, and I sat quite alone on an antique sofa with a view of a string of empty rooms whose doors stood open. It was so silent that I could hear someone coughing cautiously several rooms away. Then steady steps approached, and I jumped up and hesitatingly greeted an imposing gentleman in uniform. But, no, this too was not he. But I understood enough of what he said to gather that the President sent me his greetings and would be free very soon when a meeting of ministers was over.

Ten minutes later steady steps once more broke the silence, and this time a man with gold lace and epaulets came in. I sprang briskly from the sofa and bowed deeply. The man bowed still more deeply and led me through several rooms and up a staircase with thick carpets. Then he left me in a tiny little room with one leather-covered chair and one sofa. In came a little man in a white suit, and I waited resignedly to see where he intended to take me. But he took me nowhere, only greeted me amiably and remained standing. This was President Bustamante y Rivero.

The President had twice as much English as I had Spanish, so when we had greeted one another and he had begged me with a gesture to sit down, our common vocabulary was exhausted. Signs and gesticulations will do a lot, but they will not get one permission to build a raft in a naval harbor in Peru. The only thing I perceived was that the President did not understand what I was saying, and he grasped that still more clearly himself, for in a little while he disappeared and came back with the air minister. The air minister, General Reveredo, was a vigorous athletic man in an Air Force uniform. He spoke English splendidly with an American accent.

I apologized for the misunderstanding and said it was not to the airfield that I had been trying to ask for admission but to the naval harbor. The general laughed and explained that he had only been called in as interpreter. Bit by bit the theory was translated to the President, who listened closely and put sharp questions through General Reveredo. At last he said:

"If it is possible that the Pacific islands were first discovered from Peru, Peru has an interest in this expedition. If we can do anything for you, tell us."

I asked for a place where we could build the raft within the walls of the naval area, access to the naval workshops, a place for the storage of equipment and facilities for bringing it into the country, the use of the dry dock and of naval personnel to help us in the work, and a vessel to tow us out from the coast when we started.

"What is he asking for?" the President asked eagerly, so that I too understood.

"Nothing much," Reveredo answered, looking at me with a twinkle in his eye. And the President, satisfied, nodded as a sign of approval.

Before the meeting broke up, Reveredo promised that the foreign minister should receive orders from the President personally, and that Minister of Marine Nieto should be given a free hand to give us all the help we had asked for.

"God preserve you all!" said the General, laughing and shaking his head. The adjutant came in and escorted me out to a waiting messenger.

That day the Lima papers published a paragraph about the Norwegian raft expedition which was to start from Peru; at the same time they announced that a Swedish-Finnish scientific expedition had finished its studies among the jungle Indians in the Amazon regions. Two of the Swedish members of the Amazon expedition had come on up the river by canoe to Peru and had just arrived in Lima. One was Bengt Danielsson, from Uppsala Univeristy, who was now going to study the mountain Indians in Peru.

I cut out the paragraph, and was sitting in my hotel writing to Herman about the site for building the raft, when I was interrupted by a knock on the door. In came a tall sunburned fellow in tropical clothes, and, when he took off his white helmet, it looked as if his flaming red beard had burned his face and scorched his hair thin. That fellow came from the wilds, but his place was clearly a lecture room.

"Bengt Danielsson," I thought.

"Bengt Danielsson," said the man, introducing himself.

"He's heard about the raft," I thought and asked him to sit down.

"I've just heard of the raft plans," said the Swede.

"And now he's come to knock down the theory, because he's an ethnologist," I thought.

"And now I've come to ask if I may come with you on the raft," the Swede said peaceably. "I'm interested in the migration theory."

I knew nothing about the man except that he was a scientist and that he had come straight out of the depths of the jungle. But if a solitary Swede had the pluck to go out on a raft with five Norwegians, he could not be squeamish. And not even that imposing beard could hide his placid nature and gay humor.

Bengt became the sixth member of the crew, for the place was still vacant. And he was the only one who spoke Spanish.

When the passenger plane droned northward along the coast a few days later with me on board, I again looked down with respect on to the endless blue sea beneath us. It seemed to hang and float loose under the firmament itself. Soon we six were to be packed together like microbes on a mere speck, down there where there was so much water that it looked as if it overflowed all along the western horizon. We were to be part of a desolate world without being able to get more than a few steps away from one another. For the time being, at any rate, there was elbowroom enough between us. Herman was in Ecuador waiting for the timber. Knut Haugland and Torstein Raaby had just arrived in New York by air. Erik Hesselberg was on board ship from Oslo, bound for Panama. I myself was en route for Washington by air, and Bengt was in the hotel at Lima ready to start, waiting to meet the others.

No two of these men had met before, and they were all of entirely different types. That being so, we should have been on the raft for some weeks before we got tired of one another's stories. No storm clouds with low pressure and gusty weather held greater menace for us than the danger of psychological cloudburst among six men shut up together for months on a drifting raft. In such circumstances a good joke was often as valuable as a life belt.

Up in Washington there was still bitter winter weather when I came back—cold and snowy February. Björn had tackled the radio problem and had interested the Radio Amateur League of America in listening in for reports from the raft. Knut and Torstein were busy preparing the transmission, which was to be done partly with short-wave transmitters specially constructed for our purpose and partly with secret sabotage sets used during the war. There were a thousand things to prepare, big and small, if we were to do all that we planned on the voyage.

And the piles of paper in the files grew. Military and civilian documents—white, yellow, and blue—in English, Spanish, French, and Norwegian. Even a raft trip had to cost the paper industry half a fir tree in our practical age! Laws and regulations tied our hands everywhere, and knot after knot had to be loosened in turn.

"I'll swear this correspondence weighs twenty pounds," said Knut one day despairingly as he bent over his typewriter.

"Twenty-six," said Torstein drily. "I've weighed it."

My mother must have had a clear idea of the conditions in these days of dramatic preparation when she wrote: "And I only wish I knew you were all six safe on board the raft!"

Then one day an express telegram came from Lima. Herman had been caught in the backwash of a breaker and flung ashore, badly injured, with his neck dislocated. He was under treatment in Lima Hospital.

Torstein Raaby was sent down by air at once with Gerd Vold, the popular London secretary of the Norwegian parachute saboteurs in the war, who was now helping us in Washington. They found Herman better; he had been hung up by a strap round his head for half an hour while the doctors twisted the atlas vertebra in his neck back into position. The X-ray picture showed that the highest bone in his neck was cracked and had been turned right around. Herman's splendid condition had saved his life, and he was soon back, blue and green and stiff and rheumatic, in the naval dockyard, where he had assembled the balsa wood and started the work. He had to remain in the doctor's hands for several weeks, and it was doubtful whether he would be able to make the voyage with us. He himself never doubted it for a moment, despite his initial rough handling in the embrace of the Pacific.

Then Erik arrived by air from Panama and Knut and I from Washington, and so we were all assembled at the starting point in Lima.

Down in the naval dockyard lay the big balsa logs from the Quevedo forest. It was really a pathetic sight. Fresh-cut round logs, yellow bamboos, reeds, and green banana leaves lay in a heap, our building materials, in between rows of threatening gray submarines and destroyers. Six fair-skinned northerners and twenty brown Peruvian seamen with Inca blood in their veins swung axes and long machete knives and tugged at ropes and knots. Trim naval officers in blue and gold walked over and stared in bewilderment at these pale strangers and their crude vegetable materials which had suddenly appeared in the midst of their proud naval yard.

For the first time for hundreds of years a balsa raft was being built in Callao Bay. In these coastal waters, where Inca legends affirm that their ancestors first learned to sail such rafts from Kon-Tiki's vanished clan, modern Indians were forbidden to build such rafts by men of our own race. Sailing on an open raft can cost human lives. The descendants of the Incas have moved with the times; like us, they have creases in their trousers and are safely protected by the guns of their naval craft. Bamboo and balsa belong to the primitive past; here, too, life is marching on—to armor and steel.

The ultramodern dockyard gave us wonderful support. With Bengt as interpreter and Herman as chief constructor we had the run of the carpenter's and sailmaker's shops, as well as half the storage space as a dump for our equipment and a small floating pier where the timber was put into the water when the building began.

Nine of the thickest logs were chosen as sufficient to form the actual raft. Deep grooves were cut in the wood to prevent the ropes which were to fasten them and the whole raft together from slipping. Not a single spike, nail, or wire rope was used in the whole construction. The nine great logs were first laid loose side by side in the water so that they might all fall freely into their natural floating position before they were lashed securely together. The longest log, 45 feet long, was laid in the middle and projected a long way at both ends. Shorter and shorter logs were laid symmetrically on both sides of this, so that the sides of the raft were 30 feet long and the bow stuck out like a blunt plow. Astern the raft was cut off straight across, except that the three middle logs projected and supported a short thick block of balsa wood which lay athwart ship and held tholepins for the long steering oar. When the nine balsa logs were lashed securely together with separate lengths of inch-and-a-quarter hemp rope, the lighter balsa logs were made fast crossways over them at intervals of about 3 feet.

The raft itself was now complete, laboriously fastened together with about three hundred different lengths of rope, each firmly knotted. A deck of split bamboos was laid upon it, fastened to it in the form of separate strips and covered with loose mats of plaited bamboo reeds. In the middle of the raft, but nearer the stern, we erected a small open cabin of bamboo canes, with walls of plaited bamboo reeds and a roof of bamboo slats with leathery banana leaves overlapping one another like tiles. Forward of the cabin we set up two masts side by side. They were cut from mangrove wood, as hard as iron, and leaned toward each other, so that they were lashed together crosswise at the top. The big rectangular square sail was hauled up on a yard made of two bamboo stems bound together to secure double strength.

The nine big logs of timber which were to carry us over the sea were pointed at their forward ends in native fashion that they might glide more easily through the water, and quite low splashboards were fastened to the bow above the surface of the water.

At various places, where there were large chinks between the logs, we pushed down in all five solid fir planks which stood on their edges in the water under the raft. They were scattered about without system and went down 5 feet into the water, being 1 inch thick and 2 feet wide. They were kept in place with wedges and ropes and served as tiny parallel keels or centerboards. Centerboards of this kind were used on all the balsa rafts of Inca times, long before the time of the discoveries, and were meant to prevent the flat wooden rafts from drifting sideways with wind and sea. We did not make any rail or protection round the raft, but we had a long slim balsa log which afforded foothold along each side.

The whole construction was a faithful copy of the old vessels in Peru and Ecuador except for the low splashboards in the bow, which later proved to be entirely unnecessary. After finishing the raft itself, of course, we could arrange the details on board as we liked, so long as they had no effect on the movement and quality of the vessel. We knew that this raft was to be our whole world in the time that lay before us and that, consequently, the smallest detail on board would increase in dimensions and importance as the weeks passed.

Therefore we gave the little deck as much variation as possible. The bamboo strips did not deck in the whole raft but formed a floor forward of the bamboo cabin and along the starboard side of it where the wall was open. The port side of the cabin was a kind of back yard full of boxes and gear made fast, with a narrow edge left to walk along. Forward in the bow, and in the stern as far as the after wall of the cabin, the nine gigantic logs were not decked in at all. So, when we moved round the bamboo cabin, we stepped from yellow bamboos and wickerwork down on to the round gray logs astern and up again on to piles of cargo on the other side. It was not many steps, but the psychological effect of the irregularity gave us variation and compensated us for our limited freedom of movement. Up at the masthead we placed a wooden platform, not so much in order to have a lookout post, when at last we came to land, as to be able to clamber up while en route and look at the sea from another angle.

When the raft began to take shape and lay there among the warships, golden and fresh with ripe bamboos and green leaves, the minister of marine himself came to inspect us. We were immensely proud of our vessel as she lay there, a brave little reminder of Inca times among the threatening big warships. But the minister of marine was utterly horrified by what he saw. I was summoned to the naval office to sign a paper freeing the Navy from all responsibility for what we had built in its harbor, and to the harbor master to sign a paper saying that, if I left the harbor with men and cargo on board, it was entirely on my own responsibility and at my own risk.

Later a number of foreign naval experts and diplomats were admitted to the dockyard to see the raft. They were no more encouraging, and a few days afterward I was sent for by the ambassador of one of the Great Powers.

"Are your parents living?" he asked me. And, when I replied in the affirmative, he looked me straight in the eyes and said in a hollow voice, full of foreboding:

"Your mother and father will be very grieved when they hear of your death."

As a private individual he begged me to give up the voyage while there was yet time. An admiral who had inspected the raft had told him that we should never get across alive. In the first place, the raft's dimensions were wrong. It was so small that it would founder in a big sea; at the same time it was just long enough to be lifted up by two lines of waves at the same time, and with the raft filled with men and cargo the fragile balsa logs would break under the strain. And, what was worse, the biggest balsa exporter in the country had told him that the porous balsa logs would float only a quarter of the distance across the sea before they became so completely waterlogged that they would sink under us.

This sounded bad but, as we stuck to our guns, we were given a Bible as a present to take with us on our voyage. All in all, there was little encouragement to be had from the experts who looked at the raft. Gales and perhaps hurricanes would wash us overboard and destroy the low, open craft, which would simply lie helpless and drift in circles about the ocean before wind and sea. Even in an ordinary choppy sea we should be continually drenched with salt water which would take the skin off our legs and ruin everything on board. If we added up all that the different experts, each in turn, had pointed out as the vital flaw in the construction itself, there was not a length of rope, not a knot, not a measurement, not a piece of wood in the whole raft which would not cause us to founder at sea.

High wagers were made as to how many days the raft would last, and a flippant naval attaché bet all the whiskey the members of the expedition could drink for the rest of their lives if they reached the South Sea islands alive.

Worst of all was when a Norwegian ship came into port and we took the skipper and one or two of his most experienced sea dogs into the dockyard. We were eager to hear their practical reactions. And our disappointment was great when they all agreed that the blunt-bowed, clumsy craft would never get any help from the sail, while the skipper maintained that, if we kept afloat, the raft would take a year or two to drift across with the Humboldt Current. The boatswain looked at our lashings and shook his head. We need not worry. The raft would not hold together for a fortnight before every single rope was worn through, for when at sea the big logs would be continually moving up and down and rubbing against one another. Unless we used wire ropes or chains, we might as well pack up.

These were difficult arguments to stifle. If only one of them proved to be right, we had not a chance. I am afraid I asked myself many times if we knew what we were doing. I could not counter the warnings one by one myself because I was not a seaman. But I had in reserve one single trump in my hand, on which the whole voyage was founded. I knew all the time in my heart that a prehistoric civilization had been spread from Peru and across to the islands at a time when rafts like ours were the only vessels on that coast. And I drew the general conclusion that, if balsa wood had floated and lashings held for Kon-Tiki in 500 A.D., they would do the same for us now if we blindly made our raft an exact copy of his. Bengt and Herman had gone into the theory most thoroughly, and, while the experts lamented, all the boys took the thing quite calmly and had a royal time in Lima. There was just one evening when Torstein asked anxiously if I was sure the ocean currents went the right way. We had been to the movies and seen Dorothy Lamour dancing about in a straw skirt among palms and hula girls on a lovely South Sea island.

"That's where we must go," said Torstein. "And I'm sorry for you if the currents don't go as you say they do!"

When the day of our departure was approaching, we went to the regular passport control office to get permission to leave the country. Bengt stood first in the line as interpreter.

"What is your name?" asked a ceremonious little clerk, looking suspiciously over his spectacles at Bengt's huge beard.

"Bengt Emmerik Danielsson," Bengt answered respectfully.

The man put a long form into his typewriter.

"By what boat did you come to Peru?"

"Well, you see," Bengt explained, bending over the mild little man, "I didn't come by boat. I came to Peru by canoe."

The man looked at Bengt dumb with astonishment and tapped out "canoe" in an open space on the form.

"And by what boat are you leaving Peru?"

"Well, you see, again," said Bengt politely, "I'm not leaving Peru by boat. I'm leaving by raft."

"A likely story!" the clerk cried angrily and tore the paper out of the machine. "Will you please answer my questions properly?"

A few days before we sailed, provisions and water and all our equipment were stowed on board the raft. We took provisions for six men for four months, in the form of solid little cardboard cartons containing military rations. Herman had the idea of boiling asphalt and pouring it so as to make a level layer round each separate carton. Then we strewed sand on the cartons, to prevent them from sticking together, and stowed them, packed close, under the bamboo deck where they filled the space between the nine low crossbeams which supported the deck.

At a crystal-clear spring high up in the mountains we filled fifty-six small water cans with 275 gallons of drinking water. These, too, we made fast in between the crossbeams so that the sea might always splash round them. On the bamboo deck we lashed fast the rest of the equipment including large wicker baskets full of fruit, roots, and coconuts.

Knut and Torstein took one corner of the bamboo cabin for the radio, and inside the hut, down between the crossbeams, we made fast eight boxes. Two were reserved for scientific instruments and films; the other six were allotted one to each of us, with an intimation that each man could take with him as much private property as he could find room for in his own box. As Erik had brought several rolls of drawing paper and a guitar, his box was so full that he had to put his stockings in Torstein's. It took four seamen to carry Bengt's box on board. He brought nothing but books but he had managed to cram in seventy-three sociological and ethnological

Steering watch. We divided the day and night into watches of two hours. Although the waves often towered round us as high as our mast tops, the raft always rode over them in style. Author at the steering oar.

Above: Toward Polynesia in sunny weather. With the help of ocean currents and trade winds we moved westward without interruption. Our average speed was as much as 42½ sea miles a day.

Below: The cook's first duty in the morning was to collect all the flying fish which had landed on deck during the night.

Above: A fresh breeze. With a good wind we danced over the waves so that the raft groaned and creaked; 71 sea miles in a day was our record.
Below: View astern from the mast. Many thousand tons of water poured in astern daily and vanished between the logs.

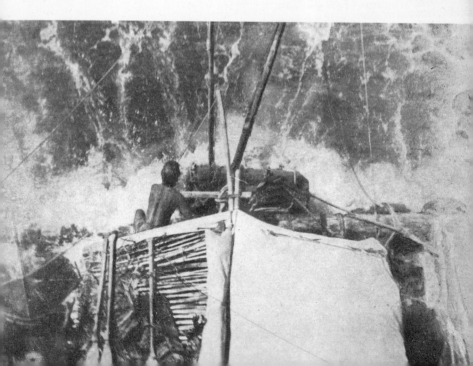

Evening. Watzinger takes the last weather observation; we eat our supper outside the cabin entrance; the lantern is hung up; and the sun sinks into the Pacific with a brilliant display of colors.

Above: An unusual bedfellow. We were the first to see a living snake mackerel (Latin name *Gempylus*). It jumped on board one night and got into Torstein's sleeping bag.
Below: A bout with a tunny was an exciting sport. There were fish enough in the sea to feed a whole flotilla of rafts.

Inside the bamboo cabin we were protected against both wind and tropical sun. The walls were of plaited bamboo and the roof of banana leaves, so that we almost felt we were in a virgin forest instead of at sea. From left: Watzinger, Haugland, Raaby, Danielsson, the author.

On opposite page: Watzinger with a bonito. This fish was certainly the best eating. It sometimes happened that bonitos swam on board with the waves.

Above: Beneath Kon-Tiki's bearded face. The head on the sail was copied from a stone carving of Kon-Tiki, the prehistoric chieftain who led a fair-skinned civilized people across the Pacific 1,500 years ago.

Below: Windless weather and tropical heat troubled us very little. When the sea was calm, we made long trips in our little rubber boat.

works. We laid plaited reed mats and our straw mattresses on top of the boxes and then we were ready to start.

First, the raft was towed out of the naval area and paddled round in the harbor for a while to see if the cargo was stowed evenly. Then she was towed across to the Callao Yacht Club, where invited guests and other persons interested were to be present at the naming of the raft the day before we sailed.

On April 27, 1947, the Norwegian flag was hoisted. Along a yard at the masthead waved the flags of the foreign countries which had given the expedition practical support. The quay was packed with people who wanted to see the strange craft christened. Both color and lineaments betrayed that many of them had remote ancestors who had sailed along the coast on balsa rafts. But there were also descendants of the old Spaniards, headed by representatives of the Peruvian Navy and the government, besides the ambassadors of the United States, Great Britian, France, China, Argentina, and Cuba; the former governor of the British colonies in the Pacific; the Swedish and Belgian ministers; and our friends from the little Norwegian colony with Consul General Bahr at their head. There were swarms of journalists and a clicking of movie cameras; indeed, the only things that were lacking were a brass band and a big drum. One thing was quite clear to us all—if the raft went to pieces outside the bay, we would paddle to Polynesia, each of us on a log, rather than dare come back here again.

Gerd Vold, the expedition's secretary and contact on the mainland, was to christen the raft with milk from a coconut, partly to be in harmony with the Stone Age and partly because, owing to a misunderstanding, the champagne had been put at the bottom of Torstein's private box. When our friends had been told in English and Spanish that the raft was named after the Incas' great forerunner—the sun-king who had vanished westward over the sea from Peru and appeared in Polynesia 1,500 years ago—Gerd Vold christened the raft *Kon-Tiki*. She smashed the coconut (previously cracked) so hard against the bow that milk and bits of coconut filled the hair of all those who stood reverently around.

Then the bamboo yard was hauled up and the sail shaken out, with Kon-Tiki's bearded head, painted in red by our artist Erik, in its center. It was a faithful copy of the sun-king's head cut in red stone on a statue in the ruined city of Tiahuanaco.

"Ah! Señor Danielsson," the foreman of our dockyard workers cried in delight when he saw the bearded face on the sail.

He had called Bengt Señor Kon-Tiki for two months, ever since we had shown him the bearded face of Kon-Tiki on a piece of paper. But now he had at last realized that Danielsson was Bengt's right name.

Before we sailed, we all had a farewell audience with the President, and then we went for a trip far up into the black mountains to look our fill on rock and scree before we drifted out into the endless ocean. While we were working on the raft down on the coast, we had stayed in a boardinghouse in a palm grove outside Lima and driven to and from Callao in an Air Ministry car with a private chauffeur whom Gerd had contrived to borrow for the expedition. Now we asked the chauffeur to drive us straight to the mountains, as far in as he could get in one day. We drove up over desert roads, along old irrigation canals from Inca times, till we came to the dizzy height of 12,000 feet above the raft's mast. Here we simply devoured rocks and mountain peaks and green grass with our eyes and tried to surfeit ourselves with the tranquil mountain mass of the Andes range that lay before us. We tried to convince ourselves that we were thoroughly tired of stone and solid earth and wanted to sail out and get to know the sea.

4.

Across
The Pacific

THERE WAS A BUSTLE IN CALLAO HARBOR THE DAY THE
Kon-Tiki was to be towed out to sea. The minister of marine had
ordered the naval tug *Guardian Rios* to tow us out of the bay and
cast us off clear of the coastal traffic, out where in times gone by the
Indians used to lie fishing from their rafts. The papers had published
the news under both red and black headlines, and there was a crowd
of people down on the quays from early in the morning of April 28.

We six who were to assemble on board all had little things to do at
the eleventh hour, and, when I came down to the quay, only Herman
was there keeping guard over the raft. I intentionally stopped the
car a long way off and walked the whole length of the mole to
stretch my legs thoroughly for the last time for no one knew how
long. I jumped on board the raft, which looked an utter chaos of
banana clusters, fruit baskets, and sacks which had been hurled on
board at the very last moment and were to be stowed and made fast.
In the middle of the heap Herman sat resignedly holding on to a
cage with a green parrot in it, a farewell present from a friendly soul
in Lima.

"Look after the parrot a minute," said Herman. "I must go ashore
and have a last glass of beer. The tug won't be here for hours."

He had hardly disappeared among the swarm on the quay when
people began to point and wave. And round the point at full speed
came the tug *Guardian Rios*. She dropped anchor on the farther
side of a waving forest of masts which blocked the way in to the
Kon-Tiki and sent in a large motorboat to tow us out between the
sailing craft. She was packed full of seamen, officers, and movie photographers, and, while orders rang out and cameras clicked, a stout
towrope was made fast to the raft's bow.

"*Un momento,*" I shouted in despair from where I sat with the parrot. "It's too early; we must wait for the others—*los expedicionarios,*" I explained and pointed toward the city.

But nobody understood. The officers only smiled politely, and the knot at our bow was made fast in more than exemplary manner. I cast off the rope and flung it overboard with all manner of signs and gesticulations. The parrot utilized the opportunity afforded by all the confusion to stick its beak out of the cage and turn the knob of the door, and when I turned round it was strutting cheerfully about the bamboo deck. I tried to catch it, but it shrieked rudely in Spanish and fluttered away over the banana clusters. With one eye on the sailors who were trying to cast a rope over the bow I started a wild chase after the parrot. It fled shrieking into the bamboo cabin, where I got it into a corner and caught it by one leg as it tried to flutter over me. When I came out again and stuffed my flapping trophy into its cage, the sailors on land had cast off the raft's moorings, and we were dancing helplessly in and out with the backwash of the long swell that came rolling in over the mole. In despair I seized a paddle and vainly tried to parry a violent bump as the raft was flung against the wooden piles of the quay. Then the motorboat started, and with a jerk the *Kon-Tiki* began her long voyage.

My only companion was a Spanish-speaking parrot which sat glaring sulkily in a cage. People on shore cheered and waved, and the swarthy movie photographers in the motorboat almost jumped into the sea in their eagerness to catch every detail of the expedition's dramatic start from Peru. Despairing and alone I stood on the raft looking out for my lost companions, but none appeared. So we came out to the *Guardian Rios,* which was lying with steam up ready to lift anchor and start. I was up the rope ladder in a twinkling and made so much row on board that the start was postponed and a boat sent back to the quay. It was away a good while, and then it came back full of pretty *señoritas* but without a single one of the *Kon-Tiki's* missing men. This was all very well but it did not solve my problems, and, while the raft swarmed with charming *señoritas*, the boat went back on a fresh search for *los expedicionarios noruegos.*

Meanwhile Erik and Bengt came sauntering down to the quay with their arms full of reading matter and odds and ends. They met the whole stream of people on its way home and were finally stopped at a police barrier by a kindly official who told them there was nothing more to see. Bengt told the officer, with an airy gesture of

his cigar, that they had not come to see anything; they themselves
were going with the raft.

"It's no use," the officer said indulgently. "The *Kon-Tiki* sailed an
hour ago."

"Impossible," said Erik, producing a parcel. "Here's the lantern!"

"And there's the navigator," said Bengt, "and I'm the steward."

They forced their way past, but the raft had gone. They trotted
desperately to and fro along the mole where they met the rest of the
party, who also were searching eagerly for the vanished raft. Then
they caught sight of the boat coming in, and so we were all six finally
united and the water was foaming round the raft as the *Guardian
Rios* towed us out to sea.

It had been late in the afternoon when at last we started, and the
Guardian Rios would not cast us off till we were clear of the coastal
traffic next morning. Directly we were clear of the mole we met
a bit of a head sea, and all the small boats which were accompanying
us turned back one by one. Only a few big yachts came with us out
to the entrance to the bay to see how things would go out there.

The *Kon-Tiki* followed the tug like an angry billy goat on a rope,
and she butted her bow into the head sea so that the water rushed
on board. This did not look very promising, for this was a calm sea
compared with what we had to expect. In the middle of the bay
the towrope broke, and our end of it sank peacefully to the bottom
while the tug steamed ahead. We flung ourselves down along the
side of the raft to fish for the end of the rope, while the yachts went
on and tried to stop the tug. Stinging jellyfish as thick as washtubs
splashed up and down with the seas alongside the raft and covered
all the ropes with a slippery, stinging coating of jelly. When the raft
rolled one way, we hung flat over the side waving our arms down
toward the surface of the water, until our fingers just touched the
slimy towrope. Then the raft rolled back again, and we all stuck
our heads deep down into the sea, while salt water and giant jellyfish poured over our backs. We spat and cursed and pulled jellyfish
fibers out of our hair, but when the tug came back the rope end
was up and ready for splicing.

When we were about to throw it on board the tug, we suddenly
drifted in under the vessel's overhanging stern and were in danger
of being crushed against her by the pressure of the water. We
dropped everything we had and tried to push ourselves clear with
bamboo sticks and paddles before it was too late. But we never got a

proper position, for when we were in the trough of the sea we could not reach the iron roof above us, and when the water rose again the *Guardian Rios* dropped her whole stern down into the water and would have crushed us flat if the suction had carried us underneath. Up on the tug's deck people were running about and shouting; at last the propeller began to turn alongside us, and it helped us clear of the backwash under the *Guardian Rios* in the last second. The bow of the raft had had a few hard knocks and had become a little crooked in the lashings, but this fault rectified itself by degrees.

"When a thing starts so damnably, it's bound to end well," said Herman. "If only this towing could stop; it'll shake the raft to bits."

The towing went on all night at a slow speed and with only one or two small hitches. The yachts had bidden us farewell long ago, and the last coast light had disappeared astern. Only a few ships' lights passed us in the darkness. We divided the night into watches to keep an eye on the towrope, and we all had a good snatch of sleep. When it grew light next morning, a thick mist lay over the coast of Peru, while we had a brilliant blue sky ahead of us to westward. The sea was running in a long quiet swell covered with little white crests, and clothes and logs and everything we took hold of were soaking wet with dew. It was chilly, and the green water round us was astonishingly cold for 12° south.

We were in the Humboldt Current, which carries its cold masses of water up from the Antarctic and sweeps them north all along the coast of Peru till they swing west and out across the sea just below the Equator. It was out here that Pizarro, Zárate, and the other early Spaniards saw for the first time the Inca Indians' big sailing rafts, which used to go out for 50 to 60 sea miles to catch tunnies and dolphins in the same Humboldt Current. All day long there was an offshore wind out here, but in the evening the onshore wind reached as far out as this and helped the rafts home if they needed it.

In the early light we saw our tug lying close by, and we took care that the raft lay far enough away from her bow while we launched our little inflated rubber dinghy. It floated on the waves like a football and danced away with Erik, Bengt, and myself till we caught hold of the *Guardian Rios'* rope ladder and clambered on board. With Bengt as interpreter we had our exact position shown us on our chart. We were 50 sea miles from land in a northwesterly direction from Callao, and we were to carry lights the first few nights so as not to be sunk by coasting ships. Farther out we would not meet a single ship, for no shipping route ran through that part of the Pacific.

We took a ceremonious farewell of all on board, and many strange looks followed us as we climbed down into the dinghy and went tumbling back over the waves to the *Kon-Tiki*. Then the towrope was cast off and the raft was alone again. Thirty-five men on board the *Guardian Rios* stood at the rail waving for as long as we could distinguish outlines. And six men sat on the boxes on board the *Kon-Tiki* and followed the tug with their eyes as long as they could see her. Not till the black column of smoke had dissolved and vanished over the horizon did we shake our heads and look at one another.

"Good-by, good-by," said Torstein. "Now we'll have to start the engine, boys!"

We laughed and felt the wind. There was a rather light breeze, which had veered from south to southeast. We hoisted the bamboo yard with the big square sail. It only hung down slack, giving Kon-Tiki's face a wrinkled, discontented appearance.

"The old man doesn't like it," said Erik. "There were fresher breezes when he was young."

"It looks as if we were losing ground," said Herman, and he threw a piece of balsa wood overboard at the bow.

"One-two-three . . . thirty-nine, forty, forty-one."

The piece of balsa wood still lay quietly in the water alongside the raft; it had not yet moved halfway along our side.

"We'll have to go over with it," said Torstein optimistically.

"Hope we don't drift astern with the evening breeze," said Bengt. "It was great fun saying good-by at Callao, but I'd just as soon miss our welcome back again!"

Now the piece of wood had reached the end of the raft. We shouted hurrah and began to stow and make fast all the things that had been flung on board at the last moment. Bengt set up a primus stove at the bottom of an empty box, and soon after we were regaling ourselves on hot cocoa and biscuits and making a hole in a fresh coconut. The bananas were not quite ripe yet.

"We're well off now in one way," Erik chuckled. He was rolling about in wide sheepskin trousers under a huge Indian hat, with the parrot on his shoulder. "There's only one thing I don't like," he added, "and that's all the little-known crosscurrents which can fling us right upon the rocks along the coast if we go on lying here like this."

We considered the possibility of paddling but agreed to wait for a wind.

And the wind came. It blew up from the southeast quietly and steadily. Soon the sail filled and bent forward like a swelling breast, with Kon-Tiki's head bursting with pugnacity. And the *Kon-Tiki* began to move. We shouted westward ho! and hauled on sheets and ropes. The steering oar was put into the water, and the watch roster began to operate. We threw balls of paper and chips of wood overboard at the bow and stood aft with our watches.

"One, two, three. . . . eighteen, nineteen—now!"

Paper and chips passed the steering oar and soon lay like pearls on a thread, dipping up and down in the trough of the waves astern. We went forward yard by yard. The *Kon-Tiki* did not plow through the sea like a sharp-prowed racing craft. Blunt and broad, heavy and solid, she splashed sedately forward over the waves. She did not hurry, but when she had once got going she pushed ahead with unshakable energy.

At the moment the steering arrangements were our greatest problem. The raft was built exactly as the Spaniards described it, but there was no one living in our time who could give us a practical advance course in sailing an Indian raft. The problem had been thoroughly discussed among the experts on shore but with meager results. They knew just as little about it as we did. As the southeasterly wind increased in strength, it was necessary to keep the raft on such a course that the sail was filled from astern. If the raft turned her side too much to the wind, the sail suddenly swung round and banged against cargo and men and bamboo cabin, while the whole raft turned round and continued on the same course stern first. It was a hard struggle, three men fighting with the sail and three others rowing with the long steering oar to get the nose of the wooden raft round and away from the wind. And, as soon as we got her round, the steersman had to take good care that the same thing did not happen again the next minute.

The steering oar, nineteen feet long, rested loose between two tholepins on a large block astern. It was the same steering oar our native friends had used when we floated the timber down the Palenque in Ecuador. The long mangrove-wood pole was as tough as steel but so heavy that it would sink if it fell overboard. At the end of the pole was a large oar blade of fir wood lashed on with ropes. It took all our strength to hold this long steering oar steady when the seas drove against it, and our fingers were tired out by the convulsive grip which was necessary to turn the pole so that the oar blade stood straight up in the water. This last problem was finally solved by our lashing a crosspiece to the handle of the steering oar so that we had a sort of lever to turn. And meanwhile the wind increased.

By the late afternoon the trade wind was already blowing at full strength. It quickly stirred up the ocean into roaring seas which swept against us from astern. For the first time we fully realized that here was the sea itself come to meet us; it was bitter earnest now—our communications were cut. Whether things went well now would depend entirely on the balsa raft's good qualities in the open sea. We knew that, from now onward, we should never get another onshore wind or chance of turning back. We were in the path of the real trade wind, and every day would carry us farther and farther out to sea. The only thing to do was to go ahead under full sail; if we tried to turn homeward, we should only drift farther out to sea stern first. There was only one possible course, to sail before the wind with our bow toward the sunset. And, after all, that was the object of our voyage—to follow the sun in its path as we thought Kon-Tiki and the old sun-worshipers must have done when they were driven out to sea from Peru.

We noted with triumph and relief how the wooden raft rose up over the first threatening wave crests that came foaming toward us. But it was impossible for the steersman to hold the oar steady when the roaring seas rolled toward him and lifted the oar out of the tholepins, or swept it to one side so that the steersman was swung round like a helpless acrobat. Not even two men at once could hold the oar steady when the seas rose against us and poured down over the steersmen aft. We hit on the idea of running ropes from the oar blade to each side of the raft; and with other ropes holding the oar in place in the tholepins it obtained a limited freedom of movement and could defy the worst seas if only we ourselves could hold on.

As the troughs of the sea gradually grew deeper, it became clear that we had moved into the swiftest part of the Humboldt Current. This sea was obviously caused by a current and not simply raised by the wind. The water was green and cold and everywhere about us; the jagged mountains of Peru had vanished into the dense cloud banks astern. When darkness crept over the waters, our first duel with the elements began. We were still not sure of the sea; we were still uncertain whether it would show itself a friend or an enemy in the intimate proximity we ourselves had sought. When, swallowed up by the darkness, we heard the general noise from the sea around us suddenly deafened by the hiss of a roller close by and saw a white crest come groping toward us on a level with the cabin roof, we held on tight and waited uneasily to feel the masses of water smash down over us and the raft.

But every time there was the same surprise and relief. The *Kon-Tiki* calmly swung up her stern and rose skyward unperturbed, while the masses of water rolled along her sides. Then we sank down again into the trough of the waves and waited for the next big sea. The biggest seas often came two or three in succession, with a long series of smaller seas in between. It was when two big seas followed each other too closely that the second broke on board aft, because the first was still holding our bow in the air. It became, therefore, an unbreakable law that the steering watch must have ropes round their waists, the other ends of which were made fast to the raft, for there were no bulwarks. Their task was to keep the sail filled by holding stern to sea and wind.

We had made an old boat's compass fast to a box aft so that Erik could check our course and calculate our position and speed. For the time being it was uncertain where we were, for the sky was overclouded and the horizon one single chaos of rollers. Two men at a time took turns as steering watch and, side by side, they had to put all their strength into the fight with the leaping oar, while the rest of us tried to snatch a little sleep inside the open bamboo cabin.

When a really big sea came, the men at the helm left the steering to the ropes and, jumping up, hung on to a bamboo pole from the cabin roof, while the masses of water thundered in over them from astern and disappeared between the logs or over the side of the raft. Then they had to fling themselves at the oar again before the raft could turn round and the sail thrash about. For, if the raft took the seas at an angle, the waves could easily pour right into the bamboo cabin. When they came from astern, they disappeared between the projecting logs at once and seldom came so far forward as the cabin wall. The round logs astern let the water pass as if through the prongs of a fork. The advantage of a raft was obviously this: the more leaks the better. Through the gaps in our floor the water ran out but never in.

About midnight a ship's light passed in a northerly direction. At three another passed on the same course. We waved our little paraffin lamp and hailed them with flashes from an electric torch, but they did not see us and the lights passed slowly northward into the darkness and disappeared. Little did those on board realize that a real Inca raft lay close to them, tumbling among the waves. And just as little did we on board the raft realize that this was our last ship and the last trace of men we should see till we had reached the other side of the ocean.

We clung like flies, two and two, to the steering oar in the darkness and felt the fresh sea water pouring off our hair while the oar hit us till we were tender both behind and before and our hands grew stiff with the exertion of hanging on. We had a good schooling those first days and nights; it turned landlubbers into seamen. For the first twenty-four hours every man, in unbroken succession, had two hours at the helm and three hours' rest. We arranged that every hour a fresh man should relieve one of the two steersmen who had been at the helm for two hours.

Every single muscle in the body was strained to the uttermost throughout the watch to cope with the steering. When we were tired out with pushing the oar, we went over to the other side and pulled, and when arms and chest were sore with pressing, we turned our backs while the oar kneaded us green and blue in front and behind. When at last the relief came, we crept half-dazed into the bamboo cabin, tied a rope round our legs, and fell asleep with our salty clothes on before we could get into our sleeping bags. Almost at the same moment there came a brutal tug at the rope; three hours had passed, and one had to go out again and relieve one of the two men at the steering oar.

The next night was still worse; the seas grew higher instead of going down. Two hours on end of struggling with the steering oar was too long; a man was not much use in the second half of his watch, and the seas got the better of us and hurled us round and sideways, while the water poured on board. Then we changed over to one hour at the helm and an hour and a half's rest. So the first sixty hours passed, in one continuous struggle against a chaos of waves that rushed upon us, one after another, without cessation. High waves and low waves, pointed waves and round waves, slanting waves and waves on top of other waves.

The one of us who suffered worst was Knut. He was let off steering watch, but to compensate for this he had to sacrifice to Neptune and suffered silent agonies in a corner of the cabin. The parrot sat sulkily in its cage, hanging on with its beak and flapping its wings every time the raft gave an unexpected pitch and the sea splashed against the wall from astern. The *Kon-Tiki* did not roll excessively. She took the seas more steadily than any boat of the same dimensions, but it was impossible to predict which way the deck would lean each time, and we never learned the art of moving about the raft easily, for she pitched as much as she rolled.

On the third night the sea went down a bit, although it was still blowing hard. About four o'clock an unexpected deluge came foaming through the darkness and knocked the raft right round before the steersmen realized what was happening. The sail thrashed against the bamboo cabin and threatened to tear both the cabin and itself to pieces. All hands had to go on deck to secure the cargo and haul on sheets and stays in the hope of getting the raft on her right course again, so that the sail might fill and curve forward peacefully. But the raft would not right herself. She would go stern foremost, and that was all. The only result of all our hauling and pushing and rowing was that two men nearly went overboard in a sea when the sail caught them in the dark.

The sea had clearly become calmer. Stiff and sore, with skinned palms and sleepy eyes, we were not worth a row of beans. Better to save our strength in case the weather should call us out to a worse passage of arms. One could never know. So we furled the sail and rolled it round the bamboo yard. The *Kon-Tiki* lay sideways on to the seas and took them like a cork. Everything on board was lashed fast, and all six of us crawled into the little bamboo cabin, huddled together, and slept like mummies in a sardine tin.

We little guessed that we had struggled through the hardest steering of the voyage. Not till we were far out on the ocean did we discover the Incas' simple and ingenious way of steering a raft.

We did not wake till well on in the day, when the parrot began to whistle and halloo and dance to and fro on its perch. Outside the sea was still running high but in long, even ridges and not so wild and confused as the day before. The first thing we saw was that the sun was beating down on the yellow bamboo deck and giving the sea all round us a bright and friendly aspect. What did it matter if the seas foamed and rose high so long as they only left us in peace on the raft? What did it matter if they rose straight up in front of our noses when we knew that in a second the raft would go over the top and flatten out the foaming ridge like a steam roller, while the heavy threatening mountain of water only lifted us up in the air and rolled groaning and gurgling under the floor? The old masters from Peru knew what they were doing when they avoided a hollow hull which could fill with water, or a vessel so long that it would not take the waves one by one. A cork steam roller—that was what the balsa raft amounted to.

Erik took our position at noon and found that, in addition to our run under sail, we had made a big deviation northward along the coast. We still lay in the Humboldt Current just 100 sea miles from land. The great question was whether we would get into the treacherous eddies south of the Galapagos Islands. This could have fatal consequences, for up there we might be swept in all directions by strong ocean currents making toward the coast of Central America. But, if things went as we calculated, we should swing west across the sea with the main current before we got as far north as the Galapagos. The wind was still blowing straight from southeast. We hoisted the sail, turned the raft stern to sea, and continued our steering watches.

Knut had now recovered from the torments of seasickness, and he and Torstein clambered up to the swaying masthead, where they experimented with mysterious radio aerials which they sent up both by balloon and by kite. Suddenly one of them shouted from the radio corner of the cabin that he could hear the naval station at Lima calling us. They were telling us that the American ambassador's plane was on its way out from the coast to bid us a last good-by and see what we looked like at sea. Soon after we obtained direct contact with the operator in the plane and then a completely unexpected chat with the secretary to the expedition, Gerd Vold, who was on board. We gave our position as exactly as we could and sent direction-finding signals for hours. The voice in the ether grew stronger and weaker as ARMY-119 circled round near and far and searched. But we did not hear the drone of the engines and never saw the plane. It was not easy to find the low raft down in the trough of the seas, and our own view was strictly limited. At last the plane had to give it up and returned to the coast. It was the last time anyone tried to search for us.

The sea ran high in the days that followed, but the waves came hissing along from the southeast with even spaces between them and the steering went more easily. We took the sea and wind on the port quarter, so that the steersman got fewer seas over him and the raft went more steadily and did not swing round. We noted anxiously that the southeast trade wind and the Humboldt Current were, day after day, sending us straight across on a course leading to the countercurrents round the Galapagos Islands. And we were going due northwest so quickly that our daily average in those days was 55 to 60 sea miles, with a record of 71 sea miles in one day.

"Are the Galapagos a nice place to go to?" Knut asked cautiously one day, looking at our chart where a string of pearls indicating our positions was marked and resembled a finger pointing balefully toward the accursed Galapagos Islands.

"Hardly," I said. "The Inca Tupak Yupanqui is said to have sailed from Ecuador to the Galapagos just before the time of Columbus, but neither he nor any other native settled there because there was no water."

"O.K.," said Knut. "Then we damned well won't go there. I hope we don't anyhow."

We were now so accustomed to having the sea dancing round us that we took no account of it. What did it matter if we danced round a bit with a thousand fathoms of water under us, so long as we and the raft were always on top? It was only that here the next question arose—how long could we count on keeping on top? It was easy to see that the balsa logs absorbed water. The aft crossbeam was worse than the others; on it we could press our whole finger tip into the soaked wood till the water squelched. Without saying anything I broke off a piece of the sodden wood and threw it overboard. It sank quietly beneath the surface and slowly vanished down into the depths. Later I saw two or three of the other fellows do exactly the same when they thought no one was looking. They stood looking reverently at the waterlogged piece of wood sinking quietly into the green water.

We had noted the water line on the raft when we started, but in the rough sea it was impossible to see how deep we lay, for one moment the logs were lifted out of the water and the next they went deep down into it. But, if we drove a knife into the timber, we saw to our joy that the wood was dry an inch or so below the surface. We calculated that, if the water continued to force its way in at the same pace, the raft would be lying and floating just under the surface of the water by the time we could expect to be approaching land.

But we hoped that the sap further in would act as an impregnation and check the absorption.

Then there was another menace which troubled our minds a little during the first weeks. The ropes. In the daytime we were so busy that we thought little about it, but, when darkness had fallen and we had crept into bed on the cabin floor, we had more time to think, feel, and listen. As we lay there, each man on his straw mattress, we could feel the reed matting under us heaving in time with the wooden logs. In addition to the movements of the raft itself all nine logs moved reciprocally. When one came up, another went down with a gentle heaving movement. They did not move much, but it was enough to make one feel as if one were lying on the back of a large breathing animal, and we preferred to lie on a log lengthways. The first two nights were the worst, but then we were too tired to bother about it. Later the ropes swelled a little in the water and kept the nine logs quieter.

But all the same there was never a flat surface on board which kept quite still in relation to its surroundings. As the foundation moved up and down and round at every joint, everything else moved with it. The bamboo deck, the double mast, the four plaited walls of the cabin, and the roof of slats with the leaves on it—all were made fast just with ropes and twisted about and lifted themselves in opposite directions. It was almost unnoticeable but it was evident enough. If one corner went up, the other corner came down, and if one half of the roof dragged all its laths forward, the other half dragged its laths astern. And, if we looked out through the open wall, there was still more life and movement, for there the sky moved quietly round in a circle while the sea leaped high toward it.

The ropes took the whole pressure. All night we could hear them creaking and groaning, chafing and squeaking. It was like one single complaining chorus round us in the dark, each rope having its own note according to its thickness and tautness.

Every morning we made a thorough inspection of the ropes. We were even let down with our heads in the water over the edge of the raft, while two men held us tight by the ankles, to see if the ropes on the bottom of the raft were all right. But the ropes held. A fortnight the seamen had said. Then all the ropes would be worn out. But, in spite of this consensus of opinion, we had not so far found the smallest sign of wear. Not till we were far out to sea did we find the solution. The balsa wood was so soft that the ropes wore their way slowly into the wood and were protected, instead of the logs wearing the ropes.

After a week or so the sea grew calmer, and we noticed that it became blue instead of green. We began to go west-northwest instead of due northwest and took this as the first faint sign that we had got out of the coastal current and had some hope of being carried out to sea.

The very first day we were left alone on the sea we had noticed fish round the raft, but we were too much occupied with the steering to think of fishing. The second day we went right into a thick shoal of sardines, and soon afterward an eight-foot blue shark came along and rolled over with its white belly uppermost as it rubbed against the raft's stern, where Herman and Bengt stood barelegged in the seas, steering. It played round us for a while but disappeared when we got the hand harpoon ready for action.

Next day we were visited by tunnies, bonitos, and dolphins, and when a big flying fish thudded on board we used it as bait and at once pulled in two large dolphins (dorados) weighing from twenty to thirty-five pounds each. This was food for several days. On steering watch we could see many fish we did not even know, and one day we came into a school of porpoises which seemed quite endless. The black backs tumbled about, packed close together, right in to the side of the raft, and sprang up here and there all over the sea as far as we could see from the masthead. And the nearer we came to the Equator, and the farther from the coast, the commoner flying fish became. When at last we came out into the blue water where the sea rolled by majestically, sunlit and serene, ruffled by gusts of wind, we could see them glittering like a rain of projectiles which shot from the water and flew in a straight line till their power of flight was exhausted and they vanished beneath the surface.

If we set the little paraffin lamp out at night, flying fish were attracted by the light and, large and small, shot over the raft. They often struck the bamboo cabin or the sail and tumbled helpless on the deck. Unable to get a take-off by swimming through the water, they just remained lying and kicking helplessly, like large-eyed herrings with long breast fins. It sometimes happened that we heard an outburst of strong language from a man on deck when a cold flying fish came unexpectedly, at a good speed, slap into his face. They always came at a good pace and snout first, and if they caught one full in the face they made it burn and tingle. But the unprovoked attack was quickly forgiven by the injured party, for, with all its drawbacks, we were in a maritime land of enchantment where delicious fish dishes came hurling through the air. We used to fry them for breakfast, and whether it was the fish, the cook, or our appetites, they reminded us of fried troutlings once we had scraped the scales off.

The cook's first duty, when he got up in the morning, was to go out on deck and collect all the flying fish that had landed on board in the course of the night. There were usually half a dozen or more, and once we found twenty-six fat flying fish on the raft. Knut was much upset one morning because, when he was standing operating with the frying pan, a flying fish struck him on the hand instead of landing right in the cooking fat.

Our neighborly intimacy with the sea was not fully realized by Torstein till he woke one morning and found a sardine on his pillow. There was so little room in the cabin that Torstein had to lie with his head in the doorway, and, if anyone inadvertently trod on his face when going out at night, he bit him in the leg. He grasped the sardine by the tail and confided to it understandingly that all sardines had his entire sympathy. We conscientiously drew in our legs so that Torstein should have more room the next night, but then something happened which caused Torstein to find himself a sleeping place on top of all the kitchen utensils in the radio corner.

It was a few nights later. It was overcast and pitch dark, and Torstein had placed the paraffin lamp close by his head, so that the night watches could see where they were treading when they crept in and out over his head. About four o'clock Torstein was awakened by the lamp tumbling over and something cold and wet flapping about his ears. "Flying fish," he thought and felt for it in the darkness to throw it away. He caught hold of something long and wet, which wriggled like a snake, and let go as if he had burned himself. The unseen visitor twisted itself away and over to Herman, while Torstein tried to get the lamp lighted again. Herman started up, too, and this made me wake, thinking of the octopus which came up at night in these waters.

When we got the lamp lighted, Herman was sitting in triumph with his hand gripping the neck of a long thin fish which wriggled in his hands like an eel. The fish was over three feet long, as slender as a snake, with dull black eyes and a long snout with a greedy jaw full of long sharp teeth. The teeth were as sharp as knives and could be folded back into the roof of the mouth to make way for what was swallowed. Under Herman's grip a large-eyed white fish, about eight inches long, was suddenly thrown up from the stomach and out of the mouth of the predatory fish, and soon after up came another like it. These were clearly two deep-water fish, much torn by the snakefish's teeth. The snakefish's thin skin was bluish violet on the back and steel blue underneath, and it came loose in flakes when we took hold of it.

Bengt too was awakened at last by all the noise, and we held the lamp and the long fish under his nose. He sat up drowsily in his sleeping bag and said solemnly:

"No, fish like that don't exist."

With which he turned over quietly and fell asleep again.

Bengt was not far wrong. It appeared later that we six sitting round the lamp in the bamboo cabin were the first men to have seen this fish alive. Only the skeleton of a fish like this one had been found a few times on the coast of South America and the Galapagos Islands; ichthyologists called it *Gempylus*, or snake mackerel, and thought it lived at the bottom of the sea at a great depth because no one had ever seen it alive. But, if it lived at a great depth, it must have done so by day when the sun blinded its big eyes. For on dark nights *Gempylus* was abroad high over the surface of the sea; we on the raft had experience of that.

A week after the rare fish had landed on Torstein's sleeping bag, we had another visit. Again it was four in the morning, and the new moon had set so that it was dark but the stars were shining. The raft was steering easily, and when my watch was over I took a turn along the edge of the raft to see if everything was shipshape for the new watch. I had a rope round my waist, as the watch always had, and, with the paraffin lamp in my hand, I was walking carefully along the outermost log to get round the mast. The log was wet and slippery, and I was furious when someone quite unexpectedly caught hold of the rope behind me and jerked till I nearly lost my balance. I turned round wrathfully with the lantern, but not a soul was to be seen. There came a new tug at the rope, and I saw something shiny lying writhing on the deck. It was a fresh *Gempylus*, and this time it had got its teeth so deep into the rope that several of them broke before I got the rope loose. Presumably the light of the lantern had flashed along the curving white rope, and our visitor from the depths of the sea had caught hold in the hope of jumping up and snatching an extra long and tasty tidbit. It ended its days in a jar of Formalin.

The sea contains many surprises for him who has his floor on a level with the surface and drifts along slowly and noiselessly. A sportsman who breaks his way through the woods may come back and say that no wild life is to be seen. Another may sit down on a stump and wait, and often rustlings and cracklings will begin and curious eyes peer out. So it is on the sea, too. We usually plow across it with roaring engines and piston strokes, with the water foaming round our bow. Then we come back and say that there is nothing to see far out on the ocean.

Not a day passed but we, as we sat floating on the surface of the sea, were visited by inquisitive guests which wriggled and waggled about us, and a few of them, such as dolphins and pilot fish, grew so familiar that they accompanied the raft across the sea and kept round us day and night.

When night had fallen and the stars were twinkling in the dark tropical sky, a phosphorescence flashed around us in rivalry with the stars, and single glowing plankton resembled round live coals so vividly that we involuntarily drew in our bare legs when the glowing pellets were washed up round our feet at the raft's stern. When we caught them, we saw that they were little brightly shining species of shrimp. On such nights we were sometimes scared when two round shining eyes suddenly rose out of the sea right alongside the raft and glared at us with an unblinking hypnotic stare. The visitors were often big squids which came up and floated on the surface with their devilish green eyes shining in the dark like phosphorus. But sometimes the shining eyes were those of deep-water fish which came up only at night and lay staring, fascinated by the glimmer of light before them. Several times, when the sea was calm, the black water round the raft was suddenly full of round heads two or three feet in diameter, lying motionless and staring at us with great glowing eyes. On other nights balls of light three feet and more in diameter would be visible down in the water, flashing at irregular intervals like electric lights turned on for a moment.

We gradually grew accustomed to having these subterranean or submarine creatures under the floor, but nevertheless we were just as surprised every time a new species appeared. About two o'clock on a cloudy night, when the man at the helm had difficulty in distinguishing black water from black sky, he caught sight of a faint illumination down in the water which slowly took the shape of a large animal. It was impossible to say whether it was plankton shining on its body, or whether the animal itself had a phosphorescent surface, but the glimmer down in the black water gave the ghostly creature obscure, wavering outlines. Sometimes it was roundish, sometimes oval, or triangular, and suddenly it split into two parts which swam to and fro under the raft independently of each other. Finally there were three of these large shining phantoms wandering round in slow circles under us.

They were real monsters, for the visible parts alone were some five fathoms long, and we all quickly collected on deck and followed the ghost dance. It went on for hour after hour, following the course of the raft. Mysterious and noiseless, our shining companions kept a good way beneath the surface, mostly on the starboard side where the light was, but often they were right under the raft or appeared on the port side. The glimmer of light on their backs revealed that the beasts were bigger than elephants but they were not whales, for they never came up to breathe. Were they giant ray fish which changed shape when they turned over on their sides? They took no notice at all if we held the light right down on the surface to lure them up, so that we might see what kind of creatures they were. And, like all proper goblins and ghosts, they had sunk into the depths when the dawn began to break.

We never got a proper explanation of this nocturnal visit from the three shining monsters, unless the solution was afforded by another visit we received a day and a half later in the full midday sunshine. It was May 24, and we were lying drifting on a leisurely swell in exactly 95° west by 7° south. It was about noon, and we had thrown overboard the guts of two big dolphins we had caught earlier in the morning. I was having a refreshing plunge overboard at the bow, lying in the water but keeping a good lookout and hanging on to a rope end, when I caught sight of a thick brown fish, six feet long, which came swimming inquisitively toward me through the crystal-clear sea water. I hopped quickly up on to the edge of the raft and sat in the hot sun looking at the fish as it passed quietly, when I heard a wild war whoop from Knut, who was sitting aft behind the bamboo cabin. He bellowed "Shark!" till his voice cracked in a falsetto, and, as we had sharks swimming alongside the raft almost daily without creating such excitement, we all realized that this must be something extra-special and flocked astern to Knut's assistance.

Knut had been squatting there, washing his pants in the swell, and when he looked up for a moment he was staring straight into the biggest and ugliest face any of us had ever seen in the whole of our lives. It was the head of a veritable sea monster, so huge and so hideous that, if the Old Man of the Sea himself had come up, he could not have made such an impression on us. The head was broad and flat like a frog's, with two small eyes right at the sides, and a toadlike jaw which was four or five feet wide and had long fringes drooping from the corners of the mouth. Behind the head was an enormous body ending in a long thin tail with a pointed tail fin which stood straight up and showed that this sea monster was not any kind of whale. The body looked brownish under the water, but both head and body were thickly covered with small white spots.

The monster came quietly, lazily swimming after us from astern. It grinned like a bulldog and lashed gently with its tail. The large round dorsal fin projected clear of the water and sometimes the tail fin as well, and, when the creature was in the trough of the swell, the water flowed about the broad back as though washing round a submerged reef. In front of the broad jaws swam a whole crowd of zebra-striped pilot fish in fan formation, and large remora fish and other parasites sat firmly attached to the huge body and traveled with it through the water, so that the whole thing looked like a curious zoological collection crowded round something that resembled a floating deep-water reef.

A twenty-five-pound dolphin, attached to six of our largest fishhooks, was hanging behind the raft as bait for sharks, and a swarm of the pilot fish shot straight off, nosed the dolphin without touching it, and then hurried back to their lord and master, the sea king. Like a mechanical monster it set its machinery going and came gliding at leisure toward the dolphin which lay, a beggarly trifle, before its jaws. We tried to pull the dolphin in, and the sea monster followed slowly, right up to the side of the raft. It did not open its mouth but just let the dolphin bump against it, as if to throw open the whole door for such an insignificant scrap was not worth while. When the giant came close up to the raft, it rubbed its back against the heavy steering oar, which was just lifted up out of the water, and now we had ample opportunity of studying the monster at the closest quarters —at such close quarters that I thought we had all gone mad, for we roared stupidly with laughter and shouted overexcitedly at the completely fantastic sight we saw. Walt Disney himself, with all his powers of imagination, could not have created a more hair-raising sea monster than that which thus suddenly lay with its terrific jaws along the raft's side.

The monster was a whale shark, the largest shark and the largest fish known in the world today. It is exceedingly rare, but scattered specimens are observed here and there in the tropical oceans. The whale shark has an average length of fifty feet, and according to zoologists it weighs fifteen tons. It is said that large specimens can attain a length of sixty feet; one harpooned baby had a liver weighing six hundred pounds and a collection of three thousand teeth in each of its broad jaws.

Our monster was so large that, when it began to swim in circles round us and under the raft, its head was visible on one side while the whole of its tail stuck out on the other. And so incredibly grotesque, inert, and stupid did it appear when seen fullface that we could not help shouting with laughter, although we realized that it had strength enough in its tail to smash both balsa logs and ropes to pieces if it attacked us. Again and again it described narrower and narrower circles just under the raft, while all we could do was to wait and see what might happen. When it appeared on the other side, it glided amiably under the steering oar and lifted it up in the air, while the oar blade slid along the creature's back.

We stood round the raft with hand harpoons ready for action, but they seemed to us like toothpicks in relation to the mammoth beast we had to deal with. There was no indication that the whale shark ever thought of leaving us again; it circled round us and followed like a faithful dog, close up to the raft. None of us had ever experienced or thought we should experience anything like it; the whole adventure, with the sea monster swimming behind and under the raft, seemed to us so completely unnatural that we could not really take it seriously.

In reality the whale shark went on encircling us for barely an hour, but to us the visit seemed to last a whole day. At last it became too exciting for Erik, who was standing at a corner of the raft with an eight-foot hand harpoon, and, encouraged by ill-considered shouts, he raised the harpoon above his head. As the whale shark came gliding slowly toward him and its broad head moved right under the corner of the raft, Erik thrust the harpoon with all his giant strength down between his legs and deep into the whale shark's gristly head. It was a second or two before the giant understood properly what was happening. Then in a flash the placid half-wit was transformed into a mountain of steel muscles.

We heard a swishing noise as the harpoon line rushed over the edge of the raft and saw a cascade of water as the giant stood on its head and plunged down into the depths. The three men who were standing nearest were flung about the place, head over heels, and two of them were flayed and burned by the line as it rushed through the air. The thick line, strong enough to hold a boat, was caught up on the side of the raft but snapped at once like a piece of twine, and a few seconds later a broken-off harpoon shaft came up to the surface two hundred yards away. A shoal of frightened pilot fish shot off through the water in a desperate attempt to keep up with their old lord and master. We waited a long time for the monster to come racing back like an infuriated submarine, but we never saw anything more of him.

We were now in the South Equatorial Current and moving in a westerly direction just 400 sea miles south of the Galapagos. There was no longer any danger of drifting into the Galapagos currents, and the only contacts we had with this group of islands were greetings from big sea turtles which no doubt had strayed far out to sea from the islands. One day we saw a thumping turtle lying struggling with its head and one great fin above the surface of the water. As the swell rose, we saw a shimmer of green and blue and gold in the water under the turtle, and we discovered that it was engaged in a life-and-death struggle with dolphins. The fight was apparently quite one-sided; it consisted in twelve to fifteen big-headed, brilliantly colored dolphins attacking the turtle's neck and fins and apparently trying to tire it out, for the turtle could not lie for days on end with its head and paddles drawn inside its shell.

When the turtle caught sight of the raft, it dived and made straight for us, pursued by the glittering fish. It came close up to the side of the raft and was showing signs of wanting to climb up on to the timber when it caught sight of us already standing there. If we had been more practiced, we could have captured it with ropes without difficulty as the huge carapace paddled quietly along the side of the raft. But we spent the time that mattered in staring, and when we had the lasso ready the giant turtle had already passed our bow. We flung the little rubber dinghy into the water, and Herman, Bengt, and Torstein went in pursuit of the turtle in the round nutshell, which was not a great deal bigger than what swam ahead of them.

Bengt, as steward, saw in his mind's eye endless meat dishes and a most delicious turtle soup.

But the faster they rowed, the faster the turtle slipped through the water just below the surface, and they were not more than a hundred yards from the raft when the turtle suddenly disappeared without a trace. But they had done one good deed at any rate. For when the little yellow rubber dinghy came dancing back over the water, it had the whole glittering school of dolphins after it. They circled round the new turtle, and the boldest snapped at the oar blades which dipped into the water like fins; meanwhile, the peaceful turtle escaped successfully from all its ignoble persecutors.

5.

Halfway

THE WEEKS PASSED. WE SAW NO SIGN EITHER OF A
ship or of drifting remains to show that there were other people in
the world. The whole sea was ours, and, with all the gates of the
horizon open, real peace and freedom were wafted down from the
firmament itself.

It was as though the fresh salt tang in the air, and all the blue
purity that surrounded us, had washed and cleansed both body and
soul. To us on the raft the great problems of civilized man appeared
false and illusory—like perverted products of the human mind. Only
the elements mattered. And the elements seemed to ignore the little
raft. Or perhaps they accepted it as a natural object, which did not
break the harmony of the sea but adapted itself to current and sea
like bird and fish. Instead of being a fearsome enemy, flinging itself
at us, the elements had become a reliable friend which steadily and
surely helped us onward. While wind and waves pushed and pro-
pelled, the ocean current lay under us and pulled, straight toward
our goal.

If a boat had cruised our way on any average day out at sea, it
would have found us bobbing quietly up and down over a long rolling
swell covered with little white-crested waves, while the trade wind
held the orange sail bent steadily toward Polynesia.

Those on board would have seen, at the stern of the raft, a brown
bearded man with no clothes on, either struggling desperately with
a long steering oar while he hauled on a tangled rope, or, in calm
weather, just sitting on a box dozing in the hot sun and keeping
a leisurely hold on the steering oar with his toes.

If this man happened not to be Bengt, the latter would have
been found lying on his stomach in the cabin door with one of his

seventy-three sociological books. Bengt had further been appointed steward and was responsible for fixing the daily rations. Herman might have been found anywhere at any time of the day—at the masthead with meteorological instruments, underneath the raft with diving goggles on checking a centerboard, or in tow in the rubber dinghy, busy with ballons and curious measuring apparatus. He was our technical chief and responsible for meteorological and hydrographical observations.

Knut and Torstein were always doing something with their wet dry batteries, soldering irons, and circuits. All their wartime training was required to keep the little radio station going in spray and dew a foot above the surface of the water.

Every night they took turns sending our reports and weather observations out into the ether, where they were picked up by chance radio amateurs who passed the reports on to the Meteorological Institute in Washington and other destinations. Erik was usually sitting patching sails and splicing ropes, or carving in wood and drawing sketches of bearded men and odd fish. And at noon every day he took the sextant and mounted a box to look at the sun and find out how far we had moved since the day before. I myself had enough to do with the logbook and reports and the collecting of plankton, fishing, and filming. Every man had his sphere of responsibility, and no one interfered with the others' work. All difficult jobs, like steering watch and cooking, were divided equally. Every man had two hours each day and two hours each night at the steering oar. And duty as cook was in accordance with a daily roster. There were few laws and regulations on board, except that the night watch must have a rope round his waist, that the lifesaving rope had its regular place, that all meals were consumed outside the cabin wall, and that the "right place" was only at the farthest end of the logs astern. If an important decision was to be taken on board, we called a powwow in Indian style and discussed the matter together before anything was settled.

An ordinary day on board the *Kon-Tiki* began with the last night watch shaking some life into the cook, who crawled out sleepily on to the dewy deck in the morning sun and began to gather flying fish. Instead of eating the fish raw, according to both Polynesian and Peruvian recipes, we fried them over a small primus stove at the bottom of a box which stood lashed fast to the deck outside the cabin door. This box was our kitchen. Here there was usually shelter from the southeast trade wind which regularly blew on to our other quarter. Only when the wind and sea juggled too much with the primus flame did it set fire to the wooden box, and once, when the cook had fallen asleep, the whole box became a mass of flames which spread to the very wall of the bamboo cabin. But the fire on the wall was quickly put out when the smoke poured into the hut, for, after all, we had never far to go for water on board the *Kon-Tiki.*

The smell of fried fish seldom managed to wake the snorers inside the bamboo cabin, so the cook usually had to stick a fork into them or sing "Breakfast's ready!" so out of tune that no one could bear to listen to him any longer. If there were no sharks' fins alongside the raft, the day began with a quick plunge in the Pacific, followed by breakfast in the open air on the edge of the raft.

The food on board was above reproach. The cuisine was divided into two experimental menus, one dedicated to the quartermaster and the twentieth century, one to Kon-Tiki and the fifth century. Torstein and Bengt were the subjects of the first experiment and restricted their diet to the slim little packages of special provisions which we had squeezed down into the hole between the logs and the bamboo deck. Fish and marine food, however, had never been their strong suit. Every few weeks we untied the lashings which held down the bamboo deck and took out fresh supplies, which we lashed fast forward of the bamboo cabin. The tough layer of asphalt outside the cardboard proved resistant, while the hermetically sealed tins lying loose beside it were penetrated and ruined by the sea water which continually washed round our provisions.

Kon-Tiki, on his original voyage across the sea, had no asphalt or hermetically sealed tins; nevertheless he had no serious food problems. In those days, too, supplies consisted of what the men took with them from land and what they obtained for themselves on the voyage. We may assume that, when Kon-Tiki sailed from the coast of Peru after his defeat by Lake Titicaca, he had one of two objectives in mind. As the spiritual representative of the sun among a solely sun-worshiping people, it is very probable that he ventured straight out to sea to follow the sun itself on its journey in the hope of finding a new and more peaceful country. An alternative possibility for him was to sail his rafts up the coast of South America in order to found a new kingdom out of reach of his persecutors. Clear of the dangerous rocky coast and hostile tribes along the shore, he would, like ourselves, fall an easy prey to the southeast trade wind and the Humboldt Current and, in the power of the elements, he would drift in exactly the same large semicircle right toward the sunset.

Whatever these sun-worshipers' plans were when they fled from their homeland, they certainly provided themselves with supplies for the voyage. Dried meat and fish and sweet potatoes were the most important part of their primitive diet. When the raftsmen of that time put to sea along the desert coast of Peru, they had ample supplies of water on board. Instead of clay vessels they generally used the skin of giant bottle gourds, which was resistant to bumps and blows, while even more adapted to raft use were the thick canes of giant bamboos. They perforated through all the knots in the center and poured water in through a little hole at the end, which they stopped with a plug or with pitch or resin. Thirty or forty of these thick bamboo canes could be lashed fast along the raft under the bamboo deck, where they lay shaded and cool with fresh sea water—about 79° Fahrenheit in the Equatorial Current—washing about them. A store of this kind would contain twice as much water as we ourselves used on our whole voyage, and still more could be taken by simply lashing on more bamboo canes in the water underneath the raft, where they weighed nothing and occupied no space.

We found that after two months fresh water began to grow stale and have a bad taste. But by then one is well through the first ocean area, in which there is little rain, and has arrived in regions where heavy rain showers can maintain the water supply. We served out a good quart of water per man daily, and it was by no means always that the ration was consumed.

Even if our predecessors had started from land with inadequate supplies, they would have managed well enough as long as they drifted across the sea with the current, in which fish abounded. There was not a day on our whole voyage on which fish were not swimming round the raft and could not easily be caught. Scarcely a day passed without flying fish, at any rate, coming on board of their own accord. It even happened that large bonitos, delicious eating, swam on board with the masses of water that came from astern and lay kicking on the raft when the water had vanished down between the logs as a sieve. To starve to death was impossible.

The old natives knew well the device which many shipwrecked men hit upon during the war—chewing thirst-quenching moisture out of raw fish. One can also press the juices out by twisting pieces

Hold on, Haugland! If the intervals between the waves were too short, water often came on board from astern, and the helmsman had a hard job to prevent himself from being washed overboard.

Above: When we were halfway across, we were about 2,000 sea miles from land both ahead and astern. We felt we were living in a strange world—"east of the sun and west of the moon."

Below: Provisions were stored between the logs and the bamboo deck. Our Peruvian parrot always came fluttering along when we opened a box of food.

Above: The whale shark which paid us a visit. It is the world's biggest fish and can be as much as 60 feet long. Its body is covered with white spots, and its jaws are nearly 5 feet wide.
Below: The dorsal fin projected menacingly from the water when the monster approached the raft.

Above: Whales often visited us, and the raft seemed pretty small alongside them. Sometimes they followed us for hours before they disappeared.
Below: The raft would certainly have come off badly in a collision with a whale. But however deliberately the whales seemed to come rushing straight toward the raft, they always dived under it at the last moment.

Catching sharks with our hands. Sharks followed us throughout the voyage and we got to know them thoroughly. Top left, a shark eating out of the author's hand. Its black head projects from the water and snaps a dolphin in half with the utmost ease. Just as it is about to dive, the author seizes its tail fin, as rough as sandpaper. The shark is slowly hauled on deck. As soon as the tail fin comes above water the shark is helpless, and when at last the stomach sinks down toward the head it is almost paralyzed.

Shark fishing (*continued*): One strong jerk and the shark is on deck. Then we have to jump out of the way and keep at a distance till the shark has ceased to snap around.

Below: A day's catch. Nine sharks, two tunnies, and a lot of bonitos. The flying fish, squids, and remora fish in the foreground all came on board of their own accord.

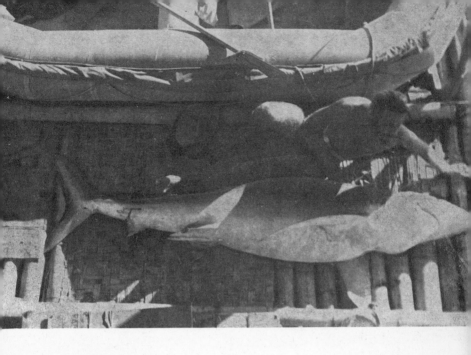

Above: A blue shark with its conqueror. Shark flesh was edible only if soaked in salt water for twenty-four hours. But we often cleared the water of sharks to be on the safe side in case one of us should fall overboard.
Below: An idyllic scene: Hesselberg playing and singing in his "watch below."

Heave ho! The ropes became slack in tropical sun and squalls, and we often had to make them taut.

of fish in a cloth, or, if the fish is large, it is a fairly simple matter to cut holes in its side, which soon become filled with ooze from the fish's lymphatic glands. It does not taste good if one has anything better to drink, but the percentage of salt is so low that one's thirst is quenched.

The necessity for drinking water was greatly reduced if we bathed regularly and lay down wet in the shady cabin. If a shark was patrolling majestically round about us and prevented a real plunge from the side of the raft, one had only to lie down on the logs aft and get a good grip of the ropes with one's fingers and toes. Then we got several bathfuls of crystal-clear Pacific pouring over us every few seconds.

When tormented by thirst in a hot climate, one generally assumes that the body needs water, and this may often lead to immoderate inroads on the water ration without any benefit whatever. On really hot days in the tropics you can pour tepid water down your throat till you taste it at the back of your mouth, and you are just as thirsty. It is not liquid the body needs then, but, curiously enough, salt. The special rations we had on board included salt tablets to be taken regularly on particularly hot days, because perspiration drains the body of salt. We experienced days like this when the wind had died away and the sun blazed down on the raft without mercy. Our water ration could be ladled into us till it squelched in our stomachs, but our throats malignantly demanded much more. On such days we added from 20 to 40 per cent of bitter, salt sea water to our fresh-water ration and found, to our surprise, that this brackish water quenched our thirst. We had the taste of sea water in our mouths for a long time afterward but never felt unwell, and moreover we had our water ration considerably increased.

One morning, as we sat at breakfast, an unexpected sea splashed into our gruel and taught us quite gratuitously that the taste of oats removed the greater part of the sickening taste of sea water!

The old Polynesians had preserved some curious traditions, according to which their earliest forefathers, when they came sailing across the sea, had with them leaves of a certain plant which they chewed, with the result that their thirst disappeared. Another effect of the plant was that in an emergency they could drink sea water without being sick. No such plants grew in the South Sea islands; they must, therefore, have originated in their ancestors' homeland. The Polynesian historians repeated these statements so often that modern scientists investigated the matter and came to the conclusion that the only known plant with such an effect was the coca plant, which grew only in Peru. And in prehistoric Peru this very coca plant, which contains cocaine, was regularly used both by the Incas and by their vanished forerunners, as is shown by discoveries in pre-Inca graves. On exhausting mountain journys and sea voyages they took with them piles of these leaves and chewed them for days on end to remove the feelings of thirst and weariness. And over a fairly short period the chewing of coca leaves will even allow one to drink sea water with a certain immunity.

We did not test coca leaves on board the *Kon-Tiki*, but we had on the foredeck large wicker baskets full of other plants, some of which had left a deeper imprint on the South Sea islands. The baskets stood lashed fast in the lee of the cabin wall, and as time passed yellow shoots and green leaves of potatoes and coconuts shot up higher from the wickerwork. It was like a little tropical garden on board the wooden raft.

When the first Europeans came to the Pacific islands, they found large plantings of sweet potatoes on Easter Island and in Hawaii and New Zealand, and the same plant was also cultivated on the other islands, but only within the Polynesian area. It was quite unknown in the part of the world which lay farther west. The sweet potato was one of the most important cultivated plants in these remote islands where the people otherwise lived mainly on fish, and many of the Polynesians' legends centered round this plant. According to tradition it had been brought by no less a personage than Tiki himself, when he came with his wife Pani from their ancestors' original homeland, where the sweet potato had been an important article of food. New Zealand legends affirm that the sweet potato was brought over the sea in vessels which were not canoes but consisted of "wood bound together with ropes."

Now, as is known, America is the only place in the rest of the world where the potato grew before the time of the Europeans. And the sweet potato Tiki brought with him to the islands, *Ipomoea batatas*, is exactly the same as that which the Indians have cultivated in Peru from the oldest times. Dried sweet potatoes were the most important travel provisions both for the seafarers of Polynesia and for the natives in old Peru. In the South Sea islands the sweet potato will grow only if carefully tended by man, and, as it cannot withstand sea water, it is idle to explain its wide distribution over these scattered islands by declaring that it could have drifted over 4,000 sea miles with ocean currents from Peru. This attempt to explain away so important a clue to the Polynesians' origin is particularly futile seeing that philologists have pointed out that on all the widely scattered South Sea islands the name of the sweet potato is *kumara,* and *kumara* is just what the sweet potato was called among the old Indians in Peru. The name followed the plant across the sea.

Another very important Polynesian cultivated plant we had with us on board the *Kon-Tiki* was the bottle gourd, *Lagenaria vulgaris.* As important as the fruit itself was the skin, which the Polynesians dried over a fire and used to hold water. This typical garden plant also, which again cannot propagate itself in a wild state by drifting across the sea alone, the old Polynesians had in common with the original population of Peru. Bottle gourds, converted into water containers, are found in prehistoric desert graves on the coast of Peru and were used by the fishing population there centuries before the first men came to the islands in the Pacific. The Polynesian name for the bottle gourd, *kimi,* is found again among the Indians in Central America, where Peruvian civilization has its deepest roots.

In addition to a few chance tropical fruits, most of which we ate up in a few weeks' time before they spoiled, we had on board a third plant which, along with the sweet potato, has played the greatest part in the history of the Pacific. We had two hundred coconuts, and they gave us exercise for our teeth and refreshing drinks. Several of the nuts soon began to sprout, and, when we had been just ten weeks at sea, we had half a dozen baby palms a foot high, which had already opened their shoots and formed thick green leaves. The coconut grew before Columbus' time both on the Isthmus of Panama and in South America. The chronicler Oviedo writes that the coconut palm was found in great numbers along the coast of Peru when the Spaniards arrived. At that time it had long existed on all the islands in the Pacific.

Botanists have still no certain proof in which direction it spread over the Pacific. But one thing has now been discovered. Not even the coconut, with its famous shell, can spread over the ocean without men's help. The nuts we had in baskets on deck remained eatable and capable of germinating the whole way to Polynesia. But we had laid about half among the special provisions below deck, with the waves washing around them. Every single one of these was ruined by the sea water. And no coconut can float over the sea faster than a balsa raft moves with the wind behind it. It was the eyes of the coconut which sucked in the sea water so that the nut spoiled. Refuse collectors, too, all over the ocean took care that no edible thing that floated should get across from one world to the other.

Solitary petrels and other sea birds which can sleep on the sea we met thousands of sea miles from the nearest land. Sometimes, on quiet days far out on the blue sea, we sailed close to a white, floating bird's feather. If, on approaching the little feather, we looked at it closely, we saw that there were two or three passengers on board it, sailing along at their ease before the wind. When the *Kon-Tiki* was about to pass, the passengers noticed that a vessel was coming which was faster and had more space, and so all came scuttling sideways at top speed over the surface and up on to the raft, leaving the feather to sail on alone. And so the *Kon-Tiki* soon began to swarm with stowaways. They were small pelagic crabs. As big as a fingernail, and now and then a good deal larger, they were tidbits for the Goliaths on board the raft, if we managed to catch them.

The small crabs were the policemen of the sea's surface, and they were not slow to look after themselves when they saw anything eatable. If one day the cook failed to notice a flying fish in between the logs, next day it was covered with from eight to ten small crabs, sitting on the fish and helping themselves with their claws. Most often they were frightened and scurried away to hide when we came in view, but aft, in a little hole by the steering block, lived a crab which was quite tame and which we named Johannes.

Like the parrot, who was everyone's amusing pet, the crab Johannes became one of our community on deck. If the man at the helm, sitting steering on a sunshiny day with his back to the cabin, had not Johannes for company, he felt utterly lonely out on the wide blue sea. While the other small crabs scurried furtively about and pilfered like cockroaches on an ordinary boat, Johannes sat broad and round in his doorway with his eyes wide open, waiting for the change of watch. Every man who came on watch had a scrap of biscuit or a bit of fish for him, and we needed only to stoop down over the hole for him to come right out on his doorstep and stretch out his hands. He took the scraps out of our fingers with his claws and ran back into the hole, where he sat down in the doorway and munched like a schoolboy, cramming his food into his mouth.

The crabs clung like flies to the soaked coconuts, which burst when they fermented, or caught plankton washed on board by the waves. And these, the tiniest organisms in the sea, were good eating too even for us Goliaths on the raft, when we learned how to catch a number of them at once so that we got a decent mouthful

It is certain that there must be a very nourishing food in these almost invisible plankton which drift about with the current on the oceans in infinite numbers. Fish and sea birds which do not eat plankton themselves live on other fish or sea animals which do, no matter how large they themselves may be. Plankton is a general name for thousands of species of visible and invisible small organisms which drift about near the surface of the sea. Some are plants (*phyto*-plankton), while others are loose fish ova and tiny living creatures (*zoo*-plankton). Animal plankton live on vegetable plankton, and vegetable plankton live on ammoniac, nitrates, and nitrites which are formed from dead animal plankton. And while they reciprocally live on one another, they all form food for everything which moves in and over the sea. What they cannot offer in size they can offer in numbers.

In good plankton waters there are thousands in a glassful. More than once persons have starved to death at sea because they did not find fish large enough to be spitted, netted, or hooked. In such cases it has often happened that they have literally been sailing about in strongly diluted, raw fish soup. If, in addition to hooks and nets, they had had a utensil for straining the soup they were sitting in, they would have found a nourishing meal—plankton. Some day in the future, perhaps, men will think of harvesting plankton from the sea to the same extent as now they harvest grain on land. A single grain is of no use, either, but in large quantities it becomes food.

The marine biologist Dr. A. D. Bajkov told us of plankton and sent us a fishing net which was suited to the creatures we were to catch. The "net" was a silk net with almost three thousand meshes per square inch. It was sewn in the shape of a funnel with a circular mouth behind an iron ring, eighteen inches across, and was towed behind the raft. Just as in other kinds of fishing, the catch varied with time and place. Catches diminished as the sea grew warmer farther west, and we got the best results at night, because many species seemed to go deeper down into the water when the sun was shining.

If we had no other way of whiling away time on board the raft, there would have been entertainment enough in lying with our noses in the plankton net. Not for the sake of the smell, for that was bad. Nor because the sight was appetizing, for it looked a horrible mess. But because, if we spread the plankton out on a board and examined each of the little creatures separately with the naked eye, we had before us fantastic shapes and colors in unending variety.

Most of them were tiny shrimplike crustaceans (*copepods*) or fish ova floating loose, but there were also larvae of fish and shellfish, curious miniature crabs in all colors, jellyfish, and an endless variety of small creatures which might have been taken from Walt Disney's *Fantasia*. Some looked like fringed, fluttering spooks cut out of cellophane paper, while others resembled tiny red-beaked birds with hard shells instead of feathers. There was no end to Nature's extravagant inventions in the plankton world; a surrealistic artist might well own himself bested here.

Where the cold Humboldt Current turned west south of the Equator, we could pour several pounds of plankton porridge out of the bag every few hours. The plankton lay packed together like cake in colored layers—brown, red, gray, and green according to the different fields of plankton through which we had passed. At night, when there was phosphorescence about, it was like hauling in a bag of sparkling jewels. But, when we got hold of it, the pirates' treasure turned into millions of tiny glittering shrimps and phosphorescent fish larvae that glowed in the dark like a heap of live coals. When we poured them into a bucket, the squashy mess ran out like a magic gruel composed of glowworms. Our night's catch looked as nasty at close quarters as it had been pretty at long range. And, bad as it smelled, it tasted correspondingly good if one just plucked up courage and put a spoonful of it into one's mouth. If this consisted of many dwarf shrimps, it tasted like shrimp paste, lobster, or crab. If it was mostly deep-sea fish ova, it tasted like caviar and now and then like oysters.

The inedible vegetable plankton were either so small that they washed away with the water through the meshes of the net, or they were so large that we could pick them up with our fingers. "Snags" in the dish were single jellylike coelenterates like glass balloons and jellyfish about half an inch long. These were bitter and had to be thrown away. Otherwise everything could be eaten, either as it was or cooked in fresh water as gruel or soup. Tastes differ. Two men on board thought plankton tasted delicious, two thought they were quite good, and for two the sight of them was more than enough. From a nutrition standpoint they stand on a level with the larger shellfish, and, spiced and properly prepared, they can certainly be a first-class dish for all who like marine food.

That these small organisms contain calories enough has been proved by the blue whale, which is the largest animal in the world and yet lives on plankton. Our own method of capture, with the little net which was often chewed up by hungry fish, seemed to us sadly primitive when we sat on the raft and saw a passing whale send up cascades of water as it simply filtered plankton through its celluloid beard. And one day we lost the whole net in the sea.

"Why don't you plankton-eaters do like him?" Torstein and Bengt said contemptuously to the rest of us, pointing to a blowing whale. "Just fill your mouths and blow the water out through your mustaches!"

I have seen whales in the distance from boats, and I have seen them stuffed in museums, but I have never felt toward the gigantic carcass as one usually feels toward proper warm-blooded animals, for example a horse or an elephant. Biologically, indeed, I had accepted the whale as a genuine mammal, but in its essence it was to all intents and purposes a large cold fish. We had a different impression when the great whales came rushing toward us, close to the side of the raft.

One day, when we were sitting as usual on the edge of the raft having a meal, so close to the water that we had only to lean back to wash out our mugs, we started when suddenly something behind us blew hard like a swimming horse and a big whale came up and stared at us, so close that we saw a shine like a polished shoe down through its blowhole. It was so unusual to hear real breathing out at sea, where all living creatures wriggle silently about without lungs and quiver their gills, that we really had a warm family feeling for our old distant cousin the whale, who like us had strayed so far out to sea. Instead of the cold, toadlike whale shark, which had not even the sense to stick up its nose for a breath of fresh air, here we had a visit from something which recalled a well-fed jovial hippopotamus in a zoological garden and which actually breathed—that made a most pleasant impression on me—before it sank into the sea again and disappeared.

We were visited by whales many times. Most often they were small porpoises and toothed whales which gamboled about us in large schools on the surface of the water, but now and then there were big cachalots, too, and other giant whales which appeared singly or in small schools. Sometimes they passed like ships on the horizon, now and again sending a cascade of water into the air, but sometimes they steered straight for us. We were prepared for a dangerous collision the first time a big whale altered course and came straight toward the raft in a purposeful manner. As it gradually grew nearer, we could hear its blowing and puffing, heavy and long drawn, each time it rolled its head out of the water. It was an enormous, thick-skinned, ungainly land animal that came toiling through the water, as unlike a fish as a bat is unlike a bird. It came straight toward our port side, where we stood gathered on the edge of the raft, while one man sat at the masthead and shouted that he could see seven or eight more making their way toward us.

The big, shining, black forehead of the first whale was not more than two yards from us when it sank beneath the surface of the water, and then we saw the enormous blue-black bulk glide quietly under the raft right beneath our feet. It lay there for a time, dark and motionless, and we held our breath as we looked down on the gigantic curved back of a mammal a good deal longer than the whole raft. Then it sank slowly through the bluish water and dis-appeared from sight. Meanwhile the whole school were close upon us, but they paid no attention to us. Whales which have abused their giant strength and sunk whaling boats with their tails have presumably been attacked first. The whole morning we had them puffing and blowing round us in the most unexpected places with-out their even pushing against the raft or the steering oar. They quite enjoyed themselves gamboling freely among the waves in the sunshine. But about noon the whole school dived as if on a given signal and disappeared for good.

It was not only whales we could see under the raft. If we lifted up the reed matting we slept on, through the chinks between the logs we saw right down into the crystal-blue water. If we lay thus for a while, we saw a breast fin or tail fin waggle past and now and again we saw a whole fish. If the chinks had been a few inches wider, we could have lain comfortably in bed with a line and fished under our mattresses.

The fish which most of all attached themselves to the raft were dolphins and pilot fish. From the moment the first dolphins joined us in the current off Callao, there was not a day on the whole voyage on which we had not large dolphins wriggling round us. What drew them to the raft we do not know, but, either there was a magical attraction in being able to swim in the shade with a moving roof above them, or there was food to be found in our kitchen garden of seaweed and barnacles that hung like garlands from all the logs and from the steering oar. It began with a thin coating of smooth green, but then the clusters of seaweed grew with astonishing speed, so that the *Kon-Tiki* looked like a bearded sea-god as she tumbled along among the waves. Inside the green seaweed was a favorite resort of tiny small fry and our stowaways, the crabs.

There was a time when ants began to get the upper hand on board. There had been small black ants in some of the logs, and, when we had got to sea and the damp began to penetrate into the wood, the ants swarmed out and into the sleeping bags. They were all over the place, and bit and tormented us till we thought they would drive us off the raft. But gradually, as it became wetter out at sea, they realized that this was not their right element, and only a few isolated specimens held out till we reached the other side. What did best on the raft, along with the crabs, were barnacles from an inch to an inch and a half long. They grew in hundreds, especially on the lee side of the raft, and as fast as we put the old ones into the soup kettle new larvae took root and grew up. The barnacles tasted fresh and delicate; we picked the seaweed as salad and it was eatable, though not so good. We never actually saw the dolphins feeding in the vegetable garden, but they were constantly turning their gleaming bellies upward and swimming under the logs.

The dolphin (dorado), which is a brilliantly colored tropical fish, must not be confused with the creature, also called the dolphin, which is a small, toothed whale. The dolphin was ordinarily from three feet three inches to four feet six inches long and had much flattened sides with an enormously high head and neck. We jerked on board one which was four feet eight inches long with a head thirteen and one-half inches high. The dolphin had a magnificent color. In the water it shone blue and green like a bluebottle with a glitter of golden-yellow fins. But if we hauled one on board, we sometimes saw a strange sight. As the fish died, it gradually changed color and became silver gray with black spots and, finally, a quite uniform silvery white. This lasted for four or five minutes, and then the old colors slowly reappeared. Even in the water the dolphin could occasionally change color like a chameleon, and often we saw a "new kind" of shining copper-colored fish, which on a closer acquaintance proved to be our old companion the dolphin.

The high forehead gave the dolphin the appearance of a bulldog flattened from the side, and it always cut through the surface of the water when the predatory fish shot off like a torpedo after a fleeing shoal of flying fish. When the dolphin was in a good humor, it turned over on its flat side, went ahead at a great speed, and then sprang high into the air and tumbled down like a flat pancake. It came down on the surface with a regular smack and a column of water rose up. It was no sooner down in the water than it came up in another leap, and yet another, away over the swell. But, when it was in a bad temper—for example, when we hauled it up on to the raft—then it bit. Torstein limped about for some time with a rag round his big toe because he had let it stray into the mouth of a dolphin, which had used the opportunity to close its jaws and chew a little harder than usual. After our return home we heard that dolphins attack and eat people when bathing. This was not very complimentary to us, seeing that we had bathed among them every day without their showing any particular interest. But they were formidable beasts of prey, for we found both squids and whole flying fish in their stomachs.

Flying fish were the dolphins' favorite food. If anything splashed on the surface of the water, they rushed at it blindly in the hope of its being a flying fish. In many a drowsy morning hour, when we crept blinking out of the cabin and, half asleep, dipped a toothbrush into the sea, we became wide-awake with a jump when a thirty-pound fish shot out like lightning from under the raft and nosed at the toothbrush in disappointment. And, when we were sitting quietly at breakfast on the edge of the raft, a dolphin might jump up and make one of its most vigorous sideway splashes, so that the sea water ran down our backs and into our food.

One day, when we were sitting at dinner, Torstein made a reality of the tallest of fish stories. He suddenly laid down his fork and put his hand into the sea, and, before we knew what was happening, the water was boiling and a big dolphin came tumbling in among us. Torstein had caught hold of the tail end of a fishing line which came quietly gliding past, and on the other end hung a completely astonished dolphin which had broken Erik's line when he was fishing a few days before.

There was not a day on which we had not six or seven dolphins following us in circles round and under the raft. On bad days there might be only two or three, but, on the other hand, as many as thirty or forty might turn up the day after. As a rule it was enough to warn the cook twenty minutes in advance if we wanted fresh fish for dinner. Then he tied a line to a short bamboo stick and put half a flying fish on the hook. A dolphin was there in a flash, plowing the surface with its head as it chased the hook, with two or three more in its wake. It was a splendid fish to play and, when freshly caught, its flesh was firm and delicious to eat, like a mixture of cod and salmon. It kept for two days, and that was all we needed, for there were fish enough in the sea.

We became acquainted with pilot fish in another way. Sharks brought them and left them to be adopted by us after the sharks' death. We had not been long at sea before the first shark visited us. And sharks soon became an almost daily occurrence. Sometimes the shark just came swimming up to inspect the raft and went on in search of prey after circling round us once or twice. But most often the sharks took up a position in our wake just behind the steering oar, and there they lay without a sound, stealing from starboard to port and occasionally giving a leisurely wag of their tails to keep pace with the raft's placid advance. The blue-gray body of the shark always looked brownish in the sunlight just below the surface, and it moved up and down with the seas so that the dorsal fin always stuck up menacingly. If there was a high sea, the shark might be lifted up by the waves high above our own level, and we had a direct side view of the shark as in a glass case as it swam toward us in a dignified manner with its fussy retinue of small pilot fish ahead of its jaws. For a few seconds it looked as if both the shark and its striped companions would swim right on board, but then the raft would lean over gracefully to leeward, rise over the ridge of waves, and descend on the other side.

To begin with, we had a great respect for sharks on account of their reputation and their alarming appearance. There was an unbridled strength in the streamlined body, consisting of one great bundle of steel muscles, and a heartless greed in the broad flat head with the small, green cat's eyes and the enormous jaws which could swallow footballs. When the man at the helm shouted "Shark alongside to starboard" or "Shark alongside to port," we used to come out in search of hand harpoons and gaffs and station ourselves along the edge of the raft. The shark usually glided round us with the dorsal fin close up to the logs. And our respect for the shark increased when we saw that the gaffs bent like spaghetti when we struck them against the sandpaper armor on the shark's back, while the spearheads of the hand harpoons were broken in the heat of the battle. All we gained by getting through the shark's skin and into the gristle or muscle was a hectic struggle, in which the water boiled round us till the shark broke loose and was off, while a little oil floated up and spread itself out over the surface.

To save our last harpoon head we fastened together a bunch of our largest fishhooks and hid them inside the carcass of a whole dolphin. We slung the bait overboard with a precautionary multiplication of steel lines fastened to a piece of our own life line. Slowly and surely the shark came, and, as it lifted its snout above the water, it opened its great crescent-shaped jaws with a jerk and let the whole dolphin slip in and down. And there it stuck. There was a struggle in which the shark lashed the water into foam, but we had a good grip on the rope and hauled the big fellow, despite its resistance, as far as the logs aft, where it lay awaiting what might come and only gaped as though to intimidate us with its parallel rows of sawlike teeth. Here we profited by a sea to slide the shark up over the low end logs, slippery with seaweed and, after casting a rope round the tail fin, we ran well out of the way till the war dance was over.

In the gristle of the first shark we caught this way we found our own harpoon head, and we thought at first that this was the reason for the shark's comparatively small fighting spirit. But later we caught shark after shark by the same method, and every time it went just as easily. Even if the shark could jerk and tug and certainly was fearfully heavy to play, it became quite spiritless and tame and never made full use of its giant strength if we only managed to hold the line tight without letting the shark gain an inch in the tug of war. The sharks we got on board were usually from six to ten feet long, and there were blue sharks as well as brown sharks. The last-named had a skin outside the mass of muscles through which we could not drive a sharp knife unless we struck with our whole strength, and often not even then. The skin of the belly was as impenetrable as that of the back; the five gill clefts behind the head on each side were the only vulnerable point.

When we hauled in a shark, black slippery remora fish were usually fixed tight to its body. By means of an oval sucking disc on the top of the flat head, they were fastened so tight that we could not get them loose by pulling their tails. But they themselves could break loose and skip away to take hold at another place in a second. If they grew tired of hanging tightly to the shark when their host gave no sign of returning to the sea, they leaped off and vanished down between the chinks in the raft to swim away and find themselves another shark. If the remora does not find a shark, it attaches itself to the skin of another fish for the time being. It is generally as long as the length of a finger up to a foot. We tried the natives' old trick which they sometimes use when they have been lucky enough to secure a live remora. They tie a line to its tail and let it swim away. It then tries to suck itself on to the first fish it sees and clings so tightly that a lucky fisherman may haul in both fishes by the remora's tail. We had no luck. Every single time we let a remora go with a line tied to its tail, it simply shot off and sucked itself fast to one of the logs of the raft, in the belief that it had found an extrafine big shark. And there it hung, however hard we tugged on the line. We gradually acquired a number of these small remoras which hung on and dangled obstinately among the shells on the side of the raft, traveling with us right across the Pacific.

But the remora was stupid and ugly and never became such an agreeable pet as its lively companion the pilot fish. The pilot fish is a small cigar-shaped fish with zebra stripes, which swims rapidly in a shoal ahead of the shark's snout. It received its name because it was thought that it piloted its half-blind friend the shark about in the sea. In reality, it simply goes along with the shark, and, if it acts independently, it is only because it catches sight of food within its own range of vision. The pilot fish accompanied its lord and master to the last second. But, as it could not cling fast to the giant's skin, as the remora does, it was completely bewildered when its old master suddenly disappeared up into the air and did not come down again. Then the pilot fish scurried about in a distracted manner, searching wildly, but always came back and wriggled along astern of the raft, where the shark had vanished skyward. But as time passed and the shark did not come down again, they had to look round for a new lord and master. And none was nearer to hand than the *Kon-Tiki* herself.

If we let ourselves down over the side of the raft, with our heads down in the brilliantly clear water, we saw the raft as the belly of a sea monster, with the steering oar as its tail and the centerboards hanging down like blunt fins. In between them all the adopted pilot fish swam, side by side, and took no notice of the bubbling human head except that one or two of them darted swiftly aside and peered right up its nose, only to wriggle back again unperturbed and take their places in the ranks of eager swimmers.

Our pilot fish patrolled in two detachments; most of them swam between the centerboards, the others in a graceful fan formation ahead of the bow. Now and then they shot away from the raft to snap up some edible trifle we passed, and after meals, when we washed our crockery in the water alongside, it was as if we had emptied a whole cigar case of striped pilot fish among the scraps. There was not a single scrap they did not examine, and, so long as it was not vegetable food, down it went. These queer little fish huddled under our protecting wings with such childlike confidence that we, like the shark, had a fatherly protective feeling toward them. They became the *Kon-Tiki's* marine pets, and it was taboo on board to lay hands on a pilot fish.

We had in our retinue pilot fish which were certainly in their childhood, for they were hardly an inch long, while most were about six inches. When the whale shark rushed off at lightning speed after Erik's harpoon had entered its skull, some of its old pilot fish strayed over to the victor; they were two feet long. After a succession of victories the *Kon-Tiki* soon had a following of forty or fifty pilot fish, and many of them liked our quiet forward movement, and our daily scraps, so much that they followed us for thousands of miles over the sea.

But occasionally some were faithless. One day, when I was at the steering oar, I suddenly noticed that the sea was boiling to southward and saw an immense shoal of dolphins come shooting across the sea like silver torpedoes. They did not come as usual, splashing along comfortably on their flat sides, but came rushing at frantic speed more through the air than through the water. The blue swell was whipped into white foam in one single turmoil of splashing fugitives, and behind them came a black back dashing along on a zigzag course like a speedboat. The desperate dolphins came shooting through and over the surface right up to the raft; here they dived, while about a hundred crowded together in a tightly packed shoal and swung away to eastward, so that the whole sea astern was a glittering mass of colors. The gleaming back behind them half rose above the surface, dived in a graceful curve under the raft, and shot astern after the shoal of dolphins. It was a devilish-big fellow of a blue shark that seemed to be nearly twenty feet long. When it disappeared, a number of our pilot fish had gone too. They had found a more exciting sea hero to go campaigning with.

The marine creature against which the experts had begged us to be most on our guard was the octopus, for it could get on board the raft. The National Geographic Society in Washington had shown us reports and dramatic magnesium photographs from an area in the Humboldt Current where monstrous octopuses had their favorite resort and came up on to the surface at night. They were so voracious that, if one of them fastened on to a piece of meat and remained on the hook, another came and began to eat its captured kinsman. They had arms which could make an end of a big shark and set ugly marks on great whales, and a devilish beak like an eagle's hidden among their tentacles. We were reminded that they lay floating in the darkness with phosphorescent eyes and that their arms were long enough to feel about in every small corner of the raft, if they did not care to come right on board. We did not at all like the prospect of feeling cold arms round our necks, dragging us out of our sleeping bags at night, and we provided ourselves with saberlike machete knives, one for each of us, in case we should wake to the embrace of fumbling tentacles. There was nothing which seemed more disagreeable to us when we started, especially as the marine experts in Peru got on to the same subject and showed us on the chart where the worst area was—right in the Humboldt Current itself.

For a long time we saw no sign of a squid, either on board or in the sea. But then one morning we had the first warning that they must be in those waters. When the sun rose, we found the progeny of an octopus on board, in the form of a little baby the size of a cat. It had come up on deck unaided in the course of the night and now lay dead with its arms twined round the bamboo outside the cabin door. A thick, black, inky liquid was smeared over the bamboo deck and lay in a pool round the squid. We wrote a page or two in the logbook with cuttlefish ink, which was like India ink, and then flung the baby overboard for the pleasure of the dolphins.

We saw in this minor incident the harbinger of larger night visitors. If the baby could clamber on board, its hungry progenitor could no doubt do the same. Our forefathers must have felt the same as we did when they sat in their Viking ships and thought of the Old Man of the Sea. But the next incident completely bewildered us. One morning we found a single smaller young squid on the top of the roof of palm leaves. This puzzled us very much. It could not have climbed up there, as the only ink marks were smeared in a ring round it in the middle of the roof. Nor had it been dropped by a sea bird, for it was completely intact with no beak marks. We came to the conclusion that it had been flung up on to the roof by a sea which had come on board, but none of those on night watch could remember any such sea that night. As the nights passed, we regularly found more young squids on board, the smallest of them the size of one's middle finger.

It was soon usual to find a small squid or two among the flying fish about the deck in the morning, even if the sea had been calm in the night. And they were young ones of the real devilish kind, with eight long arms covered with sucking discs and two still longer with thornlike hooks at the end. But large squids never gave a sign of coming on board. We saw the shine of phosphorescent eyes drifting on the surface on dark nights, and on one single occasion we saw the sea boil and bubble while something like a big wheel came up and rotated in the air, while some of our dolphins tried to escape by hurling themselves desperately through space. But why the big ones never came on board, when the small ones were constant night visitors, was a riddle to which we found no answer until two months later—two months rich in experience—after we were out of the ill-famed octopus area.

Young squids continued to come aboard. One sunny morning we all saw a glittering shoal of something which shot up out of the water and flew through the air like large raindrops, while the sea boiled with pursuing dolphins. At first we took it for a shoal of flying fish, for we had already had three different kinds of these on board. But, when they came near and some of them sailed over the raft at a height of four or five feet, one ran straight into Bengt's chest and fell slap on the deck. It was a small squid. Our astonishment was great. When we put it into a sailcloth bucket it kept on taking off and shooting up to the surface, but it did not develop speed enough in the small bucket to get more than half out of the water.

It is a known fact that the squid ordinarily swims on the principle of the rocket-propelled airplane. It pumps sea water with great force through a closed tube alongside its body and can thus shoot backward in jerks at a high speed; with all its tentacles hanging behind it in a cluster over its head it becomes streamlined like a fish. It has on its sides two round, fleshy folds of skin which are ordinarily used for steering and quiet swimming in the water. But our experience showed that defenseless young squids, which are a favorite food of many large fish, can escape their pursuers by taking to the air in the same way as flying fish. They had made the principle of the rocket aircraft a reality long before human genius hit upon the idea. They pump sea water through themselves till they get up a terrific speed, and then they steer up at an angle from the surface by unfolding the pieces of skin like wings. Like the flying fish, they make a glider flight over the waves for as far as their speed can carry them. After that, when we had to begin to pay attention, we often saw them sailing along for fifty to sixty yards, singly and in two's and three's. The fact that cuttlefish can "glide" has been a novelty to all the zoologists we have met.

As the guest of natives in the Pacific I have often eaten squid; it tastes like a mixture of lobster and India rubber. But on board the *Kon-Tiki* squid came last on the menu. If we got them on deck gratis, we just exchanged them for something else. We made the exchange by throwing out a hook, with the squid on it, and pulling it in again with a big fish kicking at the end of it. Even tunny and bonito liked young squids, and they were food which came at the head of our menu.

But we did not run up against acquaintances only, as we lay drifting over the sea's surface. The diary contains many entries of this type:

—*11/5. Today a huge marine animal twice came up to the surface alongside us as we sat at supper on the edge of the raft. It made a fearful splashing and disappeared. We have no idea what it was.*

—*6/6. Herman saw a thick dark-colored fish with a broad white body, thin tail, and spikes. It jumped clear of the sea on the starboard side several times.*

—*16/6. Curious fish sighted on port bow. Six feet long, maximum breadth one foot; long, brown, thin snout, large dorsal fin near head and a smaller one in the middle of the back, heavy sickle-shaped tail fin. Kept near surface and swam at times by wriggling its body like an eel. It dived when Herman and I went out in the rubber dinghy with a hand harpoon. Came up later but dived again and disappeared.*

—*Next day: Erik was sitting at the masthead, 12 noon, when he*

saw thirty or forty long, thin, brown fish of the same kind as yester-
day. Now they came at a high speed from the port side and disap-
peared astern like a big, brown, flat shadow in the sea.

—18/6. Knut observed a snakelike creature, two to three feet long
and thin, which stood straight up and down in the water below the
surface and dived by wriggling downward like a snake.

On several occasions we glided past a large dark mass, the size of
the floor of a room, that lay motionless under the surface of the water
like a hidden reef. It was presumably the giant ray of evil repute
but it never moved, and we never went close enough to make out
its shape clearly.

With such company in the water time never passed slowly. It was
even more entertaining when we had to dive down into the sea ourselves and inspect the ropes on the underside of the raft. One day
one of the centerboards broke loose and slipped down under the
raft, where it was caught up in the ropes without our being able to
get hold of it. Herman and Knut were the best divers. Twice Herman
swam under the raft and lay there among dolphins and pilot fish,
tugging and pulling at the board. He had just come up for the second
time, and was sitting on the edge of the raft to recover his breath,
when an eight-foot shark was detected not more than ten feet from
his legs, moving steadily up from the depths toward the tips of his
toes. Perhaps we did the shark an injustice, but we suspected it of
evil intentions and rammed a harpoon into its skull. The shark felt
aggrieved and a splashy struggle took place, as a consequence of
which the shark disappeared leaving a sheet of oil on the surface,
while the centerboard remained unsalved, lying caught up under the
raft.

Then Erik had the idea of making a diving basket. We had not
many raw materials to which we could have recourse, but we had
bamboos and ropes and an old chip basket which had contained
coconuts. We lengthened the basket upward with bamboos and
plaited ropework, and then let one another down in the basket
alongside the raft. Our enticing legs were then concealed in the
basket, and, even if the plaited ropework above had only a psychological effect on both us and the fish, in any case we could duck
down into the basket in a flash if anything with hostile intentions
made a dash at us, and have ourselves pulled up out of the water
by the others on deck.

This diving basket was not merely useful but gradually became a perfect place of entertainment for us on board. It gave us a first-class opportunity to study the floating aquarium we had under the raft floor.

When the sea was content to run in a calm swell, we crawled into the basket one by one and were let down under water for as long as our breath lasted. There was a curiously transfigured, shadow-less flow of light down in the water. As soon as we had our eyes under the surface, light no longer seemed to have a particular direction, as up in our own above-water world. Refraction of light came as much from below as from above; the sun no longer shone—it was present everywhere. If we looked up at the bottom of the raft, it was brightly illuminated all over, with the nine big logs and the whole network of rope lashings bathed in a magic light and with a flicker-ing wreath of spring-green seaweed all round the sides and along the whole length of the steering oar. The pilot fish swam formally in their ranks like zebras in fishes' skins, while big dolphins circled round with restless, vigilant, jerky movements, eager for prey. Here and there the light fell on the sappy red wood of a centerboard which stuck downward out of a chink, and on them sat peaceful colonies of white barnacles rhythmically beckoning for oxygen and food with their fringed yellow gills. If anyone came too near them, they hastily closed their red- and yellow-edged shells and shut the door till they felt the danger was over.

The light down here was wonderfully clear and soothing for us who were accustomed to the tropical sun on deck. Even when we looked down into the bottomless depths of the sea, where it is eternal black night, the night appeared to us a brilliant light blue on account of the refracted rays of the sun. To our astonishment, we saw fish far down in the depths of the clear, clean blue when we ourselves were only just below the surface. They might have been bonitos, and there were other kinds which swam at such a depth that we could not recognize them. Sometimes they were in immense shoals, and we often wondered whether the whole ocean current was full of fish, or whether those down in the depths had intentionally assembled under the *Kon-Tiki* to keep us company for a few days.

What we liked best was a dip under the surface when the great gold-finned tunnies were paying us a visit. Occasionally they came to the raft in big shoals, but most often just two or three came together and swam round us in quiet circles for several days on end, unless we were able to lure them on to the hook. From the raft they looked simply like big, heavy, brown fish without any distinctive adornment, but if we crept down to them in their own element they spontaneously changed both color and shape. The change was so bewildering that several times we had to come up and take our bearings afresh to see if it was the same fish we had been looking at across the water. The big fellows paid no attention to us whatever—they continued their majestic maneuvers unperturbed—but now they had acquired a marvelous elegance of form, the equal of which we never saw in any other fish, and their color had become metallic with a suffusion of pale violet. Powerful torpedoes of shining silver and steel, with perfect proportions and streamlined shape, they had only to move one or two fins slightly to set their 150 to 200 pounds gliding about in the water with the most consummate grace.

The closer we came into contact with the sea and what had its home there, the less strange it became and the more at home we ourselves felt. And we learned to respect the old primitive peoples who lived in close converse with the Pacific and therefore knew it from a quite different standpoint from our own. True, we have now estimated its salt content and given tunnies and dolphins Latin names. They had not done that. But, nevertheless, I am afraid that the picture the primitive peoples had of the sea was a truer one than ours.

There were not many fixed marks out here at sea. Waves and fish, sun and stars, came and went. There was not supposed to be land of any sort in the 4,300 sea miles that separated the South Sea islands from Peru. We were therefore greatly surprised when we approached 100° west and discovered that a reef was marked on the Pacific chart right ahead of us on the course we were following. It was marked as a small circle, and, as the chart had been issued the same year, we looked up the reference in *Sailing Directions for South America*. We read that "breakers were reported in 1906 and again in 1926 to exist about 600 miles southwestward of Galapagos Islands, latitude 6° 42′ S., longitude 99° 43′ W. In 1927 a steamer passed one mile westward of this position but saw no indication of breakers, and in 1934 another passed one mile southward and saw no evidence of breakers. The motor vessel 'Cowrie,' in 1935, obtained no bottom at 160 fathoms in this position."

According to the chart the place was clearly still regarded as a doubtful one for shipping, but, as a deep-draught vessel runs a greater risk by going too near a shoal than we should with a raft, we decided to steer straight for the point marked on the chart and see what we found. The reef was marked a little farther north than the point we seemed to be making for, so we laid the steering oar over to starboard and trimmed the square sail so that the bow pointed roughly north and we took sea and wind from the starboard side. Now it came about that a little more Pacific splashed into our sleeping bags than we were accustomed to, especially as at the same time the weather began to freshen considerably. But we saw to our satisfaction that the *Kon-Tiki* could be maneuvered surely and steadily at a surprisingly wide angle into the wind, so long as the wind was still on our quarter. Otherwise the sail swung round, and we had the same mad circus business to get the raft under control again.

For two days and nights we drove the raft north-northwest. The seas ran high and became incalculable as the trade wind began to fluctuate between southeast and east, but we were lifted up and down over all the waves that rushed against us. We had a constant lookout at the masthead, and when we rode over the ridges the horizon widened considerably. The crests of the seas reached six feet above the level of the roof of the bamboo cabin, and, if two vigorous seas rushed together, they rose still higher in combat and flung up a hissing watery tower which might burst down in unexpected directions. When night came, we barricaded the doorway with provision boxes, but it was a wet night's rest. We had hardly fallen asleep when the first crash on the bamboo wall came, and, while a thousand jets of water sprayed in like a fountain through the bamboo wickerwork, a foaming torrent rushed in over the provisions and on to us.

"Ring up the plumber," I heard a sleepy voice remark, as we hunched ourselves up to give the water room to run out through the floor. The plumber did not come, and we had a lot of bathwater in our beds that night. A big dolphin actually came on board unintentionally in Herman's watch.

Next day the seas were less confused, as the trade wind had decided that it would now blow for a time from due east. We relieved one another at the masthead, for now we might expect to reach the point we were making for late in the afternoon. We noticed more life than usual in the sea that day. Perhaps it was only because we kept a better lookout than usual.

During the forenoon we saw a big swordfish approaching the raft close to the surface. The two sharp pointed fins which stuck up out of the water were six feet apart, and the sword looked almost as long as the body. The swordfish swept in a curve close by the man at the helm and disappeared behind the wave crests. When we were having a rather wet and salty midday meal, the carapace, head, and sprawling fins of a large sea turtle were lifted up by a hissing sea right in front of our noses. When that wave gave place to two others, the turtle was gone as suddenly as it had appeared. This time too we saw the gleaming whitish-green of dolphins' bellies tumbling about in the water below the armored reptile. The area was unusually rich in tiny flying fish an inch long, which sailed along in big shoals and often came on board. We also noted single skuas and were regularly visited by frigate birds, with forked tails like giant swallows, which cruised over the raft. Frigate birds are usually regarded as a sign that land is near, and the optimism on board increased.

"Perhaps there is a reef or a sandbank there all the same," some of us thought. And the most optimistic said: "Suppose we find a little green grassy island—one can never know since so few people have been here before. Then we'll have discovered a new land—Kon-Tiki Island!"

From noon onward Erik was more and more diligent in climbing up on the kitchen box and standing blinking through the sextant. At 6:20 P.M. he reported our position as latitude 6° 42′ south by longitude 99° 42′ west. We were 1 sea mile due east of the reef on the chart. The bamboo yard was lowered and the sail rolled up on deck. The wind was due east and would take us slowly right to the place. When the sun went down swiftly into the sea, the full moon in turn shone out in all its brilliance and lit up the surface of the sea, which undulated in black and silver from horizon to horizon. Visibility from the masthead was good. We saw breaking seas everywhere in long rows, but no regular surf which would indicate a reef or shoal. No one would turn in; all stood looking out eagerly, and two or three men were aloft at once.

As we drifted in over the center of the marked area, we sounded all the time. All the lead sinkers we had on board were fastened to the end of a fifty-four-thread silk rope more than 500 fathoms long, and, even if the rope hung rather aslant on account of the raft's leeway, at any rate the lead hung at a depth of some 400 fathoms. There was no bottom east of the place, or in the middle of it, or west of it. We took one last look over the surface of the sea, and, when we had assured ourselves that we could safely call the area surveyed and free from shallows of any kind, we set sail and laid the oar over in its usual place, so that wind and sea were again on our port quarter.

And so we went on with the raft on her natural free course. The waves came and went as before between the open logs aft. We could now sleep and eat dry, even if the heaving seas round us took charge in earnest and raged for several days while the trade wind vacillated from east to southeast.

On this little sailing trip up to the spurious reef we had learned quite a lot about the effectiveness of the centerboards as a keel, and when, later in the voyage, Herman and Knut dived under the raft together and salved the fifth centerboard, we learned still more about these curious pieces of board, something which no one has understood since the Indians themselves gave up this forgotten sport. That the board did the work of a keel and allowed the raft to move at an angle to the wind—that was plain sailing. But when the old Spaniards declared that the Indians to a large extent "steered" their balsa rafts on the sea with "certain centerboards which they pushed down into the chinks between the timbers," this sounded incomprehensible both to us and to all who had concerned themselves with the problem. As the centerboard was simply held tight in a narrow chink, it could not be turned sideways and serve as a helm.

We discovered the secret in the following manner: The wind was steady and the sea had gone down again, so that the *Kon-Tiki* had kept a steady course for a couple of days without our touching the lashed steering oar. We pushed the recovered centerboard down into a chink aft, and in a moment the *Kon-Tiki* altered course several degrees from west toward northwest and proceeded steadily and quietly on her new course. If we pulled this centerboard up again, the raft swung back on to her previous course. But if we pulled it only halfway up, the raft swung only halfway back on her old course. By simply raising and lowering the centerboards we could effect changes of course and keep to them without touching the steering oar.

This was the Incas' ingenious system. They had worked out a simple system of balances by which pressure of the wind on the sail made the mast the fixed point. The two arms were respectively the raft forward of and the raft aft of the mast. If the aggregate centerboard surface aft was heavier, the bow swung freely round with the wind; but if the centerboard surface forward was heavier, the stern swung round with the wind. The centerboards which are nearest the mast have, of course, the least effect on account of the relation between arm and power. If the wind was due astern, the centerboards ceased to be effective, and then it was impossible to keep the raft steady without continually working the steering oar. If the raft lay thus at full length, she was a little too long to ride the seas freely. As the cabin door and the place where we had meals were on the starboard side, we always took the seas on board on our port quarter.

We could certainly have continued our voyage by making the steersman stand and pull a centerboard up and down in a chink instead of hauling sidewise on the ropes of the steering oar, but we had now grown so accustomed to the steering oar that we just set a general course with the centerboards and preferred to steer with the oar.

The next great stage on our voyage was as invisible to the eye as the shoal which existed only on the map. It was the forty-fifth day at sea; we had advanced from the 78th degree of longitude to the 108th and were exactly halfway to the first islands ahead. There were over 2,000 sea miles between us and South America to the east, and it was the same distance on to Polynesia in the west. The nearest land in any direction was the Galapagos Islands to east-northeast and Easter Island due south, both more than 500 sea miles away on the boundless ocean. We had not seen a ship, and we never did see one, because we were off the routes of all ordinary shipping traffic in the Pacific.

But we did not really feel these enormous distances, for the horizon glided along with us unnoticed as we moved and our own floating world remained always the same—a circle flung up to the vault of the sky with the raft itself as center, while the same stars rolled on over us night after night.

6.

Across
The Pacific

WHEN THE SEA WAS NOT TOO ROUGH, WE WERE OFTEN out in the little rubber dinghy taking photographs. I shall not forget the first time the sea was so calm that two men felt like putting the balloon-like little thing into the water and going for a row. They had hardly got clear of the raft when they dropped the little oars and sat roaring with laughter. And, as the swell lifted them away and they disappeared and reappeared among the seas, they laughed so loud every time they caught a glimpse of us that their voices rang out over the desolate Pacific. We looked around us with mixed feelings and saw nothing comic but our own hirsute faces; but as the two in the dinghy should be accustomed to those by now, we began to have a lurking suspicion that they had suddenly gone mad. Sunstroke, perhaps. The two fellows could hardly scramble back on board the *Kon-Tiki* for sheer laughter and, gasping, with tears in their eyes they begged us just to go and see for ourselves.

Two of us jumped down into the dancing rubber dinghy and were caught by a sea which lifted us clear. Immediately we sat down with a bump and roared with laughter. We had to scramble back on the raft as quickly as possible and calm the last two who had not been out yet, for they thought we had all gone stark staring mad.

It was ourselves and our proud vessel which made such a completely hopeless, lunatic impression on us the first time we saw the whole thing at a distance. We had never before had an outside view of ourselves in the open sea. The logs of timber disappeared behind the smallest waves, and, when we saw anything at all, it was the low cabin with the wide doorway and the bristly roof of leaves that bobbed up from among the seas. The raft looked exactly like an old

Norwegian hayloft lying helpless, drifting about in the open sea—a warped hayloft full of sunburned bearded ruffians. If anyone had come paddling after us at sea in a bathtub, we should have felt the same spontaneous urge to laughter. Even an ordinary swell rolled halfway up the cabin wall and looked as if it would pour in unhindered through the wide open door in which the bearded fellows lay gaping. But then the crazy craft came up to the surface again, and the vagabonds lay there as dry, shaggy, and intact as before. If a higher sea came racing by, cabin and sail and the whole mast might disappear behind the mountain of water, but just as certainly the cabin with its vagabonds would be there again next moment. The situation looked bad, and we could not realize that things had gone so well on board the zany craft.

Next time we rowed out to have a good laugh at ourselves we nearly had a disaster. The wind and sea were higher than we supposed, and the Kon-Tiki was cleaving a path for herself over the swell much more quickly than we realized. We in the dinghy had to row for our lives out in the open sea in an attempt to regain the unmanageable raft, which could not stop and wait and could not possibly turn around and come back. Even when the boys on board the Kon-Tiki got the sail down, the wind got such a grip on the bamboo cabin that the raft drifted away to westward as fast as we could splash after her in the dancing rubber dinghy with its tiny toy oars. There was only one thought in the head of every man—we must not be separated. Those were horrible minutes we spent out on the sea before we got hold of the runaway raft and crawled on board to the others, home again.

From that day it was strictly forbidden to go out in the rubber dinghy without having a long line made fast to the bow, so that those who remained on board could haul the dinghy in if necessary. We never went far away from the raft, thereafter, except when the wind was light and the Pacific curving itself in a gentle swell. But we had these conditions when the raft was halfway to Polynesia and the ocean, all dominating, arched itself round the globe toward every point of the compass. Then we could safely leave the Kon-Tiki and row away into the blue space between sky and sea.

When we saw the silhouette of our craft grow smaller and smaller in the distance, and the big sail at last shrunken to a vague black square on the horizon, a sensation of loneliness sometimes crept over us. The sea curved away under us as blue upon blue as the sky above, and where they met all the blue flowed together and became one. It almost seemed as if we were suspended in space. All our world was empty and blue; there was no fixed point in it but the tropical sun, golden and warm, which burned our necks. Then the distant sail of the lonely raft drew us to it like a magnetic point on the horizon. We rowed back and crept on board with a feeling that we had come home again to our own world—on board and yet on firm, safe ground. And inside the bamboo cabin we found shade and the scent of bamboos and withered palm leaves. The sunny blue purity outside was now served to us in a suitably large dose through the open cabin wall. So we were accustomed to it and so it was good for a time, till the great clear blue tempted us out again.

It was most remarkable what a psychological effect the shaky bamboo cabin had on our minds. It measured eight by fourteen feet, and to diminish the pressure of wind and sea it was built low so that we could not stand upright under the ridge of the roof. Walls and roof were made of strong bamboo canes, lashed together and guyed, and covered with a tough wickerwork of split bamboos. The green and yellow bars, with fringes of foliage hanging down from the roof, were restful to the eye as a white cabin wall never could have been, and, despite the fact that the bamboo wall on the starboard side was open for one third of its length and roof and walls let in sun and moon, this primitive lair gave us a greater feeling of security than white-painted bulkheads and closed portholes would have given in the same circumstances.

We tried to find an explanation for this curious fact and came to the following conclusion. Our consciousness was totally unaccustomed to associating a palm-covered bamboo dwelling with sea travel. There was no natural harmony between the great rolling ocean and the drafty palm hut which was floating about among the seas. Therefore, either the hut would seem entirely out of place in among the waves, or the waves would seem entirely out of place round the hut wall. So long as we kept on board, the bamboo hut and its jungle scent were plain reality, and the tossing seas seemed rather visionary. But from the rubber boat, waves and hut exchanged roles.

The fact that the balsa logs always rode the seas like a gull, and let the water right through aft if a wave broke on board, gave us an unshakable confidence in the dry part in the middle of the raft where the cabin was. The longer the voyage lasted, the safer we felt in our cozy lair, and we looked at the whitecrested waves that danced past outside our doorway as if they were an impressive movie, conveying no menace to us at all. Even though the gaping wall was only five feet from the unprotected edge of the raft and only a foot and a half above the water line, yet we felt as if we had traveled many miles away from the sea and occupied a jungle dwelling remote from the sea's perils once we had crawled inside the door. There we could lie on our backs and look up at the curious roof which twisted about like boughs in the wind, enjoying the jungle smell of raw wood, bamboos, and withered palm leaves.

Sometimes, too, we went out in the rubber boat to look at ourselves by night. Coal-black seas towered up on all sides, and a glittering myriad of tropical stars drew a faint reflection from plankton in the water. The world was simple—stars in the darkness. Whether it was 1947 B.C. or A.D. suddenly became of no significance. We lived, and that we felt with alert intensity. We realized that life had been full for men before the technical age also—in fact, fuller and richer in many ways than the life of modern man. Time and evolution somehow ceased to exist; all that was real and that mattered were the same today as they had always been and would always be. We were swallowed up in the absolute common measure of history—endless unbroken darkness under a swarm of stars.

Before us in the night the *Kon-Tiki* rose out of the seas to sink down again behind black masses of water that towered between her and us. In the moonlight there was a fantastic atmosphere about the raft. Stout, shining wooden logs fringed with seaweed, the square pitch-black outline of a Viking sail, a bristly bamboo hut with the yellow light of a paraffin lamp aft—the whole suggested a picture from a fairytale rather than an actual reality. Now and then the raft disappeared completely behind the black seas; then she rose again and stood out sharp in silhouette against the stars, while glittering water poured from the logs.

When we saw the atmosphere about the solitary raft, we could well see in our mind's eye the whole flotilla of such vessels, spread in fan formation beyond the horizon to increase the chances of finding land, when the first men made their way across this sea. The Inca Tupak Yupanqui, who had brought under his rule both Peru and Ecuador, sailed across the sea with an armada of many thousand men on balsa rafts, just before the Spaniards came, to search for islands which rumor had told of out in the Pacific. He found two islands, which some think were the Galapagos, and after eight months' absence he and his numerous paddlers succeeded in toiling their way back to Ecuador. Kon-Tiki and his followers had certainly sailed in a similar formation several hundred years before but, having discovered the Polynesian islands, they had no reason for trying to struggle back.

When we jumped on board the raft again, we often sat down in a circle round the paraffin lamp on the bamboo deck and talked of the seafarers from Peru who had had all these same experiences fifteen hundred years before us. The lamp flung huge shadows of bearded men on the sail, and we thought of the white men with the beards from Peru whom we could follow in mythology and architecture all the way from Mexico to Central America and into the northwestern area of South America as far as Peru. Here this mysterious civilization disappeared, as by the stroke of a magic wand, before the coming of the Incas and reappeared just as suddenly out on the solitary islands in the west which we were now approaching. Were the wandering teachers men of an early civilized race from across the Atlantic, who in times long past, in the same simple manner, had come over with the westerly ocean current and the trade wind from the area of the Canary Islands to the Gulf of Mexico? That was indeed a far shorter distance than the one we were covering, and we no longer believed in the sea as a completely isolating factor.

Many observers have maintained, for weighty reasons, that the great Indian civilizations, from the Aztecs in Mexico to the Incas in Peru, were inspired by sporadic intruders from over the seas in the east, while all the American Indians in general are Asiatic hunting and fishing peoples who in the course of twenty thousand years or more trickled into America from Siberia. It is certainly striking that there is not a trace of gradual development in the high civilizations which once stretched from Mexico to Peru. The deeper the archaeologists dig, the higher the culture, until a definite point is reached at which the old civilizations have clearly arisen without any foundation in the midst of primitive cultures.

And the civilizations have arisen where the current comes in from the Atlantic, in the midst of the desert and jungle regions of Central and South America, instead of in the more temperate regions where civilizations, in both old and modern times, have had easier conditions for their development.

The same cultural distribution is seen in the South Sea islands. It is the island nearest to Peru, Easter Island, which bears the deepest traces of civilization, although the insignificant little island is dry and barren and is the farthest from Asia of all the islands in the Pacific.

When we had completed half our voyage, we had sailed just the distance from Peru to Easter Island and had the legendary island due south of us. We had left land at a chance point in the middle of the coast of Peru to imitate an average raft putting to sea. If we had left the land farther south, nearer Kon Tiki's ruined city Tiahuanaco, we should have got the same wind but a weaker current, both of which would have carried us in the direction of Easter Island.

When we passed 110° west, we were within the Polynesian ocean area, inasmuch as the Polynesian Easter Island was now nearer Peru than we were. We were on a line with the first outpost of the South Sea islands, the center of the oldest island civilization. And when at night our glowing road guide, the sun, climbed down from the sky and disappeared beyond the sea in the west with his whole spectrum of colors, the gentle trade wind blew life into the stories of the strange mystery of Easter Island. While the night sky smothered all concept of time, we sat and talked and bearded giants' heads were again thrown upon the sail.

But far down south, on Easter Island, stood yet larger giants' heads cut in stone, with bearded chins and white men's features, brooding over the secret of centuries.

Thus they stood when the first Europeans discovered the island in 1722, and thus they had stood twenty-two Polynesian generations earlier, when, according to native tradition, the present inhabitants landed in great canoes and exterminated all men among an earlier population found on the island. The primitive newcomers had arrived from the islands farther west, but the Easter Island traditions claim that the earliest inhabitants, and the true discoverers of the island, had come from a distand land *toward the rising sun*. There is no land in this direction but South America. With the early extermination of the unknown local architects the giant stone heads on Easter Island have become one of the foremost symbols of the insoluble mysteries of antiquity. Here and there on the slopes of the treeless island their huge figures have risen to the sky, stone colossi splendidly carved in the shape of men and set up as a single block as high as a normal building of three or four floors. How had the men of old been able to shape, transport, and erect such gigantic stone colossi? As if the problem was not big enough, they had further succeeded in balancing an extra giant block of red stone like a colossal wig on the top of several of the heads, thirty-six feet above the ground. What did it all mean, and what kind of mechanical knowledge had the vanished architects who had mastered problems great enough for the foremost engineers of today?

If we put all the pieces together, the mystery of Easter Island is perhaps not insoluble after all, seen against a background of raftsmen from Peru. The old civilization has left on this island traces which the tooth of time has not been able to destroy.

Easter Island is the top of an ancient extinct volcano. Paved roads laid down by the old civilized inhabitants lead to well preserved landing places on the coast and show that the water level round the island was exactly the same then as it is today. This is no remains of a sunken continent but a tiny desolate island, which was as small and solitary when it was a vivid cultural center as it is today.

In the eastern corner of this wedge-shaped island lies one of the extinct craters of the Easter Island volcano, and down in the crater lies the sculptors' amazing quarry and workshop. It lies there exactly as the old artists and architects left it hundreds of years ago, when they fled in haste to the eastern extremity of the island where, according to tradition, there was a furious battle which made the present Polynesians victors and rulers of the island, whereas all grown men among the aboriginals were slain and burned in a ditch. The sudden interruption of the artists' work gives a clear cross section of an ordinary working day in the Easter Island crater. The sculptors' stone axes, hard as flint, lie strewn about their working places and show that this advanced people was as ignorant of iron as Kon-Tiki's sculptors were when they were driven in flight from Peru, leaving behind them similar gigantic stone statues on the Andes plateau. In both places the quarry can be found where the legendary white people with beards hewed blocks of stone thirty feet long or more right out of the mountainside with the help of axes of still harder stone. And in both places the gigantic blocks, weighing many tons, were transported for many miles over rough ground before being set up on end as enormous human figures, or raised on top of one another to form mysterious terraces and walls.

Many huge unfinished figures still lie where they were begun, in their niches in the crater wall on Easter Island, and show how the work was carried on in different stages. The largest human figure, which was almost completed when the builders had to flee, was sixty-six feet long; if it had been finished and set up, the head of this stone colossus would have been level with the top of an eight-floor building. Every separate figure was hewn out of a single connected block of stone, and the working niches for sculptors round the lying stone figures show that not many men were at work at the same time on each figure. Lying on their backs with their arms bent and their hands placed on their stomachs, exactly like the stone colossi in South America, the Easter Island figures were completed in every minute detail before they were removed from the workshop and transported to their destinations round about on the island. In the last stage inside the quarry the giant was attached to the cliff side by only a narrow ridge under his back; then this too was hewn away, the giant meanwhile being supported by boulders.

Large quantities of these figures were just dragged down to the bottom of the crater and set up on the slope there. But a number of the largest colossi were transported up and over the wall of the crater, and for many miles round over difficult country, before being set up on a stone platform and having an extra stone colossus of red tuff placed on their heads. This transport in itself may appear to be a complete mystery, but we cannot deny that it took place or that the architects who disappeared from Peru left in the Andes Mountains stone colossi of equal size, which show that they were absolute experts in this line. Even if the monoliths are largest and most numerous on Easter Island, and the sculptors there had acquired an individual style, the same vanished civilization erected similar giant statues in human shape on many of the other Pacific islands, but only on those nearest to America, and everywhere the monoliths were brought to their final site from out-of-the-way quarries. In the Marquesas, I heard legends of how the gigantic stones were maneuvered, and, as these corresponded exactly to the natives' stories of the transport of the stone pillars to the huge portal on Tongatabu, it can be assumed that the same people employed the same method with the columns on Easter Island.

The sculptors' work in the pit took a long time but required only a few experts. The work of transport each time a statue was completed was more quickly done but, on the other hand, required large numbers of men. Little Easter Island was then both rich in fish and thoroughly cultivated, with large plantations of Peruvian sweet potatoes, and experts believe that the island in its great days could have supported a population of seven or eight thousand. About a thousand men were quite enough to haul the huge statues up and over the steep crater wall, while five hundred were sufficient to drag them on further across the island.

Wearproof cables were plaited from bast and vegetable fibers, and, using wooden frames, the multitude dragged the stone colossus over logs and small boulders made slippery with taro roots. That old civilized peoples were masters in making ropes and cables is well known from the South Sea islands and still more from Peru, where the first Europeans found suspension bridges a hundred yards long laid across torrents and gorges by means of plaited cables as thick as a man's waist.

When the stone colossus had arrived at its chosen site and was to be set up on end, the next problem arose. The crowd built a temporary inclined plane of stone and sand and pulled the giant up the less steep side, legs first. When the statue reached the top, it shot over a sharp edge and slid straight down so that the footpiece landed in a ready-dug hole. As the complete inclined plane still stood there, rubbing against the back of the giant's head, they rolled up an extra cylinder of stone and placed it on the top of his head; then the whole temporary plane was removed. Ready-built inclined planes like this stand in several places on Easter Island, waiting for huge figures which have never come. The technique was admirable but in no way mysterious if we cease to underestimate the intelligence of men in ancient times and the amount of time and manpower which they had at their command.

But why did they make these statues? And why was it necessary to go off to another quarry four miles away from the crater workshop to find a special kind of red stone to place on the figure's head? Both in South America and in the Marquesas Islands the whole statue was often of this red stone, and the natives went great distances to get it. Red headdresses for persons of high rank were an important feature both in Polynesia and in Peru.

Let us see first whom the statues represented. When the first Europeans visited the island, they saw mysterious "white men" on shore and, in contrast to what is usual among peoples of this kind, they found men with long flowing beards, the descendants of women and children belonging to the first race on the island, who had been spared by the invaders. The natives themselves declared that some of their ancestors had been white, while others had been brown.

They calculated precisely that the last-named had immigrated from elsewhere in Polynesia twenty-two generations before, while the first had come from eastward in large vessels as much as fifty-seven generations back (*i.e., ca.* 400–500 A.D.). The race which came from the east were given the name "long-ears," because they lengthened their ears artificially by hanging weights on the lobes so that they hung down to their shoulders. These were the mysterious "long-ears" who were killed when the "short-ears" came to the island, and all the stone figures on Easter Island had large ears hanging down to their shoulders, as the sculptors themselves had had.

Now the Inca legends in Peru say that the sun-king Kon-Tiki ruled over a white people with beards who were called by the Incas "big-ears," because they had their ears artificially lengthened so that they reached down to their shoulders. The Incas emphasized that it was Kon-Tiki's "big-ears" who had erected the abandoned giant statues in the Andes Mountains before they were exterminated or driven out by the Incas themselves in the battle on an island in Lake Titicaca.

To sum up: Kon-Tiki's white "big-ears" disappeared from Peru westward with ample experience of working on colossal stone statues, and Tiki's white "long-ears" came to Easter Island from eastward skilled in exactly the same art, which they at once took up in full perfection so that not the smallest trace can be found on Easter Island of any development leading up to the masterpieces on the island.

There is often a greater resemblance between the great stone statues in South America and those on certain South Sea islands than there is between the monoliths on the different South Sea islands compared with one another. In the Marquesas Islands and Tahiti such statues were known under the generic name *Tiki*, and they represented ancestors honored in the islands' history who, after their death, had been ranked as gods. And therein undoubtedly may be found the explanation of the curious red stone caps on the Easter Island figures. At the time of the European explorations there existed on all the islands in Polynesia scattered individuals and whole families with reddish hair and fair skins, and the islanders themselves declared that it was these who were descended from the first white people on the islands. On certain islands religious festivals were held, the participators in which colored their skins white and their hair red to resemble their earliest ancestors. At annual ceremonies on Easter

Island the chief person of the festival had all his hair cut off so that his head might be painted red. And the colossal red-stone caps on the giant statues on Easter Island were carved in the shape which was typical of the local hair style; they had a round knot on the top, just as the men had their hair tied in a little traditional topknot in the middle of the head.

The statues on Easter Island had long ears because the sculptors themselves had lengthened ears. They had specially chosen red stones as wigs because the sculptors themselves had reddish hair. They had their chins carved pointed and projecting, because the sculptors themselves grew beards. They had the typical physiognomy of the white race with a straight and narrow nose and thin sharp lips, because the sculptors themselves did not belong to the Indonesian race. And when the statues had huge heads and tiny legs, with their hands laid in position of their stomachs, it was because it was just in this way the people were accustomed to make giant statues in South America. The sole decoration of the Easter Island figures is a belt which was always carved round the figure's stomach. The same symbolic belt is found on every single statue in Kon-Tiki's ancient ruins by Lake Titicaca. It is the legendary emblem of the sun-god, the rainbow belt. There was a myth on the island of Mangareva according to which the sun-god had taken off the rainbow which was his magic belt and climbed down it from the sky on to Mangareva to people the island with his white-skinned children. The sun was once regarded as the oldest original ancestor in all these islands, as well as in Peru.

We used to sit on deck under the starry sky and retell Easter Island's strange history, even though our own raft was carrying us straight into the heart of Polynesia so that we should see nothing of that remote island but its name on the map. But so full is Easter Island of traces from the east that even its name can serve as a pointer.

"Easter Island" appears on the map because some chance Dutchman "discovered" the island one Easter Sunday. And we have forgotten that the natives themselves, who already lived there, have more instructive and significant names for their home. This island has no less than three names in Polynesian.

One name is *Te-Pito-te-Henua*, which means "navel of the islands." This poetical name clearly places Easter Island in a special position in regard to the other islands farther westward and is the oldest designation for Easter Island according to the Polynesians themselves. On the eastern side of the island, near the traditional landing place of the first "long-ears," is a carefully tooled sphere of stone which is called the "golden navel" and is in turn regarded as the navel of Easter Island itself. When the poetical Polynesian ancestors carved the island navel on the east coast and selected the island nearest Peru as the navel of their myriad islands further west, it had a symbolic meaning. And when we know that Polynesian tradition refers to the discovery of their islands as the "birth" of their islands, then it is more than suggested that Easter Island of all places was considered the "navel," symbolic of the islands' birthmark and as the connecting link with their original motherland.

Easter Island's second name is Rapa Nui which means "Great Rapa," while Rapa Iti or "Little Rapa" is another island of the same size which lies a very long way west of Easter Island. Now it is the natural practice of all peoples to call their first home "Great——" while the next is called "New——" or "Little——" even if the places are of the same size. And on Little Rapa the natives have quite correctly maintained traditions that the first inhabitants of the island came from Great Rapa, Easter Island, to the eastward, nearest to America. This points directly to an original immigration from the east.

The third and last name of this key island is *Mata-Kite-Rani*, which means "the eye (which) looks (toward) heaven." At first glance this is puzzling, for the relatively low Easter Island does not look toward heaven any more than the other loftier islands—for example, Tahiti, the Marquesas, or Hawaii. But *Rani*, heaven, had a double meaning to the Polynesians. It was also their ancestors' original homeland, the holy land of the sun-god, Tiki's forsaken mountain kingdom. And it is very significant that they should have called just their easternmost island, of all the thousands of islands in the ocean, "the eye which looks toward heaven." It is all the more striking seeing that the kindred name *Mata-Rani*, which means in Polynesian "the eye of heaven," is an old Peruvian place name, that of a spot on the Pacific coast of Peru opposite Easter Island and right at the foot of Kon-Tiki's old ruined city in the Andes.

The fascination of Easter Island provided us with plenty of subjects of conversation as we sat on deck under the starry sky, feeling ourselves to be participators in the whole prehistoric adventure. We almost felt as if we had done nothing else since Tiki's days but sail about the seas under sun and stars searching for land.

We no longer had the same respect for waves and sea. We knew them and their relationship to us on the raft. Even the shark had become a part of the everyday picture; we knew it and its usual reactions. We no longer thought of the hand harpoon, and we did not even move away from the side of the raft, if a shark came up alongside. On the contrary, we were more likely to try and grasp its back fin as it glided unperturbed along the logs. This finally developed into a quite new form of sport—tug of war with shark without a line.

We began quite modestly. We caught all too easily more dolphins than we could eat. To keep a popular form of amusement going without wasting food, we hit on comic fishing without a hook for the mutual entertainment of the dolphins and ourselves. We fastened unused flying fish to a string and drew them over the surface of the water. The dolphins shot up to the surface and seized the fish, and then we tugged, each in our own direction, and had a fine circus performance, for if one dolphin let go another came in its place. We had fun, and the dolphins got the fish in the end.

Then we started the same game with the sharks. We had either a bit of fish on the end of a rope or often a bag with scraps from dinner, which we let out on a line. Instead of turning on its back, the shark pushed its snout above the water and swam forward with jaws wide to swallow the morsel. We could not help pulling on the rope just as the shark was going to close its jaws again, and the cheated animal swam on with an unspeakably foolish, patient expression and opened its jaws again for the offal, which jumped out of its mouth every time it tried to swallow it. It ended by the shark's coming right up to the logs and jumping up like a begging dog for the food which hung dangling in a bag above its nose. It was just like feeding a gaping hippopotamus in a zoological garden, and one day at the end of July, after three months on board the raft, the following entry was made in the diary:

—*We made friends with the shark which followed us today. At dinner we fed it with scraps which we poured right down into its open jaws. It has the effect of a half fierce, half good-natured and friendly dog when it swims alongside us. It cannot be denied that sharks can seem quite pleasant so long as we do not get into their jaws ourselves. At least we find it amusing to have them about us, except when we are bathing.*

One day a bamboo stick, with a bag of sharks' food tied to a string, was lying ready for use on the edge of the raft when a sea came and washed it overboard. The bamboo stick was already lying afloat a couple of hundred yards astern of the raft, when it suddenly rose upright in the water and came rushing after the raft by itself, as if it intended to put itself nicely back in its place again. When the fishing rod came swaying nearer us, we saw a ten-foot shark swimming right under it, while the bamboo stick stuck up out of the waves like a periscope. The shark had swallowed the food bag without biting off the line. The fishing rod soon overtook us, passed us quite quietly, and vanished ahead.

But, even if we gradually came to look upon the shark with quite other eyes, our respect for the five or six rows of razor-sharp teeth which lay in ambush in the huge jaws never disappeared.

One day Knut had an involuntary swim in company with a shark. No one was ever allowed to swim away from the raft, both on account of the raft's drift and because of sharks. But one day it was extra quiet and we had just pulled on board such sharks as had been following us, so permission was given for a quick dip in the sea. Knut plunged in and had gone quite a long way before he came up to the surface to crawl back. At that moment we saw from the mast a shadow bigger than himself coming up behind him, deeper down. We shouted warnings as quietly as we could so as not to create a panic, and Knut heaved himself toward the side of the raft. But the shadow below belonged to a still better swimmer, which shot up from the depths and gained on Knut. They reached the raft at the same time. While Knut was clambering on board, a six-foot shark glided past right under his stomach and stopped beside the raft. We gave it a dainty dolphin's head to thank it for not having snapped.

Generally it is smell more than sight which excites the sharks' voracity. We have sat with our legs in the water to test them, and they have swum toward us till they were two or three feet away, only quietly to turn their tails toward us again. But, if the water was in the least bloodstained, as it was when we had been cleaning fish, the sharks' fins came to life and they would suddenly collect like bluebottles from a long way off. If we flung out shark's guts, they simply went mad and dashed about in a blind frenzy. They savagely devoured the liver of their own kind and then, if we put a foot into the sea, they came for it like rockets and even dug their teeth into the logs where the foot had been. The mood of a shark may vary immensely, the animal being completely at the mercy of its own emotions.

The last stage in our encounter with sharks was that we began to pull their tails. Pulling animals' tails is held to be an inferior form of sport, but that may be because no one has tried it on a shark. For it was, in truth, a lively form of sport.

To get hold of a shark by the tail we first had to give it a real tidbit. It was ready to stick its head high out of the water to get it. Usually it had its food served dangling in a bag. For, if one has fed a shark directly by hand once, it is no longer amusing. If one feeds dogs or tame bears by hand, they set their teeth into the meat and tear and worry it till they get a bit off or until they get the whole piece for themselves. But, if one holds out a large dolphin at a safe distance from the shark's head, the shark comes up and smacks his jaws together, and, without one's having felt the slightest tug, half the dolphin is suddenly gone and one is left sitting with a tail in one's hand. We had found it a hard job to cut the dolphin in two with knives, but in a fraction of a second the shark, moving its triangular saw teeth quickly sideways, had chopped off the backbone and everything else like a sausage machine.

When the shark turned quietly to go under again, its tail flickered up above the surface and was easy to grasp. The shark's skin was just like sandpaper to hold on to, and inside the upper point of its tail there was an indentation which might have been made solely to allow of a good grip. If we once got a firm grasp there, there was no chance of our grip's not holding. Then we had to give a jerk, before the shark could collect itself, and get as much as possible of the tail pulled in tight over the logs. For a second or two the shark realized nothing, but then it began to wriggle and struggle in a spiritless manner with the fore part of its body, for without the help of its tail a shark cannot get up any speed. The other fins are only apparatus for balancing and steering. After a few desperate jerks, during which we had to keep a tight hold of the tail, the surprised shark became quite crestfallen and apathetic, and, as the loose stomach began to sink down toward the head, the shark at last became completely paralyzed.

When the shark had become quiet and, as it were, hung stiff awaiting developments, it was time for us to haul in with all our might. We seldom got more than half the heavy fish up out of the water; then the shark too woke up and did the rest itself. With violent jerks it swung its head round and up on to the logs, and then we had to tug with all our might and jump well out of the way, and that pretty quickly, if we wanted to save our legs. For now the shark was in no kindly mood. Jerking itself round in great leaps, it thrashed at the bamboo wall, using its tail as a sledge hammer. Now it no longer spared its iron muscles. The huge jaws were opened wide, and the rows of teeth bit and snapped in the air for anything they could reach. It might happen that the war dance ended in the shark's more or less involuntarily tumbling overboard and disappearing for good after its shameful humiliation, but most often the shark flung itself about at random on the logs aft, till we got a running noose round the root of its tail or till it had ceased to gnash its devilish teeth forever.

The parrot was quite thrilled when we had a shark on deck. It came scurrying out of the bamboo cabin and climbed up the wall at frantic speed till it found itself a good, safe lookout post on the palm-leaf roof, and there it sat shaking its head or fluttered to and fro along the ridge, shrieking with excitement. It had at an early date become an excellent sailor and was always bubbling over with humor and laughter. We reckoned ourselves as seven on board—six of us and the green parrot. The crab Johannes had, after all, to reconcile itself to being regarded as a cold-blooded appendage. At night the parrot crept into its cage under the roof of the bamboo cabin, but in the daytime it strutted about the deck or hung on to guy ropes and stays and did the most fascinating acrobatic exercises.

At the start of the voyage we had turnbuckles on the stays of the mast but they wore the ropes, so we replaced them by ordinary running knots. When the stays stretched and grew slack from sun and wind, all hands had to turn to and brace up the mast, so that its mangrove wood, as heavy as iron, should not bump against and cut into the ropes till they fell down. While we were hauling and pulling, at the most critical moment the parrot began to call out with its cracked voice: "Haul! Haul! Ho, ho, ho, ho, ha ha ha!" And if it made us laugh, it laughed till it shook at its own cleverness and swung round and round on the stays.

At first the parrot was the bane of our radio operators. They might be sitting happily absorbed in the radio corner with their magic earphones on and perhaps in contact with a radio "ham" in Oklahoma. Then their earphones would suddenly go dead, and they could not get a sound however much they coaxed the wires and turned the knobs. The parrot had been busy and bitten off the wire of the aerial. This was specially tempting in the early days, when the wire was sent up with a little balloon. But one day the parrot became seriously ill. It sat in its cage and moped and touched no food for two days, while its droppings glittered with golden scraps of aerial. Then the radio operators repented of their angry words and the parrot of its misdeeds, and from that day Torstein and Knut were its chosen friends and the parrot would never sleep anywhere but in the radio corner. The parrot's mother tongue was Spanish when it first came on board; Bengt declared it took to talking Spanish with a Norwegian accent long before it began to imitate Torstein's favorite ejaculations in full-blooded Norwegian.

We enjoyed the parrot's humor and brilliant colors for two months, till a big sea came on board from astern while it was on its way down the stay from the masthead. When we discovered that the parrot had gone overboard, it was too late. We did not see it. And the *Kon-Tiki* could not be turned or stopped; if anything went overboard from the raft, we had no chance of turning back for it—numerous experiences had shown that.

The loss of the parrot had a depressing effect on our spirits the first evening; we knew that exactly the same thing would happen to ourselves if we fell overboard on a solitary night watch. We tightened up on all the safety regulations, brought into use new life lines for the night watch, and frightened one another out of believing that we were safe because things had gone well in the first two months. One careless step, one thoughtless movement, could send us where the green parrot had gone, even in broad daylight.

We had several times observed the large white shells of cuttlefish eggs, lying floating like ostrich eggs or white skulls on the blue swell. On one solitary occasion we saw a squid lying wriggling underneath. We observed the snow-white balls floating on a level with ourselves and thought at first that it would be an easy matter to row out in the dinghy and get them. We thought the same that time when the rope of the plankton net broke so that the cloth net was left behind alone, floating in our wake. Each time we launched the dinghy, with a rope attached, to row back and pick up the floating object. But we saw to our surprise that the wind and sea held the dinghy off and that the line from the *Kon-Tiki* had so violent a braking effect in the water that we could never row right back to a point we had already left. We might get within a few yards of what we wanted to pick up, but then the whole line was out and the *Kon-Tiki* was pulling us away westward. "Once overboard always overboard" was a lesson that was gradually branded into our consciousness on board. If we wanted to go with the rest, we must hang on till the *Kon-Tiki* ran her bow against land on the other side.

The parrot left a blank in the radio corner, but, when the tropical sun shone out over the Pacific next day, we soon became reconciled to his loss. We hauled in many sharks the next few days, and we constantly found black curved parrots' beaks, or so we thought, among tunnies' heads and other curiosities in the shark's belly. But on closer examination the black beaks always proved to belong to assimilated cuttlefish.

The two radio operators had had a tough job in their corner since the first day they came on board. The very first day, in the Humboldt Current, sea water trickled even from the battery cases so that they had to cover the sensitive radio corner with canvas to save what could be saved in the high seas. And then they had the problem of fitting a long enough aerial on the little raft. They tried to send the aerial up with a kite, but in a gust of wind the kite simply plunged down into a wave crest and disappeared. Then they tried to send it up with a balloon, but the tropical sun burned holes in the balloon so that it collapsed and sank into the sea. And then they had the trouble with the parrot. In addition to all this, we were a fortnight in the Humboldt Current before we came out of a dead zone of the Andes in which the short wave was as dumb and lifeless as the air in an empty soapbox.

But then one night the short wave suddenly broke through, and Torstein's call signal was heard by a chance radio amateur in Los Angeles who was sitting fiddling with his transmitter to establish contact with another amateur in Sweden. The man asked what kind of set we had and, when he got a satisfactory answer to his question, he asked Torstein who he was and where he lived. When he heard that Torstein's abode was a bamboo cabin on a raft in the Pacific, there were several peculiar clickings until Torstein supplied more details. When the man on the air had pulled himself together, he told us that his name was Hal and his wife's name Anna and that she was Swedish by birth and would let our families know we were alive and well.

It was a strange thought for us that evening that a total stranger called Hal, a chance moving-picture operator far away among the swarming population of Los Angeles, was the only person in the world but ourselves who knew where we were and that we were well. From that night onward Hal, alias Harold Kempel, and his friend Frank Cuevas took it in turns to sit up every night and listen for signals from the raft, and Herman received grateful telegrams from the head of the U.S. Weather Bureau for his two daily code reports from an area for which there were extremely few reports and no statistics. Later Knut and Torstein established contact with other radio amateurs almost every night, and these passed on greetings to Norway through a radio "ham" named Egil Berg at Notodden.

When we were just a few days out in mid-ocean, there was too much salt water for the radio corner, and the station stopped working altogether. The operators stood on their heads day and night with screws and soldering irons, and all our distant radio fans thought the raft's days were ended. But then one night the signals LI 2 B burst out into the ether, and in a moment the radio corner was buzzing like a wasp's nest as several hundred American operators seized their keys simultaneously and replied to the call.

Indeed one always felt as if one were sitting down on a wasp's nest if one strayed into the radio operators' domain. It was damp with sea water, which forced its way up along the woodwork everywhere, and, even if there was a piece of raw rubber on the balsa log where the operator sat, one got electric shocks both in the hinder parts and in the finger tips if one touched the Morse key. And, if one of us outsiders tried to steal a pencil from the well-equipped corner, either his hair stood straight up on his head or he drew long sparks from the stump of the pencil. Only Torstein and Knut and the parrot could wriggle their way about in that corner unscathed, and we put up a sheet of cardboard to mark the danger zone for the rest of us.

Late one night Knut was sitting tinkering by lamplight in the radio corner when he suddenly shook me by the leg and said he had been talking to a fellow who lived just outside Oslo and was called Christian Amundsen. This was a bit of an amateur record, for the little short-wave transmitter on board the raft with its 13,990 kilocycles per second did not send out more than 6 watts, about the same strength as a small electric torch. This was August 2, and we had sailed more than sixty degrees round the earth, so that Oslo was at the opposite end of the globe. King Haakon was seventy-five years old the day after, and we sent him a message of congratulations direct from the raft; the day after that Christian was again audible and sent us a reply from the King, wishing us continued good luck and success on our voyage.

Another episode we remember as an unusual contrast to the rest of the life on the raft. We had two cameras on board, and Erik had with him a parcel of materials for developing photographs on the voyage, so that we could take duplicate snapshots of things that had not come out well. After the whale shark's visit he could contain himself no longer, and one evening he mixed the chemicals and water carefully in exact accordance with the instructions and developed two films. The negatives looked like long-distance photographs—nothing but obscure spots and wrinkles. The film was ruined. We telegraphed to our contacts for advice, but our message was picked up by a radio amateur near Hollywood. He telephoned a laboratory and soon afterward he broke in and told us that our developer was too warm; we must not use water above 60° or the negative would be wrinkled.

We thanked him for his advice and ascertained that the very lowest temperature in our surroundings was that of the ocean current itself, which was nearly 80°. Now Herman was a refrigerating engineer, and I told him by way of a joke to get the temperature of the water down to 60°. He asked to have the use of the little bottle of carbonic acid belonging to the already inflated rubber dinghy, and after some hocus-pocus in a kettle covered with a sleeping bag and a woolen vest suddenly there was snow on Herman's stubbly beard, and he came in with a big lump of white ice in the kettle.

Erik developed afresh with splendid results.

Even though the ghost words carried through the air by short wave were an unknown luxury in Kon-Tiki's early days, the long ocean waves beneath us were the same as of old and they carried the balsa raft steadily westward as they did then, fifteen hundred years ago.

The weather became a little more unsettled, with scattered rain squalls, after we had entered the area nearer the South Sea islands and the trade wind had changed its direction. It had blown steadily and surely from the southeast until we were a good way over in the Equatorial Current; then it had veered round more and more toward due east. We reached our most northerly position on June 10 with latitude 6°19′ south. We were then so close up to the Equator that it looked as if we should sail above even the most northerly islands of the Marquesas group and disappear completely in the sea without finding land. But then the trade wind swung round farther, from east to northeast, and drove us in a curve down toward the latitude of the world of islands.

It often happened that wind and sea remained unchanged for days on end, and then we clean forgot whose steering watch it was except at night, when the watch was alone on deck. For, if sea and wind were steady, the steering oar was lashed fast and the Kon-Tiki sail remained filled without our attending to it. Then the night watch could sit quietly in the cabin door and look at the stars. If the constellations changed their position in the sky, it was time for him to go out and see whether it was the steering oar or the wind that had shifted.

It was incredible how easy it was to steer by the stars when we had seen them marching across the vault of the sky for weeks on end. Indeed, there was not much else to look at at night. We knew where we could expect to see the different constellations night after night, and, when we came up toward the Equator, the Great Bear rose so clear of the horizon in the north that we were anxious lest we should catch a glimpse of the Pole Star, which appears when one comes from southward and crosses the Equator. But as the northeasterly trade wind set in, the Great Bear sank again.

The old Polynesians were great navigators. They took bearings by the sun by day and the stars by night. Their knowledge of the heavenly bodies was astonishing. They knew that the earth was round, and they had names for such abstruse conceptions as the Equator and the northern and southern tropics. In Hawaii they cut charts of the ocean on the shells of round bottle gourds, and on certain other islands they made detailed maps of plaited boughs to which shells were attached to mark the islands, while the twigs marked particular currents. The Polynesians knew five planets, which they called wandering stars, and distinguished them from the fixed stars, for which they had nearly two hundred different names. A good navigator in old Polynesia knew well in what part of the sky the different stars would rise and where they would be at different times of the night and at different times of the year. They knew which stars culminated over the different islands, and there were cases in which an island was named after a star which culminated over it night after night and year after year.

Apart from the fact that the starry sky lay like a glittering giant compass revolving from east to west, they understood that the different stars right over their heads always showed them how far north or south they were. When the Polynesians had explored and brought under their sway their present domain, which is the whole of the sea nearest to America, they maintained traffic between some of the islands for many generations to come. Historical traditions relate that, when the chiefs from Tahiti visited Hawaii, which lay more than 2,000 sea miles farther north and several degrees farther west, the helmsman steered first due north by sun and stars, till the stars right above their heads told them that they were on the latitude of Hawaii. Then they turned at a right angle and steered due west till they came so near that birds and clouds told them where the group of islands lay.

Whence had the Polynesians obtained their vast astronomical knowledge and their calendar, which was calculated with astonishing thoroughness? Certainly not from Melanesian or Malayan peoples to the westward. But the same old vanished civilized race, the "white and bearded men," who had taught Aztecs, Mayas, and Incas their amazing culture in America, had evolved a curiously similar calendar and a similar astronomical knowledge which Europe in those times could not match. In Polynesia, as in Peru, the calendar year had been so arranged as to begin on the particular day of the year when the constellation of the Pleiades first appeared above the horizon, and in both areas this constellation was considered the patron of agriculture.

In Peru, where the continent slopes down toward the Pacific, there stand to this day in the desert sand the ruins of an astronomical observatory of great antiquity, a relic of the same mysterious civilized people which carved stone collossi, erected pyramids, cultivated sweet potatoes and bottle gourds, and began their year with the rising of the Pleiades. Kon-Tiki knew the movement of the stars when he set sail upon the Pacific Ocean.

On July 2 our night watch could no longer sit in peace studying the night sky. We had a strong wind and nasty sea after several days of light northeasterly breeze. Late in the night we had brilliant moonlight and a quite fresh sailing wind. We measured our speed by counting the seconds we took to pass a chip, flung out ahead on one side of us, and found that we were establishing a speed record. While our average speed was from twelve to eighteen "chips," in the jargon current on board, we were now for a time down to "six chips," and the phosphorescence swirled in a regular wake astern of the raft.

Four men lay snoring in the bamboo cabin while Torstein sat clicking with the Morse key and I was on steering watch. Just before midnight I caught sight of a quite unusual sea which came breaking astern of us right across the whole of my disturbed field of vision. Behind it I could see here and there the foaming crests of two more huge seas like the first, following hard on its heels. If we ourselves had not just passed the place, I should have been convinced that what I saw was high surf flung up over a dangerous shoal. I gave a warning shout, as the first sea came like a long wall sweeping after us in the moonlight, and wrenched the raft into position to take what was coming.

When the first sea reached us, the raft flung her stern up sideways and rose up over the wave back which had just broken, so that it hissed and boiled all along the crest. We rode through the welter of boiling foam which poured along both sides of the raft, while the heavy sea itself rolled by under us. The bow flung itself up last as the wave passed, and we slid, stern first, down into a broad trough of the waves. Immediately after the next wall of water came on and rose up, while we were again lifted hurriedly into the air and the clear water masses broke over us aft as we shot over the edge. As a result the raft was flung right broadside on to the seas, and it was impossible to wrench her round quickly enough.

The next sea came on and rose out of the stripes of foam like a glittering wall which began to fall along its upper edge just as it reached us. When it plunged down, I saw nothing else to do but hang on as tight as I could to a projecting bamboo pole of the cabin roof; there I held my breath while I felt that we were flung sky-high and everything round me carried away in roaring whirlpools of foam. In a second we and the *Kon-Tiki* were above water again and gliding quietly down a gentle wave back on the other side. Then the seas were normal again. The three great wave walls raced on before us, and astern in the moonlight a string of coconuts lay bobbing in the water.

The last wave had given the cabin a violent blow, so that Torstein was flung head over heels into the radio corner and the others woke, scared by the noise, while the water gushed up between the logs and in through the wall. On the port side of the foredeck the bamboo wickerwork was blown open like a small crater, and the diving basket had been knocked flat up in the bow, but everything else was as it had been. Where the three big seas came from, we have never been able to explain with certainty, unless they were due to disturbances on the sea bottom, which are not so uncommon in these regions.

Two days later we had our first storm. It started by the trade wind dying away completely, and the feathery, white tradewind clouds, which were drifting over our heads up in the topmost blue, being suddenly invaded by a thick black cloud bank which rolled up over the horizon from southward. Then there came gusts of wind from the most unexpected directions, so that it was impossible for the steering watch to keep control. As quickly as we got our stern turned to the new direction of the wind, so that the sail bellied out stiff and safe, just as quickly the gusts came at us from another quarter, squeezed the proud bulge out of the sail, and made it swing round and thrash about to the peril of both crew and cargo. But then the wind suddenly set in to blow straight from the quarter whence the bad weather came, and, as the black clouds rolled over us, the breeze increased to a fresh wind which worked itself up into a real storm.

In the course of an incredibly short time the seas round about us were flung up to a height of fifteen feet, while single crests were hissing twenty and twenty-five feet above the trough of the sea, so that we had them on a level with our masthead when we ourselves were down in the trough. All hands had to scramble about on deck bent double, while the wind shook the bamboo wall and whistled and howled in all the rigging.

To protect the radio corner we stretched canvas over the rear wall and port side of the cabin. All loose cargo was lashed securely, and the sail was hauled down and made fast around the bamboo yard. When the sky clouded over, the sea grew dark and threatening, and in every direction it was white-crested with breaking waves. Long tracks of dead foam lay like stripes to windward down the backs of the long seas; and everywhere, where the wave ridges had broken and plunged down, green patches like wounds lay frothing for a long time in the blue-black sea. The crests blew away as they broke, and the spray stood like salt rain over the sea. When the tropical rain poured over us in horizontal squalls and whipped the surface of the sea, invisible all round us, the water that ran from our hair and beards tasted brackish, while we crawled about the deck naked and frozen, seeing that all the gear was in order to weather the storm.

When the storm rushed up over the horizon and gathered about us for the first time, strained anticipation and anxiety were discernible in our looks. But when it was upon us in earnest, and the *Kon-Tiki* took everything that came her way with ease and buoyancy, the storm became an exciting form of sport, and we all delighted in the fury round about us which the balsa raft mastered so adroitly, always seeing that she herself lay on the wave tops like a cork, while all the main weight of the raging water was always a few inches beneath. The sea had much in common with the mountains in such weather. It was like being out in the wilds in a storm, up on the highest mountain plateaus, naked and gray. Even though we were right in the heart of the tropics, when the raft glided up and down over the smoking waste of sea we always thought of racing downhill among snowdrifts and rock faces.

The steering watch had to keep its eyes open in such weather. When the steepest seas passed under the forward half of the raft, the logs aft rose right out of the water, but the next second they plunged down again to climb up over the next crest. Each time the seas came so close upon one another that the hindmost reached us while the first was still holding the bow in the air. Then the solid sheets of water thundered in over the steering watch in a terrifying welter, but next second the stern went up and the flood disappeared as through the prongs of a fork.

We calculated that in an ordinary calm sea, where there were usually seven seconds between the highest waves, we took in about two hundred tons of water astern in twenty-four hours. But we hardly noticed it because it just flowed in quietly round the bare legs of the steering watch and as quietly disappeared again between the logs. But in a heavy storm more than ten thousand tons of water poured on board astern in the course of twenty-four hours, seeing that loads varying from a few gallons to two or three cubic yards, and occasionally much more, flowed on board every five seconds. It sometimes broke on board with a deafening thunderclap, so that the helmsman stood in water up to his waist and felt as if he were forcing his way against the current in a swift river. The raft seemed to stand trembling for a moment, but then the cruel load that weighed her down astern disappeared overboard again in great cascades.

Herman was out all the time with his anemometer measuring the squalls of gale force, which lasted for twenty-four hours. Then they gradually dropped to a stiff breeze with scattered rain squalls, which continued to keep the seas boiling round us as we tumbled on westward with a good sailing wind. To obtain accurate wind measurements down among the towering seas Herman had, whenever possible, to make his way up to the swaying masthead, where it was all he could do to hold on.

When the weather moderated, it was as though the big fish around us had become completely infuriated. The water round the raft was full of sharks, tunnies, dolphins, and a few dazed bonitos, all wriggling about close under the timber of the raft and in the waves nearest to it. It was a ceaseless life-and-death struggle; the backs of big fishes arched themselves over the water and shot off like rockets, one chasing another in pairs, while the water round the raft was repeatedly tinged with thick blood. The combatants were mainly tunnies and dolphins, and the dolphins came in big shoals which moved much more quickly and alertly than usual. The tunnies were the assailants; often a fish of 150 to 200 pounds would leap high into the air holding a dolphin's bloody head in its mouth. But, even if individual dolphins dashed off with tunnies hard on their heels, the actual shoal of dolphins did not give ground, although there were often several wriggling round with big gaping wounds in their necks. Now and again the sharks, too, seemed to become blind with rage, and we saw them catch and fight with big tunnies, which met in the shark a superior enemy.

Not one single peaceful little pilot fish was to be seen. They had been devoured by the furious tunnies, or they had hidden in the chinks under the raft or fled far away from the battlefield. We dared not put our heads down into the water to see.

I had a nasty shock—and could not help laughing afterward at my own complete bewilderment—when I was aft, obeying a call of nature. We were accustomed to a bit of a swell in the water closet, but it seemed contrary to all reasonable probabilities when I quite unexpectedly received a violent punch astern from something large and cold and very heavy, which came butting up against me like a shark's head in the sea. I was actually on my way up the mast stay, with a feeling that I had a shark hanging on to my hindquarters, before I collected myself. Herman, who was hanging over the steering oar doubled up with laughter, was able to tell me that a huge tunny had delivered a sideways smack at my nakedness with his 160 pounds or so of cold fish. Afterward, when Herman and then Torstein were on watch, the same fish tried to jump on board with the seas from astern, and twice the big fellow was right up on the end of the logs, but each time it flung itself overboard again before we could get a grip of the slippery body.

After that a stout bewildered bonito came right on board with a sea, and with that, and a tunny caught the day before, we decided to fish, to bring order into the sanguinary chaos that surrounded us.

Our diary says:

—*A six-foot shark was hooked first and hauled on board. As soon as the hook was out again, it was swallowed by an eight-foot shark, and we hauled that on board. When the hook came out again, we got a fresh six-foot shark and had hauled it over the edge of the raft when it broke loose and dived. The hook went out again at once, and an eight-foot shark came on to it and gave us a hard tussle. We had its head over the logs when all four steel lines were cut through and the shark dived into the depths. New hook out, and a seven-foot shark was hauled on board. It was now dangerous to stand on the slippery logs aft fishing, because the three sharks kept on throwing up their heads and snapping, long after one would have thought they were dead. We dragged the sharks forward by the tail into a heap on the foredeck, and soon afterward a big tunny was hooked and gave us more of a fight than any shark before we got it on board. It was so fat and heavy that none of us could lift it by the tail.*

The sea was just as full of furious fish backs. Another shark was hooked but broke away just when it was being pulled on board. But then we got a six-foot shark safely on board. After that a five-foot shark, which also came on board. Then we caught yet another six-foot shark and hauled it up. When the hook came out again, we hauled in a seven-foot shark.

Wherever we walked on deck, there were big sharks lying in the way, beating their tails convulsively on the deck or thrashing against the bamboo cabin as they snapped around them. Already tired and worn out when we began to fish after the storm, we became completely befuddled as to which sharks were quite dead, which were still snapping convulsively if we went near them, and which were quite alive and were lying in ambush for us with their green cat's eyes. When we had nine big sharks lying round us in every direction, we were so weary of hauling on heavy lines and fighting with the twisting and snapping giants that we gave up after five hours' toil.

Next day there were fewer dolphins and tunnies but just as many sharks. We began to fish and haul them in again but soon stopped when we perceived that all the fresh shark's blood that ran off the raft only attracted still more sharks. We threw all the dead sharks overboard and washed the whole deck clean of blood. The bamboo mats were torn by shark teeth and rough sharkskin, and we threw the bloodiest and most torn of them overboard and replaced them with new golden-yellow bamboo mats, several layers of which were lashed fast on the foredeck.

When we turned in on these evenings in our mind's eye we saw greedy, open shark jaws and blood. And the smell of shark meat stuck in our nostrils. We could eat shark—it tasted like haddock if we got the ammoniac out of the pieces by putting them in sea water for twenty-four hours—but bonito and tunny were infinitely better.

That evening, for the first time, I heard one of the fellows say that it would soon be pleasant to be able to stretch oneself out comfortably on the green grass on a palm island; he would be glad to see something other than cold fish and rough sea.

The weather had become quite quiet again, but it was never as constant and dependable as before. Incalculable, violent gusts of wind from time to time brought with them heavy showers, which we were glad to see because a large part of our water supply had begun to go bad and tasted like evil-smelling marsh water. When it was pouring the hardest, we collected water from the cabin roof and stood on deck naked, thoroughly to enjoy the luxury of having the salt washed off with fresh water.

The pilot fish were wriggling along again in their usual places, but whether they were the same old ones which had returned after the blood bath, or whether they were new followers taken over in the heat of the battle, we could not say.

On July 21 the wind suddenly died away again. It was oppressive and absolutely still, and we knew from previous experience what this might mean. And, right enough, after a few violent gusts from east and west and south, the wind freshened up to a breeze from southward, where black, threatening clouds had again rushed up over the horizon. Herman was out with his anemometer all the time, measuring already fifty feet and more per second, when suddenly Torstein's sleeping bag went overboard. And what happened in the next few seconds took a much shorter time than it takes to tell it.

Herman tried to catch the bag as it went, took a rash step, and fell overboard. We heard a faint cry for help amid the noise of the waves, and saw Herman's head and a waving arm as well as some vague green object twirling about in the water near him. He was struggling for life to get back to the raft through the high seas which had lifted him out from the port side. Torstein, who was at the steering oar aft, and I myself, up in the bow, were the first to perceive him, and we went cold with fear. We bellowed "Man overboard!" at the top of our lungs as we rushed to the nearest life-saving gear. The others had not heard Herman's cry because of the noise of the sea, but in a trice there was life and bustle on deck. Herman was an excellent swimmer, and, though we realized at once that his life was at stake, we had a fair hope that he would manage to crawl back to the edge of the raft before it was too late.

Torstein, who was nearest, seized the bamboo drum round which was the line we used for the lifeboat, for this was within his reach. It was the only time on the whole voyage that this line got caught up. Herman was now on a level with the stern of the raft but a few yards away, and his last hope was to crawl to the blade of the steering oar and hang on to it. As he missed the end of the logs, he reached out for the oar blade, but it slipped away from him. And there he lay, just where experience had shown we could get nothing back. While Bengt and I launched the dinghy, Knut and Erik threw out the life belt. Carrying a long line, it hung ready for use on the corner of the cabin roof, but today the wind was so strong that when it was thrown it was simply blown back to the raft. After a few unsuccessful throws Herman was already far astern of the steering oar, swimming desperately to keep up with the raft, while the distance increased with each gust of wind. He realized that henceforth the gap would simply go on increasing, but he set a faint hope on the dinghy which we had now got into the water. Without the line, which acted as a brake, it would perhaps be possible to drive the rubber raft to meet the swimming man, but whether the rubber raft would ever get back to the *Kon-Tiki* was another matter. Nevertheless, three men in a rubber dinghy had some chance; one man in the sea had none.

Then we suddenly saw Knut take off and plunge headfirst into the sea. He had the life belt in one hand and was heaving himself along. Every time Herman's head appeared on a wave back Knut was gone, and every time Knut came up Herman was not there. But then we saw both heads at once; they had swum to meet each other and both were hanging on to the life belt. Knut waved his arm, and, as the rubber raft had meanwhile been hauled on board, all four of us took hold of the line of the life belt and hauled for dear life, with our eyes fixed on the great dark object which was visible just behind the two men. This same mysterious beast in the water was pushing a big greenish-black triangle up above the wave crests; it almost gave Knut a shock when he was on his way over to Herman. Only Herman knew then that the triangle did not belong to a shark or any other sea monster. It was an inflated corner of Torstein's watertight sleeping bag. But the sleeping bag did not remain floating for long after we had hauled the two men safe and sound on board. Whatever dragged the sleeping bag down into the depths had just missed a better prey.

"Glad I wasn't in it," said Torstein and took hold of the steering oar where he had let it go.

But otherwise there were not many wisecracks that evening. We all felt a chill running through nerve and bone for a long time afterward. But the cold shivers were mingled with a warm thankfulness that there were still six of us on board.

We had a lot of nice things to say to Knut that day—Herman and the rest of us, too.

But there was not much time to think about what had already happened, for as the sky grew black over our heads the gusts of wind increased in strength, and before night a new storm was upon us. We finally got the life belt to hang astern of the raft on a long line, so that we had something behind the steering oar toward which to swim if one of us should fall overboard again in a squall. Then it grew pitch dark around us as night fell and hid the raft and the sea. Bouncing wildly up and down in the darkness, we only heard and felt the gale howling in masts and guy ropes, while the gusts pressed with smashing force against the springy bamboo cabin till we thought it would fly overboard. But it was covered with canvas and well guyed. And we felt the *Kon-Tiki* tossing with the foaming seas, while the logs moved up and down with the movement of the waves like the keys of an instrument. We were astonished that cascades of water did not gush up through the wide chinks in the floor, but they only acted as a regular bellows through which damp air rushed up and down.

For five whole days the weather varied between full storm and light gale; the sea was dug up into wide valleys filled with the smoke from foaming gray-blue seas, which seemed to have their backs pressed out long and flat under the onset of the wind. Then on the fifth day the heavens split to show a glimpse of blue, and the malignant, black cloud cover gave place to the ever victorious blue sky as the storm passed on. We had come through the gale with the steering oar smashed and the sail rent; the centerboards hung loose and banged about like crowbars among the logs, because all the ropes which had tightened them up under water were worn through. But we ourselves and the cargo were completely undamaged.

After the two storms the *Kon-Tiki* had become a good deal weaker in the joints. The strain of working over the steep wave backs had stretched all the ropes, and the continuously working logs had made the ropes eat into the balsa wood. We thanked Providence that we had followed the Incas' custom and had not used wire ropes, which would simply have sawed the whole raft into matchwood in the gale. And, if we had used bone-dry, high-floating balsa at the start, the raft would long ago have sunk into the sea under us, saturated with sea water. It was the sap in the fresh logs which served as an impregnation and prevented the water from filtering in through the porous balsa wood.

But now the ropes had become so loose that it was dangerous to let one's foot slip down between two logs, for it could be crushed when they came together violently. Forward and aft, where there was no bamboo deck, we had to give at the knees when we stood with our feet wide apart on two logs at the same time. The logs aft were as slippery as banana leaves with wet seaweed, and, even though we had made a regular path through the greenery where we usually walked and had laid down a broad plank for the steering watch to stand on, it was not easy to keep one's foothold when a sea struck the raft. On the port side one of the nine giants bumped and banged against the crossbeams with dull, wet thuds both by night and by day. There came also new and fearful creakings from the ropes which held the two sloping masts together at the masthead, for the steps of the masts worked about independently of each other, because they rested on two different logs.

We got the steering oar spliced and lashed with long billets of mangrove wood, as hard as iron, and with Erik and Bengt as sailmakers Kon-Tiki soon raised his head again and swelled his breast in a stiff bulge toward Polynesia, while the steering oar danced behind in seas which the fine weather had made soft and gentle. But the centerboards never again became quite what they had been; they did not meet the pressure of the water with their full strength but gave way and hung, dangling loose and unguyed, under the raft. It was useless to try to inspect the ropes on the underside, for they were completely overgrown with seaweed. On taking up the whole bamboo deck we found only three of the main ropes broken; they had been lying crooked and pressed against the cargo, which had worn them away. It was evident that the logs had absorbed a great weight of water but, since the cargo had been lightened, this was roughly canceled out. Most of our provisions and drinking water were already used up, likewise the radio operators' dry batteries.

Nevertheless, after the last storm it was clear enough that we should both float and hold together for the short distance that separated us from the islands ahead. Now quite another problem came into the foreground—how would the voyage end?

The *Kon-Tiki* would slog on inexorably westward until she ran her bow into a solid rock or some other fixed object which would stop her drifting. But our voyage would not be ended until all hands had landed safe and sound on one of the numerous Polynesian islands ahead.

When we came through the last storm, it was quite uncertain where the raft would end up. We were at an equal distance from the Marquesas Islands and the Tuamotu group, and in a position which meant that we could very easily pass right between the two groups of islands without having a glimpse of one of them. The nearest island in the Marquesas group lay 300 sea miles northwest, and the nearest island in the Tuamotu group lay 300 sea miles southwest, while wind and current were uncertain, with their general direction westerly and toward the wide ocean gap between the two island groups.

The island which lay nearest to the northwest was no other than Fatu Hiva, the little jungle-clad mountainous island where I had lived in a hut built on piles on the beach and heard the old man's vivid stories of the ancestral hero Tiki. If the *Kon-Tiki* stood in to that same beach, I should meet many acquaintances, but hardly the old man himself. He must have departed long ago, with a fair hope of meeting the real Tiki again. If the raft headed in toward the mountain ranges of the Marquesas group, I knew the few islands in the group were a long way apart and the sea thundered unchecked against perpendicular cliffs where we should have to keep our eyes open while steering for the mouths of the few valleys, which always ended in narrow strips of beach.

If, on the contrary, she headed down toward the coral reefs of the Tuamotu group, there the numerous islands lay close together and covered a wide space of sea. But this group of islands is also known as the Low or Dangerous Archipelago, because the whole formation has been built up entirely by coral polyps and consists of treacherous submerged reefs and palmclad atolls which rise only six or ten feet above the surface of the sea. Dangerous ring-shaped reefs fling themselves protectingly round every single atoll and are a menace to shipping throughout the area. But, even if coral polyps built the Tuamotu atolls while the Marquesas Islands are remains of extinct volcanoes, both groups are inhabited by the same Polynesian race, and the royal families in both regard Tiki as their primeval ancestor.

As early as July 3, when we were still 1,000 sea miles from Polynesia, Nature herself was able to tell us, as she was able to tell the primitive raftsmen from Peru in their time, that there really was land ahead somewhere out in the sea. Until we were a good thousand sea miles out from the coast of Peru we had noted small flocks of frigate birds. They disappeared at about 100° west, and after that we saw only small petrels which have their home on the sea. But on July 3 the frigate birds reappeared, at 125° west, and from now onward small flocks of frigate birds were often to be seen, either high up in the sky or shooting down over the wave crests, where they snapped up flying fish which had taken to the air to escape from dolphins. As these birds did not come from America astern of us, they must have their homes in another country ahead.

On July 16 Nature betrayed herself still more obviously. On that day we hauled up a nine-foot shark, which threw up from its stomach a large undigested starfish which it had recently brought from some coast out here in the ocean.

And the very next day we had the first definite visitor straight from the islands of Polynesia.

It was a great moment on board when two large boobies were spotted above the horizon to westward and soon afterward came sailing in over our mast, flying low. With a wingspread of five feet they circled round us many times, then folded their wings and settled on the sea alongside us. Dolphins rushed to the spot at once and wriggled inquisitively round the great swimming birds, but neither party touched the other. These were the first living messengers that came to bid us welcome to Polynesia. They did not go back in the evening but rested on the sea, and after midnight we still heard them flying in circles round the mast, uttering hoarse cries.

The flying fish which came on board were now of another and much larger species; I recognized them from fishing trips I had taken with the natives along the coast of Fatu Hiva.

For three days and nights we made straight toward Fatu Hiva, but then a strong northeast wind came on and sent us down in the direction of the Tuamotu atolls. We were now blown out of the real South Equatorial Current, and the ocean currents were no longer behaving dependably. One day they were there; another day they were gone. The currents could run like invisible rivers branching out all over the sea. If the current was swift, there was usually more swell and the temperature of the water usually fell one degree. It showed its direction and strength every day by the difference between Erik's calculated and his measured position.

On the threshold of Polynesia the wind said "Pass," having handed us over to a weak branch of the current which, to our alarm, had its course in the direction of the Antarctic. The wind did not become absolutely still—we never experienced that throughout the voyage—and when it was feeble we hoisted every rag we had to collect what little there was. There was not one day on which we moved backward toward America, and our smallest distance in twenty-four hours was 9 sea miles, while our average run for the voyage as a whole was 42½ sea miles in twenty-four hours.

The trade wind, after all, had not the heart to fail us right in the last lap. It reported for duty again and pushed and shoved at the ramshackle craft which was preparing her entry into a new and strange part of the world.

With each day that passed, larger flocks of sea birds came and circled over us aimlessly in all directions. One evening, when the sun was about to sink into the sea, we noticed that the birds had received a violent impetus. They were flying away in a westerly direction without paying any attention to us or the flying fish beneath them. From the masthead we could see that, as they came over, they all flew straight on on exactly the same course. Perhaps they saw something from up above which we did not see. Perhaps they were flying by instinct. In any case they were flying with a plan, straight home to the nearest island, their breeding place.

We twisted the steering oar and set our course exactly in the direction in which the birds had disappeared. Even after it was dark, we heard the cries of stragglers flying over us against the starry sky on exactly the same course as that which we were now following.

It was a wonderful night; the moon was nearly full for the third time in the course of the *Kon-Tiki's* voyage.

Next day there were still more birds over us, but we did not need to wait for them to show us our way again in the evening. This time we had detected a curious stationary cloud above the horizon. The other clouds were small feathery wisps of wool which came up in the south and passed across the vault of the sky with the trade wind till they disappeared over the horizon in the west. So I had once come to know the drifting trade-wind clouds on Fatu Hiva, and so we had seen them over us night and day on board the *Kon-Tiki*. But the lonely cloud on the horizon to the southwest did not move; it just rose like a motionless column of smoke while the trade-wind clouds drifted by. The Polynesians knew land lay under such clouds. For, when the tropical sun bakes the hot sand, a stream of warm air is created which rises up and causes its vapor content to condense up in the colder strata of air.

We steered on the cloud till it disappeared after sunset. The wind was steady, and with the steering oar lashed tight the *Kon-Tiki* kept to her course unaided. The steering watch's job was now to sit on the plank at the masthead, shiny with wear, and keep a lookout for anything that indicated land.

There was a deafening screaming of birds over us all that night. And the moon was nearly full.

7.

To the South
Sea Islands

Our daily bread. Dolphins followed us throughout the voyage and were the best eating imaginable. They bit at once if we used flying fish as bait.

Above: Haugland goes down to inspect the lashings on the raft's bottom. The author holds him firmly by the legs.

Below: Where Haugland went down, a shark was hauled up—an easy matter, as the deck was only a foot or two above the surface of the water.

Hesselberg making a diving basket. If we received unwelcome attentions when we dived under the raft, we just crouched inside the basket and were quickly hauled on board.

At left: Studying the chart. Hesselberg took observations daily and marked our drift on the chart. Not till after three months, when we reached the Tuamotu group, did a serious navigation problem arise—how were we to land?

Below: Raaby in the radio corner. Haugland and Raaby had their radio station behind a cardboard partition decorated by Danielsson. They were in contact with amateurs in many different countries and sent regular reports to the U.S. Weather Bureau.

MENU №1
FIRST HALF OF
5' RATIONS

At right: The first birds from Polynesia which welcomed us. We followed the same course as they when they flew home at evening.

Below: Land in sight! After 93 days we sighted land for the first time. It was the island Puka Puka. But the wind and current took us out to sea again.

Above: Kon-Tiki approaching land. The tricolor was hoisted as we steered toward the French island Angatau. We had reached Polynesia.
Below: The first natives coming out. Toward evening several canoes appeared with natives eager to help us ashore. But the raft drifted out to sea again, and finally Angatau disappeared astern.

Above: A reef with a witches' caldron of seething breakers barred the approach to the island Raroia. The raft was heavily pounded and finally flung up by the waves on to the coral reef surrounding the island.
Below: The wreck was washed higher up on to the reef every day. The Raroia reef—25 miles long—is (like all the other islands in the Tuamotu group) the work of industrious little coral polyps.

Salvage work. Danielsson
—safe and sound, but his
head still aching from a
blow from the mast—
dragging his mattress out
of the wreckage. The
most important cargo has
already been salvaged.

Chaos. After the strand-
ing the raft was hardly
recognizable. The masts
were broken, the cabin
crushed, the bamboo deck
twisted up to form a bar-
ricade, and our belong-
ings strewn all over the
place.

On the night before July 30 there was a new and strange atmosphere about the *Kon-Tiki*. Perhaps it was the deafening clamor from all the sea birds over us which showed that something fresh was brewing. The screaming of birds with many voices sounded hectic and earthly after the dead creaking of lifeless ropes, which was all we had heard above the noise of the sea in the three months we had behind us. And the moon seemed larger and rounder than ever as it sailed over the lookout at the masthead. In our fancy it reflected palm tops and warm-blooded romance; it did not shine with such a yellow light over the cold fishes out at sea.

At six o'clock Bengt came down from the masthead, woke Herman, and turned in. When Herman clambered up the creaking, swaying mast, the day had begun to break. Ten minutes later he was down the rope ladder again and was shaking me by the leg.

"Come out and have a look at your island!"

His face was radiant and I jumped up, followed by Bengt who had not quite gone to sleep yet. Hard on one another's heels, we huddled together as high as we could climb, at the point where the masts crossed. There were many birds around us, and a faint violet-blue veil over the sky was reflected in the sea as a last relic of the departing night. But over the whole horizon away to the east a ruddy glow had begun to spread, and far down to the southeast it gradually formed a blood-red background for a faint shadow, like a blue pencil line, drawn for a short way along the edge of the sea.

Land! An island! We devoured it greedily with our eyes and woke the others, who tumbled out drowsily and stared in all directions as if they thought our bow was about to run on to a beach. Screaming sea birds formed a bridge across the sky in the direction of the distant island, which stood out sharper against the horizon as the red background widened and turned gold with the approach of the sun and the full daylight.

Our first thought was that the island did not lie where it should. As the island could not have drifted, the raft must have been caught up in a northward current in the course of the night. We had only to cast one glance over the sea to perceive at once, from the direction of the waves, that we had lost our chance in the darkness. Where we now lay, the wind no longer allowed us to press the raft on a course toward the island. The region round the Tuamotu Archipelago was full of strong, local ocean currents which twisted in all directions as they ran up against land; many of them varied in direction as they met powerful tidal currents flowing in and out over reefs and lagoons.

We laid the steering oar over, but we knew quite well that it was useless. At half-past six the sun rose out of the sea and climbed straight up as it does in the tropics. The island lay some few sea miles away and had the appearance of a quite low strip of forest creeping along the horizon. The trees were crowded close together behind a narrow light-colored beach, which lay so low that it was hidden behind the seas at regular intervals. According to Erik's positions this island was Puka Puka, the first outpost of the Tuamotu group. *Sailing Directions for Pacific Islands 1940*, our two different charts, and Erik's observations gave, in all, four quite different positions for this island, but as there were no other islands in all that neighborhood there could be no doubt that the island we saw was Puka Puka.

No extravagant outbursts were to be heard on board. After the sail had been trimmed and the oar laid over, we all formed a silent group at the masthead or stood on deck staring toward the land which had suddenly cropped up out in the middle of the endless, all-dominating sea. At last we had a visible proof that we had really been moving in all these months; we had not just been lying tumbling about in the center of the same eternal circular horizon. To us it seemed as if the island were mobile and had suddenly entered the circle of blue and empty sea in the center of which we had our permanent abode; as if the island were drifting slowly across our own domain, heading for the eastern horizon. We were all filled with a warm, quiet satisfaction at having actually reached Polynesia, mingled with a faint momentary disappointment at having to submit helplessly to seeing the island lie there like a mirage while we continued our eternal drift across the sea westward.

Just after sunrise a thick black column of smoke rose above the treetops to the left of the middle of the island. We followed it with our eyes and thought to ourselves that the natives were rising and getting their breakfast. We had no idea then that native lookout posts had seen us and were sending up smoke signals to invite us to land. About seven o'clock we scented a faint breath of burned *borao* wood which tickled our salted nostrils. It awoke in me at once slumbering memories of the fire on the beach on Fatu Hiva. Half an hour later we caught the smell of newly cut wood and of forest. The island had now begun to shrink and lay astern of us so that we received flickering wafts of breeze from it. For a quarter of an hour Herman and I clung to the masthead and let the warm smell of leaves and greenery filter in through our nostrils. This was Polynesia—a beautiful, rich smell of dry land after ninety-three salty days down among the waves. Bengt already lay snoring in his sleeping bag again. Erik and Torstein lay on their backs in the cabin meditating, and Knut ran in and out and sniffed the smell of leaves and wrote in his diary.

At half-past eight Puka Puka sank into the sea astern of us, but right on till eleven o'clock we could see, on climbing to the masthead, that there was a faint blue streak above the horizon in the east. Then that too was gone, and a high cumulo-nimbus cloud, rising motionless skyward, was all that showed where Puka Puka lay. The birds disappeared. They kept by preference to windward of the islands so that they had the wind with them when they returned home in the evening with full bellies. The dolphins also had become noticeably scarcer, and there were again only a few pilot fish under the raft.

That night Bengt said he longed for a table and chair, for it was so tiring to lie and turn from back to stomach while reading. Otherwise he was glad we had missed our landing, for he still had three books to read. Torstein suddenly had a desire for an apple, and I myself woke up in the night because I definitely smelled a delicious odor of steak and onions. But it turned out to be only a dirty shirt.

The very next morning we detected two new clouds rising up like the steam from two locomotives below the horizon. The map was able to tell us that the names of the coral islands they came from were Fangahina and Angatau. The cloud over Angatau lay the most favorably for us as the wind was blowing, so we set our course for that, lashed the oar fast, and enjoyed the wonderful peace and freedom of the Pacific. So lovely was life on this fine day on the bamboo deck of the *Kon-Tiki* that we drank in all the impressions in the certainty that the journey would soon be over now, whatever might await us.

For three days and nights we steered on the cloud over Angatau; the weather was brilliant, the oar alone held us on our course, and the current played us no tricks. On the fourth morning Torstein relieved Herman after the 4–6 watch and was told that Herman thought he had seen the outlines of a low island in the moonlight. When the sun rose just afterward, Torstein stuck his head in at the cabin door and shouted:

"Land ahead!"

We all plunged out on deck, and what we saw made us hoist all our flags. First the Norwegian aft, then the French at the masthead because we were heading for a French colony. Soon the raft's entire collection of flags was fluttering in the fresh trade wind—the American, British, Peruvian, and Swedish flags besides the flag of the Explorers Club—so there was no doubt on board that now the *Kon-Tiki* was dressed. The island was ideally placed this time, right in our own course and a little farther away from us than Puka Puka had been when it cropped up at sunrise four days before. As the sun rose straight up over the sky astern of us, we could see a clear green glimmer high up toward the misty sky over the island. It was the reflection of the still, green lagoon on the inside of the surrounding reef. Some of the low atolls throw up mirages of this kind for many thousand feet into the air, so that they show their positions to primitive seafarers many days before the island itself is visible above the horizon.

About ten o'clock we took charge of the steering oar ourselves; we must now decide toward which part of the island we should steer. We could already distinguish individual treetops from the others and could see rows of tree trunks shining in the sun, which stood out against the background of dense shadowy foliage.

We knew that somewhere between us and the island there was a dangerous submerged shoal, lying in ambush for anything that approached the innocent island. This reef lay right under the deep, free roll of the swell from the east, and, as the huge masses of water lost their balance above the shoal, they wavered skyward and plunged down, thundering and foaming, over the sharp coral reef.

Many vessels have been caught in the terrible suction against the submerged reefs in the Tuamotu group and have been smashed to pieces against the coral.

From the sea we saw nothing of this insidious trap. We sailed in, following the direction of the waves, and saw only the curved shining back of sea after sea disappearing toward the island. Both the reef and the whole frothing witches' dance over it were hidden behind rising rows of broad wave backs ahead of us. But along both ends of the island where we saw the beach in profile, both north and south, we saw that a few hundred yards from land the sea was one white boiling mass flinging itself high into the air.

We laid our course so as to graze the outside of the witches' kitchen off the southern point of the island, hoping, when we got there, to be able to steer along the atoll till we came round the point on the lee side or till we touched, before we drifted past, a place where it was so shallow that we could stop our drift with a makeshift anchor and wait till the wind changed and placed us under the lee of the island.

About noon we could see through the glass that the vegetation on shore consisted of young green coconut palms, which stood with their tops close together over a waving hedge of luxuriant undergrowth in the foreground. On the beach in front of them a number of large coral blocks lay strewn about on the bright sand. Otherwise there was no sign of life, apart from white birds sailing over the palm tufts.

At two o'clock we had come so close that we began to sail along the island, just outside the baffling reef. As we gradually approached, we heard the roar of the breakers like a steady waterfall against the reef, and soon they sounded like an endless express train running parallel with us a few hundred yards from our starboard side. Now, too, we could see the white spray which was occasionally flung high into the air behind the curly, breaking wave backs just in there where the "train" was roaring along.

Two men at the same time stood turning the steering oar; they were behind the bamboo cabin and so had no view ahead whatever. Erik, as navigator, stood on the top of the kitchen box and gave directions to the two men at the heavy oar. Our plan was to keep as close in to the dangerous reef as was safe. We kept a continuous lookout from the masthead for a gap or opening in the reef where we could try to slip the raft through. The current was now driving us along the whole length of the reef and played us no tricks. The loose centerboards allowed us to steer at an angle of about 20° to the wind on both sides, and the wind was blowing along the reef.

While Erik directed our zigzag course and took his loops as near the reef as was advisable in view of the suction, Herman and I went out in the rubber dinghy at the end of a rope. When the raft was on the inward tack, we swung after her on the rope and came so close to the thundering reef that we caught a glimpse of the glass-green wall of water that was rolling away from us and saw how, when the seas sucked themselves back, the naked reef exposed itself, resembling a torn-up barricade of rusty iron ore. As far as we could see along the coast there was no gap or passage. So Erik trimmed the sail by tightening the port and loosening the starboard sheets, and the helmsman followed with the steering oar, so that the *Kon-Tiki* turned her nose out again and tumbled away from the danger zone till her next drive inward.

Each time the *Kon-Tiki* stood in toward the reef and swung out again, we two who were in tow in the dinghy sat with our hearts in our mouths, for each time we came so close in that we felt the beat of the seas becoming nervous as it rose higher and fiercer. And each time we were convinced that this time Erik had gone too far, that this time there was no hope of getting the *Kon-Tiki* out again clear of the breakers which drew us in toward the devilish red reef. But each time Erik got clear with a smart maneuver, and the *Kon-Tiki* ran safely out into the open sea again, well out of the clutch of the suction. All the time we were gliding along the island, so close that we saw every detail on shore; yet the heavenly beauty there was inaccessible to us because of the frothing moat that lay between.

About three o'clock the forest of palms ashore opened, and through a wide gap we saw right into a blue glassy lagoon. But the surrounding reef lay as compact as ever, gnashing its blood-red teeth ominously in the foam. There was no passage, and the palm forest closed again as we plodded on along the island with the wind at our backs. Later the palm forest became thinner and thinner and gave us a view into the interior of the coral island. This consisted of the fairest, brightest salt-water lagoon, like a great silent tarn, surrounded by swaying coconut palms and shining bathing beaches. The seductive, green palm island itself formed a broad, soft ring of sand round the hospitable lagoon, and a second ring ran round the whole island —the rust-red sword which defended the gates of heaven.

All day we zigzagged along Angatau and had its beauty at close quarters, just outside the cabin door. The sun beat down on all the palms, and all was Paradise and joy on the island within. As our maneuvers gradually became a matter of routine, Erik got out his guitar and stood on deck in a huge Peruvian sun hat playing and singing sentimental South Sea songs, while Bengt served an excellent dinner on the edge of the raft. We opened an old coconut from Peru and drank to the young fresh nuts which hung on the trees inside. The whole atmosphere—the peace over the bright, green palm forest which stood deep-rooted and beckoned toward us, the peace over the white birds that sailed round the palm tops, the peace over the glassy lagoon and the soft sand beach, and the viciousness of the red reef, the cannonading and roll of drums in the air—all made an overwhelming impression on the six of us who had come in from the sea. An impression which can never be effaced from our memories. There was no doubt that now we had reached the other side; we should never see a more genuine South Sea island. Landing or no landing, we had nonetheless reached Polynesia; the expanse of sea lay behind us for all time.

It happened that this festal day off Angatau was the ninety-seventh day on board. Strangely enough, it was ninety-seven days that we had estimated in New York as the absolute minimum time in which, in theoretically ideal conditions, we could reach the nearest islands of Polynesia.

About five o'clock we passed two palm-roofed huts which lay among the trees on shore. There was no smoke and no sign of life.

At half-past five we stood in toward the reef again; we had sailed along the whole south coast and were getting near the west end of the island, and must have a last look round in the hope of finding a passage before we passed. The sun now stood so low that it blinded us when we looked ahead, but we saw a little rainbow in the air where the sea broke against the reef a few hundred yards beyond the last point of the island. This now lay as a silhouette ahead of us. On the beach inside we detected a cluster of motionless black spots. Suddenly one of them moved slowly down toward the water, while several of the others made off at full speed up to the edge of the woods. They were people! We steered along the reef as close in as we dared; the wind had died down so that we felt we were within an inch of getting under the lee of the island. Now we saw a canoe being launched, and two individuals jumped on board and paddled off on the other side of the reef. Farther down they turned the boat's head out, and we saw the canoe lifted high in the air by the seas as it shot through a passage in the reef and came straight out toward us.

The opening in the reef, then, was down there; there was our only hope. Now, too, we could see the whole village lying in among the palm trunks. But the shadows were already growing long.

The two men in the canoe waved. We waved back eagerly, and they increased their speed. It was a Polynesian outrigger canoe; two brown figures in singlets sat paddling, facing ahead. Now there would be fresh language difficulties. I alone of those on board remembered a few words of Marquesan from my stay on Fatu Hiva, but Polynesian is a difficult language to keep up, for lack of practice in our northern countries.

We felt some relief, therefore, when the canoe bumped against the raft's side and the two men leaped on board, for one of them grinned all over his face and held out a brown hand, exclaiming in English:

"Good night!"

"Good night," I replied in astonishment. "Do you speak English?" The man grinned again and nodded.

"Good night," he said. "Good night."

This was his entire vocabulary in foreign languages, and thereby he scored heavily over his more modest friend, who just stood in the background and grinned, much impressed, at his experienced comrade.

"Angatau?" I asked, pointing toward the island.

"H'angatau," the man nodded affirmatively.

Erik nodded proudly. He had been right; we were where the sun had told him that we were.

"Maimai hee iuta," I tried.

According to my knowlege acquired on Fatu Hiva this should mean approximately, "Want to go to land."

They both pointed toward the invisible passage in the reef, and we laid the oar over and decided to take our chance.

At that moment fresher gusts of wind came from the interior of the island. A small rain cloud lay over the lagoon. The wind threatened to force us away from the reef, and we saw that the *Kon-Tiki* was not answering the steering oar at a wide enough angle to be able to reach the mouth of the opening in the reef. We tried to find bottom, but the anchor rope was not long enough. Now we had to have resort to the paddles, and pretty quickly, too, before the wind got a fair hold of us. We hauled down the sail at top speed and each of us got out his big paddle.

I wanted to give an extra paddle to each of the two natives, who stood enjoying the cigarettes they had been given on board. They only shook their heads vigorously, pointed out the course, and looked confused. I made signs that we must all paddle and repeated the words, "Want to go to land!" Then the most advanced of the two bent down, made a cranking motion in the air with his right hand, and said:

"Brrrrrrrrr-!"

There was no doubt whatever that he wanted us to start the engine. They thought they were standing on the deck of a curiously deep loaded boat. We took them aft and made them feel under the logs to show them that we had no propeller or screw. They were dumbfounded and, putting out their cigarettes, flung themselves down on the side of the raft where we sat—four men on each outside log, dipping our paddles into the water. At the same time the sun sank straight into the sea behind the point, and the gusts of wind from the interior of the island freshened. It did not look as if we were moving an inch. The natives looked frightened, jumped back into the canoe, and disappeared. It grew dark, and we were alone once more, paddling desperately so as not to drift out to sea again.

As darkness fell over the island, four canoes came dancing out from behind the reef, and soon there was a crowd of Polynesians on board, all wanting to shake hands and get cigarettes. With these fellows on board, who had local knowledge, there was no danger. They would not let us go out to sea again and out of sight, so we should be ashore that evening!

We quickly had ropes made fast from the sterns of all the canoes to the bow of the *Kon-Tiki*, and the four sturdy outrigger canoes spread out in fan formation, like a dog team, ahead of the wooden raft. Knut jumped into the dinghy and found a place as draft dog in among the canoes, and we others, with paddles, posted ourselves on the two outside logs of the *Kon-Tiki*. And so began, for the first time, a struggle against the east wind which had been at our back for so long.

It was now pitch dark until the moon rose, and there was a fresh wind. On land the inhabitants of the village had collected brushwood and lighted a big fire to show us the direction of the passage through the reef. The thundering from the reef surrounded us in the darkness like a ceaselessly roaring waterfall, and at first the noise grew louder and louder.

We could not see the team that was pulling us in the canoes ahead, but we heard them singing exhilarating war songs in Polynesian at the top of their lungs. We could hear that Knut was with them, for every time the Polynesian music died away we heard Knut's solitary voice singing Norwegian folk songs in the midst of the Polynesians' chorus. To complete the chaos we on board the raft chimed in with "Tom Brown's baby had a pimple on his nose," and both white and brown men heaved at their paddles with laughter and song.

We were overflowing with high spirits. Ninety-seven days. Arrived in Polynesia. There would be a feast in the village that evening. The natives cheered and bellowed and shouted. There was a landing on Angatau only once a year, when the copra schooner came from Tahiti to fetch coconut kernels. So there would indeed be a feast round the fire on land that evening.

But the angry wind blew stubbornly. We toiled till every limb ached. We held our ground, but the fire did not come any nearer and the thunder from the reef was just the same as before. Gradually the singing died away. All grew still. It was all and more the men could do to row. The fire did not move; it only danced up and down as we fell and rose with the seas. Three hours passed, and it was now nine o'clock. Gradually we began to lose ground. We were tired.

We made the natives understand that we needed more help from land. They explained to us that there were plenty of people ashore, but they had only these four seagoing canoes in the whole island.

Then Knut appeared out of the darkness with the dinghy. He had an idea; he could row in in the rubber dinghy and fetch more natives. Five or six men could sit crowded together in the dinghy at a pinch.

This was too risky. Knut had no local knowledge; he would never be able to feel his way forward to the opening in the coral reef in that pitch-black darkness. He then proposed to take with him the leader of the natives, who could show him the way. I did not think this plan a safe one, either, for the native had no experience in maneuvering a clumsy rubber dinghy through the narrow and dangerous passage. But I asked Knut to fetch the leader, who was sitting paddling in the darkness ahead of us, so that we might hear what he thought of the situation. It was clear enough that we were no longer able to prevent ourselves from drifting astern.

Knut disappeared into the darkness to find the leader. When some time had passed and Knut had not returned with the leader, we shouted for them but received no answer except from a cackling chorus of Polynesians ahead. Knut had vanished into the darkness. At that moment we understood what had happened. In all the bustle, noise, and turmoil Knut had misunderstood his instructions and rowed shoreward with the leader. All our shouting was useless, for where Knut now was all other sounds were drowned by the thunder all along the barrier.

We quickly got hold of a Morse lamp, and a man climbed up to the masthead and signaled, "Come back. Come back."

But no one came back.

With two men away and one continuously signaling at the masthead our drift astern increased, and the rest of us had begun to grow really tired. We threw marks overboard and saw that we were moving slowly but surely the wrong way. The fire grew smaller and the noise from the breakers less. And the farther we emerged from under the lee of the palm forest, the firmer hold of us the eternal east wind took. We felt it again now; it was almost as it had been out at sea. We gradually realized that all hope had gone—we were drifting out to sea. But we must not slacken our paddling. We must put the brake on the drift astern with all our might till Knut was safe on board again.

Five minutes went. Ten minutes. Half an hour. The fire grew smaller; now and then it disappeared altogether when we ourselves slid down into the trough of the sea. The breakers became a distant murmur. Now the moon rose; we could just see the glimmer of its disk behind the palm tops on land, but the sky seemed misty and half clouded over. We heard the natives beginning to murmur and exchange words. Suddenly we noticed that one of the canoes had cast off its rope into the sea and disappeared. The men in the other three canoes were tired and frightened and were no longer pulling their full weight. The *Kon-Tiki* went on drifting out over the open sea.

Soon the three remaining ropes slackened and the three canoes bumped against the side of the raft. One of the natives came on board and said quietly with a jerk of his head:

"*Iuta* (To land)."

He looked anxiously at the fire, which now disappeared for long periods at a time and only flashed out now and again like a spark. We were drifting fast. The breakers were silent; only the sea roared as it used to, and all the ropes on board the *Kon-Tiki* creaked and groaned.

We plied the natives with cigarettes, and I hurriedly scrawled a note which they were to take with them and give to Knut if they found him. It ran:

"Take two natives with you in a canoe with the dinghy in tow. Do NOT come back in the dinghy alone."

We counted on the helpful islanders being willing to take Knut with them in a canoe, assuming they thought it advisable to put to sea at all; if they did not think it advisable, it would be madness for Knut to venture out on to the ocean in the dinghy in the hope of overtaking the runaway raft.

The natives took the scrap of paper, jumped into the canoes, and disappeared into the night. The last we heard was the shrill voice of our first friend out in the darkness calling politely:

"Good night!"

There was murmur of appreciation from the less accomplished linguists, and then all was as silent, as free from sounds from without, as when we were 2,000 sea miles from the nearest land.

It was useless for us four to do anything more with the paddles out here in the open sea, under the full pressure of the wind, but we continued the light signals from the masthead. We dared not send "Come back" any longer; we now sent out only regular flashes. It was pitch dark. The moon appeared only through occasional rifts in the bank of clouds. It must have been Angatau's cumulo-nimbus cloud which was hanging over us.

At ten o'clock we gave up the last faint hope of seeing Knut again. We sat down in silence on the edge of the raft and munched a few biscuits, while we took turns flashing signals from the masthead, which seemed just a naked projection without the broad *Kon-Tiki* sail.

We decided to keep the lamp-signaling going all night, so long as we did not know where Knut was. We refused to believe that he had been caught by the breakers. Knut always landed on his feet, whether it was heavy water or breakers; he was alive all right. Only it was so damnable to have him stuck down among Polynesians on an out-of-the-way island in the Pacific. An accursed business!

After all that long voyage all we could do was to nip in and land a man on a remote South Sea island and sail off again. No sooner had the first Polynesians come smiling on board then they had to clear out headlong to escape being themselves caught up in the *Kon-Tiki's* wild, incontinent rush westward. It was the devil of a situation. And the ropes were creaking horribly that night. Not one of us showed a sign of wanting to sleep.

It was half-past ten. Bengt was coming down to be relieved at the swaying masthead. Then we all started. We had heard voices clearly, out on the sea in the darkness. There it was again. It was Polynesians talking. We shouted into the black night with all the strength of our lungs. They shouted back, and—there was Knut's voice among the rest! We were mad with excitement. Our tiredness had gone; the whole thundercloud had lifted. What did it matter if we drifted away from Angatau? There were other islands in the sea. Now the nine balsa logs, so fond of travel, could drift where they liked, so long as all six of us were assembled on board again.

Three outrigger canoes emerged from the darkness, riding over the swell, and Knut was the first man to jump across to the dear old *Kon-Tiki*, followed by six brown men. There was little time for explanations; the natives must have presents and be off on their adventurous journey back to the island. Without seeing light or land, and with hardly any stars, they had to find their course by paddling against wind and sea till they saw the light from the fire. We rewarded them amply with provisions, cigarettes, and other gifts, and each of them shook us heartily by the hand in a last farewell.

They were clearly anxious on our account; they pointed westward, indicating that we were heading toward dangerous reefs. The leader had tears in his eyes and kissed me tenderly on the chin, which made me thank Providence for my beard. Then they crept into the canoes, and we six comrades were left on the raft, together and alone.

We left the raft to her own devices and listened to Knut's story.

Knut had in good faith made for land in the dinghy with the native leader on board. The native himself was sitting at the little oars and rowing toward the opening in the reef, when Knut to his surprise saw the light signals from the *Kon-Tiki* asking him to come back. He made signs to the rower to turn, but the native refused to obey. Then Knut took hold of the oars himself, but the native tore his hands away, and with the reef thundering around them it was no use starting a fight. They had bounded right in through the opening in the reef and gone on inside it, until they were lifted right up on to a solid coral block on the island itself. A crowd of natives caught hold of the dinghy and dragged it high up on the shore, and Knut stood alone under the palm trees surrounded by a huge crowd of natives chattering away in an unknown lingo. Brown, barelegged men, women, and children of all ages flocked round him and felt the material of his shirt and trousers. They themselves wore ragged old European clothes, but there were no white men on the island.

Knut got hold of some of the smartest fellows and made signs to them that they should go out in the dinghy with him. Then a big fat man came waddling up who Knut presumed must be the chief, for he had an old uniform cap on his head and talked in a loud, authoritative voice. All made way for him. Knut explained both in Norwegian and in English that he needed men and must get back to the raft before we others drifted away. The chief beamed and understood nothing, and Knut, despite his most vehement protests, was pushed over to the village by the whole shouting crowd. There he was received by dogs and pigs and pretty South Sea girls who came along carrying fresh fruit. It was clear that the natives were prepared to make Knut's stay as agreeable as possible, but Knut was not to be enticed; he thought sadly of the raft which was vanishing westward. The natives' intention was obvious. They badly wanted our company, and they knew that there were a lot of good things on board white men's ships. If they could keep Knut ashore, the rest of us and the queer boat would certainly come in also. No vessel would leave a white man behind on such an out-of-the-way island as Angatau.

After more curious experiences Knut got away and hurried down to the dinghy, surrounded by admirers of both sexes. His international speech and gesticulations could no longer be misunderstood; they realized that he must and would return to the odd craft out in the night, which was in such a hurry that she had to go on at once.

Then the natives tried a trick; they indicated by signs that the rest of us were coming ashore on the other side of the point. Knut was puzzled for a few minutes, but then loud voices were heard down on the beach, where women and children were tending the flickering fire. The three canoes had come back, and the men brought Knut the note. He was in a desperate situation. Here were instructions not to row out on the sea alone, and all the natives absolutely refused to go with him.

There followed a high-pitched, noisy argument among all the natives. Those who had been out and seen the raft understood perfectly well that it was of little use to keep Knut back in the hope of getting the rest of us ashore. The end of it was that Knut's promises and threats in international accents induced the crews of three canoes to accompany him out to sea in pursuit of the *Kon-Tiki*. They put out to sea in the tropical night with the dinghy dancing along in tow, while the natives stood motionless by the dying fire and watched their new blond friend disappear as quickly as he had come.

Knut and his companions could see the faint light signals from the raft far out to sea when the swell lifted the canoes. The long, slim Polynesian canoes, stiffened by pointed side floats, cut through the water like knives, but it seemed an eternity to Knut before he felt the thick round logs of the *Kon-Tiki* under his feet again.

"Have a good time ashore?" Torstein asked enviously.

"Oho, you just should have seen the hula girls!" Knut teased him.

We left the sail down and the oar inboard, and all six of us crept into the bamboo cabin and slept like boulders on the beach at Angatau.

For three days we drifted across the sea without a sight of land.

We were drifting straight toward the ominous Takume and Raroia reefs, which together blocked up forty to fifty miles of the sea ahead of us. We made desperate efforts to steer clear, to the north of these dangerous reefs, and things seemed to be going well till one night the watch came hurrying in and called us all out.

The wind had changed. We were heading straight for the Takume reef. It had begun to rain, and there was no visibility at all. The reef could not be far off.

In the middle of night we held a council of war. It was a question of saving our lives now. To get past on the north side was now hopeless; we must try to get through on the south side instead. We trimmed the sail, laid the oar over, and began a dangerous piece of sailing with the uncertain north wind behind us. If the east wind came back before we had passed the whole façade of the fifty-mile-long reefs, we should be hurled in among the breakers, at their mercy.

We agreed on all that should be done if shipwreck was imminent. We would stay on board the *Kon-Tiki* at all costs. We would not climb up the mast, from which we should be shaken down like rotten fruit, but would cling tight to the stays of the mast when the seas poured over us. We laid the rubber raft loose on the deck and made fast to it a small watertight radio transmitter, a small quantity of provisions, waterbottles, and medical stores. This would be washed ashore independently of us if we ourselves should get over the reef safe but empty-handed. In the stern of the Kon-Tiki we made fast a long rope with a float which also would be washed ashore, so that we could try to pull in the raft if she were stranded out on the reef. And so we crept into bed and left the watch to the helmsman out in the rain.

As long as the north wind held, we glided slowly but surely down along the façade of the coral reefs which lay in ambush below the horizon. But then one afternoon the wind died away, and when it returned it had gone round into the east. According to Erik's position we were already so far down that we now had some hope of steering clear of the southernmost point of the Raroia reef. We would try to get round it and into shelter before going on to other reefs beyond it.

When night came, we had been a hundred days at sea.

Late in the night I woke, feeling restless and uneasy. There was something unusual in the movement of the waves. The *Kon-Tiki's* motion was a little different from what it usually was in such conditions. We had become sensitive to changes in the rhythm of the logs. I thought at once of suction from a coast, which was drawing near, and was continually out on deck and up the mast. Nothing but sea was visible. But I could get no quiet sleep. Time passed.

At dawn, just before six, Torstein came hurrying down from the masthead. He could see a whole line of small palm-clad islands far ahead. Before doing anything else we laid the oar over to southward as far as we could. What Torstein had seen must be the small coral islands which lay strewn like pearls on a string behind the Raroia reef. A northward current must have caught us.

At half-past seven palm-clad islets had appeared in a row all along the horizon to westward. The southernmost lay roughly ahead of our bow, and thence there were islands and clumps of palms all along the horizon on our starboard side till they disappeared as dots away to northward. The nearest were four or five sea miles away.

A survey from the masthead showed that, even if our bow pointed toward the bottom island in the chain, our drift sideways was so great that we were not advancing in the direction in which our bow pointed. We were drifting diagonally right in toward the reef. With fixed centerboards we should still have had some hope of steering clear. But sharks were following close astern, so that it was impossible to dive under the raft and tighten up the loose center-boards with fresh guy ropes.

We saw that we had now only a few hours more on board the *Kon-Tiki*. They must be used in preparation for our inevitable wreck on the coral reef. Every man learned what he had to do when the moment came; each one of us knew where his own limited sphere of responsibility lay, so that we should not fly round treading on one another's toes when the time came and seconds counted. The *Kon-Tiki* pitched up and down, up and down, as the wind forced us in. There was no doubt that here was the turmoil of waves created by the reef—some waves advancing while others were hurled back after beating vainly against the surrounding wall.

We were still under full sail in the hope of even now being able to steer clear. As we gradually drifted nearer, half sideways, we saw from the mast how the whole string of palm-clad isles was connected with a coral reef, part above and part under water, which lay like a mole where the sea was white with foam and leaped high into the air. The Raroia atoll is oval in shape and has a diameter of twenty-five miles, not counting the adjoining reefs of Takume. The whole of its longer side faces the sea to eastward, where we came pitching in. The reef itself, which runs in one line from horizon to horizon, is only a few hundred yards clear, and behind it idyllic islets lie in a string round the still lagoon inside.

It was with mixed feelings that we saw the blue Pacific being ruthlessly torn up and hurled into the air all along the horizon ahead of us. I knew what awaited us; I had visited the Tuamotu group before and had stood safe on land looking out over the immense spectacle in the east, where the surf from the open Pacific broke in over the reef. New reefs and islands kept on gradually appearing to southward. We must be lying off the middle of the façade of the coral wall.

On board the *Kon-Tiki* all preparations for the end of the voyage were being made. Everything of value was carried into the cabin and lashed fast. Documents and papers were packed into water-tight bags, along with films and other things which would not stand a dip in the sea. The whole bamboo cabin was covered with canvas, and especially strong ropes were lashed across it. When we saw that all hope was gone, we opened up the bamboo deck and cut off with machete knives all the ropes which held the centerboards down. It was a hard job to get the centerboards drawn up, because they were all thickly covered with stout barnacles. With the centerboards up the draught of our vessel was no deeper than to the bottom of the timber logs, and we would therefore be more easily washed in over the reef. With no centerboards and with the sail down, the raft lay completely sideways on and was entirely at the mercy of wind and sea.

We tied the longest rope we had to the homemade anchor and made it fast to the step of the port mast, so that the *Kon-Tiki* would go into the surf stern first when the anchor was thrown overboard. The anchor itself consisted of empty water cans filled with used radio batteries and heavy scrap, and solid mangrove-wood sticks projected from it, set crosswise.

Order number one, which came first and last, was: Hold on to the raft! Whatever happened, we must hang on tight on board and let the nine great logs take the pressure from the reef. We ourselves had more than enough to do to withstand the weight of the water. If we jumped overboard, we should become helpless victims of the suction which would fling us in and out over the sharp corals. The rubber raft would capsize in the steep seas or, heavily loaded with us in it, it would be torn to ribbons against the reef. But the wooden logs would sooner or later be cast ashore, and we with them, if we only managed to hold fast.

Next, all hands were told to put on their shoes for the first time in a hundred days and to have their life belts ready. The last precaution, however, was not of much value, for if a man fell overboard he would be battered to death, not drowned. We had time, too, to put our passports and such few dollars as we had left into our pockets. But it was not lack of time that was troubling us.

Those were anxious hours in which we lay drifting helplessly sideways, step after step, in toward the reef. It was noticeably quiet on board; we all crept in and out from cabin to bamboo deck, silent or laconic, and carried on with our jobs. Our serious faces showed that no one was in doubt as to what awaited us, and the absence of nervousness showed that we had all gradually acquired an unshakable confidence in the raft. If it had brought us across the sea, it would also manage to bring us ashore alive.

Inside the cabin there was a complete chaos of provision cartons and cargo, lashed fast. Torstein had barely found room for himself in the radio corner, where he had got the shortwave transmitter working. We were now over 4,000 sea miles from our old base at

Callao, where the Peruvian Naval War School had maintained regular contact with us, and still farther from Hal and Frank and the other radio amateurs in the United States. But, as chance willed, we had on the previous day got in touch with a capable radio "ham" who had a set on Rarotonga in the Cook Islands, and the operators, quite contrary to all our usual practice, had arranged for an extra contact with him early in the morning. All the time we were drifting closer and closer in to the reef, Torstein was sitting tapping his key and calling Rarotonga.

Entries in the *Kon-Tiki's* log ran:

—*8:15: We are slowly approaching land. We can now make out with the naked eye the separate palm trees inside on the starboard side.*

—*8:45: The wind has veered into a still more unfavorable quarter for us, so we have no hope of getting clear. No nervousness on board, but hectic preparations on deck. There is something lying on the reef ahead of us which looks like the wreck of a sailing vessel, but it may be only a heap of driftwood.*

—*9:45: The wind is taking us straight toward the last island but one we see behind the reef. We can now see the whole coral reef clearly; here it is built up like a white and red speckled wall which barely sticks up out of the water as a belt in front of all the islands. All along the reef white foaming surf is flung up toward the sky. Bengt is just serving up a good hot meal, the last before the great action!*

It is a wreck lying in there on the reef. We are so close now that we can see right across the shining lagoon behind the reef and see the outlines of other islands on the other side of the lagoon.

As this was written, the dull drone of the surf came near again; it came from the whole reef and filled the air like thrilling rolls of the drum, heralding the exciting last act of the *Kon-Tiki*.

—*9:50: Very close now. Drifting along the reef. Only a hundred yards or so away. Torstein is talking to the man on Rarotonga. All clear. Must pack up log now. All in good spirits; it looks bad, but we shall make it!*

A few minutes later the anchor rushed overboard and caught hold of the bottom, so that the *Kon-Tiki* swung around and turned her stern inward toward the breakers. It held us for a few valuable minutes, while Torstein sat hammering like mad on the key. He had got Rarotonga now. The breakers thundered in the air and the sea rose and fell furiously. All hands were at work on deck, and now Torstein got his message through. He said we were drifting toward the Raroia reef. He asked Rarotonga to listen in on the same wave length every hour. If we were silent for more than thirty-six hours, Rarotonga must let the Norwegian Embassy in Washington know. Torstein's lasts words were:

"O.K. Fifty yards left. Here we go. Good-by."

Then he closed down the station, Knut sealed up the papers, and both crawled out on deck as fast as they could to join the rest of us, for it was clear now that the anchor was giving way.

The swell grew heavier and heavier, with deep troughs between the waves, and we felt the raft being swung up and down, up and down, higher and higher.

Again the order was shouted: "Hold on, never mind about the cargo, hold on!"

We were now so near the waterfall inside that we no longer heard the steady continuous roar from all along the reef. We now heard only a separate boom each time the nearest breaker crashed down on the rocks.

All hands stood in readiness, each clinging fast to the rope he thought the most secure. Only Erik crept into the cabin at the last moment; there was one part of the program he had not yet carried out—he had not found his shoes!

No one stood aft, for it was there the shock from the reef would come. Nor were the two firm stays which ran from the masthead down to the stern safe. For if the mast fell they would be left hanging overboard, over the reef. Herman, Bengt, and Torstein had climbed up on some boxes which were lashed fast forward of the cabin wall, and, while Herman clung on to the guy ropes from the ridge of the roof, the other two held on to the ropes from the masthead by which the sail at other times was hauled up. Knut and I chose the stay running from the bow up to the masthead, for, if mast and cabin and everything else went overboard, we thought the rope from the bow would nevertheless remain lying inboard, as we were now head on to the seas.

When we realized that the seas had got hold of us, the anchor rope was cut and we were off. A sea rose straight up under us, and we felt the *Kon-Tiki* being lifted up in the air. The great moment had come; we were riding on the wave back at breathless speed, our ramshackle craft creaking and groaning as she quivered under us. The excitement made one's blood boil. I remember that, having no other inspiration, I waved my arm and bellowed "Hurrah!" at the top of my lungs; it afforded a certain relief and could do no harm anyway. The others certainly thought I had gone mad, but they all beamed and grinned enthusiastically. On we ran with seas rushing in behind us; this was the *Kon-Tiki's* baptism of fire. All must and would go well.

But our elation was soon dampened. A new sea rose high up astern of us like a glittering, green glass wall. As we sank down it came rolling after us, and, in the same second in which I saw it high above me, I felt a violent blow and was submerged under floods of water. I felt the suction through my whole body, with such great power that I had to strain every single muscle in my frame and think of one thing only—hold on, hold on! I think that in such a desperate situation the arms will be torn off before the brain consents to let go, evident as the outcome is. Then I felt that the mountain of water was passing on and relaxing its devilish grip of my body. When the whole mountain had rushed on, with an ear-splitting roaring and crashing, I saw Knut again hanging on beside me, doubled up into a ball. Seen from behind, the great sea was almost flat and gray. As it rushed on, it swept over the ridge of the cabin roof which projected from the water, and there hung the three others, pressed against the cabin roof as the water passed over them.

We were still afloat.

In an instant I renewed my hold, with arms and legs bent round the strong rope. Knut let himself down and with a tiger's leap joined the others on the boxes, where the cabin took the strain. I heard reassuring exclamations from them, but at the same time I saw a new green wall rise up and come towering toward us. I shouted a warning and made myself as small and hard as I could where I hung. In an instant hell was over us again, and the *Kon-Tiki* disappeared completely under the masses of water. The sea tugged and pulled with all the force it could bring to bear at the poor little bundles of human bodies. The second sea rushed over us, to be followed by a third like it.

Then I heard a triumphant shout from Knut, who was now hanging on to the rope ladder:

"Look at the raft—she's holding!"

After three seas only the double mast and the cabin had been knocked a bit crooked. Again we had a feeling of triumph over the elements, and the elation of victory gave us new strength.

Then I saw the next sea come towering up, higher than all the rest, and again I bellowed a warning aft to the others as I climbed up the stay, as high as I could get in a hurry, and hung on fast. Then I myself disappeared sideways into the midst of the green wall which towered high over us. The others, who were farther aft and saw me disappear first, estimated the height of the wall of water at twenty-five feet, while the foaming crest passed by fifteen feet above the part of the glassy wall into which I had vanished. Then the great wave reached them, and we had all one single thought—hold on, hold on, hold, hold, hold!

We must have hit the reef that time. I myself felt only the strain on the stay, which seemed to bend and slacken jerkily. But whether the bumps came from above or below I could not tell, hanging there. The whole submersion lasted only seconds, but it demanded more endurance than we usually have in our bodies. There is greater strength in the human mechanism than that of the muscles alone. I determined that, if I was to die, I would die in this position, like a knot on the stay. The sea thundered on, over and past, and as it roared by it revealed a hideous sight. The *Kon-Tiki* was wholly changed, as by the stroke of a magic wand. The vessel we knew from weeks and months at sea was no more; in a few seconds our pleasant world had become a shattered wreck.

I saw only one man on board besides myself. He lay pressed flat across the ridge of the cabin roof, face downward with his arms stretched out on both sides, while the cabin itself was crushed in, like a house of cards, toward the stern and toward the starboard side. The motionless figure was Herman. There was no other sign of life, while the hill of water thundered by, in across the reef. The hardwood mast on the starboard side was broken like a match, and the upper stump, in its fall, had smashed right through the cabin roof, so that the mast and all its gear slanted at a low angle over the reef on the starboard side. Astern, the steering block was twisted round lengthways and the crossbeam broken, while the steering oar was smashed to splinters. The splashboards at the bow were broken like cigar boxes, and the whole deck was torn up and pasted like wet paper against the forward wall of the cabin, along with boxes, cans, canvas, and other cargo. Bamboo sticks and rope ends stuck up everywhere, and the general effect was of complete chaos.

I felt cold fear run through my whole body. What was the good of my holding on? If I lost one single man here, in the run in, the whole thing would be ruined, and for the moment there was only one human figure to be seen after the last buffet. In that second Torstein's hunched-up form appeared outside the raft. He was hanging like a monkey in the ropes from the masthead and managed to get on to the logs again, where he crawled up on to the debris forward of the cabin. Herman, too, now turned his head and gave me a forced grin of encouragement, but did not move. I bellowed in the faint hope of locating the others and heard Bengt's calm voice call out that all hands were aboard. They were lying holding on to the ropes behind the tangled barricade which the tough plaiting from the bamboo deck had built up.

All this happened in the course of a few seconds, while the *Kon-Tiki* was being drawn out of the witches' caldron by the backwash, and a fresh sea came rolling over her. For the last time I bellowed "Hang on!" at the top of my lungs amid the uproar, and that was all I myself did; I hung on and disappeared in the masses of water which rushed over and past in those endless two or three seconds. That was enough for me. I saw the ends of the logs knocking and bumping against a sharp step in the coral reef without going over it. Then we were sucked out again. I also saw the two men who lay stretched out across the ridge of the cabin roof, but none of us smiled any longer. Behind the chaos of bamboo I heard a calm voice call out:
"This won't do."

I myself felt equally discouraged. As the masthead sank farther and farther out over the starboard side, I found myself hanging on to a slack line outside the raft. The next sea came. When it had gone by I was dead tired, and my only thought was to get up on to the logs and lie behind the barricade. When the backwash retreated, I saw for the first time the rugged red reef naked beneath us and perceived Torstein standing, bent double, on gleaming red corals, holding on to a bunch of rope ends from the mast. Knut, standing aft, was about to jump. I shouted that we must all keep on the logs, and Torstein, who had been washed overboard by the pressure of water, sprang up again like a cat.

Two or three more seas rolled over us with diminishing force, and what happened then I do not remember, except that water foamed in and out and I myself sank lower and lower toward the red reef over which we were being lifted in. Then only crests of foam full of salt spray came whirling in, and I was able to work my way in on to the raft, where we all made for the after end of the logs which was highest up on the reef.

At the same moment Knut crouched down and sprang up on to the reef with the line which lay clear astern. While the backwash was running out, he waded through the whirling water some thirty yards in and stood safely at the end of the line when the next sea foamed in toward him, died down, and ran back from the flat reef like a board stream.

Then Erik came crawling out of the collapsed cabin, with his shoes on. If we had all done as he did, we should have got off cheaply. As the cabin had not been washed overboard but had been pressed down pretty flat under the canvas, Erik lay quietly stretched out among the cargo and heard the peals of thunder crashing above him while the collapsed bamboo walls curved downward. Bengt had had a slight concussion when the mast fell but managed to crawl under the wrecked cabin alongside Erik. We should all of us have been lying there if we had realized in advance how firmly the countless lashings and plaited bamboo sheets would hang on to the main logs under the pressure of the water.

Erik was now standing ready on the logs aft, and when the sea retired he, too, jumped up on to the reef. It was Herman's turn next, and then Bengt's. Each time the raft was pushed a bit farther in, and, when Torstein's turn and my own came, the raft already lay so far in on the reef that there was no longer any ground for abandoning her. All hands began the work of salvage.

We were now twenty yards away from that devilish step up on the reef, and it was there and beyond it that the breakers came rolling after one another in long lines. The coral polyps had taken care to build the atoll so high that only the very tops of the breakers were able to send a fresh stream of sea water past us and into the lagoon, which abounded in fish. Here inside was the corals' own world, and they disported themselves in the strangest shapes and colors.

A long way in on the reef the others found the rubber raft, lying drifting and quite waterlogged. They emptied it and dragged it back to the wreck, and we loaded it to the full with the most important equipment, like the radio set, provisions, and water bottles. We dragged all this in across the reef and piled it up on the top of a huge block of coral, which lay alone on the inside of the reef like a large meteorite. Then we went back to the wreck for fresh loads. We could never know what the sea would be up to when the tidal currents got to work around us.

In the shallow water inside the reef we saw something bright shining in the sun. When we waded over to pick it up, to our astonishment we saw two empty tins. This was not exactly what we had expected to find there, and we were still more surprised when we saw that the little boxes were quite bright and newly opened and stamped "Pineapple," with the same inscription as that on the new field rations we ourselves were testing for the quartermaster. They were indeed two of our own pineapple tins which we had thrown overboard after our last meal on board the *Kon-Tiki*. We had followed close behind them up on the reef.

We were standing on sharp, rugged coral blocks, and on the uneven bottom we waded now ankle-deep, now chest-deep, according to the channels and stream beds in the reef. Anemones and corals gave the whole reef the appearance of a rock garden covered with mosses and cactus and fossilized plants, red and green and yellow and white. There was no color that was not represented, either in corals or algae or in shells and sea slugs and fantastic fish, which were wriggling about everywhere. In the deeper channels small sharks about four feet long came sneaking up to us in the crystal-clear water. But we had only to smack the water with the palms of our hands for them to turn about and keep at a distance.

Where we had stranded, we had only pools of water and wet patches of coral about us; farther in lay the calm blue lagoon. The tide was going out, and we continually saw more corals sticking up out of the water round us, while the surf which thundered without interruption along the reef sank down, as it were, a floor lower. What would happen there on the narrow reef when the tide began to flow again was uncertain. We must get away.

The reef stretched like a half-submerged fortress wall up to the north and down to the south. In the extreme south was a long island densely covered with tall palm forest. And just above us to the north, only 600 or 700 yards away, lay another but considerably smaller palm island. It lay inside the reef, with palm tops rising into the sky and snow-white sandy beaches running out into the still lagoon. The whole island looked like a bulging green basket of flowers, or a little bit of concentrated paradise.

This island we chose.

Herman stood beside me beaming all over his bearded face. He did not say a word, only stretched out his hand and laughed quietly. The *Kon-Tiki* still lay far out on the reef with the spray flying over her. She was a wreck, but an honorable wreck. Everything above deck was smashed up, but the nine balsa logs from the Quevedo forest in Ecuador were as intact as ever. They had saved our lives. The sea had claimed but little of the cargo, and none of what we had stowed inside the cabin. We ourselves had stripped the raft of everything of real value, which now lay in safety on the top of the great sunsmitten rock inside the reef.

Since I had jumped off the raft, I had genuinely missed the sight of all the pilot fish wriggling in front of our bow. Now the great balsa logs lay up on the reef in six inches of water, and brown sea slugs lay writhing under the bows. The pilot fish were gone. The dolphins were gone. Only unknown flat fish with peacock patterns and blunt tails wriggled inquisitively in and out between the logs. We had arrived in a new world. Johannes had left his hole. He had doubtless found another lurking place here.

I took a last look round on board the wreck and caught sight of a little baby palm in a flattened basket. It projected from an eye in a coconut to a length of eighteen inches, and two roots stuck out below. I waded in toward the island with the nut in my hand. A little way ahead I saw Knut wading happily landward with a model of the raft, which he had made with much labor on the voyage, under his arm. We soon passed Bengt. He was a splendid steward. With a lump on his forehead and sea water dripping from his beard, he was walking bent double pushing a box, which danced along before him every time the breakers outside sent a stream over into the lagoon. He lifted the lid proudly. It was the kitchen box, and in it were the primus and cooking utensils in good order.

I shall never forget that wade across the reef toward the heavenly palm island that grew larger as it came to meet us. When I reached the sunny sand beach, I slipped off my shoes and thrust my bare toes down into the warm, bone-dry sand. It was as though I enjoyed the sight of every footprint which dug itself into the virgin sand beach that led up to the palm trunks. Soon the palm tops closed over my head, and I went on, right in toward the center of the tiny island. Green coconuts hung under the palm tufts, and some luxuriant bushes were thickly covered with snow-white blossoms, which smelled so sweet and seductive that I felt quite faint. In the interior of the island two quite tame terns flew about my shoulders. They were as white and light as wisps of cloud. Small lizards shot away from my feet, and the most important inhabitants of the island were large blood-red hermit crabs which lumbered along in every direction with stolen snail shells as large as eggs adhering to their soft hinder parts.

I was completely overwhelmed. I sank down on my knees and thrust my fingers deep down into the dry warm sand.

The voyage was over. We were all alive. We had run ashore on a small uninhabited South Sea island. And what an island! Torstein came in, flung away a sack, threw himself flat on his back and looked up at the palm tops and the white birds, light as down, which circled noiselessly just above us. Soon we were all six lying there. Herman, always energetic, climbed up a small palm and pulled down a cluster of large green coconuts. We cut off their soft tops with our machete knives, as if they were eggs, and poured down our throats the most delicious refreshing drink in the world—sweet, cold milk from young and seedless palm fruit. On the reef outside resounded the monotonous drum beats from the guard at the gates of paradise.

"Purgatory was a bit damp," said Bengt, "but heaven is more or less as I'd imagined it."

We stretched ourselves luxuriously on the ground and smiled up at the white trade-wind clouds drifting by westward up above the palm tops. Now we were no longer following them helplessly; now we lay on a fixed, motionless island, in Polynesia.

And as we lay and stretched ourselves, the breakers outside us rumbled like a train, to and fro, to and fro, all along the horizon.

Bengt was right; this was heaven.

8.

Among
Polynesians

OUR LITTLE ISLAND WAS UNINHABITED. WE SOON GOT TO
know every palm clump and every beach, for the island was barely
two hundred yards across. The highest point was less than six feet
above the lagoon.

Over our heads, in the palm tops, there hung great clusters of
green coconut husks, which insulated their contents of cold coconut
milk from the tropical sun, so we should not be thirsty in the first
weeks. There were also ripe coconuts, a swarm of hermit crabs, and
all sorts of fish in the lagoon; we should be well off.

On the north side of the island we found the remnants of an old,
unpainted wooden cross, half buried in the coral sand. Here there
was the view northward along the reef to the stripped wreck, which
we had first seen closer in as we drifted by on the way to our strand-
ing. Still farther northward we saw in a bluish haze the palm tufts
of another small island. The island to southward, on which the trees
grew thickly, was much closer. We saw no sign of life there, either,
but for the time we had other matters to think about.

Robinson Crusoe Hesselberg came limping up in his big straw hat
with his arms full of crawling hermit crabs. Knut set fire to some dry
wood, and soon we had crab and coconut milk with coffee for des-
sert.

"Feels all right being ashore, doesn't it, boys?" Knut asked delightedly.

He had himself enjoyed this feeling once before on the voyage,
at Angatau. As he spoke, he stumbled and poured half a kettle of
boiling water over Bengt's bare feet. We were all of us a bit unsteady
the first day ashore, after 101 days on board the raft, and would sud-

denly begin reeling about among the palm trunks because we had put out a foot to counter a sea that did not come.

When Bengt handed over to us our respective mess utensils, Erik grinned broadly. I remember that, after the last meal on board, I had leaned over the side of the raft and washed up as usual, while Erik looked in across the reef, saying: "I don't think I shall bother to wash up today." When he found his things in the kitchen box, they were as clean as mine.

After the meal and a good stretch on the ground we set about putting together the soaked radio apparatus; we must do it quickly so that Torstein and Knut might get on the air before the man on Rarotonga sent out a report of our sad end.

Most of the radio equipment had already been brought ashore, and among the things which lay drifting on the reef Bengt found a box, on which he laid hands. He jumped high into the air from an electric shock; there was no doubt that the contents belonged to the radio section. While the operators unscrewed, coupled, and put together, we others set about pitching camp.

Out on the wreck we found the heavy waterlogged sail and dragged it ashore. We stretched it between two big palms in a little opening, looking on to the lagoon, and supported two other corners with bamboo sticks which came drifting in from the wreck. A thick hedge of wild flowering bushes forced the sail together so that we had a roof and three walls and, moreover, a clear view of the shining lagoon, while our nostrils were filled with an insinuating scent of blossoms. It was good to be here. We all laughed quietly and enjoyed our ease; we each made our beds of fresh palm leaves, pulling up loose branches of coral which stuck up inconveniently out of the sand. Before night fell we had a very pleasant rest, and over our heads we saw the big bearded face of good old Kon-Tiki. No longer did he swell out his breast with the east wind behind him. He now lay motionless on his back looking up at the stars which came twinkling out over Polynesia.

On the bushes round us hung wet flags and sleeping bags, and soaked articles lay on the sand to dry. Another day on this island of sunshine and everything would be nicely dry. Even the radio boys had to give it up until the sun had a chance of drying the inside of their apparatus next day. We took the sleeping bags down from the trees and turned in, disputing boastfully as to who had the driest

Above: An uninhabited South Sea island, protected by the coral reef, was our first home across the ocean. It was a curious experience to feel solid ground under our feet again after 101 days at sea.

Below: We were able to save most of our equipment and carried it to the island in our rubber boat, which we had found a long way in on the reef. We waded across to the island seen in the background, but that too was uninhabited.

A coconut from Peru was planted on the island where we had been shipwrecked. The coconut palm grew on the coast of tropical America and in the South Sea islands before Columbus' time. As the nuts will not withstand sea water for any length of time, they must have been spread with man's assistance.

Big fresh green coconuts hung from the trees in clusters. With coconuts, hermit crabs, and fish we were not short of food.

"All well, all well"—
Raaby and Haugland
sent out this message
hour after hour to prevent
relief expeditions from
coming to search for us.
"If all's well, why worry?" asked an American
radio "ham" who picked
up the message. In the
foreground Hesselberg is
shown turning the hand
generator.

Polynesians arrive. After
a week on our desert island an outrigger canoe
appeared. The natives on
board lived in a village
on the other side of the
lagoon; they had found
wreckage and seen a light
from our island.

At left: "Ke-ke-te-huru-huru (Heave ho)!" shouted the natives as they dragged the raft to land. After several days she had finally been washed over the reef.

Below: Kon-Tiki in the Raroia lagoon. It may be safely assumed that no other vessel will repeat our raft's exploit in clearing the breakers and then sailing as trimly over land as over water.

At top: The raft arrives at Tahiti in tow of the government schooner "Tamara."
Below, left: Tiki was the name of the first great chief on Tahiti. He was
regarded by the inhabitants as their divine ancestor, and stone statues of
South American type were erected in his honor on many of the islands.
Below, right: Teriieroo a Teriierooiterai is the name of the last chief on Tahiti.
He was on the quay to meet us when we arrived. Ten years before he had
adopted the author as his son and had given him the name Terai Mateata
(Blue Sky).

Above: The country which Tiki found. Low coral islands, like those of the Tuamotu group, and lofty mountainous islands like Tahiti and Moorea were found by Kon-Tiki, Son of the Sun, when he came from Peru with the first men on balsa rafts.

At left: Hula dance on Tahiti. Purea was related to the last queen of the island. After Tiki another Indian race came to these islands in big double canoes from British Columbia via Hawaii. The Polynesian race is a mixture of these two immigrant peoples.

A Tahitian belle. When we came to the native village on Raroia, the natives started festivities that lasted the fourteen days we spent on the island. Our stay on Tahiti was of the same nature, but lasted longer.

At the White House. After our return to Washington, President Truman
received the members of the expedition. The American flag that had accom-
panied us across the Pacific was presented to him. From left: (half hidden)
Knut Haugland, the author, Herman Watzinger, President Truman, Mr.
Lykke (counselor to the Embassy), Erik Hesselberg, and Torstein Raaby.
Bengt Danielsson had remained on the west coast.

bag. Bengt won, for his did not squelch when he turned over. Heavens, how good it was to be able to sleep!

When we woke next morning at sunrise, the sail was bent down and full of rain water as pure as crystal. Bengt took charge of this asset and then ambled down to the lagoon and jerked ashore some curious breakfast fish which he decoyed into channels in the sand.

That night Herman had had pains in the neck and back where he had injured himself before the start from Lima, and Erik had a return of his vanished lumbago. Otherwise we had come out of the trip over the reef astonishingly lightly, with scratches and small wounds, except for Bengt who had had a blow on the forehead when the mast fell and had a slight concussion. I myself looked most peculiar, with my arms and legs bruised blue black all over by the pressure against the rope.

But none of us was in such a bad state that the sparkling clear lagoon did not entice him to a brisk swim before breakfast. It was an immense lagoon. Far out it was blue and rippled by the trade wind, and it was so wide that we could only just see the tops of a row of misty, blue palm islands which marked the curve of the atoll on the other side. But here, in the lee of the islands, the trade wind rustled peacefully in the fringed palm tops, making them stir and sway, while the lagoon lay like a motionless mirror below and reflected all their beauty. The bitter salt water was so pure and clear that gaily colored corals in nine feet of water seemed so near the surface that we thought we should cut our toes on them in swimming. And the water abounded in beautiful varieties of colorful fish. It was a marvelous world in which to disport oneself. The water was just cold enough to be refreshing, and the air was pleasantly warm and dry from the sun. But we must get ashore again quickly today; Rarotonga would broadcast alarming news if nothing had been heard from the raft at the end of the day.

Coils and radio parts lay drying in the tropical sun on slabs of coral, and Torstein and Knut coupled and screwed. The whole day passed, and the atmosphere grew more and more hectic. The rest of us abandoned all other jobs and crowded round the radio in the hope of being able to give assistance. We must be on the air before 10 P.M. Then the thirty-six hours' time limit would be up, and the radio amateur on Rarotonga would send out appeals for airplane and relief expeditions.

Noon came, afternoon came, and the sun set. If only the man on

Rarotonga would contain himself! Seven o'clock, eight, nine. The tension was at breaking point. Not a sign of life in the transmitter, but the receiver, an NC–173, began to liven up somewhere at the bottom of the scale and we heard faint music. But not on the amateur wave length. It was eating its way up, however; perhaps it was a wet coil which was drying inward from one end. The transmitter was still stone-dead—short circuits and sparks everywhere.

There was less than an hour left. This would never do. The regular transmitter was given up, and a little sabotage transmitter from wartime was tried again. We had tested it several times before in the course of the day, but without result. Now perhaps it had become a little drier. All the batteries were completely ruined, and we got power by cranking a tiny hand generator. It was heavy, and we four who were laymen in radio matters took turns all day long sitting and turning the infernal thing.

The thirty-six hours would soon be up. I remember someone whispering "Seven minutes more," "Five minutes more," and then no one would look at his watch again. The transmitter was dumb as ever, but the receiver was sputtering upward toward the right wave length. Suddenly it crackled on the Rarotonga man's frequency, and we gathered that he was in full contact with the telegraph station in Tahiti. Soon afterward we picked up the following fragment of a message sent out from Rarotonga:

". . . no plane this side of Samoa. I am quite sure. . . ."

Then it died away again. The tension was unbearable. What was brewing out there? Had they already begun to send out plane and rescue expeditions? Now, no doubt, messages concerning us were going over the air in every direction.

The two operators worked feverishly. The sweat trickled from their faces as freely as it did from ours who sat turning the handle. Power began slowly to come into the transmitter's aerial, and Torstein pointed ecstatically to an arrow which swung slowly up over a scale when he held the Morse key down. Now it was coming!

We turned the handle madly while Torstein called Rarotonga. No one heard us. Once more. Now the receiver was working again, but Rarotonga did not hear us. We called Hal and Frank at Los angeles and the Naval School at Lima, but no one heard us.

Then Torstein sent out a CQ message: that is to say, he called all the stations in the world which could hear us on our special amateur wave length.

That was of some use. Now a faint voice out in the ether began to call us slowly. We called again and said that we heard him. Then the slow voice out in the ether said:

"My name is Paul—I live in Colorado. What is your name and where do you live?"

This was a radio amateur. Torstein seized the key, while we turned the handle, and replied:

"This is the *Kon-Tiki*. We are stranded on a desert island in the Pacific."

Paul did not believe the message. He thought it was a radio amateur in the next street pulling his leg, and he did not come on the air again. We tore our hair in desperation. Here were we, sitting under the palm tops on a starry night on a desert island, and no one even believed what we said.

Torstein did not give up; he was at the key again sending "All well, all well, all well" unceasingly. We must at all costs stop all this rescue machinery from starting out across the Pacific.

Then we heard, rather faintly, in the receiver:

"If all's well, why worry?"

Then all was quiet in the ether. That was all.

We could have leaped into the air and shaken down all the coconuts for sheer desperation, and heaven knows what we should have done if both Rarotonga and good old Hal had not suddenly heard us. Hal wept for delight, he said, at hearing LI 2 B again. All the tension stopped immediately; we were once more alone and undisturbed on our South Sea island and turned in, worn out, on our beds of palm leaves.

Nest day we took it easy and enjoyed life to the full. Some bathed, others fished or went out exploring on the reef in search of curious marine creatures, while the most energetic cleared up in camp and made our surroundings pleasant. Out on the point which looked toward the *Kon-Tiki* we dug a hole on the edge of the trees, lined it with leaves, and planted in it the sprouting coconut from Peru. A cairn of corals was erected beside it, opposite the place where the *Kon-Tiki* had run ashore.

The *Kon-Tiki* had been washed still farther in during the night and lay almost dry in a few pools of water, squeezed in among a group of big coral blocks a long way through the reef.

After a thorough baking in the warm sand Erik and Herman were in fine fettle again and were anxious to go southward along the reef in the hope of getting over to the large island which lay down there. I warned them more against eels than against sharks, and each of them stuck his long machete knife into his belt. I knew the coral reef was the habitat of a frightful eel with long poisonous teeth which could easily tear off a man's leg. They wriggle to the attack with lightning rapidity and are the terror of the natives, who are not afraid to swim round a shark.

The two men were able to wade over long stretches of the reef to southward, but there were occasional channels of deeper water running this way and that where they had to jump in and swim. They reached the big island safely and waded ashore. The island, long and narrow and covered with palm forest, ran farther south between sunny beaches under the shelter of the reef. The two continued along the island till they came to the southern point. From here the reef, covered with white foam, ran on southward to other distant islands. They found the wreck of a big ship down there; she had four masts and lay on the shore cut in two. She was an old Spanish sailing vessel which had been loaded with rails, and rusty rails lay scattered all along the reef. They returned along the other side of the island but did not find so much as a track in the sand.

On the way back across the reef they were continually coming upon curious fish and were trying to catch some of them when they were suddenly attacked by no fewer than eight large eels. They saw them coming in the clear water and jumped up on to a large coral block, round and under which the eels writhed. The slimy brutes were as thick as a man's calf and speckled green and black like poisonous snakes, with small heads, malignant snake eyes, and teeth an inch long and as sharp as an awl. The men hacked with their machete knives at the little swaying heads which came writhing toward them; they cut the head off one and another was injured. The blood in the sea attracted a whole flock of young blue sharks which attacked the dead and injured eels, while Erik and Herman were able to jump over to another block of coral and get away.

On the same day I was wading in toward the island when something, with a lightning movement, caught hold of my ankle on both sides and held on tight. It was a cuttlefish. It was not large, but it was a horrible feeling to have the cold gripping arms about one's limb and to exchange looks with the evil little eyes in the bluish-red, beaked sack which constituted the body. I jerked in my foot as hard as I could, and the squid, which was barely three feet long, followed it without letting go. It must have been the bandage on my foot which attracted it. I dragged myself in jerks toward the beach with the disgusting carcass hanging on to my foot. Only when I reached the edge of the dry sand did it let go and retreat slowly through the shallow water, with arms outstretched and eyes directed shoreward, as though ready for a new attack if I wanted one. When I threw a few lumps of coral at it, it darted away.

Our various experiences out on the reef only added a spice to our heavenly existence on the island within. But we could not spend all our lives here, and we must begin to think about how we should get back to the outer world. After a week the *Kon-Tiki* had bumped her way in to the middle of the reef, where she lay stuck fast on dry land. The great logs had pushed away and broken off large slabs of coral in the effort to force their way forward to the lagoon, but now the wooden raft lay immovable, and all our pulling and all our pushing were equally unavailing. If we could only get the wreck into the lagoon, we could always splice the mast and rig her sufficiently to be able to sail with the wind across the friendly lagoon and see what we found on the other side. If any of the islands were inhabited, it must be some of those which lay along the horizon away in the east, where the atoll turned its façade toward the lee side.

The days passed.

Then one morning some of the fellows came tearing up and said they had seen a white sail on the lagoon. From up among the palm trunks we could see a tiny speck which was curiously white against the opal-blue lagoon. It was evidently a sail close to land on the other side. We could see that it was tacking. Soon another appeared.

They grew in size, as the morning went on, and came nearer. They came straight toward us. We hoisted the French flag on a palm tree and waved our own Norwegian flag on a pole. One of the sails was now so near that we could see that it belonged to a Polynesian outrigger canoe. The rig was of more recent type. Two brown figures stood on board gazing at us. We waved. They waved back and sailed straight in on to the shallows.

"*Ia-ora-na*," we greeted them in Polynesian.

"*Ia-ora-na*," they shouted back in chorus, and one jumped out and dragged his canoe after him as he came wading over the sandy shallows straight toward us.

The two men had white men's clothes but brown men's bodies.

They were barelegged, well built, and wore homemade straw hats to protect them from the sun. They landed and approached us rather uncertainly, but, when we smiled and shook hands with them in turn, they beamed on us with rows of pearly teeth which said more than words.

Our Polynesian greeting had astonished and encouraged the two canoers in exactly the same way as we ourselves had been deceived when their kinsman off Angatau had called out "Good night," and they reeled off a long rhapsody in Polynesian before they realized that their outpourings were going wide of the mark. Then they had nothing more to say but giggled amiably and pointed to the other canoe which was approaching.

There were three men in this, and, when they waded ashore and greeted us, it appeared that one of them could talk a little French. We learned that there was a native village on one of the islands across the lagoon, and from it the Polynesians had seen our fire several nights earlier. Now there was only one passage leading in through the Raroia reef to the circle of islands around the lagoon, and, as this passage ran right past the village, no one could approach these islands inside the reef without being seen by the inhabitants of the village. The old people in the village, therefore, had come to the conclusion that the light they saw on the reef to eastward could not be the work of men but must be something supernatural. This had quenched in them all desire to go across and see for themselves. But then part of a box had come drifting across the lagoon, and on it some signs were painted. Two of the natives, who had been on Tahiti and learned the alphabet, had deciphered the inscription and read TIKI in big black letters on the slab of wood. Then there was no longer any doubt that there were ghosts on the reef, for Tiki was the long-dead founder of their own race—they all knew that. But then tinned bread, cigarettes, cocoa, and a box with an old shoe in it came drifting across the lagoon. Now they all realized that there had been a shipwreck on the eastern side of the reef, and the chief sent out two canoes to search for the survivors whose fire they had seen on the island.

Urged on by the others, the brown man who spoke French asked why the slab of wood that drifted across the lagoon had "Tiki" on it. We explained that "Kon-Tiki" was on all our equipment and that it was the name of the vessel in which we had come.

Our new friends were loud in their astonishment when they heard that all on board had been saved, when the vessel stranded, and that the flattened wreck out on the reef was actually the craft in which we had come. They wanted to put us all into the canoes at once and take us across to the village. We thanked them and refused, as we wanted to stay till we had got the *Kon-Tiki* off the reef. They looked aghast at the flat contraption out on the reef; surely we could not dream of getting that collapsed hull afloat again! Finally the spokesman said emphatically that we must go with them; the chief had given them strict orders not to return without us.

We then decided that one of us should go with the natives as envoy to the chief and should then come back and report to us on the conditions on the other island. We would not let the raft remain on the reef and could not abandon all the equipment on our little island. Bengt went with the natives. The two canoes were pushed off from the sand and soon disappeared westward with a fair wind.

Next day the horizon swarmed with white sails. Now, it seemed, the natives were coming to fetch us with all the craft they had.

The whole convoy tacked across toward us, and, when they came near, we saw our good friend Bengt waving his hat in the first canoe, surrounded by brown figures. He shouted to us that the chief himself was with him, and the five of us formed up respecfully down on the beach where they were wading ashore.

Bengt presented us to the chief with great ceremony. The chief's name, Bengt said, was Tepiuraiarii Teriifaatau, but he would understand whom we meant if we called him Teka. We called him Teka.

Teka was a tall, slender Polynesian with uncommonly intelligent eyes. He was an important person, a descendant of the old royal line in Tahiti, and was chief of both the Raroia and the Takume islands. He had been to school in Tahiti, so that he spoke French and could both read and write. He told me that the capital of Norway was called Christiania and asked if I knew Bing Crosby. He also told us that only three foreign vessels had called at Raroia in the last ten years, but that the village was visited several times a year by the native copra schooner from Tahiti, which brought merchandise and took away coconut kernels in exchange. They had been expecting the schooner for some weeks now, so she might come at any time.

Bengt's report, summarized, was that there was no school, radio, or any white men on Raroia, but that the 127 Polnesians in the village had done all they could to make us confortable there and had prepared a great reception for us when we came over.

The chief's request was to see the boat which had brought us ashore on the reef alive. We waded out toward the *Kon-Tiki* with a string of natives after us. When we drew near, the natives suddenly stopped and uttered loud exclamations, all talking at once. We could now see the logs of the *Kon-Tiki* plainly, and one of the natives burst out:

"That's not a boat, it's a *pae-pae!*"

"*Pae-pae!*" they all repeated in chorus.

They splashed out across the reef at a gallop and clambered up on to the *Kon-Tiki*. They scrambled about everywhere like excited children, feeling the logs, the bamboo plaiting, and the ropes. The chief was in as high spirits as the others; he came back and repeated with an inquiring expression:

"The *Tiki* isn't a boat, she's a *pae-pae*."

Pae-pae is the Polynesian word for "raft" and "platform," and on Easter Island it is also the word used for the natives' canoes. The chief told us that such *pae-pae* no longer existed, but that the oldest men in the village could relate old traditions of them. The natives all outshouted one another in admiration for the great balsa logs, but they turned up their noses at the ropes. Ropes like that did not last many months in salt water and sun. They showed us with pride the lashings on their own outriggers; they had plaited them themselves of coconut hemp, and such ropes remained as good as new for five years at sea.

When we waded back to our little island, it was named Fenua Kon-Tiki, or Kon-Tiki Island. This was a name we could all pronounce, but our brown friends had a hard job trying to pronounce our short Nordic Christian names. They were delighted when I said they could call me Terai Mateata, for the great chief in Tahiti had given me that name when adopting me as his "son" the first time I was in those parts.

The natives brought out fowls and eggs and breadfruit from the canoes, while others speared big fish in the lagoon with three-pronged spears, and we had a feast round the campfire. We had to narrate all our experiences with the *pae-pae* at sea, and they wanted to hear about the whale shark again and again. And every time we came to the point at which Erik rammed the harpoon into its skull, they uttered the same cries of excitement. They recognized at once every single fish of which we showed them sketches and promptly gave us the names in Polynesian. But they had never seen or heard of the whale shark or the *Gempylus*.

When the evening came, we turned on the radio, to the great delight of the whole assemblage. Church music was most to their taste until, to our own astonishment, we picked up real hula music from America. Then the liveliest of them began to wriggle with their arms curved over their heads, and soon the whole company sprang up on their haunches and danced the hula-hula in time with the music. When night came, all camped round a fire on the beach. It was as much of an adventure to the natives as it was to us.

When we awoke next morning, they were already up and frying newly caught fish, while six freshly opened coconut shells stood ready for us to quench our morning thirst.

The reef was thundering more than usual that day; the wind had increased in strength, and surf was whipping high into the air out there behind the wreck.

"The *Tiki* will come in today," said the chief, pointing to the wreck. "There'll be a high tide."

About eleven o'clock the water began to flow past us into the lagoon. The lagoon began to fill like a big basin, and the water rose all round the island. Later in the day the real inflow from the sea came. The water came rolling in, terrace after terrace, and more and more of the reef sank below the surface of the sea. The masses of water rolled forward along both sides of the island. They tore away large coral blocks and dug up great sandbanks which disappeared like flour before the wind, while others were built up. Loose bamboos from the wreck came sailing past us, and the *Kon-Tiki* began to move. Everything that was lying along the beach had to be carried up into the interior of the island so that it might not be caught by the tide. Soon only the highest stones on the reef were visible, and all the beaches round our island had gone, while the water flowed up toward the herbage of the pancake island. This was eerie. It looked as if the whole sea were invading us. The *Kon-Tiki* swung right round and drifted until she was caught by some other coral blocks.

The natives flung themselves into the water and swam and waded through the eddies till, moving from bank to bank, they reached the raft. Knut and Erik followed. Ropes lay ready on board the raft, and, when she rolled over the last coral blocks and broke loose from the reef, the natives jumped overboard and tried to hold her. They did not know the *Kon-Tiki* and her ungovernable urge to push on westward; so they were towed along helplessly with her. She was soon moving at a good speed right across the reef and into the lagoon. She became slightly at a loss when she reached quieter water and seemed to be looking round as though to obtain a survey of further possibilities. Before she began to move again and discovered the exit across the lagoon, the natives had already succeeded in getting the end of the rope around a palm on land. And there the *Kon-Tiki* hung, tied up fast in the lagoon. The craft that went over land and water had made her way across the barricade and into the lagoon in the interior of Raroia.

With inspiring war cries, to which *"ke-ke-te-huru-huru"* formed an animating refrain, we hauled the *Kon-Tiki* by our combined efforts in to the shore of the island of her own name. The tide reached a point four feet above normal high water. We had thought the whole island was going to disappear before our eyes.

The wind-whipped waves were breaking all over the lagoon, and we could not get much of our equipment into the narrow, wet canoes. The natives had to get back to the village in a hurry, and Bengt and Herman went with them to see a small boy who lay dying in a hut in the village. The boy had an abscess on his head, and we had penicillin.

Next day we four were alone on Kon-Tiki Island. The east wind was now so strong that the natives could not come across the lagoon, which was studded with sharp coral formations and shoals. The tide, which had somewhat receded, flowed in again fiercely, in long, rushing step formations.

Next day it was quieter again. We were now able to dive under the *Kon-Tiki* and ascertain that the nine logs were intact, even if the reef had planed an inch or two off the bottom. The cordage lay so deep in its grooves that only four of the numerous ropes had been cut by the corals. We set about clearing up on board. Our proud vessel looked better when the mess had been removed from the deck, and cabin pulled out again like a concertina, and the mast spliced and set upright.

In the course of the day the sails appeared on the horizon again; the natives were coming to fetch us and the rest of the cargo. Herman and Bengt were with them, and they told us that the natives had prepared great festivities in the village. When we got over to the other island, we must not leave the canoes till the chief himself had indicated that we might do so.

We ran across the lagoon, which here was seven miles wide, before a fresh breeze. It was with real sorrow that we saw the familiar palms on Kon-Tiki Island waving us good-by as they changed into a clump and shrank into one small indefinable island like all the others along the eastern reef. But ahead of us larger islands were broadening out. And on one of them we saw a jetty and smoke rising from huts among the palm trunks.

The village looked quite dead; not a soul was to be seen. What was brewing now? Down on the beach, behind a jetty of coral blocks, stood two solitary figures, one tall and thin and one big and stout as a barrel. As we came in, we saluted them both. They were the chief Teka and the vice-chief Tupuhoe. We all fell for Tupuhoe's broad hearty smile. Teka was a clear brain and a diplomat, but Tupuhoe was a pure child of nature and a sterling fellow, with a humor and a primitive force the like of which one meets but rarely. With his powerful body and kingly features he was exactly what one expects a Polynesian chief to be. Tupuhoe was, indeed, the real chief on the island, but Teka had gradually acquired the supreme position because he could speak French and count and write, so that the village was not cheated when the schooner came from Tahiti to fetch copra.

Teka explained that we were to march together up to the meeting-house in the village, and when all the boys had come ashore we set off thither in ceremonial procession, Herman first with the flag waving on a harpoon shaft, and then I myself between the two chiefs.

The village bore obvious marks of the copra trade with Tahiti; both planks and corrugated iron had been imported in the schooner. While some huts were built in a picturesque old-fashioned style, with twigs and plaited palm leaves, others were knocked together with nails and planks as small tropical bungalows. A large house built of planks, standing alone among the palms, was the new village meetinghouse; there we six whites were to stay. We marched in with the flag by a small back door and out on to a broad flight of steps before the façade. Before us in the square stood everyone in the village who could walk or crawl—women and children, old and young. All were intensely serious; even our cheerful friends from Kon-Tiki Island stood drawn up among the others and did not give us a sign of recognition.

When we had all come out on the steps, the whole assembly opened their mouths simultaneously and joined in singing—the "Marseillaise"! Teka, who knew the words, led the singing, and it went fairly well in spite of a few old women getting stuck up on the high notes. They had been training hard for this. The French and Norwegian flags were hoisted in front of the steps, and this ended the official reception by the chief Teka. He retired quietly into the background, and now stout Tupuhoe sprang forward and became master of the ceremonies. Tupuhoe gave a quick sign, on which the whole assembly burst into a new song. This time it went better, for the tune was composed by themselves and the words, too, were in their language—and sing their own hula they could. The melody was so fascinating, in all its touching simplicity, that we felt a tingling down our backs as the South Sea came roaring toward us. A few individuals led the singing and the whole choir joined in regularly; there were variations in the melody, though the words were always the same:

"Good day, Terai Mateata and your men, who have come across the sea on a *pae-pae* to us on Raroia; yes, good day, may you remain long among us and share memories with us so that we can always be together, even when you go away to a far land. Good day."

We had to ask them to sing the song over again, and more and more life came into the whole assembly as they began to feel less constrained. Then Tupuhoe asked me to say a few words to the people as to why we had come across the sea on a *pae-pae;* they had all been counting on this. I was to speak in French, and Teka would translate bit by bit.

It was an uneducated but highly intelligent gathering of brown people that stood waiting for me to speak. I told them that I had been among their kinsmen out here in the South Sea islands before, and that I had heard of their first chief, Tiki, who had brought their forefathers out to the islands from a mysterious country whose whereabouts no one knew any longer. But in a distant land called Peru, I said, a mighty chief had once ruled whose name was Tiki. The people called him Kon-Tiki, or Sun-Tiki, because he said he was descended from the sun. Tiki and a number of followers had at last disappeared from their country on big *pae-paes;* therefore we six thought that he was the same Tiki who had come to those islands.

As nobody would believe that a *pae-pae* could make the voyage across the sea, we ourselves had set out from Peru on a *pae-pae*, and here we were, so it could be done.

When the little speech was translated by Teka, Tupuhoe was all fire and flame and sprang forward in front of the assembly in a kind of ecstasy. He rumbled away in Polynesian, flung out his arms, pointed to heaven and us, and in his flood of speech constantly repeated the word Tiki. He talked so fast that it was impossible to follow the thread of what he said, but the whole assembly swallowed every word and was visibly excited. Teka, on the contrary, looked quite embarrassed when he had to translate.

Tupuhoe had said that his father and grandfather, and his fathers before him, had told of Tiki and had said that Tiki was their first chief who was now in heaven. But then the white men came and said that the traditions of their ancestors were lies. Tiki had never existed. He was not in heaven at all, for Jehovah was there. Tiki was a heathen god, and they must not believe in him any longer. But now we six had come to them across the sea on a *pae-pae*. We were the first whites who had admitted that their fathers had spoken the truth. Tiki had lived, he had been real, but now he was dead and in heaven.

Horrified at the thought of upsetting the missionaries' work, I had to hurry forward and explain that Tiki had lived, that was sure and certain, and now he was dead. But whether he was in heaven or in hell today only Jehovah knew, for Jehovah was in heaven while Tiki himself had been a mortal man, a great chief like Teka and Tupuhoe, perhaps still greater.

This produced both cheerfulness and contentment among the brown men, and the nodding and mumbling among them showed clearly that the explanation had fallen on good soil. Tiki had lived— that was the main thing. If he was in hell now, no one was any the worse for it but himself; on the contrary, Tupuhoe suggested, perhaps it increased the chances of seeing him again.

Three old men pushed forward and wanted to shake hands with us. There was no doubt that it was they who had kept the memories of Tiki alive among the people, and the chief told us that one of the old men knew an immense number of traditions and historical ballads from his forefathers' time. I asked the old man if there was, in the traditions, any hint of the direction from which Tiki had come. No, none of the old men could remember having heard that. But after long and careful reflection the oldest of the three said that Tiki had with him a near relation who was called Maui, and in the ballad of Maui it was said that he had come to the islands from Pura and *pura* was the word for the part of the sky where the sun rose. If Maui had come from Pura, the old man said, Tiki had no doubt come from the same place, and we six on the *pae-pae* had also come from *pura*—that was sure enough.

I told the brown men that on a lonely island near Easter Island, called Mangareva, the people had never learned the use of canoes and had continued to use big *pae-paes* at sea right down to our time. This the old men did not know, but they knew that their forefathers also had used big *pae-paes*. However, they had gradually gone out of use, and now they had nothing but the name and traditions left. In really ancient times they had been called *rongo-rongo*, the oldest man said, but that was a word which no longer existed in the language. *Rongo-rongo* were mentioned in the most ancient legends.

This name was interesting, for Rongo—on certain islands pronounced "Lono"—was the name of one of the Polynesians' best-known legendary ancestors. He was expressly described as white and fair-haired. When Captain Cook first came to Hawaii, he was received with open arms by the islanders because they thought he was their white kinsman Rongo, who, after an absence of generations, had come back from their ancestors' homeland in his big sailing ship. And on Easter Island the word *"rongo-rongo"* was the designation for the mysterious hieroglyphs the secret of which was lost with the last "Long-ears" who could write.

While the old men wanted to discuss Tiki and *rongo-rongo*, the young ones wanted to hear about the whale shark and the voyage across the sea. But the food was waiting, and Teka was tired of interpreting.

Now the whole village was allowed to come up and shake hands with each of us. The men mumbled *"ia-ora-na"* and almost shook our hands out of joint, while the girls squirmed forward and greeted us coquettishly yet shyly and the old women babbled and cackled and pointed to our beards and the color of our skin. Friendliness beamed from every face, so it was quite immaterial that there was a hubbub of linguistic confusion. If they said something incomprehensible to us in Polynesian, we gave them tit for tat in Norwegian. We had the greatest fun together. The first native word we all learned was the word for "like," and when, moreover, one could point to what one liked and count on getting it at once, it was all very simple. If one wrinkled one's nose when "like" was said, it meant "don't like," and on this basis we got along pretty well.

As soon as we had become acquainted with the 127 inhabitants of the village, a long table was laid for the two chiefs and the six of us, and the village girls came round bearing the most delicious dishes. While some arranged the table, others came and hung plaited wreaths of flowers round our necks and smaller wreaths round our heads. These exhaled a lingering scent and were cool and refreshing in the heat. And so a feast of welcome began which did not end till we left the island weeks after. Our eyes opened wide and our mouths watered, for the tables were loaded with roast suckling pigs, chickens, roast ducks, fresh lobsters, Polynesian fish dishes, breadfruit, papaya, and coconut milk. While we attacked the dishes, we were entertained by the crowd singing hula songs, while young girls danced round the table.

The boys laughed and thoroughly enjoyed themselves, each of us looking more absurd than the next as we sat and gorged like starving men, with flowing beards and wreaths of flowers in our hair. The two chiefs were enjoying life as wholeheartedly as ourselves.

After the meal there was hula dancing on a grand scale. The village wanted to show us their local folk dances. While we six and Teka and Tupuhoe were each given stools in the orchestra, two guitar players advanced, squatted down, and began to strum real South Sea melodies. Two ranks of dancing men and women, with rustling skirts of palm leaves round their hips, came gliding and wriggling forward through the ring of spectators who squatted and sang. They had a lively and spirited leading singer in a luxuriantly fat *vahine*, who had had one arm bitten off by a shark. At first the dancers seemed a little self-conscious and nervous, but when they saw that the white men from the *pae-pae* did not turn up their noses at their ancestors' folk dances, the dancing became more and more animated. Some of the older people joined in; they had a splendid rhythm and could dance dances which were obviously no longer in common use. As the sun sank into the Pacific, the dancing under the palm trees became livelier and livelier, and the applause of the spectators more and more spontaneous. They had forgotten that we who sat watching them were six strangers; we were now six of their own people, enjoying ourselves with them.

The repertory was endless; one fascinating display followed another. Finally a crowd of young men squatted down in a close ring just in front of us, and at a sign from Tupuhoe they began to beat time rhythmically on the ground with the palms of their hands. First slowly, then more quickly, and the rhythm grew more and more and more perfect when a drummer suddenly joined in and accompanied them, beating at a furious pace with two sticks on a bonedry, hollowed block of wood which emitted a sharp, intense sound. When the rhythm reached the desired degree of animation, the singing began, and suddenly a hula girl with a wreath of flowers round her neck and flowers behind one ear leaped into the ring. She kept time to the music with bare feet and bent knees, swaying rhythmically at the hips and curving her arms above her head in true Polynesian style. She danced splendidly, and soon the whole assembly were beating time with their hands. Another girl leaped into the ring, and after her another. They moved with incredible supplenness in perfect rhythm, gliding round one another in the dance like graceful shadows. The dull beating of hands on the ground, the singing, and the cheerful wooden drum increased their tempo faster and faster and the dance grew wilder and wilder, while the spectators howled and clapped in perfect rhythm.

This was the South Seas life as the old days had known it. The stars twinkled and the palms waved. The night was mild and long and full of the scent of flowers and the song of crickets. Tupuhoe beamed and slapped me on the shoulder.

"*Maitai?*" he asked.

"Yes, *maitai*," I replied.

"*Maitai?*" he asked all the others.

"*Maitai*," they all replied emphatically, and they all really meant it.

"*Maitai*," Tupuhoe nodded, pointing to himself; he too was enjoying himself now.

Even Teka thought it was a very good feast; it was the first time white men had been present at their dances on Raroia, he said. Faster and faster, faster and faster, went the rolls of the drums, the clapping, singing, and dancing. Now one of the girl dancers ceased to move round the ring and remained on the same spot, performing a wriggling dance at a terrific tempo with her arms stretched out toward Herman. Herman snickered behind his beard; he did not quite know how to take it.

"Be a good sport," I whispered. "You're a good dancer."

To the boundless delight of the crowd Herman sprang into the ring and, half crouching, tackled all the difficult wriggling movements of the hula. The jubilation was unbounded. Soon Bengt and Torstein leaped into the dance, striving till the perspiration streamed down their faces to keep up with the tempo, which rose and rose to a furious pace till the drum alone was beating in one prolonged drone and the three real hula dancers quivering in time like aspen leaves. Then they sank down in the finales and the drumbeats ceased abruptly.

Now the evening was ours. There was no end to the enthusiasm.

The next item on the program was the bird dance, which was one of the oldest ceremonies on Raroia. Men and women in two ranks jumped forward in a rhythmic dance, imitating flocks of birds following a leader. The dance leader had the title of chief of the birds and performed curious maneuvers without actually joining in the dance. When the dance was over, Tupuhoe explained that it had been performed in honor of the raft and would now be repeated, but the dance leader would be relieved by myself. As the dance leader's main task appeared to me to consist in uttering wild howls, hopping around on his haunches, wriggling his backside, and waving his hands over his head, I pulled the wreath of flowers well down over my head and marched out into the arena. While I was curving myself in the dance, I saw old Tupuhoe laughing till he nearly fell off his stool, and the music grew feeble because the singers and players followed Tupuhoe's example.

Now everyone wanted to dance, old and young alike, and soon the drummer and earth-beaters were there again, giving the lead to a fiery hula-hula dance. First the hula girls sprang into the ring and started the dance at a tempo that grew wilder and wilder, and then we were invited to dance in turn, while more and more men and women followed, stamping and writhing along, faster and faster.

But Erik could not be made to stir. The drafts and damp on board the raft had revived his vanished lumbago and he sat like an old yacht skipper, stiff and bearded, puffing at his pipe. He would not be moved by the hula girls who tried to lure him into the arena. He had put on a pair of wide sheepskin trousers which he had worn at night in the coldest spells in the Humboldt Current, and, sitting under the palms with his big beard, body bare to the waist, and sheepskin breeches, he was a faithful copy of Robinson Crusoe. One pretty girl after another tried to ingratiate herself, but in vain. He only sat gravely puffing his pipe, with the wreath of flowers in his bushy hair.

Then a well-developed matron with powerful muscles entered the arena, executed a few more or less graceful hula steps, and then marched determinedly toward Erik. He looked alarmed, but the amazon smiled ingratiatingly, caught him resolutely by the arm, and pulled him off of his stool. Erik's comic pair of breeches had the sheep's wool inside and the skin outside, and they had a rent behind so that a white spot of wool stuck out like a rabbit's tail. Erik followed most reluctantly and limped into the ring with his pipe in one hand and the other pressed against the spot where his lumbago hurt him. When he tried to jump round, he had to let go of his trousers to save his wreath which was threatening to fall off, and then, with the wreath on one side, he had to catch hold of his trousers again, which were coming down of their own weight. The stout dame who was hobbling round in the hula in front of him was just as funny, and tears of laughter trickled down our beards. Soon all the others who were in the ring stopped, and salvos of laughter rang through the palm grove as Hula Erik and the female heavyweight circled gracefully round. At last even they had to stop, because both singers and musicians had more than they could do to hold their sides for laughter at the comic sight.

The feast went on till broad daylight, when we were allowed to have a little pause, after again shaking hands with every one of the 127. We shook hands with every one of them every morning and every evening throughout our stay on the island. Six beds were scraped together from all the huts in the village and placed side by side along the wall in the meetinghouse, and in these we slept in a row like the seven little dwarfs in the fairy story, with sweet-smelling wreaths of flowers hanging above our beds.

Next day the boy of six who had an abscess on his head seemed to be in a bad way. He had a temperature of 106°, and the abscess was as large as a man's fist and throbbed painfully.

Teka declared that they had lost a number of children in this way and that, if none of us could do any doctoring, the boy had not many days to live. We had bottles of penicillin in a new tablet form, but we did not know what dose a small child could stand. If the boy died under our treatment, it might have serious consequences for all of us.

Knut and Torstein got the radio out again and slung up an aerial between the tallest coconut palms. When evening came they got in touch again with our unseen friends, Hal and Frank, sitting in their rooms at home in Los Angeles. Frank called a doctor on the telephone, and we signaled with the Morse key all the boy's symptoms and a list of what we had available in our medical chest. Frank passed on the doctor's reply, and that night we went off to the hut where little Haumata lay tossing in a fever with half the village weeping and making a noise about him.

Herman and Knut were to do the doctoring, while we others had more than enough to do to keep the villagers outside. The mother became hysterical when we came with a sharp knife and asked for boiling water. All the hair was shaved off the boy's head and the abscess was opened. The pus squirted up almost to the roof, and several of the natives forced their way in in a state of fury and had to be turned out. It was a grave moment. When the abscess was drained and sterilized, the boy's head was bound up and we began the penicillin cure. For two days and nights, while the fever was at its maximum, the boy was treated every four hours, and the abscess was kept open. And each evening the doctor in Los Angeles was consulted. Then the boy's temperature fell suddenly, the pus was replaced by plasma which was allowed to heal, and the boy was beaming and wanting to look at pictures from the white man's strange world where there were motorcars and cows and houses with several floors.

A week later Haumata was playing on the beach with the other children, his head bound up in a big bandage which he was soon allowed to take off.

When this had gone well, there was no end to the maladies which cropped up in the village. Toothache and gastric troubles were everywhere, and both old and young had boils in one place or another. We referred the patients to Dr. Knut and Dr. Herman, who ordered diets and emptied the medicine chest of pills and ointments. Some were cured and none became worse, and, when the medicine chest was empty, we made oatmeal porridge and cocoa, which were admirably efficacious with hysterical women.

We had not been among our brown admirers for many days before the festivities culminated in a fresh ceremony. We were to be adopted as citizens of Raroia and receive Polynesian names. I myself was no longer to be Terai Mateata; I could be called that in Tahiti, but not here among them.

Six stools were placed for us in the middle of the square, and the whole village was out early to get good places in the circle round. Teka sat solemnly among them; he was chief all right, but not where old local ceremonies were concerned. Then Tupuhoe took over.

All sat waiting, silent and profoundly serious, while portly Tupuhoe approached solemnly and slowly with his stout knotted stick. He was conscious of the gravity of the moment, and the eyes of all were upon him as he came up, deep in thought, and took up his position in front of us. He was the born chief—a brilliant speaker and actor.

He turned to the chief singers, drummers, and dance leaders, pointed at them in turn with his knotted stick, and gave them curt orders in low, measured tones. Then he turned to us again, and suddenly opened his great eyes wide, so that the large white eyeballs shone as bright as the teeth in his expressive copper-brown face. He raised the knotted stick and, the words streaming from his lips in an uninterrupted flow, he recited ancient rituals which none but the oldest members understood, because they were in an old forgotten dialect.

Then he told us, with Teka as interpreter, that Tikaroa was the name of the first king who had established himself on the island, and that he had reigned over this same atoll from north to south, from east to west, and up into the sky above men's heads.

While the whole choir joined in the old ballad about King Tikaroa, Tupuhoe laid his great hand on my chest and, turning to the audience, said that he was naming me Varoa Tikaroa, or Tikaroa's Spirit.

When the song died away, it was the turn of Herman and Bengt. They had the big brown hand laid upon their chests in turn and received the names Tupuhoe-Itetahua and Topakino. These were the names of two old-time heroes who had fought a savage sea monster and killed it at the entrance to the Raroia reef.

The drummer delivered a few vigorous rolls, and two robust men with knotted-up loincloths and a long spear in each hand sprang forward. They broke into a march in double-quick time, with their knees raised to their chests and their spears pointing upward, and turned their heads from side to side. At a fresh beat of the drum they leaped into the air and, in perfect rhythm, began a ceremonial battle in the purest ballet style. The whole thing was short and swift and represented the heroes' fight with the sea monster. Then Torstein was named with song and ceremony; he was called Maroake, after a former king in the present village, and Erik and Knut received the names of Tane-Matarau and Tefaunui after two navigators and sea heroes of the past. The long monotonous recitation which accompanied their naming was delivered at breakneck speed and with a continuous flow of words, the incredible rapidity of which was calculated both to impress and amuse.

The ceremony was over. Once more there were white and bearded chiefs among the Polynesian people on Raroia. Two ranks of male and female dancers came forward in plaited straw skirts with swaying bast crowns on their heads. They danced forward to us and transferred the crowns from their own heads to ours; we had rustling straw skirts put round our waists, and the festivities continued.

One night the flower-clad radio operators got into touch with the radio amateur on Rarotonga, who passed on a message to us from Tahiti. It was a cordial welcome from the governor of the French Pacific colonies.

On instructions from Paris he had sent the government schooner "Tamara" to fetch us to Tahiti, so we should not have to wait for the uncertain arrival of the copra schooner. Tahiti was the central point of the French colonies and the only island which had contact with the world in general. We should have to go via Tahiti to get the regular boat home to our own world.

The festivities continued on Raroia. One night some strange hoots were heard from out at sea, and lookout men came down from the palm tops and reported that a vessel was lying at the entrance to the lagoon. We ran through the palm forest and down to the beach on the lee side. Here we looked out over the sea in the opposite direction to that from which we had come. There were much smaller breakers on this side, which lay under the shelter of the entire atoll and the reef.

Just outside the entrance to the lagoon we saw the lights of a vessel. Since the night was clear and starry, we could distinguish the outlines of a broad-beamed schooner with two masts. Was this the governor's ship which was coming for us? Why did she not come in?

The natives grew more and more uneasy. Now we too saw what was happening. The vessel had a heavy list and threatened to capsize. She was aground on an invisible coral reef under the surface.

Torstein got hold of a light and signaled:

"*Quel bateau?*"

" 'Maoae,' " was flashed back.

The "Maoae" was the copra schooner which ran between the islands. She was on her way to Raroia to fetch copra. There was a Polynesian captain and crew on board, and they knew the reefs inside out. But the current out of the lagoon was treacherous in darkness. It was lucky that the schooner lay under the lee of the island and that the weather was quiet. The list of the "Maoae" became heavier and heavier, and the crew took to the boat. Strong ropes were made fast to her mastheads and rowed in to the land, where the natives fastened them round coconut palms to prevent the schooner from capsizing. The crew, with other ropes, stationed themselves off the opening in the reef in their boat, in the hope of rowing the "Maoae" off when the tidal current ran out of the lagoon. The people of the village launched all their canoes and set out to salvage the cargo. There were ninety tons of valuable copra on board. Load after load of sacks of copra was transferred from the rolling schooner and brought on to dry land.

At high water the "Maoae" was still aground, bumping and rolling against the corals until she sprang a leak. When day broke she was lying in a worse position on the reef than ever. The crew could do nothing; it was useless to try to haul the heavy 150-ton schooner off the reef with her own boat and the canoes. If she continued to lie bumping where she was, she would knock herself to pieces, and, if the weather changed, she would be lifted in by the suction and be a total loss in the surf which beat against the atoll.

The "Maoae" had no radio, but we had. But it would be impossible to get a salvage vessel from Tahiti until the "Maoae" would have had ample time to roll herself into wreckage. Yet for the second time that month the Raroia reef was balked of its prey.

About noon the same day the schooner "Tamara" came in sight on the horizon to westward. She had been sent to fetch us from Raroia, and those on board were not a little astonished when they saw, instead of a raft, the two masts of a large schooner lying and rolling helplessly on the reef.

On board the "Tamara" was the French administrator of the Tuamotu and Tubuai groups, M. Frédéric Ahnne, whom the governor had sent with the vessel from Tahiti to meet us. There were also a French movie photographer and a French telegrapher on board, but the captain and crew were Polynesian. M. Ahnne himself had been born in Tahiti of French parents and was a splendid seaman. He took over the command of the vessel with the consent of the Tahitian captain, who was delighted to be freed from the responsibility in those dangerous waters. While the "Tamara" was avoiding a myriad of submerged reefs and eddies, stout hawsers were stretched between the two schooners and M. Ahnne began his skillful and dangerous evolutions, while the tide threatened to drag both vessels on to the same coral bank.

At high tide the "Maoae" came off the reef, and the "Tamara" towed her out into deep water. But now water poured through the hull of the "Maoae," and she had to be hauled with all speed on to the shallows in the lagoon. For three days the "Maoae" lay off the village in a sinking condition, with all pumps going day and night. The best pearl divers among our friends on the island went down with lead plates and nails and stopped the worst leaks, so that the "Maoae" could be escorted by the "Tamara" to the dockyard in Tahiti with her pumps working.

When the "Maoae" was ready to be escorted, M. Ahnne maneuvered the "Tamara" between the coral shallows in the lagoon and across to Kon-Tiki Island. The raft was taken in tow, and then he set his course back to the opening with the *Kon-Tiki* in tow and the "Maoae" so close behind that the crew could be taken off if the leaks got the upper hand out at sea.

Our farewell to Raroia was more than sad. Everyone who could walk or crawl was down on the jetty, playing and singing our favorite tunes as the ship's boat took us out to the "Tamara."

Tupuhoe bulked large in the center, holding little Haumata by the hand. Haumata was crying, and tears trickled down the cheeks of the powerful chief. There was not a dry eye on the jetty, but they kept the singing and music going long, long after the breakers from the reef drowned all other sounds in our ears.

Those faithful souls who stood on the jetty singing were losing six friends. We who stood mute at the rail of the "Tamara" till the jetty was hidden by the palms and the palms sank into the sea were losing 127. We still heard the strange music with our inner ear:

"—and share memories with us so that we can always be together, even when you go away to a far land. Good day."

Four days later Tahiti rose out of the sea. Not like a string of pearls with palm tufts. As wild jagged blue mountains flung skyward, with wisps of cloud like wreaths round the peaks.

As we gradually approached, the blue mountains showed green slopes. Green upon green, the lush vegetation of the south rolled down over rust-red hills and cliffs, till it plunged down into deep ravines and valleys running out toward the sea. When the coast came near, we saw slender palms standing close packed up all the valleys and all along the coast behind a golden beach. Tahiti was built by old volcanoes. They were dead now and the coral polyps had slung their protecting reef about the island so that the sea could not erode it away.

Early one morning we headed through an opening in the reef into the harbor of Papeete. Before us lay church spires and red roofs half hidden by the foliage of giant trees and palm tops. Papeete was the capital of Tahiti, the only town in French Oceania. It was a city of pleasure, the seat of government, and the center of all traffic in the eastern Pacific.

When we came into the harbor, the population of Tahiti stood waiting, packed tight like a gaily colored living wall. News spreads like the wind in Tahiti, and the *pae-pae* which had come from America was something everyone wanted to see.

The *Kon-Tiki* was given the place of honor alongside the shore promenade, the mayor of Papeete welcomed us, and a little Polynesian girl presented us with an enormous wheel of Tahitian wild flowers on behalf of the Polynesian Society. Then young girls came forward and hung sweet-smelling white wreaths of flowers round our necks as a welcome to Tahiti, the pearl of the South Seas.

There was one particular face I was looking for in the multitude, that of my old adoptive father in Tahiti, the chief Teriieroo, head of the seventeen native chiefs on the island. He was not missing. Big and bulky, and as bright and alive as in the old days, he emerged from the crowd calling, "Terai Mateata!" and beaming all over his broad face. He had become an old man, but he was the same impressive chieftainly figure.

"You come late," he said smiling, "but you come with good news. Your *pae-pae* has in truth brought blue sky (*terai mateata*) to Tahiti, for now we know where our fathers came from."

There was a reception at the governor's palace and a party at the town hall, and invitations poured in from every corner of the hospitable island.

As in former days, a great feast was given by the chief Teriieroo at his house in the Papeno Valley which I knew so well, and, as Raroia was not Tahiti, there was a new ceremony at which Tahitian names were given those who had none before.

Those were carefree days under sun and drifting clouds. We bathed in the lagoon, climbed in the mountains, and danced the hula on the grass under the palms. The days passed and became weeks. It seemed as if the weeks would become months before a ship came which could take us home to the duties that awaited us.

Then came a message from Norway saying that Lars Christensen had ordered the 4,000-tonner "Thor I" to proceed from Samoa to Tahiti to pick up the expedition and take it to America.

Early one morning the big Norwegian steamer glided into Papeete harbor, and the *Kon-Tiki* was towed out by a French naval craft to the side of her large compatriot, which swung out a huge iron arm and lifted her small kinsman up on to her deck. Loud blasts of the ship's siren echoed over the palm-clad island. Brown and white people thronged the quay of Papeete and poured on board with fare-well gifts and wreaths of flowers. We stood at the rail stretching out our necks like giraffes to get our chins free from the ever growing load of flowers.

"If you wish to come back to Tahiti," Chief Teriieroo cried as the whistle sounded over the island for the last time, "you must throw a wreath out into the lagoon when the boat goes!"

The ropes were cast off, the engines roared, and the propeller whipped the water green as we slid sideways away from the quay.

Soon the red roofs disappeared behind the palms, and the palms were swallowed up in the blue of the mountains which sank like shadows into the Pacific.

Waves were breaking out on the blue sea. We could no longer reach down to them. White trade-wind clouds drifted across the blue sky. We were no longer traveling their way. We were defying Nature now. We were going back to the twentieth century which lay so far, far away.

But the six of us on deck, standing beside our nine dear balsa logs, were grateful to be all alive. And in the lagoon at Tahiti six white wreaths lay alone, washing in and out, in and out, with the wavelets on the beach.

Publisher's Note

MR. HEYERDAHL'S MANUSCRIPT, "POLYNESIA AND America: A Study of Prehistoric Relations," mentioned in the first two chapters of KON-TIKI as presenting the author's scientific arguments in favor of his migration theory, has now been published by Rand McNally & Company under the title, AMERICAN INDIANS IN THE PACIFIC: THE THEORY BEHIND THE KON-TIKI EXPEDITION.

Index